NO LONGER THE
PROPERTY OF
ELON UNIVERSITY LIBRARY

6.6.72

MASS VIOLENCE IN AMERICA

Advisory editors:

ROBERT M. FOGELSON   RICHARD E. RUBENSTEIN

MASS VIOLENCE IN AMERICA

HEARINGS ON

THE KU KLUX KLAN

1921

ARNO PRESS & THE NEW YORK TIMES

New York • 1969

90236

Introduction copyright © 1969 by Arno Press, Inc.
All rights reserved

*

Library of Congress Catalog Card No. 72–90203

*

Reprinted from a copy in
The Library of Congress

*

Manufactured in the United States of America

Editorial Note

NATIONS, LIKE MEN, ARE SOMETIMES INTERESTED IN BURYING THE PAST. In early 1968, after more than five years marked by political assassinations, racial uprisings, campus disorders, mass demonstrations and the violent suppression of protest, *The New York Times Magazine* asked a group of distinguished scholars to reply to the question, "Is America by nature a violent society?" In answer, University of Chicago anthropologist Clifford Geertz wrote:

"We do not know very well what kind of society we live in, what kind of history we have had, what kind of people we are. We are just now beginning to find out, the hard way . . ."

The proposition was astonishing but correct: what was least understood about domestic political violence was its role in American history. It was common knowledge that the United States had had a Revolution, a Civil War, some trouble with the Indians and a period of labor-management conflict. But one could search the shelves of the nation's great libraries without discovering more than a handful of works on the subject of violence in American history, and these hopelessly out of date.

Historians had generally ignored or soft-pedaled the history of farmer uprisings, native vigilantism, labor-management struggles, ethnic conflicts and race riots; comparative work in the history of social conflict was particularly weak. Sociologists and political scientists in the grip of "consensus" theory tended to treat episodes of mass violence in America as insignificant or aberrational—temporary exceptions to the norm of peaceful progress. Psychologists and behavioral scientists discussed "mob violence" in terms which suggested that riots, revolts, insurrections and official violence were the products of individual or group pathology. All such interpretations had the effect not only of minimizing group violence in America, but of depriving it of political content—hence, of relevance to the present.

As a result, as late as 1968, the rich, multifarious and often terrifying history of domestic political violence was still largely *terra incognita*. So long as most Americans wished to keep certain skeletons locked away in their closets, few scholars would attempt to open doors. Conversely, once the American people, frightened yet emboldened by the sudden reappearance of intense social conflict, began to ask new questions about the past, so did the scholars.

Our purpose in helping Arno Press and *The New York Times* select and publish significant documents in the history of political violence has not been to compound past errors by overemphasizing the role of conflict in American history. On the contrary, our aim has been to provide materials which will aid in the search for an accurate perspective on the present. MASS VIOLENCE IN AMERICA includes eyewitness reports, government documents and other descriptive and analytic material relating to mass political violence in the United States. These documents not only provide information—they give the "feel" or "flavor" of past eras of civil disorder by evoking the emotional and political context in which revolts took place. Most of them have long been out of print and are obtainable, if at all, only in the nation's largest libraries.

The scope of this series is wide, ranging from accounts of Indian warfare to descriptions of labor-management violence, from narratives of colonial insurrections to reports on modern racial uprisings. It is not, however, limitless, nor were the constituent volumes carelessly selected. The principle of coherence which guided the selections is implicit in the phrase "mass political violence." "Mass" denotes activity engaged in by large groups rather than individuals acting alone; "political" suggests a relationship between such activity and competition among domestic groups for power, property and prestige; and "violence" is narrowly construed as resulting in physical damage to persons or property. In short, the materials reproduced herein are intended to illuminate the resort to violence by American groups seeking to change or to preserve the status quo. Although historical, they are of interest to any who wishes to understand the causes, nature and direction of domestic political violence, whether they be social scientists, historians or just interested Americans.

Of course, we are particularly hopeful that these volumes will prove useful to those now engaged in curriculum-revision and the teaching of high school and college courses in the area of American studies. What Christopher Jencks and David Reisman term "the Academic Revolution" has made difficult demands on all educators, not the least of which is the demand for courses which are both relevant to the condition of modern America and of the highest academic quality. These volumes are meant to provide raw material for such courses—primary source matter which will help both instructors and students to deepen and enrich their views of the American experience.

Most important, the editors and publisher recognize that these volumes appear during a national crisis which is also a crisis of the spirit, a time in which the public response to various manifestations of civil disorder is increasingly governed by anger, fear and hysteria. In such an atmosphere it is important to recognize that one is not alone in time—that such events have taken place before in America and, unless fundamental changes in our social and political life take place, will probably recur in the future. Our fondest hope is that this work, and others like it, will help to keep alive, in a time of growing unreason, the spirit of reasoned inquiry.

RICHARD E. RUBENSTEIN
The Adlai Stevenson Institute
Chicago, Illinois

ROBERT M. FOGELSON
Harvard-MIT Joint Center
for Urban Studies
Cambridge, Massachusetts

HEARINGS ON
THE KU KLUX KLAN
1921

THE KU-KLUX KLAN

HEARINGS

BEFORE

THE COMMITTEE ON RULES

HOUSE OF REPRESENTATIVES

SIXTY-SEVENTH CONGRESS
FIRST SESSION

WASHINGTON
GOVERNMENT PRINTING OFFICE
1921

COMMITTEE ON RULES.

HOUSE OF REPRESENTATIVES.

SIXTY-SEVENTH CONGRESS, FIRST SESSION.

PHILIP P. CAMPBELL, Kansas, *Chairman.*

BERTRAND H. SNELL, New York.
WILLIAM A. RODENBERG, Illinois.
SIMEON D. FESS, Ohio.
AARON S. KREIDER, Pennsylvania.
PORTER H. DALE, Vermont.
ROYAL C. JOHNSON, South Dakota.
THOMAS D. SCHALL, Minnesota.

EDWARD W. POU, North Carolina.
FINIS J. GARRETT, Tennessee.
JAMES C. CANTRILL, Kentucky.
DANIEL J. RIORDAN, New York.

ALFRED G. ARMSTRONG, *Clerk.*
JOHN J. McCUNE, *Assistant Clerk.*

2

THE KU-KLUX KLAN.

COMMITTEE ON RULES,
HOUSE OF REPRESENTATIVES,
Tuesday, October 11, 1921.

The committee met at 10.30 o'clock a. m., Hon. Philip P. Campbell (chairman) presiding.

Mr. CAMPBELL. A number of resolutions have been introduced in the House of Representatives having for their purpose an investigation of an order known as the Knights of the Ku-Klux Klan. The resolutions have the usual whereases and invite to a very wide field of discovery. The resolving clauses themselves, however, direct attention to two specific matters. First of all, has the organization used the mails in such a way as to, or for the purpose of, defrauding, in violation of Federal statutes. That question no doubt will have attention, if evidence of it is developed, from the proper authorities of the Government. Another question that is presented in the resolutions is that of overt acts alleged to have been committed by men wearing masks, which overt acts would probably not be committed by men who did not wear such masks. If overt acts have been committed, amounting to assault, disturbances of the peace of citizens and of communities, these are matters cognizable by State authorities and should have the attention of such authorities. The invitation to go into a wide field of discovery should be resisted as far as possible if that range of discovery does not lead to a corrective, either under the laws as they now exist or the necessity for legislation to meet such conditions as may be disclosed. The resolutions that have been introduced, in their order is, first, the resolution (H. Res. 188) introduced by Mr. Tague, of Massachusetts. I will ask Mr. Tague to make a statement to the committee as to his purpose and what he has in mind with respect to the investigation.

STATEMENT OF HON. PETER F. TAGUE, A REPRESENTATIVE IN CONGRESS FROM THE STATE OF MASSACHUSETTS.

Mr. TAGUE. Mr. Chairman and gentlemen of the committee, some seven or eight months ago, through some traveling men who had been in the South, my attention was called to the activities of the Ku-Klux Klan organization. At that time they told of the terrible things being done to innocent people; how the rights of citizens throughout that section of the country in which they had traveled had been violated, and that they had not been protected in those rights which are allowed and given to them under the Constitution of the United States. When I received that notice I immediately took up the matter with the Department of Justice. I called it to their attention and they assured me of an immediate investigation. Congress adjourned a little later, while the investigation was in progress, and a change of administration took place. When the new Congress convened I again called the matter to the attention of the Department of Justice and they informed me they were investigating the matter. I told them then I was going to put in a resolution asking for an investigation. They asked me at that time to withhold my resolution because of the fact that they had been investigating and had found that not only what I had said to them was true but had found the most glaring instances of a violation of the Constitution of the United States and the rights of the people.

I do not know, personally, any member of this organization. A day or two ago in my own city a gentleman gave an interview to the newspapers in which he said that he was organizing this so-called American organization that goes around in the dark, covered with a mask, defying the laws of this land.

I believed with such conditions prevailing in this country that it was time for an investigation, and so I introduced this resolution asking for a special committee of Congress. My reason for asking for a special committee is this: I believed that this was of sufficient importance to take up the time of men who would give their entire attention to it. If one-third of all that has been said of this organization is true, then, Mr. Chairman and gentlemen of this committee, there should be an investigation and the law should be made so strong, not only in the future, but to go back and inflict the punishment of the law upon any man or men who would go around in the dark like cowards, afraid to show their faces, and go into the home of an innocent man or woman and take him out in the street, tar and feather him, and cruelly punish him.

Mr. Chairman, I have in my possession any number of letters from men in the sections of the country where these acts have been committed, and I will submit them to the committee, if they wish them, at any time they are desired.

I have studied the law in my limited capacity as a layman, and find that some time ago there was an organization somewhat similar to this, or similar in name at least, that had gone forth and violated every law of the land, so far as the rights of men are concerned, and immediately Congress stepped in and passed a law that forbade that and disbanded that organization. Now, I can conceive of no right that any men have, no matter how they so organize themselves, that will permit them to go out in the night and in the dark into my home because of my race or my religion or because of the color of a man, go into that man's home, take me out, or take my wife and children out, upon the highways and cruelly punish them, when the Constitution of the United States gives me protection as a free man in this land so long as I live up to the laws of the land, whether I am black or white, whether I am Catholic, Jew, or belong to any other race or religion.

Now, Mr. Chairman, these are the things that are going on. The great news-papers of the country—for instance, the New York World—has made an exhaustive study, and Mr. Hearst has made an exhaustive study, and the news-papers, many of whose clippings I have here and many hundreds of which I have in my office, which I will gladly give to the committee, have investigated these things, and they declare everything that is published as being the facts. Now, if they are true, then the time has come for the Congress of the United States to put out its hand and to say that the Constitution of the United States is not a scrap of paper, and that it will be upheld at any cost.

Now, what else? According to the statements of their own members, given in the press, they claim they have over 500,000 members, and these members have paid all the way from $10 to $40 apiece for their membership. Upon inves-tigation, there are no returns made to the United States of America under the internal revenue laws for more than $30,000,000, which you gentlemen [indicat-ing] have collected in violation of the law and from which this Government has had no return.

A few days ago the New York World was investigating in Atlanta the cases of some of the members, whose names I will not use, because the chairman wants me to be brief in order to give others a chance to be heard. Upon investiga-tion, according to the New York World, this organization was so powerful that they could go into the very courts of the land and of the State and destroy the records of that court.

We have been told there are Members of Congress who are members of this organization. Mr. Chairman, I do not believe it. I would hate to believe that any Member of the Congress of the United States would so far forget his oath of office as to be a member of any organization that goes out and deliberately violates the law of the land. There is no place in this country, to my mind, for any organization that attempts to do that. The Constitution protects us all. If the Constitution is of no value, then the Congress of the Unied States should try at least to present it to the people of the United States so it will be amended to mean something. But it is not within the power of any imperial grand wizard or goblin or goshen, or whatever he may call himself, to travel through my State or my city—and we welcome them up in my city. We would be glad to have them come up and parade in their garb and violate the law up there, but they would not get very far with it, Mr. Chairman and gentlemen. I represent one of the greatest cosmopolitan districts in this Congress of the United States. I have almost every nationality and race and color that there is in the United States, and I appear here as their representative, protesting against any organization that will step in and deprive any one of them, no matter who they may be, or how great or how humble they may be, of their right of citizenship and their right of protection. For that reason, Mr. Chairman, first, that they are violating and desecrating the law, and, second, that they are depriving every man they meet of his rights under the law, and, third, that they have violated the law in so far as they have deliberately gone out and collected money from the public for the purpose of destroying the law, and then in their same cowardly manner, the same manner that they carry out their threats, the same manner that they parade under a cloak, they deprive the Government of just taxes that you and I are trying every day to collect in order to decrease the taxation of this country.

I ask you, gentlemen of this committee, to pass this resolution so that Congress will give this special committee power to conduct an investigation, which, I understand, they welcome. If they welcome it, then give it to us. Let the country know whether the laws of the land amount to anything or not; let the country know whether a black man can walk down the street without being molested or interfered with; let the country know whether a Jew can go through the street without being interfered with; let the country know that 30,000,000 Catholics in this country stand up and oppose their actions, and we ask Congress for a fair investigation, and the Catholics, the Jews, and the colored people of this country will abide by the decision of Congress and live under the law just as they have always lived under it.

I would go further, if I could, with my resolution, and say, Mr. Chairman, that this Congress should pass an act that would give the Attorney General of the United States the power to investigate every organization in this country, no matter how big or how great they may be; so that he may not only know their membership and their officers, but that he may have the power to go in and prosecute them for any violation of the law. That is how far I would go, and then there would be no question——

Mr. Pou [interposing]. The courts have that authority, anyway, have they not, Mr. Tague?

Mr. Tague. Well, it is very evident, Mr. Pou, that the courts have not used that authority where these gentlemen have been working. They have been unable until now to find out who the officers of this organization are, and for the first time the United States of America knows who the leading officers of this organization are, and only after the most trying and searching investigation, thanks to the great newspapers of this country.

Now, Mr. Burns, of the Department of Justice, is here, and I understand you are going to call upon him. His department has investigated, and I am willing to rest my case——

Mr. Pou (interposing). What I meant by my question was this: Of course, if these people are guilty of any violation of the law there is no obstacle in the way of a prosecution.

Mr. Tague. Well, I understand, Mr. Pou, that in some of the States, in the State of Texas especially, in the legislature a few days ago a member of the legislature put in a resolution to give the courts the power and ask the courts of their land to investigate and punish the men who were causing these hardships and murders in the State of Texas. It is very evident that some of the authorities have been negligent.

Mr. Pou. You would not think such a resolution as that was necessary, would you?

Mr. Tague. I do under the present conditions; yes, sir; positively, because there is no question but what the whole land knows what is going on, and there has been no court that has started any proceedings against them so far as I can learn.

Mr. Rodenberg. Your position is that even the courts are intimidated in certain localities?

Mr. Tague. It has been proven right down South, where they walk right in and take the records of the court and destroy them and then go out and say that no man knows how it happened. Somebody must have known or they could not get to the records of the court, because they openly boast that not only Members of Congress but members of the judiciary, officers of the courts, and officers of the police departments in the towns where they are doing their work are members of their organization. Now, if that is the protection they receive, then the people of the country are entitled to further protection under the law, and I ask, Mr. Chairman, that the committee give this matter consideration, and I also ask for the passage of the resolution.

Mr. Campbell. Mr. Dyer, do you desire to be heard now?

STATEMENT OF HON. LEONIDAS C. DYER, A REPRESENTATIVE IN CONGRESS FROM THE STATE OF MISSOURI.

Mr DYER. Mr. Chairman and gentlemen of the committee: The resolution (H. Res. 192) which I have presented for the consideration of the Committee on Rules is somewhat different from the others in that it provides that this matter shall be investigated by the Committee on the Judiciary. Of course, all of you gentlemen, who are really great Congressmen, know there is only one committee in the House that is competent to investigate a great matter such as this, and that is the Judiciary Committee.

Mr. RODENBERG. You are a member of that committee?

Mr. DYER. Yes.

Mr. Chairman, my attention to this matter has been called by the people whom I have the honor to represent in the Congress, the people of the city of St. Louis, and for that reason I have been led to ask for an investigation. Of course, what affects the people of my city largely affects those of the entire country.

I have no desire to ask of this committee or of the Congress any investigation, so far as this organization may be concerned, as to what it does in its lodge rooms, behind its doors. I think that is a matter about which we have no concern. My only complaint is what it does as an organization on the outside, either in this regalia in which they hide themselves or otherwise. I think that is fundamentally wrong and against free government and against the rights of all humankind.

I have been told, and I believe it is quite true, that this organization has set itself up in many communities to say what should be or should not be done with reference to individuals in connection with violations of law, etc. I have received a number of letters, and a reference to one or two of them might bring to the attention of the committee just what I have in mind in saying that this organization has no right, as a secret organization, to go out upon the streets and highways for the purpose of trying to correct the morals of individuals, and if they are doing that they are violating the law of the land and should be dealt with. and in order to obtain full information as to whether or not that is so, it is necessary that a committee be appointed, because there are many complaints and many people are willing to testify about them.

Here is a letter I have received from a party who gives his name and address in Muskogee, Okla.—and, by the way, he says he knows me and that he helped to elect me to Congress, and that I ought to get off of this kind of doings, because he praises up this organization. He says, among other things, that he has had his eyes opened to the good that the Ku-Klux Klan has been and is doing in Oklahoma and Texas. He says:

"In the oil towns filled with the bad and 'no counts' of men and females and where no school girl or lady is safe from this tough and rough bootleg element, one 'visit' and the town is almost a 'Sunday-school class.'

"I could mention three or four towns I have been in and personally took the trouble to see if good had come out of this 'new way' of deal ng with this bad and tough element, and naturally, being a good Missourian who helped elect you, I don't want to see you get off on the wrong foot. I find that the very best Americans in all these towns speak out in its favor and * * *.

"I have not seen a case, not a single one, that all the leading good people of the town have not said, 'It's a good thing, push it along.' It moves out the gangster, bootlegger, chock shop, fast and loose females, and the man who abuses and neglects his children and his wife. It certainly was born of a great necessity in this oil country, as also was made necessary on the western frontier the 'vigilance committee' that put a stop to crime by using a rope. The delay in our laws is a protection to the criminal class, and the people, taxed to the limit, are taking this method to put a stop to this cost on the towns and county."

In other words, this and similar letters are to the effect that this organization has set up themselves as the ones that are to be the censors of the morality of the communities wherein they are organized, and if they believe that a man or woman is violating the laws, moral or other laws, that they are charged to go out and punish those people, and they apparently have done that in many portions of the country, especially in the South.

Now, here is another letter from a gentleman from Alabama. He says:

"I notice your action in regards to the K. K. K. in the columns of the New York World "——

Mr. Chairman, at this point, before reading this letter, I want to express to the New York World my great appreciation of the work it has done in bringing the facts to the attention of the public. My resolution started by mentioning a St. Louis paper, the Post Dispatch, and also mentioning the World. The Post Dispatch belongs to the same people that the World belongs to, but the credit for the investigation is due to the New York World and to the other 23 or 24 papers which obtained the news, as the Post Dispatch did, from the New York World, and then have given it to the public.

Now, here is a letter along similar lines:

"I notice your action in regards to the K. K. K. in the columns of the New York World, and I want to ask you to assist me to get a Federal warrant issued for members of this gang. They have ruined me physically, broken up my home, and forced me to sacrifice my business that I worked 17 years for, threatened me with death if I did not leave my native State and have driven me away from my wife and home. All evidence is now in the hands of Mr. Burns, Department of Justice, and I appeal to you also to assist me."

This is signed by a gentleman who gives his name and address.

I have also received similar letters, and I believe it is the duty of this Congress to see to it that the facts are brought out. I know and you know that this organization has been terrorizing various communities. Just let me give you two or three instances, Mr. Chairman, and then I shall close. It has been charged that violent and criminal assaults on individuals have been made, and that has been published in the papers of this country. During the past year constant succession of such acts, consisting of abductions, floggings, brandings, irreparable mutilations, applications of tar and feathers to men and women, and, in several instances, murders have been reported from various parts of the country. All these acts were marked by two characteristics. They purport to be punishments inflicted on violators of the statute or moral law, and they were inflicted almost without exception during the hours of darkness and with precaution to insure secrecy, and we have had interference of peace officers by bodies of men whose identity was concealed by masks. The New York World printed a list of these crimes, and the exact number or even the approximate number of such instances can not be and probably never will be known unless a Federal investigation develops such information. This New York paper listed 65 such criminal acts. In one of these instances the Klan at Beaumont, Tex., over its official seal, proclaimed to the public its full responsibility for it.

One of the things, Mr. Chairman, that has been and is being done by this organization is to terrorize certain classes of people in this country, and one, especially, is the negro population of America. Terrorization, active or passive, of the colored people of American communities has been one of its principal objects. It has been the result sometimes of public parades of klansmen in their uniform, sometimes of posted or published warnings put out in the name of the klan, sometimes merely of statements given to the press or spread by rumor that the K. K. K. was organizing or organized in a community. The name Ku-Klux alone is enough to thoroughly frighten the average ignorant negro.

Particularly marked instances of the active and premeditated use of such terrorization have been the holding of Ku-Klux parades in southern communities on the eve of an election, as happened last year at Ocoee and Jacksonville, Fla. Observers on the spot have reported that following such demonstrations only a fraction of the registered colored voters ventured to come to the polls. Passive terrorization has gone wherever the klan has gone. A single instance is that the klan has no sooner stated this last summer that it was organizing in New Jersey than the colored populace deluged the State authorities with pleas that the masked order be kept out; and when the authorities replied that they could do nothing until the klan had committed some overt act, the Negroes began buying arms and ammunition for the avowed purpose of defending their persons and homes, all of which has and does result in riots, disturbing the peace of communities and the Nation by violent propaganda of suspicion and dislike against selected religious and racial groups. Abundant evidence exists that such propaganda of hatred, directed particularly against those American citizens who happen to be Catholics or Jews, has been actively circulated by the professional solicitors who have been making a living getting members into the klan on a commission basis. Corollary evidence that the klan is systematically cultivating such militant bigotry among its members is found in the contents of its semiofficial publication, the Searchlight, of Atlanta, the pages of which literally drip with venomous and frequently totally baseless attacks on the Catholics and Jews. They refuse to take any man into their order who is a Catholic.

They have the right, of course—as any organization has the right—to say who they shall receive into this organization; but what they do on the outside in preaching and practicing against the Catholics, the Jews, and the Negroes is what I complain of; not that they do not accept these people into their klan.

Mr. Chairman, I could go on and give to you many instances wherein this organization is not for the best interests of the country; and I trust this committee will give favorable consideration to the pleas set forth in the resolutions which have been presented, and that a committee will be appointed—whether one of the standing committees or of the House itself—for the purpose of giving this matter the investigation and publicity to which it is entitled, and to find whether there are any laws upon the statute books—and if not, to see that such laws are enacted—which will prevent such things as have been happening by reason of the organization of this order. I thank you.

Mr. CAMPBELL. Is Mr. Thomas present?

Mr. THOMAS. Yes.

Mr. CAMPBELL. Before you proceed we will hear Mr. Ryan, of New York, who has introduced a resolution.

STATEMENT OF HON. THOMAS J. RYAN, A REPRESENTATIVE IN CONGRESS FROM THE STATE OF NEW YORK.

Mr. RYAN. Mr. Chairman and gentlemen of the committee, I introduced a resolution (H. Res. 191) directed against the Ku-Klux Klan, and I believe it is a matter that should receive the attention of Congress irrespective of the fact that it might be handled in the local courts. It is a matter that concerns the very principles upon which this country of ours was founded. Any organization that is anti-Catholic, anti-Negro, anti-Jew, and against the foreign element in this country, which comprises over 25 per cent of the voting strength of the country, is really a menace to the community. I do not insist that my particular feelings in this matter would in any way cast any aspersions upon the Ku-Klux Klan, but I have certain data, certain witnesses, certain men who are members of the Ku-Klux Klan, and certain information received from the Internal Revenue Department that would show certain violations of the law by the Ku-Klux Klan and certain omissions by the officers and members of the Ku-Kluk Klan that deserve and merit the attention of Congress.

My thoughts were first directed to this by certain men calling at the office and leaving letters and affidavits, and then by the investigation conducted by the New York World and the New York American. Both investigators employed members of the Ku-Klux Klan, and where we have members of the klan itself making statements against the klan, where we have income-tax reports that do not show the financial strength of the klan, do not show how their moneys were obtained, do not show how they are used or how they are kept, I think a condition is presented that calls for investigation by Congress. Then, again, when certain members of the klan commit acts that are recognized by the klan after those acts are committed that is full recognition by the klan of those acts and the klan is responsible for them.

I am willing to submit my evidence, my witnesses, and my data to the committee on reasonable notice. In two weeks' time I could supply the committee with all the information and all the data I might have.

Mr. CAMPBELL. Now, Mr. Thomas, do you desire to make a statement or submit to questions?

Mr. THOMAS. Whichever way the committee thinks will best bring out the points it wishes to reach.

Mr. CAMPBELL. I suggest that you make a statement in your own way of what you know about the matter to which attention is directed by these resolutions.

STATEMENT OF MR. ROWLAND THOMAS.

Mr. THOMAS. Mr. Chairman and gentlemen of the committee, what I have to say——

Mr. CAMPBELL (interposing). State your name, whom you represent, and what your activities have been in connection with this matter.

Mr. THOMAS. My name is Rowland Thomas. I am a member of the editorial staff of the New York World. At the beginning of July I was assigned to the duty of investigating the Ku-Klux Klan That investigation occupied the months of July, August, and September. It was made as thoroughly as a newspaper investigation, without the right of subpœna or any other access to papers, can be made. We investigated in Atlanta. We sent two men of our staff there separately to examine condit'ons, and we investigated also by means of our local representatives in, perhaps, 30—possibly more—cities in the United States. In our investigation in those smaller communities we were governed by the same rules of accuracy which always govern a newspaper. We attempted always without bias to get an accurate statement of the facts as known. As a result of this investigation in September we began publishing a series of articles in which we stated the facts as we had found them.

In speaking to the committee now, i want always to be understood as indicating what seemed to me the conditions as they appeared on the surface. I can not pretend to go thoroughly to the bottom for the very fact I have spoken of, that a newspaper has no power of subpœna or search. A great deal of what comes to it has to come by rumor and it has to be followed up.

Perhaps the outstanding fact in our investigation is that during the last year a great number of acts of violence against individuals have been reported in the press throughout the United States. The acts I refer to are all marked by two characteristics. They were, or pretended to be, punishments administered to individuals for the violation of statute law or objectionable moral conduct. The second thing that marked them is the fact that almost without exception these punishments were administere˙ in the hours of darkness by men whose identity was completely concealed by masks and whose responsibility for the acts, therefore, could not easily be established. Practically without exception when such acts were reported in the papers they were referred to as acts of the Ku-Klux Klan, or Ku-Klux outrages; always the name Ku-Klux came in. As we investigated in the communities from which these acts were reported we found it a matter of common public belief that they were Ku-Klux acts. As we went on we found one instance in which a klan of the Ku-Klux, using its own seal and signing itself "Ku-Klux Klan," had sent to the newspapers of Beaumont, Tex., a statement of some 4,000 words covering one of these acts of violence, with the request that the newspapers publish this statement. In the statement the Beaumont klan accepted complete responsibility for an act of outrageous and lawless violence which consisted in abducting a citizen of Beaumont, taking him to an isolated spot at night, inflicting a flogging on him, giving him a coat of tar and feathers, bringing him back nude, except for the tar and feathers, to the central portion of Beaumont, dumping him in the street there, according to the statement, as a warning to the community and to other of his kind, and giving him a warning that if he did not leave town permanently within a short time something worse would happen to him. The imperial authorities of the Ku-Klux Klan denied—they did two things, and you will find, gentlemen, as you go on that this is quite typical. They made a statement from Atlanta——

Mr. CAMPBELL (interposing). I understand the local klan at Beaumont assumed the responsibility?

Mr. THOMAS. The local klan at Beaumont assumed the responsibility, and a copy of the statement which they gave to the local papers is in the office of the editor of one of the local papers in Beaumont, bearing the seal of the klan. A photograph of that portion of that statement is in the office of the New York World and can be made available to the committee on 24 hours' notice, just long enough to have it mailed over. The imperial authorities first announced through their press service that they had suspended the charter of this klan. Information reaching me from Beaumont is to the effect that the klan has never, so far as known. ceased is activities there. I mean by that that there is still a klan in Beaumont; men who are members recognize themselves as still members and have their meetings. After that statement, that the charter had been suspended, from imperial headquarters once again it was announced that the klan had made an investigation and had found out that some party or parties unknown, actuated by malice against this order, had not only done the deed but had somehow stolen the official seal of the klan and affixed it to this false statement. The many other outrages which have been reported—I think we in the World carried some 64 other cases—are not linked closely with the klan in that way. As I say, they are all marked by those two sets of characteristics. There are punishments and there are punishments inflicted under the protection of masks, and local report and local belief in all these communities is that they were Ku-Klux work. That seems to me one of the strongest reasons why an investigation should be made. The whole subject is so exceedingly difficult that light needs to be let in on the thing to the very fullest degree possible.

Another thing which we found in investigating this order is that it seems to be rooted in hatred and prejudice. This aspect of the thing first came to.my attention in some official correspondence which passed between the king kleagle of the State of Tennessee and one of his kleagles. Perhaps I should say here that when you strip the fancy language from all that a kleagle is nothing more or less than a salesman of.memberships in the klan, working on a commission basis, and a king kleagle is nothing more or less than a State sales manager, the official or business.superior of the kleagles. A letter came into my possession from the king kleagle of Tennessee, whose name is McArthur, saying to this kleagle that the klan itself did not print copies of the Knights of Columbus oath but they could easily be obtained, and that they, the king kleagles, found them of great use in certain selected instances. "However," he said, "I find this dope is contained in that Washington paper, The Protestant, of which I am sending you a bundle of copies." He said, "Of course, also, you must get all copies of The Searchlight, because they also are extremely useful." Following that lead, I procured a copy of the so called Knights of Columbus oath, such as had been used in Tennessee after this word of advice from the king kleagle. I dare say all you gentlemen have seen copies of that oath. It first appeared, I think, about 1912 or 1913, in an election case here in the House of Representatives, a case from Pennsylvania, Bonniwell and Butler. As part of the proceedings in that election case it was printed in the Congressional Record. Since that time it has repeatedly been circulated in all parts of the United States, always bearing at the bottom the statement that it is a part of the Congressional Record, the inference being that, therefore, it has been officially signed and sealed by the Congress of the United States as a true version of the oath assumed by fourth-degree members of the Knights of Columbus.

Mr. JOHNSON. Do you know whether that has ever been circulated under a frank?

Mr. THOMAS. I do not know that. This oath is as thoroughly calculated to stir up hatred against a certain class of American citizens as anything could be. I have a copy here which I will give the committee if they care to have it.

Mr. POU. A copy of what?

Mr. THOMAS. Of the bogus oath of the fourth degree of the Knights of Columbus, the thing that was printed in the Congressional Record.

Mr. POU. You mean it is not the real oath?

Mr. THOMAS. It is not the real oath, Mr. Pou. The real oath has been made known in court proceedings and forms a part of the record of a case in Minnesota in a libel suit.

Mr. POU. Could you have the two oaths, the bogus oath and the real oath, inserted in the record side by side?

Mr. THOMAS. They can be inserted side by side. They are, I believe, included in a mass of documents which is to come to the committee from another source of investigation in the course of this hearing, but if other copies are wanted I can furnish them easily. I also got copies of the paper called the Protestant, which was referred to. I found that also was given to the most rabid expressions of bigotry against members of the Catholic church. For the purposes of the record, let me state here that my mother's family has been a New England Congregationalist family ever since there was a New England, and that my father's people are Welsh dissenters and have been dissenters, even from the established Church of England, for some 600 years. So that any sympathy I might have for the Church of Rome is only the sympathy of fair play in this particular case.

Now, as we came to look into the activities of the kleagles, or salesmen, of this order in New York City, we found that they were using this same bitter attack on Catholics constantly to secure members. We also found that they were using a similar attack on Jewish citizens of the United States. In the case of the Jews the attack was not so open, but it was persistent nevertheless. We found also that they attempted always to play on any prejudice which might exist against foreign-born persons who had become citizens of the United States by naturalization, their cry constantly being, "We are 100 per cent Americans," the implication being that anyone who was not one of them was hardly 100 per cent. He may have been as pure as Ivory soap, but he did not come up to that little notch of perfection.

This attitude, of course, appears in their official documents. In the questionnaire, which is a preliminary to admission to the order, a candidate has to state that he is native born, white, a Gentile, and owes no allegiance of any sort to any foreign body, organization, potentate, ruler, and so on and so forth, the reference to the foreign body and potentate, and all that, being made perfectly clear in other literature as a reference to the Pope and to the Roman Catholic Church. We find, or have found, that as a result of this active cutivation of prejudice strong feeling is being aroused where the klan goes, with the result that the peace of communities is put in jeopardy. The most striking instance of the thing which came to my attention came in the home city of the klan, Atlanta, where some few months ago a member of the school board insisted that a teacher, Miss Julia Riordan, who had been in the service of the Atlanta schools for some 20 years and who had constantly given satisfaction, should be discharged. He stated in an open meeting of the Atlanta School Board that the reason Miss Riordan must be discharged was because she was a Catholic and that no Catholic could be allowed to be a teacher in the public schools of Georgia. During the last fortnight another member of the Atlanta governing body, Sims, of the Common Council of Atlanta, introduced a resolution in the Atlanta Common Council for the investigation of the Knights of Columbus, basing the reason for this investigation on this same bogus fourth-degree oath, which I spoke of earlier. That resolution, as I remember it, was passed unanimously, but a little later was, with equal unanimity, rescinded. The man who in the school board insisted on and procured the discharge of Miss Riordan is not known to be a member of the klan. He is known, however, to be one of the associate editors of that newspaper called the Searchlight, which is, by rumor, owned largely by Mrs. Elizabeth Tyler, the business partner of Edward Young Clarke, who manages the business affairs of the Ku-Klux Klan, and Hutchison is a law partner of one J. O. Wood, who is set down at the masthead of the Searchlight as its editor. The connection between the parties is suggestive.

Mr. RODENBERG. Is that the official organ of the Ku-Klux Klan?

Mr. THOMAS. They have never admitted that it was the official organ. I have to come constantly to the process of calling attention to the significance of certain things that have happened. About the middle of September—let me see; I can give you the exact date—on the 18th of September, which was a Monday morning, the World had reason to publish an article calling attention to a criminal record which existed in the cases of Edward Young Clarke and Mrs. Elizabeth Tyler——

Mr. CAMPBELL (interposing.) I suggest that that matter might be omitted.

Mr. THOMAS. Very well, sir; I can bring out the point I was making without going into the details of that. After a certain article was published in the New York World of the 18th of September, which bore on the personalities of certain members and officers of the Ku-Klux Klan, the Searchlight, which had up to that time been a weekly paper, announced in its columns that beginning the following Monday it would become a daily paper and that it would be used to meet the attacks of the New York World and other newspapers on the Ku-Klux Klan and some of its members and officers. The Searchlight has published interviews with Col. Simmons, the imperial wizard of the order; it has run a column conducted by the Rev. Caleb Ridley, the imperial chaplain of the order, and as the committee examines the Searchlight it will find a very close connection between Ku-Klux affairs and that newspaper, closer than it can find in any other publication. Another thing which developed in the course of our investigation was the fact that this awakening of the spirit of violence which was, to say the least, suspiciously connected with the Ku-Klux Klan, and this spreading of the spirit of racial and religious prejudice and hatred, was being done as a part of a campaign to get money and that this campaign to get money was apparently highly successful. We had no sooner begun to make this exposure than officials of the klan announced through the press that they were going to bring libel suits, amounting to some $10,000,000, against us and other newspapers, and that they were retaining 200 of the most prominent lawyers of the country to see them through in those suits. They also have made statements that they were going to spend a million and a half dollars on their imperial palace headquarters and another million or two on a manufacturing plant so that they could get all the profit out of the regalia, stationery, lodge furniture and supplies, and all those things which were used throughout the klan. They talked in millions, and so far as we could find out with our limited facilities of inquiry, they were justified in talking in millions.

They claimed to have some 650,000 or 700,000 members, these figures being given out by Imperial Kleagle Clarke, who had complete charge of all the work of securing members and had been made by Col. Simmons, the business manager of all the affairs of the klan.

It was known that every person who joined the klan made a contribution of $10 before he could be admitted. So that if their figures were correct, some six and a half or seven mill on dollars had passed in the matter of membership admissions alone. We knew also that every member was required to have the regalia and that this regalia was ordered from Col. Simmons with an initial down payment of $6.50. So that on their membership figures there came in another three and a half or four million dollars. We found out that lodge furniture had to be procured by all the different lodges by order through Col. Simmons at high prices. We had no means of estimating what the income had been.

It was obvious that the Searchlight was bringing in a considerable income, and there were other sources of income which other people can point out more accurately than I can. So that altogether they had had access to a very large amount of money, this income being the fruit of the spread of that spirit of violence and that propaganda of group dislike, suspicion, and hatred.

We found also that they boasted or declared that they were setting up an invisible empire here in the United States. We found that their chief man had taken the title of emperor and that he issued imperial and secret decrees from an imperial palace. We found also, having secured a copy of their oath, that every man who joined this order pledged himself to obey without question all the instructions of the emperor, who had been elected for life. We found that severe penalties were threatened to him if he failed ever in obedience. We found that part of this oath was a pledge of impenetrable secrecy surrounding all the doings of the klan. We found that each member promised to keep at all costs, even that of life, in the face of any coercion, persecution, or punishment, all secrets of the klan and all knowledge of the klan committed to him, with only four exceptions. He was not obliged to keep to himself a violation of the oath of the klan, treason against the United States of America, malicious murder, and rape. Those four secrets, apparently, he could give up to other persons, three of them the crimes, supposedly, he was at liberty to reveal to peace officers and judicial officers of the United States Government. All others, as far as the phraseology of the oath can be read, he was to keep to himself. They belong to the klan and to the invisible empire and not to the United States of America.

We found them boasting that they had succeeded in securing as members bound by this oath and made citizens in this invisible empire many men who are also officials of the visible, constituted Government of the United States. Emperor Simmons more than once made statements that Members of the Congress of the United States—both Representatives and Senators—belonged to his invisible empire, and therefore were under his imperial orders. He boasted that governors, mayors, and other administrative officers, members of city councils, were citizens of this invisible government, and that sheriffs, policemen, police chiefs were citizens of the invisible empire and that judges on the bench were members of it.

The statement has been made publicly in print that it amused a klansman when he read in the press that a judge had charged a grand jury to investigate the klan, because all klansmen knew that a substantial part of the membership of that grand jury would be klansmen; that the judge was a joke in making such a suggestion of investigation.

Of course, another point which you do not care to have taken up now concerns the known and proven character of the people who had secured control of this invisible empire and were directing its affairs. That, I dare say, will come in through other sources which will be more direct than my own investigations were.

This, in brief, is my statement of the basic findings of our investigation.

Mr. CAMPBELL. Your findings covered the question of violence to citizens in how many States?

Mr. THOMAS. You want an approximate answer?

Mr. CAMPBELL. Yes; just an approximation.

Mr. THOMAS. Florida and Texas seemed to be the hotbeds. Other cases were reported from Georgia, from Alabama, and, as I remember it, from Mississippi, from Oklahoma, and, I think, one case from Missouri.

Mr. CAMPBELL. You have cited one case of violence to a citizen. Have you any others in mind of a different character?

Mr. THOMAS. There is a case which happened in Atlanta last winter which seems to me to be in need of the most thorough probing. I have not the exact date in mind, but sometime in March three men, not disguised, went to a so-called weiner stand in Atlanta, kept by a man named Thomas, and representing to him that there was some trouble about a bad check and that the chief of police wanted to see Thomas, they got him into an automobile with them. My information is that the driver of this car was named H. R. Pitts, that the second member of the party was named Shute, and that the third member of the party was Thompson. After these three men got Thomas into the car, they told him they wanted to drive out and pick up a couple more men whom the chief of police wanted to see also, and under that pretense, they got him out in the outskirts of Atlanta, near Lakewood Park, where they got him out of the car and attempted to tie him to a tree, telling him they were going to give him a flogging. By the way, I should have prefaced this actual incident by stating that Thomas had received several anonymous notes of warning previous to this time, telling him that he was going around with a woman and that that activity would not be stood for. They got him out and attempted to tie him to a tree. Thomas drew a knife and killed Thompson, severely slashed Pitts, and, my recollection is, he also slashed the other man, and got away. He was arrested, indicted for manslaughter, tried, and acquitted.

At the inquest into the death of Thompson, the other two members of the abducting party, Pitts and Shute, were examined by the coroner's jury, and Pitts was represented there by an Atlanta lawyer by the name of Capt. W. S. Coburn, who was publicly known and acknowledge in Atlanta at that time as the supreme attorney of the Ku-Klux Klan.

Later, after the acquittal of Thomas on the manslaughter charge, Pitts and Shute were brought to trial on the charge of abducting Thomas, and on that occasion, also, Pitts was once more defended by Coburn, the supreme attorney of the Ku-Klux Klan. At this abduction trial no mention was made in the record of the Ku-Klux Klan. Thomas, the victim of the abduction, declined to appear and press the charges against the two men, stating that he had had satisfaction enough, and the charges against them were dismissed.

I have been informed by the men who were attorneys for Thomas in the manslaughter trial that during their preparation of the case and during the trial they received many threats, either anonymous or initialed K. K. K., which written threats are in their possession at the present time.

Here again comes one of those points which I wish to insert merely for its significance——

Mr. FESS (interposing). Were these threats made through the mail?

Mr. THOMAS. I am unable to say, Dr. Fess, whether they came through the mail or were delivered otherwise. That could easily be ascertained from these attorneys in Atlanta.

Following the dismissal of the abduction case against Shute and Pitts, Capt. Coburn was sent to California as the grand goblin or district sales manager of the so-called domain of the Pacific coast, and Pitts was sent to California to work under him as a kleagle or salesman. My latest information is that Coburn is still functioning in Los Angeles as grand goblin and that Pitts is still working in Fresno, Calif., as kleagle.

Mr. KREIDER. As grand goblin, what are his duties?

Mr. THOMAS. The grand goblin is a part of the propagation department. The committee will find that there seems to be a dual activity in this thing. There is the business side and there is the intensively secret, fraternal order side. The business so far has consisted largely of securing members; in fact, only in July Imperial Wizard Simmons gave an interview to the Searchlight, which was printed, I think, on the 2d of July. In that statement Col. Simmons stated he had just received a report from Imperial Kleagle Clarke, and was greatly gratified by the rapid progress being made in securing members, who were then flocking in at the rate of some 5,000 a week. He said the klan had been under attack, but that it did not mind the attack; that at the present time it was doing nothing but organizing, and probably for a long time would do nothing but organize, because it did not intend to attempt any activity until it was so strong that it was sure any activity attempted would prove successful. He said that he would advise those interested in fireworks, verbal or otherwise, to wait patiently, for the time of the klan was coming. He reiterated his statement that they were now only organizing and intended to get busy later, and said that at the present "We are only keeping watch and making records, but the day is coming when all those who have attacked us will find themselves in an exceedingly unpleasant situation."

As I say, the business activity so far has been largely a drive for members at $10 per head. That has been in charge of the so-called propagation department, of which the superior, in fact, and by appointment of the imperial head of the order, is Edward Young Clarke, of Atlanta, who before taking up with the Ku-Klux Klan had been a drive promoter for a number of charitable things.

Mr. RODENBERG. Did I understand you to say in the beginning of your statement that your investigation covered approximately 68 cases of outrages on individuals?

Mr. THOMAS. We listed 65 cases, Mr. Rodenberg. We know, of course, that that is a very incomplete list, indeed. Those are merely cases which fell under our classification and were published through regular press sources.

Mr. FESS. Can you give the committee that list?

Mr. THOMAS. I can; yes, Dr. Fess. This propagation activity and other business activity runs on under the direction of Mr. Clarke as the imperial kleagle.

Mr. KREIDER. I would like to know about this goblin business. Is he the financial manager?

Mr. THOMAS. The goblin is one of the employees of the propagation department, and at the head of the propagation department is this imperial kleagle.

Mr. KREIDER. Is the kleagle over the goblin or is the goblin over the kleagle?

Mr. THOMAS. The imperial kleagle is over everybody else except the imperial wizard, who has no superior. Under the imperial kleagle comes eight district sales managers called grand goblins, and they are in charge of domains. I realize this phraseology is highly complicated. A domain is a group of States, with one exception. The domain of the Capital comprises only the District of Columbia, but the other seven domains comprise groups of States, each in charge of a grand goblin.

Mr. FESS. Does the order cover the whole United States?

Mr. THOMAS. It does; yes. Under the grand goblin is a State sales manager bearing the title of king kleagle and under the king kleagle is a group of legwork men or kleagles. They are the house to house solicitors or peddlers for membership.

It may interest the committee to know what we learned about the distribution of the membership fees. These membership fees are $10 a head, and they are camouflaged so that they escape any income tax question by being called donations to the propagation fund of the Knights of the Ku-Klux Klan. Of this $10, in th normal course of procedure, the kleagle who signs the candidate on the dotted line gets $4 at once. He sends the other $6 on to his king kleagle or State sales manager, who takes out $1 for himself and sends the remaining $5 on to the grand goblin or district sales manager. The grand goblin subtracts 50 cents for his part and sends $4.50 to Atlanta.

Now, what becomes of the thing in Atlanta we never succeeded in learning from any statements made by the Ku-Klux officers in Atlanta. I believe that investigators for one department of the Federal Government have now learned what division is purported to be made of that $4.50 after it reaches Atlanta.

Mr. CAMPBELL Do you desire to make any further statement?

Mr. THOMAS. I think not, Mr. Chairman.

Mr. CAMPBELL. The material you have is at the disposal of the committee?

Mr. THOMAS. Any material I have is at the disposal of the committee; yes, sir.

Mr. GARRETT. I would like to ask the gentlemen a question.

Mr. GALLIVAN. If the gentleman has finished——

Mr. CAMPBELL (interposing). Mr. Garrett, of the committee, desires to ask a question.

Mr. GARRETT. Mr. Thomas, I want to ask you whether the investigations made by the World convinced you that the statement as to the membership was approximately correct?

Mr. THOMAS. It did not. Mr. Garrett. I felt that these gentlemen were entitled to the benefit of their own staements to a certain extent. I discounted their statement of 650,000 to 700,000 and stated that there might be 500,000 members of the outfit at the present time, but even that is simply taking their statement about the thing. They are the only people who know how many members they have.

Mr. GARRETT. I believe you said there were eight districts?

Mr. THOMAS. Yes.

Mr. GARRETT. Did those eight districts cover the entire United States?

Mr. THOMAS. They did.

Mr. GARRETT. Continental United States alone?

Mr. THOMAS. Continental United States only. I should say that a branch of the klan is now reported to be attempting to operate in Canada, but that is quite a recent development.

Mr. GARRETT. How extensively, geographically, do you think the organization extends from the investigations made in the United States?

Mr. THOMAS. I have had reports of klans established all the way from Connecticut to Portland, Oreg., and those statements were given out to the newspapers by men who represented themselves as qualified organizers for the order, and from North to South there have been organizations reported from the Canadian border; that is, from Chicago, we will say, to the extreme South. There has been the organization of the klan reported from Arizona and from California.

Mr. GARRETT. When you say from Connecticut to Portland, Oreg., do you mean that that covers practically all the territory between those two points?

Mr. THOMAS. A klan has been organized in Omaha; a klan has been organized in Wisconsin, in Michigan, in Iowa, and I think I have reports, but I am not positive about this, of a klan organization in the two Dakotas. The organization in the North is a great deal more sporadic than in the South at present, because the organizing activity was just getting up to carry its peak load in the north at the time when this exposure came, and this exposure has checked a good deal of that organizing activity.

Mr. JOHNSON. Mr. Chairman, I would like to ask the gentleman a question. Do you know who originated this plan of organization and of a division of the commission and where it came from?

Mr. THOMAS. I only have the information which has been given to me in some instances by persons who were members of the klan and in other instances by residents of Atlanta who had a good deal of familiarity with the course of events in Atlanta.

Mr. JOHNSON. I have noticed such a striking similarity between this plan of organization of the Ku-Klux Klan and an organization that has been in the West called the Nonpartisan League, with about the same sort of division of commission, and I am wondering whether you could say whether the Nonpartisan League got the plan of organization from the klan or whether the klan may have secured it from the league?

Mr. THOMAS. I think it would take a Congressional investigation perhaps to determine that question.

Mr. FESS. Is there any organization in the District of Columbia?

Mr. THOMAS. There is; yes, Dr. Fess.

Mr. GARRETT. Mr. Thomas, I believe you stated that so far as your investigation extended the alleged acts of punishment committed by the klan or those alleged to belong to the klan were confined to cases of violation of statutory law and moral law?

Mr. THOMAS. And moral law; yes, sir.

Mr. GARRETT. There were no cases, so far as your investigations extended, that went outside of those two things?

Mr. THOMAS. So far as my investigations went, I know of no cases where, at least, the allegation was not made to the victim that he was being punished for some violation of moral or statutory law.

Mr. GARRETT. There was no case of punishment on account of any religious belief, so far as your investigations showed?

Mr. THOMAS. None that was so stated to the victim, so far as my investigation went.

Mr. GARRETT. And I suppose there were none, so far as your investigations went, that indicated that any punishment was being inflicted on account of the racial characteristics of the person punished?

Mr. THOMAS. I came across no such statement made to the victim by the band of regulators.

Mr. RODENBERG. Did you interview the victims themselves?

Mr. THOMAS. I did not. That was beyond my power, to attempt to go to all those communities and interview those persons.

Mr. CAMPBELL. I think that is all, Mr. Thomas.

STATEMENT OF MR. C. ANDERSON WRIGHT.

Mr. CAMPBELL. Mr. Wright, will you state your name to the stenographer?

Mr. WRIGHT. C. Anderson Wright.

Mr. CAMPBELL. State where you reside.

Mr. WRIGHT. New York City. I was formerly a member——

Mr. TERRELL (interposing). Mr. Chairman, pardon me, but will you ask the gentleman to turn around so we over here can hear what he has to say?

Mr. WRIGHT. I was formerly a member of the New York klan, king kleagle, assigned as chief of staff of the invisible planet, Knights of the Air. Gentlemen, I urge an——

Mr. CAMPBELL (interposing). When were you a member of the klan?

Mr. WRIGHT. When was I a member?

Mr. CAMPBELL. Yes.

Mr. WRIGHT. Up until the 14th of this month; I mean last month.

Mr. CAMPBELL. The 14th of last September?

Mr. WRIGHT. No; this October.

Mr. CAMPBELL. This is October.

Mr. WRIGHT. I mean the month before that, September.

Mr. CAMPBELL. You were a member up to the 14th of September last?

Mr. WRIGHT. Yes, sir.

Mr. CAMPBELL. State again what empire or part of the empire you had jurisdiction over.

Mr. WRIGHT. The aeronautical unit known as the Knights of the Air.

Mr. CAMPBELL. What was your jurisdiction?

Mr. WRIGHT. The whole United States in this department.

Mr. CAMPBELL. Who appointed you?

Mr. WRIGHT. Edward Young Clarke, the imperial kleagle.

Mr. CAMPBELL. From Atlanta?

Mr. WRIGHT. From Atlanta. I was stationed in Atlanta.

Mr. CAMPBELL. When was this appointment made?

Mr. WRIGHT. It was made last March or April. I could not state positively. I have not my papers with me to-day.

I wish to say, gentlemen, that the investigation should be made on account of race and religious hatred above all, and especially that the real power behind the klan is a woman, Mrs. Elizabeth Tyler, copartner of Edward Young Clarke, owners of the Southern Publicity Association; that Mrs. Tyler absolutely dominates and runs the klan through Imperial Kleagle Clarke, and everything is done by her direction.

Mr. CAMPBELL. Is she over the imperial wizard?

Mr. WRIGHT. Not officially, no, sir; but unofficially, yes. It is an absolute fact—there is no question about it—that Mrs. Tyler and Mr. Clarke own the klan and control the klan in every way. All documents are issued by Clarke, possibly signed by Col. Simmons or possibly signed by his secretary, Mr. Wade, using his signature at Mr. Clarke's direction. Mrs. Taylor and Mr. Clarke, as has been brought out in the papers, at the time I was in Atlanta were living together on an estate. I visited their home many times; I can prove by witnesses.

Mr. CAMPBELL. We do not care to go into that phase of it at this time.

Mr. WRIGHT. I can back all this up by documentary evidence I have and have published in the New York American and affiliated papers throughout the country in my articles. I claim that they have evaded the war tax or income tax; that they call their initiation a donation to get away from any initiation fees; they call their dues klectokens; that they make an enormous profit on their regalia; that their Searchlight, the semiofficial organ, which is owned by Mrs. Tyler, prints treason, and it goes through the mails. I think the basis of inquiry for this should be on their evasion of war tax or income tax and the use of the mails to publish the Searchlight and have it go through the mails. I will be very willing to answer any questions, as I was in the imperial palace for quite a time and knew everything that went on there.

Mr. RODENBERG. How did you happen to be assigned to this aeronautical division?

Mr. WRIGHT. I was in the Air Service, and I am a reserve in the Army to-day. Through that I was interested in aeronautics. I joined the klan in New York and was very much interested in it at that time, as I was in other fraternal orders of which I am a member, and thought it was a very good thing until I got to Atlanta, when I found out that Col. Simmons really had absolutely no control over anything. My business, directions and everything were received from Mr. Clarke and Mrs. Tyler. I was given my instructions by her.

Mr. POU. How long were you in Atlanta?

Mr. WRIGHT. I was there two months. I was there twice.

Mr. RODENBERG. As I understand, you say Clarke assigned you as king kleagle for New York?

Mr. WRIGHT. No; I was unassigned and was automatically placed in charge of the Knights of the Air as chief of staff. It was an affiliated branch. I have documentary evidence to prove that over his signature and seal of the klan.

Mr. CAMPBELL. Have you that with you?

Mr. WRIGHT. I have it in my safe-deposit vault; I do not have it here, but it has been reproduced in the Washington Times and in all the press of the country.

Mr. POU. Did you see active service during the war?

Mr. WRIGHT. Yes, sir.

Mr. POU. Abroad?

Mr. WRIGHT. Both abroad and on this side.

Mr. POU. As an Army aviator?

Mr. WRIGHT. Yes, sir. And I have been the publisher of the largest aeronautical paper in the country, known as the Tail Spin, which was formerly a Government paper and which I took over. It was a corporation in which I still have the controlling stock, but I have had to put it up on the shelf for the time being, because it was not a paying proposition.

Mr. CAMPBELL. Give us some idea of the office force and the office locations in Atlanta.

Mr. WRIGHT. Since I have left Atlanta——

Mr. CAMPBELL (interposing). Describe first the imperial palace.

Mr. WRIGHT. The imperial palace when I was in Atlanta—which I understand has since been moved—was located on the third floor of the Haynes Building; it was formerly a loft and was fitted up by Clarke for this use. It had in it the general offices of the klan, which only attended to the chartered klans.

Mr. CAMPBELL. How many rooms are in the imperial palace?

Mr. WRIGHT. There was the general room, where all the clerks were, and it was divided into three sections; there was an outer office where Mr. Clarke and his assistants had their offices, and there was a private office that Col. Simmons had at the end of the hall, or off of that room. The imperial palace only attended, however, to the chartered klans; the unchartered klans and field forces were all run from the Flatiron Building, where the headquarters of the Southern Publicity Association are.

Mr. KREIDER. The Flatiron Building in New York?

Mr. WRIGHT. No; Atlanta, Ga. The Southern Publicity Association has half a floor, and Mrs. Tyler is in absolute and supreme command of everything that goes on. She has charge of all the field forces. Mr. Clarke—of course, a woman is not eligible for membership, so her partner was the member.

Mr. RODENBERG. She is the directing genius?

Mr. WRIGHT. Yes. I would like to tell from Clarke's own words how he came into the klan and how he happened to come into the order itself. He stated he joined the klan in Atlanta after he had finished his war work, which consisted of advancing drives for the Salvation Army, the Y. M. C. A., the Red Cross, etc., which they took care of in Georgia during the war and built up a large business. They were looking around for something, and Clarke, in the meantime, had joined the klan. The klan was in very poor financial shape, had no money whatsoever. Col. Simmons, while very sincere, had no money to go ahead with the work. Mr. Clarke told me he talked this over with Mrs. Tyler, and they saw the possibilities of a wonderful revival of this name—Ku-Klux Klan—which would strike the public's fancy. So they went and made Col. Simmons a proposition to handle the business end.

Mr. CAMPBELL. How long ago was this?

Mr. WRIGHT. This was just a little over a year ago. At that time, as I am told by Mr. Edward Young Clarke, the klan had about 1,000 or 2,000 members; to-day they boast of 700,000 members. Whether that is true I can not say, because I did not have access to their records, but that is what they claim. With the $10 initiation fee you can readily see how much money they have taken in. I can tell you the division of that money even further than it has been told. Of the $10 originally taken $4 goes to the field man or kleagle; $1 goes to the State man, who is the sales manager of that State, known as the king kleagle, and 50 cents goes to the grand goblin of that district, who is district sales manager; the remaining $4.50 goes into the imperial palace, and I am told by Mr. Clarke that he receives $3 of this remaining $4.50, which he uses in any way he sees fit for the Southern Publicity Association, and the remaining $1.50 goes into the treasury and is subject to the check·of the imperial wizard. Now, I am sure that if they have 700,000 members, as they claim, that reports have not been shown where all this money has been spent or returns have not been made of it.

Mr. Fess. Is this $10 an admittance fee or an annual fee?

Mr. Wright. They call it a donation fee; it is an initiation fee but they call it a donation.

Mr. Fess. Does it pay for complete membership?

Mr. Wright. It pays for the first degree; it pays for the initiation of the first degree.

Mr. Rodenberg. Do you know whether the members are assessed annual dues?

Mr. Wright. Yes, sir.

Mr. Rodenberg. Which go to the imperial palace?

Mr. Wright. Yes, sir.

Mr. Rodenberg. How much are they?

Mr. Wright. They range from $5 up. It depends on how much is set, but I understand that $3 must come into the imperial treasury from each member each year, and what the local klans charge is up to them, like in any other order.

Mr. Rodenberg. Your understanding is that each individual member of the klan must contribute $3 a year to the imperial office?

Mr. Wright. Yes, sir; but that is collected by the local klans.

Mr. Rodenberg. Three times 700,000 would be $2,100,000 a year of income that the klan would have from its present membership?

Mr. Wright. Yes, sir.

Mr. Rodenberg. And you say that is exclusive of the initiation fee?

Mr. Wright. Yes; it is exclusive of the initiation fee, and that is not even counting the sale of their robes, which Mr. Clarke admits cost $1.25 to manufacture and which he compels every klansman to buy and pay $6.50 for; the price was $7.50 until just lately. The robes range in price up to the grand goblin's robes. It depends on how fine it is and the regalia required.

I have covered everything fully in my newspaper articles and I will be very glad to submit the whole report to this committee. I do not think when a klansman joins the order he realizes the conditions or the race hatred that is preached until he is in. I joined the klan in a class which the imperial kleagle says consisted of 1,000 members, but it did not consist of at the most over 250, as I was in the class. After we were initiated meetings were held by Grand Goblin Lloyd P. Hooper, who was at the Embassy Hotel, in New York, which was the local headquarters. These rooms were checked up under the name of Edward Young Clarke, the imperial kleagle; the negotiations were made by him for this suite at the Embassy. The work was carried on there secretly. Small classes were put through as they were very afraid of the New York police, in fact, such instances are told me by the proprietor of that hotel, Mr. Levin, that strict orders were given by Mr. Hooper that if anybody called and asked for him he was not at the Embassy Hotel, but if they called and asked for room so-and-so they would get Mr. Hooper. The New York police authorities had repeatedly stated that the klan could not meet in New York.

Mr. Campbell. How many degrees are in the initiation?

Mr. Wright. There are four degrees to the order, but that is something to come. The first degree is the only one in operation to-day. You can become a member in one degree; you just simply pay $10 and you receive all the mystic ritual and oaths.

Mr. Rodenberg. That is, $10 for the first degree?

Mr. Wright. Yes.

Mr. Rodenberg. What do they charge for the third degree?

Mr. Wright. The other degrees are not in operation yet, but the plans are to charge $10 for each degree. Then they were also to have a funny degree which would be something of a rival to the Grotto and Shrine in Masonry, which they would call the Knights of Mirth. Mr. Clarke told this to me in detail several times, and this was to be an exclusive degree, in which they could sit back and see their work accomplished and be satisfied. Their work on racial hatred, etc., would come on during the different degrees. The idea was this, as was told to me many times by the officers, that after they had gotten everybody in the first degree who was 100 per cent American, so called by the klan—they must be protestants, gentiles, and native born—then they would take those men up and offer them the second degree, and they would let down the bars of the first degree and get $10 from the foreign borr. They would then take men in the second degree into the third and let in a few more, where possible the Catholics, although that was not definitely decided on, and so up into the degrees until they had gotten everybody in the first degree, and then the people in the top degree could look down and know who were in the lower degrees, but the men in the lower degrees would not know who the men were in the higher degree.

Mr. CAMPBELL. Is there an open roster of the members?

Mr. WRIGHT. No, sir. They have a very elaborate file system in Atlanta in the imperial palace; each member in each klan is kept in a certain division of very expensive steel files; each drawer is pulled out and it has a list of the members card by card, but those are not accessible to anybody but the secretary of the order, the imperial secretary.

Mr. CAMPBELL. You say there was a class of 200 when you were initiated?

Mr. WRIGHT. Yes, sir.

Mr. CAMPBELL. Were the members of that class made known to their friends?

Mr. WRIGHT. No, sir; nobody knew who was in the class, as everybody was afraid of the thing; they did not know what it was all about, and the men who were putting on the work were very timid. Mr. Clarke came to New York for the occasion to officiate at the conferring of this first degree. It was done in the Masonic Temple in New York City, in one of lodge rooms. Clarke tells about how he put on the first class and how he fooled the police of New York City. He has boasted many times that a captain of the New York police force went into the order at this time, and that Enright had his squad looking for Clarke all over New York and these members; that this captain of police sent this squad, which was the bomb squad in New York, off in another direction while the men were sent notice to meet at this Masonic Temple room, where the degree was conferred. Everybody was a stranger to each other that night, and the ceremony was kind of bungled without question, and after everybody was getting very nervous and just about ready to go out, finally three robed figures appeared in the regalia of the klan, and after they had obligated everybody by going through a very short part of the ritual and the oaths they removed their masks, and these men were Edward Young Clarke, the imperial kleagle; William Coburn, who was at that time in charge of the work here in Washington, D. C., in your city here, and later became the supreme attorney of the order, and the last time I heard of him he was grand goblin on the Pacific coast; the other man was Lloyd P. Hooper, who was the organizer, salesman, and field worker. He had seen the possibilities of the name Ku-Klux Klan and had gone to Atlanta to negotiate and had come back here with authority to organize the Ku-Klux Klan.

Mr. CAMPBELL. Is there a book in New York containing the names of those who were initiated the night you were initiated?

Mr. WRIGHT. There is bound to be in Mr. Hooper's possession. Everybody upon joining the order must sign a charter petition, which goes to the imperial wizard or emperor, as he is called, calling upon them to charter this klan. They do not charter a klan until they think they have their maximum number, because they do not want to let down their efficiency of getting new members.

Mr. CAMPBELL. What were your instructions with respect to whom you should regulate and how, and how you were to serve the klan or uplift the community?

Mr. WRIGHT. My instructions as a klansman were simply starting in and giving the Jews the dickens in New York. Their idea was this, as preached by Clarke and Hooper in my presence, with several other prospective members whom I brought up, that the Jew patronizes the Jew, if possible; therefore, we, as klansmen, the only real 100 per cent Americans, will only patronize klansmen. Now, the idea was this, to simply organize everybody that was of their belief and religious belief into this order and they would practice not only moral clannishness but also practical clannishness; in other words, a klansman would be compelled to buy from another klansman if possible. That was how it was explained to us by Hooper. He did not really know much about it at that time; he was simply out for the money he could make out of it, and that was also explained by Clarke. They said, "In New York City here we have all the Jews; they are controlling New York; we will get under here and when we have 10,000 members here, if we do not want a certain man to do a certain thing, if this man receives 10,000 letters or telegrams stating that he should not do this thing, he is not very apt to do it."

In other words, if a member of the klan should be brought on trial before a certain judge or jury, if that judge or jury received 10,000 requests from New York to do a certain thing, they would be pretty apt to do it. That was their idea of gaining control of the courts.

Mr. CAMPBELL. What, if anything, were you told about the wearing of the mask, or were you told it was important that you should do that?

Mr. WRIGHT. You only wore the mask, according to imperial instructions, when you were in the klavern or klan, and then only when what they called the aliens or strangers or people to be initiated were present. Of course, in official parades it was up to the exalted cyclops, which is the title——

Mr. FESS (interposing). Who is he?

Mr. WRIGHT. He is the ruler of the klan after it is chartered. Up until the time the klan is chartered the field man or kleagle or king kleagle is in absolute charge. He can go out and sign up any man who will pay him $10 and take him into the order without any vote; after a klan is chartered, then it is up to the vote of the membership. The idea is this, and I have seen instances of it in my work, where one klan would be chartered and there would be objection to a certain member, so they would immediately go and get enough men to form another klan and take him in there, where nobody could vote against him. In other words, the idea of Clarke and Mrs. Tyler, no matter how sincere the idea of Col. Simmons has been, is to get the money.

Mr. CAMPBELL. He would not deny anybody admission who had the $10.

Mr. WRIGHT. Not if he would answer the charges, and if they were eligible for admittance into the order, no matter what their character was or anything else. There was no investigation made of any man who went into an unchartered klan.

Mr. RODENBERG. In other words, the man who solicited them passed on their qualifications?

Mr. WRIGHT. He wanted to earn his $4, so it would not be very hard to pass on him.

Mr. POU. You think Col. Simmons was not after the money?

Mr. WRIGHT. I think Col. Simmons was absolutely sincere; I think he has simply been led astray, or not astray but simply was in such a position financially and believed in the order sincerely, and was simply made just a figurehead by this Mrs. Tyler. There is no question about it in the world. I have found that out in my arguments over expenses, and am told that Col. Simmons received $100 a week, which is his total income from the order, and all the money is spent subject to Edward Young Clarke and Mrs. Elizabeth Tyler. Col. Simmons, when I was down there, was living in a little cottage with his family on a side street, and a suggestion came out to all of the klansmen to donate so much money to buy the imperial wizard a home.

Of course, the klansmen in the East were against it and the opposition was terrible against it; but Clarke had to make good, so he and Mrs. Tyler went out and bought a fine mansion, and had a wonderful tablet made which said, "Presented by the klansmen of America." I know absolutely that there was no money collected in the East, and if there was it did not amount to anything, but there might have been some collected in the South.

Mr. FESS. In whose name is that title?

Mr. WRIGHT. Well, that I can not say, because I have never seen the deed, but that could be very easily looked up. I am sure it is not in the colonel's name.

Mr. RODENBERG. You refer to Col. Simmons; was he ever in the military service?

Mr. WRIGHT. I do not know, but I have always known him as " Colonel."

Mr. RODENBERG. We can find that out from him.

Mr. KREIDER. You had charge of this aerial department?

Mr. WRIGHT. Yes, sir.

Mr. KREIDER. What was the object to be accomplished, or what were the duties of the aerial service?

Mr. WRIGHT. I will tell you what my idea is and what the ideas of the flyers of this country were. We saw that the Aero Club of America and other organizations were absolutely going out of existence; they were decaying; and we felt that we should get a fraternal order together of flyers to promote commercial aviation and give the boys a chance to fly. We are all reserve officers, or some of us are, and since we have been out of the Army we have never seen an airplane. If we take our reserve documents and go to a field to fly we are told there are no ships available, and we have to go through a certain medical examination, which is ridiculous, but we can not fly. So we got several together, and I will name a few of the men, including Reed Landis, one of our famous aces and son of Judge Landis, of Chicago; Jack Swaab, also one of our aces, who, by the way, is part Jewish, and Sydney Owens, who is an ace and lives in Philadelphia, and Maj. Biddle, also an ace and lives in Philadelphia.

We all got together and tried to do something for the flyers. Then along came the Ku-Klux Klan and I looked at it very favorably; it looked like a most wonderful organization, and it looked like this man who was behind it, Col. Simmons, as I then thought, was the man to get behind the flyers and organize them into units. We knew, of course, that Col. Simmons was not an aviator, and therefore nobody could point to him and say he was doing it for personal reasons. After taking this matter up with Clarke several times he wire'l me to come to Atlanta and go over the matter. I am sure that at that time Col. Simmons was absolutely sincere in the matter, and he said, "If you can bring back to me petitions from the leading aeronautical people of America I will agree to head this order." I then came back to Philadelphia. I had no money, absolutely, and the idea was to get the colonel to finance it, or the klan. When I was down there they jumped me from a plain klansman to a king kleagle, which was then the highest rank in the order, and I was given this commission and this document, and it was told me by Mr. Clarke that it would never do to send out these petitions from the South, because they would know it was the Ku-Klux Klan. Now, understand, the Knights of the Air was not to bar anybody on account of religious beliefs; it was simply to get the flyers together; that was my intention. So under agreement with Clarke I came back to Philadelphia, where my office of the Tail Spin was established, and sent out these petitions all over the country. There were several hundred returned signed, and they said, "We will wait upon you to appoint Col. Simmons as the head of the Knights of the Air." They all said it was a good thing. A very strong letter went out with these petitions. I took these petitions and went back to Atlanta. When I got to Atlanta I, of course, saw Mr. Clarke; I had very little dealings with Col. Simmons, because he was out of town most of the time. I saw immediately that Clarke was not running things, but Mrs. Tyler, because I was immediately ushered in to her and told the whole thing. Then, shortly afterward, they had the annual conclave or convention of the klan.

Mr. CAMPBELL. What did Mrs. Tyler do?

Mr. WRIGHT. She told me to go ahead and what to do; in other words, the directions were always given me by Mrs. Tyler or by Mr. Clarke, never by the colonel.

Mr. POU. What were the directions?

Mr. WRIGHT. To go ahead; until the convention was over to just help as a kind of reception committee, and after that to get down to actual work, open up offices away from the klan under the name of the Knights of the Air, and get all the flyers as members. I followed these instructions, and talked over with Mr. Clarke what I had decided for the Knights of the Air, as I was supposed to be chief of staff. The real head was supposed to be Col. Simmons, but he had no time to direct it. And I went over and took Mr. Clarke into the Haynes Build'ng, and he signed the lease under the name of the Southern Publicity Association and assigned to me, as chief assistant and to represent the klan, as I was a northerner and could not be trusted too much, a gentleman by the name of Paydon. Mr. Paydon was made secretary and I was made ch'ef of staff. After we got under way a few days, all of a sudden into the office burst Mrs. Elizabeth Tyler; she looked around and said the office was very fine and all that, and who was to pay for this? I sa'd, "Why, Mr. Clarke s'gned the lease and told me to furnish it; I suppose the klan is." She said, "Well, Mr. Clarke did this without my authority, and I won't have it." Well, the result of the whole thing was thát the newspapers about that time got on to the idea that the Knights of the Air was a money-making scheme. It was not intended to be that originally, but Clarke had taken Mr. Paydon and I out to this place of Mrs. Tyler's, or his place; I do not know whose place it is, but it is a very elaborate place out in the country, with even a lake in it, boats and everything, and he has every animal on it from a bear to a peacock, and I was taken out there for two days.

Mr. RODENBERG. Any goblins on it?

Mr. WRIGHT. Well, there are plenty of guinea pigs. While Mr. Clarke told the world he was sick, we were out there with him for two days outlining the plans of the Knights of the Air. Then suddenly something happened; I do not know what it was, but I had never drawn any salary up to th s time except expenses, and my agreement was to do this work on purely a commission basis.

Mr. CAMPBELL. What commission were you to get?

Mr. WRIGHT. That had not been decided, but I presume 25 cents a member. We tried the thing and, as I have said, I have absolutely no money and did not have any——

Mr. KREIDER [interposing]. Did all the members of this organization, known as the Knights of the Air, have to be members of the Ku-Klux Klan?

Mr. WRIGHT. No, sir; but here is where the hitch came, as decided by Clarke; he said, "No man can become an officer of the Knights of the Air who is not a klansman; we will absolutely control the Knights of the Air through having only klansmen as officers." That was the first thing; and then Clarke decided that the equipment that the klan got should be placed in his name and not in the name of the Knights of the Air, his idea being to absolutely control it with an iron hand. As I say, out there it was talked over for two days what we were going to do, and he was very visionary, and he saw Edward Young Clarke controlling the air in America, without question or belief. Then, Mrs. Tyler said, "The papers are attacking us too fiercely; we will have to lay off for the time being."

I was dumbfounded. She had called me in, and I said. "Mrs. Tyler, my dealings have been with Mr. Clarke and Col. Simmons. What right have you to give directions as to what I should do?" She said, "Well, Mr. Wright, Col. Simmons is sick and compelled to be away part of the time, and you know that Mr. Clarke has been sick at home now for several days, so therefore I am in charge and am really the Ku-Klux Klan."

Mr. KREIDER. Was this organization to be used later on or at any time to terrorize men?

Mr. WRIGHT. Oh, no. The Knights of the Air was simply started into being with the flyers as something to get us together, and was capitalized by Clarke as a money-making plan; that is all. I afterwards saw letters, after I left Atlanta, being sent out under the name of Mr. Cherry, who was a klansman, and an assistant over in the office, who had never seen an airplane, I think, to all the aero clubs and flyers throughout the country, saying what a great thing the Knights of the Air was; in fact, after I left there, there was nobody that I know of that was a flyer or a reserve officer in the Army. It was simply a case of Clarke's ideas being absolutely so that no man could conscientiously go into it as a reserve officer in the United States Army. There is no question about it. The whole Ku-Klux Klan is simply based on treason against the country, in this way, that they have planned and schemed and would have, if not publicly exposed, gotten control of practically every seat of government through their tremendous voting power. In the State of Texas to-day I venture to say that practically all the smaller cities are absoluteely controlled by the klan from the mayor on down. Texas should be the headquarters of the Ku-Klux Klan and not Georgia, because in Georgia they all look upon it more as a joke—the Atlanta people.

I will cite one instance which I think caused Mrs. Tyler to be bitter against me. Mr. Paydon and I decided we would get an apartment to live in instead of living at the hotels. So Clarke said, "Be sure to get an apartment big enough for me to have a room at." That was the start, I think, of Mrs. Tyler getting suspicious of Clarke, and then she started to call a halt on both Mr. Paydon and me. I was then sent to Washington, to this city, with a great many ideas in mind, which it is too long to relate here, but the problem was when I got here that Mr. Terrell, who was then king kleagle—I understand now a grand goblin in charge of this domain—stated they were meeting terrible opposition here from the police, and that the police were controlled by other factions and they were afrid to make a move. I had come up here under instructions from the imperial palace to talk to him and he said that nothing could be done. So I went from here into the Chicago domain. The real reason was that I was trying to work myself out of the klan gradually. As I say, I was absolutely broke. They had not lived up to their obligation, or I should say Clarke had not, to give me any kind of a drawing account or salary, and I was pretty nearly up against it. So they kept sending me from city to city, and finally I got out of the klan entirely and resigned from the order last month.

Mr. FESS. What is the purpose of the parades we hear about?

Mr. WRIGHT. The parades?

Mr. Fess. Yes; we have had statements about terrorizing.

Mr. Wright. Well, the idea is this, which I can prove and will be very glad to file before the committee, by their own semiofficial organ, the Searchlight—the idea was simply to terrorize people by showing their strength. To cite an instance of that, in Dallas. Tex., they were having trouble there with a certain class of the building trades—I do not know just exactly what it was—and the klan decided they would hold a parade to show their strength. So it seems like it was all arranged with the city authorities and the parade was held in Dallas, and they marched down the street in full regalia, and about the time they appeared the lights were all extinguished, and the next day the people were back at work. This is cited in their semiofficial organ and in the press throughout the country.

Mr. Fess. Who extinguished the lights?

Mr. Wright. That is why I say the State of Texas must be controlled by the klan as everything worked in harmony with it. If they had a parade, everything was done silently and without question.

Mr. Rodenberg. Mr. Wright, since you have severed your connection with this organization and exposed some of its inner workings, has any attempt been made to visit punishment upon you?

Mr. Wright. With official sanction it has not, sir; but it is very strange that only last Friday I received a letter from the executive head of the organization of which I was sales manager telling me that I would immediately have to resign, without a day's notice, for my exposure of the Ku-Klux Klan. I have that letter or a photograph of it in my pocket now.

Mr. Pou. Mr. Wright, would you have continued your membership if the officers had lived up to their agreement with you?

Mr. Wright. No, sir; not in the Knights of the Air; absolutely not. I had to go out of the klan easily. As I say, they had me powerless in Atlanta. I had no money, and I have a wife and two children and it was necessary for me to do a little traveling, which was more inspection work than anything else, in order to get back East, so I could resign and get out. I got back to the Middle West and immediately took another position just as soon as I could get there. When I found out the real plan of Clarke, which was simple—well, he has the most visionary plans of any man I ever heard of in my life. One thing he planned on doing was to go into every city and have a flying squadron there and have myself and Mr. Paydon or others of us there. We had a very beautiful uniform designed for the Knights of the Air. We were to make speeches at the various chambers of commerce and rotary clubs, all based upon real facts, American air supremacy, which should go forward, and the idea then would be suggested that then the chamber of commerce should give us a strip of land in this city for a flying field, but Clarke had it planned that these titles would not be in the name of the Knights of the Air, but in the name of Edward Young Clarke. His idea was to be the wealthiest man in America, and he told me he would either make me a power in America if I stuck to him or else he would crush me. He certainly tried to crush me without question when I did not live up to his plans.

Mr. Snell. How many other secret societies do you belong to, Mr. Wright?

Mr. Wright. I am a thirty-second-degree Mason, a Shriner, and an Elk.

Mr. Snell. You have never withdrawn from any other order?

Mr. Wright. No, sir; I am in good standing in every one of my organizations.

Mr. Snell. Did you know something about this organization before you joined it—the Ku-Klux Klan?

Mr. Wright. Only the printed literature which is practically the same as any fraternal order, simply waiving the flag in front of your face and saying it is a great thing and we are going to do great things for America.

Mr. Snell. But you had heard of it before, in a general way?

Mr. Wright. In a general way, and I can say right here, and I would like to say that as Clarke told me, who was responsible for the growth of the Ku-Klux Klan, it is not only the cleverness of Mrs. Tyler but also the newspapers of the country, and more especially the Herald in New York—the Herald sent down a correspondent to Atlanta. The publicity was shooting out from Mrs. Tyler with talk about this wonderful organization, and this correspondent, of course, saw things only from the outside and thought it was a very good thing. He came back to New York and carried a series of articles on this great new revival of the Ku-Klux Klan, which ran in the Herald of New York. Of course, thousands of people read these articles, and I know from being in Atlanta that the membership from the East began to grow, and request after request came in to know about it. How they would find out about a man was not by a personal investigation, but they would send him a questionnaire and when this questionnaire was filled out it would show whether he was eligible for membership, and then they would send a man to see him and sign him up just like they did me.

Mr. CAMPBELL. We will now take a recess until 2.45.

The committee met at 2.45 p. m., pursuant to the recess.

STATEMENT OF MR. C. ANDERSON WRIGHT—Continued.

Mr. POU. Mr. Wright, during your connection with the Ku-Klux Klan, do you know of any violations of the law by members of the klan?

Mr. WRIGHT. Nothing that I could prove, sir; just what I have heard boasted of, but no documents. My work, understand, was not in the field. It was purely to organize this aeronautical unit. I was given my commission for that reason only.

Mr. RODENBERG. Boasted of by whom?

Mr. POU. You were a dweller at the imperial palace for a while, were you not?

Mr. WRIGHT. The so-called imperial palace; yes, sir; but the imperial palace did not know much about what was going on in the individual realms, in fact, I am sure that the imperial palace would not dare sanction any violations direct, but the exalted cyclops of each klan has enough authority to go ahead and do anything he wants to. In other words, that is where the danger lies—not what the palace orders, but when any man has the authority to have so many armed men, and as they boast in their newsletters, as branches and as deputies of the police department, when it is not up to the courts at all; it is up to the exalted cyclops to assign certain men to do certain things, and they go and do it. In other words, it makes the exalted cyclops, no matter who he is, above everybody, if they wish to go into anything like punishing anybody.

Mr. POU. Do you know of any violation? I believe you said you know of no violations of the law except on hearsay.

Mr. WRIGHT. Well, when I was in Atlanta everybody was frightened stiff. They did not know what was going to happen on account of this Lakewood tragedy.

Mr. RODENBERG. What was the Lakewood tragedy?

Mr. WRIGHT. It seems that the klan was going to punish a certain man who, as I understand, ran a hot-dog stand and news stand combined or a small store or something of that kind, because he was familiar with the Negroes or was trading or selling to the Negroes. They warned him not to do this, and I understand they went by, as he claims—and this all came out in the testimony in court—and got this man and put him in an automobile to take him out near Lakewood to punish him for daring to defy the laws of the Ku-Klux Klan. When he got out there it seems he did not submit so easily to these things and he pulled out a knife and killed one of the klansmen and stabbed two others.

Mr. SNELL. That is the matter that was referred to by Mr. Thomas this morning?

Mr. WRIGHT. Then you know the circumstances of that.

Mr. RODENBERG. And the thing they accused him of—let me get this clear—the thing he was guilty of or that they accused this man of doing was selling weiners to the Negroes?

Mr. WRIGHT. Or whatever it was that he was selling. That is what he said in his testimony in court in Atlanta.

Mr. RODENBERG. That was the crime he was charged with?

Mr. WRIGHT. By the klan.

Mr. RODENBERG. Yes; by the klan.

Mr. WRIGHT. Yes; and he did not submit to their flogging or tarring and feathering or whatever it was to be, and put up a fight, as the records will show. At that time the supreme attorney of the order, Capt. Coburn, who was an Army officer overseas and used to be in charge here in Washington, defended these people in court. Capt. Coburn afterwards showed me a check for $500 from the imperial wizard which he had been paid to defend this case. They claimed it was not being defended by the klan. I have evidence now that I just gathered which I will be able to submit a little later on on that subject.

Mr. RODENBERG. Did you read the record in this case; that is, the Thomas case?

Mr. WRIGHT. Yes.

Mr. RODENBERG. And you mean to say—let me get this thing clear—the only thing this man was charged with by the klan was that he had some business dealings with the Negroes?

Mr. WRIGHT. And did not stop when they told him to?

Mr. RODENBERG. And did not stop when they told him to. and for that he was taken out and flogged?

Mr. WRIGHT. They brought in a lot of other things regarding women and things like that, but that was the specific charge that they charged him with according to his testimony.

Mr. RODENBERG. And that was not disputed in court or not successfully disputed?

Mr. WRIGHT. I was not at the trial. I simply know that everybody in the imperial palace was frightened to death about it and the local secretary was so frightened that he left town and did not show up again for a long time. I am not speaking now of the palace but the klan in Atlanta, whi is under the exalted cyclops, a man named—I can not think of his name w, Knowland or Norton.

Mr. POU. When did that take place?

Mr. WRIGHT. This took place, I think, in April. I would not say precisely.

Mr. POU. In April?

Mr. WRIGHT. I think so.

Mr. POU. How long after that did you continue your connection with the klan?

Mr. WRIGHT. Approximately three weeks at Atlanta, and then when I came on up here it was some time longer before I finally quit.

Mr. POU. When did you finally sever your connection?

Mr. WRIGHT. On the 13th of September, 1921. That is when I resigned, not as an officer, but as a klansman. I would like very much to put in the minutes my letter of resignation which covers everything and is not very long, if that would suit you.

Mr. POU. If you knew of all these circumstances that you are detailing here now. why did you not have something to say about it immediately?

Mr. WRIGHT. I was in no position where I could make a fight. I intended to get out of it as easily as I could. I never attended but one klan meeting after that, after I left Atlanta, and it was only upon solicitation. after it became public property, that I was waited upon by a great many members in fraternal orders whom I had induced to go into the order, and to some of them I had given the oath of allegiance myself. When they knew these real facts they came after me and said. "Why did you get us into a thing like this." and I said, "Just the same as I got into it myself, because I thought it was a good thing," and it was only following that and upon the solicitation of the press that I exposed my series of articles. In other words, I did not feel I was in position to do this myself. I had work to look after and my position.

Mr. FESS. Mr. Wright, I believe you stated you went into this because of some commercial advantage?

Mr. WRIGHT. No, sir ; no commercial advantage. I simply joined it more on the idea that people I knew came to me and approached me, who were brothers in another fraternal order.

Mr. FESS. I think the committee understood from your testimony that the advantage you sought was to organize the air force.

Mr. WRIGHT. Yes, sir.

Mr. FESS. Rather upon the basis of a commercial advantage, so that the boys might find an agency through which to fly.

Mr. WRIGHT. Not as a commercial advantage. but merely to get the boys together in such a way that the Government would sanction it and there would be enough reserve officers so that the Government would be glad to give them equipment to use just as they have other aero clubs ; but to do that would have required something 'n the way of ritualistic or secret work to make it interesting and to have a hold on them.

Mr. FESS. The money advantage then is confined to officers and not to members?

Mr. WRIGHT. The money to be derived from the plan of having the Knights of the Air?

Mr. FESS. Yes.

Mr; WRIGHT. That was all the imperial palace or Mr. Clarke personally. No officer. was to get any money out of it except the men who went out and signed them up.

Mr. RODENBERG. Mr. Wright, you said oefore recess that no attempt was ever made by the klan to visit punishment upon you. Have you rece.ved any threatening letters?

Mr. WRIGHT. I have received hundreos of them. My articles have appeared in 26 newspapers, and every day they send me a pack of them, but I do not attach any importance to that. The only thing I attach any importance to is that I have been very successful in the position I held and I was giv-. one day's notice to get out, with the only excuse that I had become notorious in the Ku-Klux Klan mix-up.

Mr. RODENBERG. No attempt at physical violence has ever been made in your case?

Mr. WRIGHT. No, sir; the New York police department have seen to that. They have continuously had men with me.

Mr. SNELL. What induced you to disclose the se _ets of the klan?

Mr. WRIGHT. Why did I?

Mr. SNELL. Yes; anything special?

Mr. WRIGHT. Yes, sir. My reason was simply this: I have nothing against the mass of klansmen. They go into it in ignorance, and I knew that. My idea was not to expose so much race hatred, which would drive lots of people into the klan. In other words, there are enough narrow-minded people who would be glad enough to join an order against the Jews, Catholics, foreign born, and Negroes; but if you can show a man where he was simply taken in and made a goat of in order to get money out of him by selling all these mystic contrivances and show him how his money went and the men it was making wealthy and the women who were behind the whole thing and show him where the man at the head of the order was not receiving any money or the imperial treasury was not receiving any money, I figured the klansmen should know that and would be glad to know that, whether they had done any violence or anything else. In other words, I think to-day the more the papers preach on the Ku-Klux Klan as preaching racial hatred, the more members they are going to get, because there are so many narrow-minded people who will join, but when you can show them where their money goes and what a fool he is made and the character of the people getting it, then I think the klansmen of the country will realize and wake up to what they have gone into.

Mr. SNELL. That is, your only interest was to show the foolishness of the whole proposition?

Mr. WRIGHT. To show the people who were getting the money; that was it.

Mr. RODENBERG. And how they were being duped into this organization?

Mr. WRIGHT. To show how they were being duped and show up this woman who was really the power behind the whole thing. Also, the klan are preaching the chastity of the home and the purity of the womanhood of our country, when the real leading spirit of the klan, I found out absolutely, and the one behind the throne, was a notorious sporting-house keeper in Atlanta, which has been proven in court records, and the man who is the imperial kleagle, the real man who is the head of the order, and this woman were living in adultery together in Atlanta on a beautiful estate which has been bought with their supplies, and then I thought it was up to them to know who were running the klan and preaching morality, and so forth.

Mr. JOHNSON. Mr. Wright, something has been said somewhere in this testimony or in a letter sent to Members of the House by Mr. Terrell, their attorney, that Members of the Senate and House were members of this Ku-Klux Klan; do you know anything about that?

Mr. WRIGHT. Only by boasting. I have never sat in conclave assembly or klan lodge room with anybody I knew to be a high official of the United States Government or of any eastern department. I do know that the governor of Georgia was bitterly against the klan, the former governor of Georgia, Gov. Dorsey, and openly attacked it, and the prosecuting attorney of Atlanta admitted he was a klansman when this trial came up about this Lakewood tragedy.

Mr. JOHNSON. Did the imperial wizard or any of these goblins or cyclops ever tell you that Members of Congress belonged to the klan?

Mr. WRIGHT. Oh. yes, sir. It was openly boasted all the time, especially by Clarke, how they would soon control Congress.

Mr. JOHNSON. Clarke told you that?

Mr. WRIGHT. He told it not only to me but in the convention. On May 6 the annual conclave, the big gathering of the klan, took place and he openly boasted of it, how they were going to control and were getting Congress with them. However, when I came to Washington, when Mr. Terrell was in command here—I know nothing about Washington because I only visited him once and was here one day—but he told me that there were Members of Congress, but that the opposition was so great from the chief of police, and so forth, that they did not dare to show their hand and they were not enrolling any members at that time.

Mr. JOHNSON. Mr. Terrell told you that?

Mr. RODENBERG. He did not give you the name?

Mr. WRIGHT. No, sir; he did not.

Mr. JOHNSON. Who do you say told you that?

Mr. WRIGHT. Mr. Terrell.

Mr. JOHNSON. Is Mr. Terrell in the room?

Mr. WRIGHT. Yes, sir.

Mr. TERRELL. Yes, sir; I am.

Mr. JOHNSON. Did the imperial wizard ever tell you that Members of Congress belonged to the order—that is, Col. Simmons?

Mr. WRIGHT. I could not say definitely whether he did, sir; but his spokesman, Mr. Clarke, certainly referred to it numerous times.

Mr. POU. Mr. Wright, I simply want to ask you these questions in winding up. When you became a klansman, did you take an oath?

Mr. WRIGHT. Yes, sir; I took a very stringent oath.

Mr. POU. Now, since you have ceased to be a klansman, have you divulged any of the things that you swore you would not divulge?

Mr. WRIGHT. I have, sir.

Mr. POU. You have?

Mr. WRIGHT. Yes, sir. I have done that purely and simply for this reason, that when the heads of the order have violated every sacred oath, as they call it, toward me, and have used every weapon within their power to put me out of existence, then certainly my oath which I gave to such people as those that were in the imperial palace—if the imperial palace can go back on their oath, certainly they can not hold a klansman to it.

Mr. POU. You claim that as your justification for violating the oath that you yourself voluntarily took?

Mr. WRIGHT. Yes, sir. I did not publicly make the oath public property until that had been done in the press. I referred to it several times, but I openly did not publish it. I simply refused to obey the oaths any longer, and in my letter of resignation and telegram I stated that.

Mr. POU. And you also have divulged things you solemnly swore you would not divulge under any circumstances?

Mr. WRIGHT. I have; yes, sir.

Mr. RODENBERG. Of course, before you subscribed to the oath, you did not know just exactly what it was going to be?

Mr. WRIGHT. I knew absolutely nothing about it. It was told in the oath that there was nothing in it that would be against any man's citizenship.

Mr. POU. You found out afterwards about it?

Mr. WRIGHT. That there were such things, and I found out after carefully going over it many times that a man who is an officer in the United States Army, whether on active or inactive status, could not live up to an oath like that and at the same time live up to the oath of his office.

Mr. POU. You say that thereafter you did carefully go over the oath several times?

Mr. WRIGHT. Yes, sir.

Mr. POU. You knew exactly what you had sworn to at the time that you, according to your statement, divulged things you swore you would not divulge?

Mr. WRIGHT. Yes, sir.

Mr. POU. That is all.

Mr. CAMPBELL. Mr. Wright, Mr. Garrett may want to ask you some questions after he returns. He is not here now and you can just stand aside for the present.

STATEMENT OF MR. O. B. WILLIAMSON.

Mr. CAMPBELL. Mr. Williamson, state your name and your business.

Mr. WILLIAMSON. O. B. Williamson; I am a post-office inspector.

Mr. CAMPBELL. As a post-office inspector, have you made any investigation of the order of the Knights of the Ku-Klux Klan?

Mr. WILLIAMSON. Yes, sir. I have made an investigation of the order. I spent some seven days in Atlanta, and have made a preliminary investigation of the business of that concern.

While in Atlanta I interviewed Mr. Clarke, Mrs. Tyler, and Col. Simmons. Mr. Clarke very freely gave me all the information I asked for. The same is true of Col. Simmons and Mrs. Tyler. I asked Mr. Clarke for the literature which had been printed for the klan, and he gave me these pieces which I have here in my hand and which include the so-called kloran—that is, the secret work, some advertising pamphlets, the charter of the order, and the constitution and laws of the klan.

I have looked over this constitution and each law and I do not see anything in there that would have a tendency to incite murder, but in the beginning I find what is called the Imperial Proclamation. Do you want me to read a part of that?

Mr. CAMPBELL. You may read it.

Mr. WILLIAMSON. This is one paragraph:

" To all nations, people, tribes, and tongues, and to the lovers of law and order, peace and justice of the whole world, greetings :

" I and the citizens of the invisible empire through me proclaim to you as follows : We, the members of this order, desiring to promote real patriotism toward our civil government, honorable peace among men and nations, protection for and happiness in the homes of our people, love, real brotherhood, mirth and manhood among ourselves and liberty, justice and fraternity among all mankind, and believing we can best accomplish these noble purposes through the channel of a high class mystic, social, patriotic, benevolent association, having a perfected lodge system, with an exalted ritualistic form of work and an effective form of government, not for selfish profit but for the mutual betterment, benefit and protection of all our oath-bound associates, their welfare, physically, socially, morally and vocationally and their loved ones, do proclaim to the whole world." etc.

Now, the statement there as to whether this order was formed not for selfish profit was made the starting point of my investigation, and I talked to Clarke concerning the various charges which had been made against him and his order, and I got from Mr. Clarke his statement as to what had happened concerning the so-called imperial palace, the property given to Col. Simmons and the connection between the klan and the Lanier University, and I have here before me his statement which was taken by a stenographer and transcribed, and if you desire I will read the statement :

" The imperial palace is the old Durant Home on Peachtree Road. It was bought the last of June, 1921, from Mr. E. M. Durant, Hurt Building, Atlanta. It was bought by Mr. Clarke, individually, and the title passed to him individually. The consideration was $35,000, $10,000 of which was paid in cash, the money being secured from the treasury of the Ku-Klux Klan (Inc.). The remaining $25,000 was secured by notes given by Mr. Clarke, personally, to Mr. Durant—the payments are to cover five years. Mr. Clarke's recollection is that he wrote a letter to Col. Simmons saying that the property was being purchased in his (Mr. Clarke's) name, but, of course, the property would belong to the klan whenever it assumed or paid the obligations then existing.

" The reasons for handling this property individually are as follows : First, Mr. Clarke and the others did not want the klan known in the deal. Second, the klan at the time was supposed to have plenty of money and it was believed that for this the price would have been raised beyond reason. Third, the property is located in a residential section and it was believed the neighbors might object to the use to which the property was to be put in view of the criticism which was being made in the press against the klan. Fourth, all titles to property in this particular section have a clause to the effect that it can only be used for residential purposes and not business buildings erected thereon, and this clause would have given the neighbors an opportunity to start litigation to secure an injunction, at least temporary, to prevent taking over the property by the Ku-Klux Klan.

" Mr. Clarke, through one of the attorneys for the klan, Mr. Ben H. Sullivan, of the Hurt Building, is to-day, October 4, 1921, making deed of this property to the klan."

That was the day I went out there to begin the investigation.

" It is to be understood that the $10,000 already paid out is from the $2 part of the $10, which is retained by the klan in its treasury after having reimbursed Mr. Clarke and all others for the services rendered."

That is the information I have regarding that deal. Then I have this information regarding the property now being occupied by Col. Simmons.

Mr. CAMPBELL. Now, this property is the imperial palace?

Mr. WILLIAMSON. Yes, sir; that is right.

Mr. CAMPBELL. Where the business of the klan is conducted?

Mr. WILLIAMSON. Yes, sir; that is right.

Mr. SNELL. Does Clarke live there?

Mr. WILLIAMSON. That is the place where all the help is engaged and where Clarke himself has his office and where all the business is conducted. It is a private residence made into a business office; that is about what it is.

Now, this is concerning the property which is now being occupied by Col. Simmons. This statement was made by Mr. Clarke:

"This property was purchased in April, 1921. It is located at 1840 Peachtree Road. It was purchased from John Bratton, a retired capitalist of Atlanta, for $25,500. The arrangement as to payment is as follows: Ten thousand dollars was paid in cash and one note for $15,500 was given; this note is due October 15, 192. Mr. Bratton made the deed to Mr. Clarke, and the property is still in Mr. Clarke's name. The $10,000 which was paid on the property was secured in this way: One thousand dollars by subscriptions from klan members; $5,000 was loaned by the klan; $3,000 was loaned by Mr. Clarke and Mrs. Tyler.

"The loan form the klan fund is in two parts. The first part, consisting of $3,000, was from the general fund; that is to say, the fund other than that which is made up by the $2 coming from the donation. The second part, consisting of $3,000, is from that fund made up by the $2 part of the donation."

Mr. Clarke further made this statement:

"This use of the klan funds for what would appear to be a private purpose is justified in this way, that Col. Simmons was at the time living at an unpretentious part of the city and in no way, as I viewed it, in keeping with his position, and it was therefore in the interest of the klan to put him a better home and one that would reflect credit on the organization. Moreover, Col. Simmons earned this and more too, because for four or five years he had devoted almost his entire time to the creation and preservation of this organization, at times actually going hungry in order that the bills of the klan might be met and the work kept alive."

That is all the information I have concerning that property. Then I found that some of the klan funds had been used in a deal with the Lanier University, a small school in Atlanta, and Mr. Clarke made these statements to me concerning that:

"The Lanier University has existed for only a few years. It has been a Baptist institution of learning, operating under a charter granted by the State of Georgia and controlled by a board of trustees of 15 men. Some time in July this year representatives of this university approached Col. Simmons and myself with a proposition to purchase the university outright and assume, of course, its debts, which amounted to $50,000. We had 'our attorney to investigate the matter fully and we found the indebtedness much larger than claimed. We therefore rejected the proposition to purchase and submitted a counter proposition. The counter proposition was accepted and was in substance as follows: First, that the managing board elect Col. Simmons president of the university. Second, that they agree to make it nonsectarian. Third, that the present existing board elect new trustees, as named by Col. Simmons, the present board resigning in their favor."

Now, following that is other information, the material part of which is that the klan paid to this university $22,474.32, a part of which was out of the klan treasury and which is not secured in any way.

I also secured from Mr. Clarke detailed information concerning the way the membership proposition is handled. This is in question and answer form, and if you desire I will read it to you.

Mr. CAMPBELL. You may read it.

Mr. WILLIAMSON (reading):

"Q. Mr. Clarke, who first manufactured the robes used by klansmen?—A. W. E. Floding, a secret-order paraphernalia manufacturer, whose plant was located on Mitchell Street, in Atlanta, Ga.

"Q. When did he first begin to manufacture these robes?—A. Shortly after the chartering of the institution, in 1915.

"Q. How long did he continue manufacturing them?—A. About four years; up to some time during the summer or fall of 1920.

" Q. Did this man operate under a contract?—A. He operated under an agreement with the imperial wizard to manufacture the robes at so much per robe; I presume it was a written contract.

" Q. Can you give the substance of the contract?—A. Yes. That we were to turn over all robe orders to him and that he was to manufacture the robes at a certain price per robe, regardless of what price we might get for the robe.

" Q. Did this price vary during the life of his contract?—A. I don't think so.

" Q. What was the price that he received for each robe?—A. I think the price was $5 or $6, but can not say positively.

" Q. When the Floding contract terminated who then was given the contract?—A. Mr. C. B. Davis, operating as The Gates City Manufacturing Co. of Atlanta, Ga.

" Q. Has this company made the robes from that date to the present?—A. They have.

" Q. Does this company operate under a written contract?—A. It does.

" Q. What in substance are the terms of the contract?—A. The contract is that the robes shall be manufactured at a stipulated price, the price to vary according to the cost of manufacturing, either up or down. The price for the past several months has been $4 for robe and helmet. My impression is that we paid more previously, but this matter was handled by Col. Simmons.

" Q. What price do you get for these robes from the klan?—A. $6.50.

" Q. This, then, is one of the principal sources of revenue of the order?—A. It is one.

" Q. What are all the sources?"

Now, this answer explains what is done with the $10 which is paid by a member when he joins the klan:

" The sources of revenue to the general treasury of the order are: First, $2 from the donation; second, an imperial palace tax of $1.80 per year per member. The imperial palace has no supervision over or connection with the funds of a local klan, and has nothing to do with the setting of the amount of the dues of members of local klans, but because of the fact that the secretary of each local klan must send $1.80 per member in good standing per year to the imperial palace (in quarterly installments), in setting their local dues the local klan must regard as a fixed charge the sum of $1.80 per year per member. Therefore, the local dues can not be less than that amount."

Mr. CAMPBELL. Mr. Williamson, Mr. Gallivan, who has a resolution pending here, is anxious to get away on a train in a very short time. Will you suspend while he makes a brief statement to the committee?

STATEMENT OF HON. JAMES A. GALLIVAN, A REPRESENTATIVE IN CONGRESS FROM THE STATE OF MASSACHUSETTS.

Mr. GALLIVAN. Mr. Chairman and gentlemen of the committee. I do not intend to detain this committee for any great length of time. I have introduced a resolution (H. Con. Res. 29). It is sort of supplementary to what you are now listening to and in a way action on it depends upon the action your committee takes on the resolutions which you are now considering. I presented it not representing any district, any State, any faith, or any party, but we have heard enough here to-day, uncontradicted, to show that at least $8,000,000 has been collected and that not all of it has gone to the cyclopians, goblins, or kleagles, and perhaps some of it went for political purposes.

Now, my resolution provides that a special joint committee be created, etc., to be composed of three Members of the Senate and three Members of the House to investigate and determine whether any Members of Congress are members of the Knights of the Ku-Klux Klan. As I say, unless your committee believes that one of these resolutions or all of these resolutions ought to be referred to an investigating committee I realize that nothing will happen to my resolution, but if your committee considers that these resolutions, either individually or a consolidated resolution formed out of them, should be presented to the House for its consideration I hope that you will include in it the suggestion of an investigation as to whether any Members of the Senate or of the House of Representatives are members of the Ku-Klux Klan.

Ah, my mind goes back less than a year ago when the primaries were on and we heard that there were contests in this State and in that State, and it all depended upon whether a candidate in this State or that State would join the Ku-Klux Klan. Of course, it was all gossip and rumor, but certain members were elected, and all around the congressional halls went the word that the candidates nominated had joined the Ku-Klux Klan.

Now, $8,000,000 was collected, according to evidence presented to this committee. That may be disputed. The other side has not been heard and I am not taking an unfair advantage of that fact, but what I want to impress upon this committee is this: That in considering these resolutions I sincerely hope that you will consider them all together and that you will not forget that my resolution is not intended in any other way than as a supplement to the resolutions already suggested, and also to help the committee, if it needs any help, find out whether we have in Congress men who have violated the Constitution of the United States in violation of their oaths of office.

Mr. JOHNSON. I would like to ask you a question.

Mr. GALLIVAN. Certainly.

Mr. JOHNSON. Would the gentleman from Massachusetts think that the Rules Committee of the House would have any jurisdiction over an investigation to determine whether or not Members of the Senate belong to this or any other organization?

Mr. GALLIVAN. I would suggest that you eliminate the honorable Senate.

Mr. RODENBERG. This is a joint resolution.

Mr. GALLIVAN. I beg your pardon; I forgot to say to the Representative from South Dakota that mine is a joint resolution, so that the Senate will have to act on my resolution. But in view of the fact that the House speedily began this investigation I thought it was my place to be here and bring it to the attention of this committee that I have presented the resolution and to say what I have already said. I thank you, gentlemen.

STATEMENT OF MR. O. B. WILLIAMSON—Resumed.

Mr. CAMPBELL. Now, Mr. Williamson, you may resume.

Mr. WILLIAMSON. I started to explain the sources of revenue of this order and said that first was the $2 taken from the donation and, second, that $1.80 was levied on each member of each local klan and was called the imperial tax. Now, reading from the statement:

"Third, an item of income is profits accruing from the sale price over the cost price on robes or other paraphernalia."

That of course bears on the question as to whether this is an institution organized for profit or whether it is what it says—an institution organized on benevolent lines.

Mr. Clarke explained to me that he was at the head of what is called the propagation department and that this department was operated by Mrs. Tyler and himself, and that it was organized for profit. He explained that he had entered into a contract with the klan under which he was operating this department, and he gave me a copy of that contract, which I will hand the committee and will read it if you desire.

Mr. CAMPBELL. We will not take the time to read it, but it may be made a part of the record.

(Said contract follows:)

ATLANTA, GA., *Fulton County, ss.:*

In person before me, a notary public authorized to administer oaths, appeared E. Y. Clarke, who being first duly sworn on oath, deposes and says that the copy of the contract hereto attached is marked in the handwriting of the said E. Y. Clarke as follows: "Copy of original contract, E. Y. Clarke, 10-4-21," and that said copy is a full, complete, and correct copy of the original contract between himself and the Knights of the Ku-Klux Klan; and that the said contract sets forth in full his agreement with the said Knights of the Ku-Klux Klan, and that said contract is the only agreement, contract, or understanding of any nature which now exists or has ever existed between himself and the said Knights of the Ku-Klux Klan.

EDWARD YOUNG CLARKE.

Sworn to and subscribed before me this the 4th day of October, 1921.

B. H. SULLIVAN,
Notary Public, Fulton County, Ga.

IMPERIAL KLEAGLE'S CONTRACT.

STATE OF GEORGIA,
County of Fulton, ss:

This agreement, made and entered into on this the 7th day of June, A. D. 1920, by and between the Knights of the Ku-Klux Klan, a corporation, of said county, acting by its imperial wizard (president), W. J. Simmons, party of the first part, and Edward Young Clarke, of said county, party of the second part.

Witnesseth that the said party of the second part hereto having by virtue of this agreement been appointed imperial kleagle (general superintendent of the organization department) of said first party, and it being desirable that the details of his rights, privileges, powers, duties, responsibilities, and compensation, etc., in addition to that laid down in the constitution and laws of the said corporation be definitely fixed:

Therefore it is agreed by the said parties hereto that this contract shall continue so long as it is mutually agreeable; that it shall remain of force and may be canceled by either party hereto without previous notice of any intention to do so.

It is agreed that said second party may employ, subject to the approval and appointment of the said imperial wizard (president) of the corporation aforesaid, and subject to the right and power of said imperial wizard (president) to revoke all such appointments, such assistant organizers as he (the said second party) may deem necessary in order to properly carry out the plans for the propagation and extension of said corporation: Provided, That such persons so appointed or employed by members of the said corporation in good and regular standing prior to their appointment, and that they maintain their good standing therein as an essential condition on which their appointment is made.

It is agreed that in all things the said second party shall be subordinate to the said imperial wizard (president) and shall attempt no plans or methods of work without the consent or approval of the said imperial wizard.

It is agreed that the said second party shall receive as in full compensation and expenses of himself and his duly appointed and commissioned subordinate organizers the sum of $8 for each and every new member brought into the said corporation by himself and his assistant subordinate organizers, and in addition to the $8 he shall receive $2 for each new member added to all klans organized by himself or his subordinate organizers within a period of six months after the date of the charter of all such klans organized by himself and his subordinate organizers.

It is agreed that no expense or debts shall be made or incurred by the said Edward Young Clarke or his subordinate organizers, and no obligation entered into with any firm, company, corporation, or person for which the said first party hereto or the said imperial wizard (president) shall be bound to make any outlay of or expenditure of money unless there be a specific approval of the particular item; or items of all such expenditures prior to the incurring of same by the said imperial wizard (president) of the said corporation.

It is agreed that the said second party shall advance from time to time, as may be necessary, the office rent and all other expenses incident to the proper conduct and furnishing of the main office of the aforesaid corporation and in addition thereto a sum of not less than $75 per week and traveling expenses of the said imperial wizard (president) of the aforesaid corporation, reimbursing himself for such expenditures or advancements out of the $2 due by him to the aforesaid corporation on account of each member received into the aforesaid corporation by him and his duly appointed and commissioned subordinate organizers.

Duly executed in duplicate in the city of Atlanta, Ga., on the day and date above written.

KNIGHTS OF THE KU-KLUX KLAN (INC.),
By ————— ———,
Imperial Wizard (President).

This is to certify that the above and foregoing is a true and correct copy of the only contract existing between E. Y. Clarke and the Knights of the Ku-Klux Klan.

————— ———,
Imperial Wizard.

Mr. WILLIAMSON. Now, I secured from Mr. Clarke a financial statement of the operations of the so-called propagating department, and this shows that he has received from all sources the sum of $860,393.50.

Mr. RODENBERG. In how long a period of time?

Mr. WILLIAMSON. That covers the period from June 1, 1920, to September 24, 1921.

Mr. FESS. Does that represent the $2?

Mr. WILLIAMSON. That represents the $10. Now, in disbursing that I find that $15,247 has gone for executive salaries; that $170,252 has gone to the treasury of the klan. That is the $2.

Mr. RODENBERG. That would indicate a growth of 85,000 in that period of time?

Mr. WILLIAMSON. Yes, sir. Mr. Clarke has spent $49,875.46 for advertising, and he has listed under the heading, "Organization work," the sum of $103,000. His bookkeeper told me that that represented the salaries paid salaried men who went out into the field in advance of the kleagles and prepared the way for the kleagles. Mr. Clarke has loaned to field men the sum of $20,308.21, and has in the bank $12,415.26. That accounts for the funds of the propagating department.

(The statement in full follows:)

Financial statement of Edward Young Clarke, imperial kleagle, from June 1, 1920, to September 24, 1921, inclusive.

Receipts:

From klectokens	$851,260.00
Commissions from new chartered klans	----------
Total	860,393.50

Disbursements:

Salaries, executive	15,247.00
Salaries, clerical	9,503.63
Commissions to field men	464,572.66
Commissions to klan	170,252.00
Publicity	49,875.46
Organization work	103,000.00
Supplies	2,596.99
Postage	2,064.66
Telephone	290.05
Telegraph	1,054.55
Multigraphing	613.53
Traveling expense	2,895.54
Miscellaneous expense	4,683.45
Rent	1,019.91
Loans	20,308.21
Balance in bank	12,415.26
Total	860,393.50

Assets and liabilities:

Loans	20,308.21
Cash in bank	12,415.26
Total	32,723.47
Profit	32,723.47
Total	32,723.47

Mr. WILLIAMSON. I have here a statement showing how the $170,252 has been spent; that is, the $2 part of the $10 collected, and this is taken from the books of the klan proper, not from the books of the propagating department. I will leave that with the committee.

(Said statement follows:)

Balance sheet Consolidated Knights of the Ku Klux Klan (Inc.), propagation fund and general fund, Oct. 1, 1921.

	Disbursements.	Receipts.		Disbursements.	Receipts.
Propagation commissions, 85,126 members, at $2...		$170,252.00	Kleagles kostumes account...	$828.90	
Traveling expense...	$25,139.69		Interest and exchange...	304.31	
Miscellaneous expense...	3,849.48		Express, freight, and drayage...	1,873.68	
Office expense...	2,877.26		Gold bond account...		$773.51
Field work salaries...	19,361.70		Bills receivable...	4,480.10	
Office salaries...	17,891.12		Bond retirement...	1,104.00	
Postage...	1,773.55		Lanier university...	22,474.32	
Furniture and equipment	14,486.36		Insurance account...	770.00	
Speakings and specials...	6,769.35		Accounts receivable...	17,197.67	
Office supplies...	3,767.89		Building and ground expense...	820.00	
W. J. Simmons (salary)..	12,600.00		Office rent...	2,175.00	
Advertising...	13,760.72		Typewriter and furniture rent...	258.00	
Publicity...	11,244.57		Telephone and telegraph account...	5,347.05	
Klan commissions, propagation department...	3,134.00		Multigraphing...	613.23	
Imperial kloncilium expense...	805.26		New York bureau...	1,031.84	
Legal service...	4,773.69		Knights of the air...	2,778.66	
May celebration...	5,549.14		Auto account...	1,468.08	
Washington bureau...	6,395.87	10.10	Employees bond premiums...		1,180.67
Reserve fund account...		21,996.65	Imperial palace property...	10,000.00	
Repairs to building...	3,446.80		Department of investigation...	823.57	
Printing...	19,279.94		Atlanta klan...	3,050.94	
Property improvement...	1,890.40		Simmons home fund...	3,000.00	
W. J. Simmons, special account...	186.50	547.35	National Motor Specialty Corporation...	600.00	
Bond sale expense...	1,394.20		Cash on hand...	500.00	
Propagation fund account	14,459.45	14,359.45	Bank accounts...	3,873.68	24,833.49
Kostumes account...	13,079.05				
Klan supplies account...	15,372.40		Total...	308,661.42	308,661.42
Klan account receivable..		9,254.32			
Accounts payable...		35,727.73			
Klan bond premiums...		1,257.30			
Klan klectokons...		21,200.00			
Klan dues...		7,268.85			

Consolidation assets and liabilities, Knights of the Ku-Klux Klan, propagation fund and general fund, Oct. 1, 1921.

	Assets.	Liabilities.
Furniture equipment...	$14,486.36	
Propagation fund...	14,459.45	$14,359.45
W. J. Simmons, special account...	186.50	547.35
Auto account...	1,468.08	
Imperial palace property...	10,000.00	
Atlanta klan...	3,050.94	
Simmons home fund...	6,000.00	
Accounts receivable...	14,197.67	
Revolving fund, cash on hand...	500.00	
Bank balance (propagation fund)...	3,873.68	
Bank balance (general fund, see schedule No. 1)...	1,755.05	
Employees, bond premiums...		1,180.67
Klan accounts receivable...		9,254.32
Accounts payable...		35,727.73
Klan bond premiums...		1,257.30
Bills receivable...	4,480.10	
Lanier University...	22,474.32	
Approximate furniture and fixtures, not booked...	8,000.00	
Total...	104,932.15	62,326.82
Assets above liabilities...		42,605.32
Total...	104,932.15	104,932.15

Mr. CAMPBELL. Will you give a summary of the statement?

Mr. WILLIAMSON. Well, it shows that commissions, as they call the $2, have been paid from 85,126 members; that $10,000 of this money has been paid on the imperial palace property. This is the property which was in Mr. Clarke's name until the afternoon of the day when I began the investigation in earnest. It also shows that $3,000 has been paid on the Simmons home. This is the property which is in the name of Mr. Clarke. Now, in addition to the $10 received from new members, as I explained, the klan has other sources of revenue, and I have a statement here showing the other sources. The bookkeeper explained to me that there are no books showing the disposition of the other sources of revenue prior to June 15, 1921; he said that up to that date $151,088.72 had been received and that $102,000, in round numbers, had been disbursed, but he did not know how it had been disbursed. The books, however, are very accurate from June 15 on, and the statement which I have shows that there has been received $137,228.75 from all sources of revenue other than the $2 out of the $10.

Mr. CAMPBELL. Have you any information as to how the remainder of that money was spent?

Mr. WILLIAMSON. I have a detailed statement showing how it was all spent.

Mr. CAMPBELL. I understood you to say that there was no record of how some of it was spent. Have you any information as to how the money received prior to June was spent?

Mr. WILLIAMSON. I have none.

Mr. GARRETT. June, 1921?

Mr. CAMPBELL. Yes.

Mr. JONES. The item there indicating that the books do not show anything previous to 1921 is probably a typographical error, because that should have been June, 1920, the date the Clarke contract started, and the figures represent from 1920 up to 1921, this year. .His answer was that it shows from June, 1921.

Mr. RODENBERG. What is your connection with this matter?

Mr. JONES. I have no connection with it except that I am a friend of Col. Simmons. I do not belong to the klan and have no connection with the klan.

Mr. CAMPBELL. We simply want to get some identification of your statement for the record. What are your initials, Mr. Jones, and where do you live?

Mr. JONES. N. P.

Mr. RODENBERG. How do you get those facts so accurately?

Mr. JONES. I went over the matter with Col. Simmons and the books. I have no connection with the klan and do not belong to the klan, but I am a friend of Col. Simmons.

Mr. JOHNSON. Are you a resident of Atlanta, Mr. Jones?

Mr. JONES. Yes.

Mr. WILLIAMSON. I can now give the committee some information as to the gross receipts from all sources. The receipts, as estimated from the old records, $151,088.72; taken in from 85,126 members, $851,260; received from chartered klans, $9,133.50; received from sources under the heading, "general fund," $137,228.75. This shows that there has been taken in from all sources, from the date the klan was organized to date, the sum of $1,148,710.97.

Mr. SNELL. That is quite different from what was testified to here this morning.

Mr. WILLIAMSON. Yes, sir; it is.

Mr. SNELL. These are actual figures that you have?

Mr. WILLIAMSON. They are.

Mr. FESS. That 85,000 is the number of members——

Mr. RODENBERG (interposing). Taken in since June of last year.

Mr. WILLIAMSON. I was told by Mr. Clarke that they now had, in round numbers, 126,000 members. Of course, these figures do not account for that many and I can not explain the discrepancy. I am merely giving you what the books show.

Mr. CAMPBELL. Your figures and the books account for about 85,000 members?

Mr. WILLIAMSON. Yes, sir. To be exact, 85,126.

Mr. RODENBERG. Do I understand that the 85,126 represent the increase since June of last year and up to September of this year?

Mr. WILLIAMSON. Yes.

Mr. RODENBERG. That is not the total membership now, Mr. Campbell; that is the increase since last June.

Mr. WILLIAMSON. That represents the amount taken in through the so-called propagation department.

Mr. RODENBERG. Since last June?

Mr. WILLIAMSON. Since the date of the contract, which is about a year from last June.

Mr. GARRETT. You gave some figures showing the amount taken in since the beginning of the organization?

Mr. WILLIAMSON. Yes; but those are estimated; there are no books from which to get those figures, and the figures I gave you were $151,088.72.

Mr. GARRETT. Whose estimate was that?

Mr. WILLIAMSON. That is the estimate of the bookkeeper employed by the klan.

Mr. FESS. Have you ever seen the statement that the membership is from 600,000 to 700,000?

Mr. WILLIAMSON. I think I have in the press.

Mr. FESS. On any posters?

Mr. WILLIAMSON. I think not.

Mr. POU. Your investigation would hardly justify any such membership as that, would it?

Mr. WILLIAMSON. It would not. Of course, I am only giving you what these books show. They may be wrong, but I have every reason to believe that they are correct. They are figures given me by a competent bookkeeper, employed by the klan, and who was turned over to me by the klan for the purpose of getting whatever the books showed.

Mr. KREIDER. The difference between the membership, which Mr. Clarke said was about 125,000, and 85,126 might represent a large portion of those who were members prior to this time.

Mr. WILLIAMSON. Pior to the date of the contract.

Mr. KREIDER. And included in the 126,000, and which the $152,000 on hand would represent?

Mr. WILLIAMSON. $151,000; yes, sir.

Mr. RODENBERG. Mr. Clarke made the statement as late as this month that the total membership, according to the best of his knowledge. was 126,000.

Mr. WILLIAMSON. He made that on October 4, the date I got these statements. I have here some information as to what has been received by Mr. Clarke and Mrs. Tyler through the so-called propagation department. From the chartered klans they have received $9,133.50; they have received as executive salaries, $15,247, and they have a bank balance of $12,415.26. That makes a total of $36,795.76. The statement shows that they have loaned to field men—and they have the loans listed as assets—the sum of $20,308.21, the total being $57,103.97.

While I was in Atlanta, Mrs. Tyler gave me copies of what they call weekly news letters. These are issued under numbers, from 1 on. From the news letter dated March 4, 1921, the following is taken:

" Washington, D. C., was the next objective of the imperial kleagle, and there he encountered many interesting experiences. He found that several Senators and Representatives had been naturalized among others, due to the activity of Capt. William S. Coburn."

Mr. FESS. Was that news letter for the press?

Mr. WILLIAMSON. That is a news letter sent to the kleagles in the field from headquarters in Atlanta.

Mr. FESS. It is not in the public press, then?

Mr. WILLIAMSON. No, sir; it is not. The following is taken from the weekly news letter dated April 22, 1921:

" It is announced that one of the big features of the gathering will be the presentation of a moving picture known as The Face at your Window. It strikingly depicts the serious workings of those forces which are antagonistic to all the principles for which the Ku-Klux Klan stands and which would tear down and scatter to the four winds those principles, ideals, and institutions inseparably associated with our Government and which the Ku-Klux Klan is determined shall be preserved. It shows the hooded figures of the knights of the Ku-Klux Klan riding to the rescue and portrays the final triumph of decent and orderly government by real Americans over the alien influences now at work in our midst. By special arrangement this picture is to be shown on this occasion for the first time, and thereafter it will be exhibited throughout the country. This is not a picture prepared as propaganda by the Ku-Klux Klan, but has the backing of higher powers which we are not now at liberty to disclose."

The following is taken from the weekly news letter dated June 10, 1921:

"We have just taken in the chief of police. He is a fine upstanding fellow, a major in the World War. We had a hard time getting information regarding him, but when we found he was eligible we had no trouble enlisting him in our ranks, and when he was initiated you never saw such a pleased fellow; he radiated it, and when he learned he was to have our support in upholding the law he was certainly pleased, especially with our military organization, which we offered him in case of trouble."

This is a quotation from a news letter from Norfolk, Va. It goes on to say: "He then informed us that the city is insufficiently protected and that we are sitting on a volcano regarding the Negro question; that there is a great deal of unrest among them and that we might have a riot at any time, and that he was very much worried. He told me that not many months ago there was a riot in the Negro district caused by Negro soldiers attacking a district police station to release a Negro prisoner, but it never got into the papers, so it was news to all of us. He welcomed us, and the military company is to be trained and 200 repeating rifles will be turned over to us in time of trouble. I asked how many in the 300 present at the meeting would be willing to join the organization to assist the chief, and every one of them stood up."

Further down in the same letter this language appears: "Just received intelligence from Kligrapp, of Shreveport, La., klan that a number of propaganda spreaders for the Nationl Association for the Advancment of Colored People, fresh from Tulsa, Okla., were run out of Shreveport, La., by our organization, and we understand are headed for this place, where they will certainly meet with a warm reception. Natchez klan has been notified. Notify all Tennessee, Arkansas, Mississippi, and Alabama klans."

Mr. Fess. Do you know what the military organization referred to there is?

Mr. Williamson. I do not; I have no information on that. From a news letter dated June 24, 1921, this appears:

"Mobile has its ups and downs, but we are again going forward and going forward fast. The National Association for the Advancement of Colored People is well represented here. They are preaching to the Negroes here that there is only one way for them to have social equality, and that is to fight for it and that now is the time to begin to fight. This is only bringing on a race riot. We are going to take steps to run the instigators out of town. We wish to offer through the columns of the News Weekly an invitation to our neighboring klans and have them come the night of the Fourth of July, as we wish to have a large parade in this city, at which time all the law violators will receive their warnings."

Mr. Rodenberg. Mr. Williamson, during your investigation did you visit that magnificent estate that is supposed to be occupied jointly by Mr. Clarke and Mrs. Tyler?

Mr. Williamson. I did not.

Mr. Rodenberg. There was nothing in the record to show how they secured that or that it was paid for out of the funds of the klan?

Mr. Williamson. I could not find any such estate down there. I do not believe Mr. Clarke and Mrs. Tyler are living together in any place of that sort at this time.

Mr. Rodenberg. At this time?

Mr. Williamson. No. My information is that Mrs. Tyler is building herself a home in the outskirts and is now living there.

Mr. Rodenberg. Had you not heard of this estate, this magnificent place?

Mr. Williamson. I never did before.

Mr. Pou. You did not hear of it in your investigations while you were in Atlanta?

Mr. Williamson. I did not.

Mr. Pou. Then you believe it to be mythical?

Mr. Williamson. It must be.

Mr. Pou. You say it must be?

Mr. Williamson. At this time.

Mr. Campbell. In any event, that would be a matter for the authorities in Atlanta?

Mr. Williamson. I presume so.

Mr. Campbell. And not of this committee?

Mr. Williamson. I do not know anything about it.

Mr. Campbell. Or for the klan, as I understand they clean up things of that kind?

Mr. Williamson. I do not believe I have any more information.

Mr. Pou. Was not that the place described by one of the former witnesses and did he not say he spent a part of his time there? Mr. Wright, if I did not misunderstand him, described a visit to this place. That is true, is it not, Mr. Rodenberg?

Mr. Rodenberg. Yes. I understand you to say that you did not find any such place and that you do not believe any such place exists.

Mr. Williamson. Not as far as I know; I did not find any such place.

Mr. Rodenberg. Did you make an inquiry?

Mr. Williamson. I made an inquiry of people who know the local situation and got no information of such a place.

Mr. Snell. Then you had heard about it?

Mr. Williamson. I heard the scandal hinted at by the World, and that was why I made such an inquiry.

Mr. Rodenberg. If such a place is 'n existence it would surely be a matter eas'ly ascertained.

Mr. Pou. Surely.

Mr. Rodenberg I would rather believe your statement that it does not exist because I would not think much of your inspection if you had not found it and it existed.

Mr. Williamson. I talked to Mrs. Tyler about it and, of course, I got her story that there was no such place.

Mr. Snell. Where did Clarke live at that t'me?

Mr. Williamson. I do not know. I saw him at the 'mperial palace; he was in charge of things there and he seems to be the head of the whole thing; he is the business man at the head of it.

Mr. Campbell. Mr. Williamson, in your investigation of the sources of revenues that have been secured by the organization, the Knights of the Ku-Klux Klan, was there anything in the propaganda that would lead you to believe that they had used the mails in connection with their work?

Mr. Williamson. Yes, sir; those news letters from which these quotation were taken have all been sent through the mails. Those are merely copies that I secured in the offices of what had been used.

Mr. Campbell. And those news letters were sent out for what purpose?

Mr. Williamson. They were sent to kleagles who were out securing memberships—I presume to stimulate them in their work.

Mr. Campbell. The ritual of the order and the proclamation hold out the order as one for benevolent and high purposes?

Mr. Williamson. Yes, sir; and not for selfish profit.

Mr. Campbell. What did you discover with respect to the use of money for beneficial purposes to the public?

Mr. Williamson. Well, when I went to Atlanta I found that the imperial palace itself, which had been bought in part with klan funds was in the name of Mr. Clarke. I found that the home of Mr. Simmons, which had been bought in part with klan funds, was in Mr. Clarke's name. I found also that some $21,000 of klan funds had been given the Lanier University without security. And in that connection I might say this: That whenever anybody pays his $10 for the purpose of joining this klan, he is given a receipt which says that this money is received in trust for the Knights of the Ku-Klux Klan (Inc.). That is printed on each and every receipt.

Mr. Campbell. What is the amount that has been paid out for salaries of officers in Atlanta—out of the money that has been collected, if you know?

Mr. Williamson. Well, I can tell you that, from the propagation department alone, $15,247 has been paid as executive salaries.

Mr. Campbell. To whom has that been paid?

Mr. Williamson. Well, I take it, from the word "executive," that it must be Mr. Clarke and Mrs. Tyler, because they are the two executives of that department. Then the field men—they are the kleagles—have been paid, in round numbers, $464,000. That would be $5 out of the $10, of which $4 would go to the kleagle and $1 would go to the king kleagle. That uses up $5. Then 50 cents goes to the grand goblin. And it is all used up but $, and $2 goes to the klan.

Mr. Campbell. And all of the $8, then, is used up in paying officers or agents of the klan?

Mr. Williamson. That is true.

Mr. Campbell. How much of the remaining $2 has been spent, if you know, for the benefit of needy people, or for helpful purposes in communities—charitable purposes?

Mr. WILLIAMSON. Well, if you call Mr. Simmons a needy person, then some thousands of dollars have been spent for him. But general charity, I do not think, has received any of it; at least it does not appear on the accounts.

Mr. CAMPBELL. What is Mr. Simmons' salary, if you know?

Mr. WILLLIAMSON. Mr. Simmons at present gets $1,000 a month. He has been getting that since the 1st of August.

Mr. CAMPBELL. Since the first of last August?

Mr. WILLIAMSON. Yes, sir; before that time he was receiving $100 per week. Mr. Clarke and Mrs. Tyler are not receiving salaries. Their compensation comes out of the propagation fund; whatever they make out of that is theirs—50–50.

Mr. CAMPBELL. Whatever amount comes into the propagation fund they divide equally between themselves?

Mr. WILLIAMSON. That is correct.

Mr. JOHNSON. Well, how much have they divided up to now?

Mr. WILLIAMSON. Well, I can not quite tell you that.

Mr. JOHNSON. Approximately?

Mr. WILLIAMSON. But I can tell you what they have in the bank to divide; that is $12,415.26. Now, they have loaned to field men $20,000, in round numbers. I take it that that is a good debt; it is merely an advance to a man who is working for the propagation department.

Mr. CAMPBELL. Who fixes the amount of the propagation fund?

Mr. WILLIAMSON. That is fixed by the contract, Clarke getting so much and the klan as a corporation getting so much.

Mr. RODENBERG. Mr. Williamson, did you answer the chairman's question in full a moment ago? You gave the two items, twelve thousand and some dollars, and $20,000 field fund. What is the balance that is in that propagation fund? You did not finish your statement; let us get that complete.

Mr. WILLIAMSON. As I have it from these statements, there is a sum of $57,103.97. Now, that includes cash in bank, loans to field men, executive salaries, which have already been paid, and what Clarke receives from the chartered klans; he gets $2 per member for the first six months, after the thing starts to going; that is in addition to the $8 out of $10 which goes to his department.

Mr. SNELL. This $2 simply goes to the propagation fund?

Mr. WILLIAMSON. That goes to Clarke and Mrs. Tyler, as the heads of the propagation department.

Mr. JOHNSON. Then, according to your figures, Mrs. Tyler and Mr. Clarke have divided or will divide approximately $57,000; is that correct?

Mr. WILLIAMSON. Yes, sir.

Mr. JOHNSON. Now, between what dates would that be?

Mr. WILLIAMSON. That covers the whole period from the beginning to the date of my investigation.

Mr. POU. You mean running back to 1915?

Mr. CAMPBELL. From the date of the contract, June, 1920?

Mr. WILLIAMSON. Yes. Now, that is what they have net, you understand. They have spent hundreds of thousands in paying these helpers of theirs—the field men.

Mr. CAMPBELL. How many field men have they?

Mr. WILLIAMSON. I have no idea, sir; I did not inquire. I was told this, however, that the klans had been organized in every State in the United States, and that their large following in the North was in Chicago; that they had not been so successful in New York, due to the World's articles; and that they had something like 300 members in the District of Columbia.

Mr. JOHNSON. May I ask one more question, Mr. Chairman? Mr. Williamson, I was informed recently by a Member of Congress that the New York American published an article recently to the effect that these people sold a quart of Chattahoochee River water for $10 a quart, for annointing purposes in some of their ceremonies. Did you find any record of that? [Laughter.]

Mr. WILLIAMSON. I did not. I do not believe it. I did talk to Mrs. Tyler about that; she told me it was not true.

Mr. JOHNSON. She said it was not true?

Mr. WILLIAMSON. Yes, sir.

Mr. CAMPBELL. Almost everyone who has any information about this order speaks of Mrs. Tyler. Are women eligible for membership?

Mr. WILLIAMSON. They are not.

Mr. CAMPBELL. Did you learn while in Atlanta the secret of Mrs. Tyler's executive authority in the order?

Mr. WILLIAMSON. Mrs. Tyler is not an officer of the order. She is merely a business woman working with Clarke at the head of the propaganda department, which is entirely separate from the klan. The officers of the propagation department are in the city; the klan headquarters are some 6 miles out of the city, on what is called "Peachtree Road." She is working at that as a business. She is a publicity woman. She and Clarke have been together before, in the Southern Publicity Association, and they are now working in this together.

Mr. CAMPBELL. It is purely a business proposition, so far as she is concerned?

Mr. WILLIAMSON. Absolutely.

Mr. CAMPBELL. She is using the mysticism, the regalia, the paraphernalia, the masks, and all of the literature of the order for the purpose of making money out of it? Is that correct?

Mr. WILLIAMSON. That is correct. In fact, she told me at least twice that she was in the business for the purpose of making money, just like she was in any other business for that same purpose. She is not, as I say, an officer.

Mr. CAMPBELL. Well, does Clarke, a member of the order, cooperate with her in that work?

Mr. WILLIAMSON. Yes. But Mr. Clarke at the present time is running the klan. Mrs. Tyler at the present time is running this department.

Mr. CAMPBELL. What is the imperial wizard doing while Mr. Clarke is running the klan?

Mr. WILLIAMSON. He was trying to get well of a severe cold when I was down there, and was not doing anything in the klan offices.

Mr. CAMPBELL. Well, can Clarke use the wizard's authority in the administration of the business of the klan?

Mr. WILLIAMSON. Mr. Clarke is called the imperial kleagle, which is the second officer in authority, the wizard being the highest. When the imperial wizard was sick Mr. Clarke was at the head of the order. As I saw it, he was doing everything necessary to be done; he was the highest officer there.

Mr. CAMPBELL. Oh, that is by the ritual, or by the rules and laws of the order?

Mr. WILLIAMSON. That is by the constitution and laws.

Mr. CAMPBELL. The constitution and laws?

Mr. WILLIAMSON. Yes, sir; he is the second officer.

Mr. CAMPBELL. Yes. Did you talk with the imperial wizard while you were there?

Mr. WILLIAMSON. I did.

Mr. CAMPBELL. Did he know of the financial uses to which the name of the order was being put by Clarke and Mrs. Tyler?

Mr. WILLIAMSON. He did not so indicate. Mr. Clarke told me that he doubted if Col. Simmons knew that the house was in his, Clarke's, name.

Mr. CAMPBELL. That is the house that——

Mr. WILLIAMSON. That the colonel was living in.

Mr. CAMPBELL. That Col. Simmons was living in?

Mr. WILLIAMSON. Yes, sir.

Mr. CAMPBELL. Then, in your investigation, did you discover whether or not Col. Simmons knew very much about what was going on in the local klan, or in the imperial klan at Atlanta?

Mr. WILLIAMSON. Well, if I may be permitted to venture an opinion, I should say that he did not know a great deal about the business operations of the klan.

Mr. CAMPBELL. He is credited with originating the ritual?

Mr. WILLIAMSON. Yes, sir.

Mr. CAMPBELL. And the mystic symbols?

Mr. WILLIAMSON. Yes, sir.

Mr. CAMPBELL. The founder of the reorganized Knights of the Ku-Klux Klan?

Mr. WILLIAMSON. Yes, sir. He told me that but one degree had been made; that two other degrees were in process of formation, but had not yet been "communicated," as he termed it.

Mr. CAMPBELL. That was Col. Simmons that told you that?

Mr. WILLIAMSON. Yes, sir.

Mr. CAMPBELL. Is there a treasurer?

Mr. WILLIAMSON. I think so.

Mr. CAMPBELL. Do you know who the treasurer is?

Mr. WILLIAMSON. Mr. Furney acts in that capacity and keeps the books.

Mr. CAMPBELL. When deposits are made of klan funds—for instance, the $2— in whose name is that deposit made?

Mr. WILLIAMSON. That is made in the name of the klan, as I understand it. Mr. Furney has accounted for all of that and seems to have charge of the finances of the klan.

Mr. CAMPBELL. How can that be checked up?

Mr. WILLIAMSON. I am not sure about that. My impression is that Mr. Furney can draw a check, thought I am not sure.

Mr. CAMPBELL. Mr. Furney being the treasurer?

Mr. WILLIAMSON. Yes.

Mr. CAMPBELL. I ask you this for the purpose of finding out whether or not all sources of information with respect to the use of this money for benevolent purposes were exhausted by you?

Mr. WILLIAMSON. I think you will find on those financial statements an item heading showing the use to which that particular item was put. I do not see anything there that indicates that any great amount has been expended for charity—general charity—or, in fact, any amount.

Mr. CAMPBELL. Any great amount?

Mr. WILLIAMSON. Any amount.

Mr. CAMPBELL. Any amount at all. Mr. Garrett, do you wish to ask any questions?

Mr. GARRETT. Yes, Mr. Chairman. Mr. Williamson, what was the attitude of this man Clarke and this lady about exposing their records to your investigation?

Mr. WILLIAMSON. They made no objection, but gave me everything I called for.

Mr. GARRETT. From what you saw there, do you think you saw all the records they had?

Mr. WILLIAMSON. I think I did.

Mr. GARRETT. Do you think you have exhausted the possible sources of information as to the funds that have come in to this organization?

Mr. WILLIAMSON. No, sir. You can not do that in seven days. This is merely a preliminary investigation.

Mr. GARRETT. Well, I will not ask you about what other lines you desire to pursue, because that is a matter for the Post Office Department to take up, and perhaps ought not to be exposed to this committee. But I will ask you if, so far as the records in Atlanta are concerned, you think you have exhausted them?

Mr. WILLIAMSON. No, sir. I should like to see the original vouchers showing where this money was spent. I should like to know something more about that one hundred and fifty-one and odd thousand dollars which was disbursed.

Mr. GARRETT. Now, that is the fund that it was estimated was received before this contract?

Mr. WILLIAMSON. Yes.

Mr. GARRETT. Well, I suppose Clarke and Mrs. Tyler knew nothing about that, because they were not connected with the organization at that time—or did they?

Mr. WILLIAMSON. Mr. Furney gave me all the information on that that I have. He told me that that was handled by Col. Simmons himself, and that Col. Simmons was a very poor bookkeeper and things were somewhat confused, and that he had not been able to get heads nor tails out of it.

Mr. GARRETT. Well, did you see anything or learn anything there to lead you to believe that more than that amount might have been received?

Mr. WILLIAMSON. I can hardly harmonize those figures with the statement that 126,000 members had been received. If you multiply that by $10 you will get more money than I have covered in these accounts.

Mr. GARRETT. That would give $1,260,000. You have accounted, I believe you said, for $480,000 paid to field kleagles, or whatever they are?

Mr. WILLIAMSON. I have accounted for $1,148,000, in round numbers.

Mr. RIORDAN. That is, from all sources?

Mr. WILLIAMSON. All sources. Now, of course, a great part of that is from the so-called general fund, which does not come in from any part of the $10.

Mr. GARRETT. Well, you are not through with your investigations, then?

Mr. WILLIAMSON. No, sir.

Mr. GARRETT. You expect to return there shortly, or some one will return there shortly—or is it proper to ask that question? I will withdraw that question.

Mr. CAMPBELL. Dr. Fess, do you desire to ask any questions?

Mr. FESS. Mr. Williamson, you stated that Col. Simmons received $100 a week up to a certain time, and then it was made $1,000 a month?

Mr. WILLIAMSON. Yes, sir.

Mr. FESS. Was there any agreement to pay any back salary, and has there been any paid?

Mr. WILLIAMSON. I do not know that.

Mr. FESS. You know nothing of that?

Mr. WILLIAMSON. No.

Mr. FESS. That would be an unusual increase at one time, from $400 to $1,000 a month; how do you account for that?

Mr. WILLIAMSON. I have no way of accounting for that, excepting that I just found it on the books that way, and I was told by Mr. Furney that that part had been and would be paid.

Mr. FESS. It has gotten about in some fugitive way that there is something like $25,000 that has been agreed to be paid in back salary; did you hear anything about that?

Mr. WILLIAMSON. I have no information about that.

Mr. JOHNSON. Mr. Williamson, what are Mr. Furney's initials, and how do you spell his name?

Mr. WILLIAMSON. N. N. F-u-r-n-e-y.

Mr. JOHNSON. Do you know what city he comes from?

Mr. WILLIAMSON. No; I do not.

Mr. JOHNSON. Just one or two more questions: I have been very much interested in this scheme of propagation and division of this money that comes in. It is being used by promoters all over the United States; for instance, out in the West there is the nonpartisan league that has an imperial wizard, A. C. Townley—although they do not call him that—and that has the same identical scheme as this Ku-Klux Klan of the division of the fee by goblins, and cyclops, and one thing or another, although they do not call them that. I would like to know if your investigation developed whether this promotion scheme came originally from the promoters of the nonpartisan league or from the promoters of the Ku-Klux Klan?

Mr. WILLIAMSON. I have no information of that.

Mr. JOHNSON. You do not know who thought of the idea and gave it to Mr. Clarke and Mrs. Tyler?

Mr. WILLIAMSON. I do not.

Mr. JOHNSON. That is all I have.

STATEMENT OF HON. WILLIAM J. BURNS, DIRECTOR OF THE BUREAU OF INVESTIGATION, DEPARTMENT OF JUSTICE.

Mr. CAMPBELL. Mr. Burns, will you state your full name to the stenographer?

Mr. BURNS. William J. Burns.

Mr. CAMPBELL. You are connected with the Department of Justice?

Mr. BURNS. Director of the Bureau of Investigation.

Mr. CAMPBELL. It was stated here this morning—I think by Mr. Tague—that complaints had been made to the Department of Justice with respect to the activities of the Knights of the Ku-Klux Klan?

Mr. BURNS. Yes.

Mr. CAMPBELL. Are you making an investigation of that matter?

Mr. BURNS. We are.

Mr. CAMPBELL. Have you concluded your investigation?

Mr. BURNS. No.

Mr. CAMPBELL. Are you ready to make a report?

Mr. BURNS. Not yet.

Mr. CAMPBELL. You are making the investigation for the Department of Justice?

Mr. BURNS. Yes.

Mr. CAMPBELL. Have you any statement that you care to make?

Mr. BURNS. None.

Mr. CAMPBELL. I believe that is all, unless other members of the committee wish to ask questions.

Mr. GARRETT. That investigation is being pursued now, is it?

Mr. BURNS. Yes, sir.

Mr. GARRETT. It has not been stopped pending this congressional investigation?

Mr. BURNS. No.
Mr. GARRETT. It is going right along?
Mr. BURNS. Yes, sir.
Mr. GARRETT. That is all.
We will now recall Mr. Wright.

ADDITIONAL STATEMENT OF MR. C. ANDERSON WRIGHT.

Mr. GARRETT. Mr. Wright, I want to see if I got the right impression this morning. You became a member of this klan, did you?
Mr. WRIGHT. Yes, sir.
Mr. GARRETT. A full-fledged member?
Mr. WRIGHT. Yes, sir.
Mr. GARRETT. And were appointed to seek other members—that is, as a kleagle?
Mr. WRIGHT. I had a commission to that extent, but I was never used in that official capacity. That was simply an honorary title, given me so that I would have a rank equal to the highest officer.
Mr. GARRETT. I did not get clearly in my mind just why it was that those of you who were interested in the development came into this—or was it aircraft, or the use of aircraft?
Mr. WRIGHT. Well, it was more to get the flyers together in some kind of a body where we could get ships to fly, and have a real big order to that extent. Flyers were not the only ones eligible to it; anybody interested in air ships, or any women, would be. That was the original plan of the order.
Mr. GARRETT. Well, flying for commercial purposes, or——
Mr. WRIGHT. Oh, no; simply to keep in training; simply to keep the boy in training who were flyers during the war, and the younger generation growing up who wished to learn how to fly, but, of course, could not afford to take instruction.
Mr. GARRETT. And you wanted to be supplied with machines?
Mr. WRIGHT. We wanted to have enough together so we could have machines to fly in in all sections of the country, and it simply was put up to—at first, I thought the correspondence was all going to Col. Simmons, but I found out later that it was to Mr. Clarke and Mrs. Tyler, and that he did not know much about it, when I got down there.
Mr. GARRETT. Was it upon the initiative of those interested in the development of the air service that this matter was taken up with the klan?
Mr. WRIGHT. Yes, sir.
Mr. GARRETT. You sought it; you sought the cooperation of the klan?
Mr. WRIGHT. I sought the cooperation, not of the klan, but of Col. Simmons, who I imagined to be a very wealthy man and a man of great organizing ability, who would be strong enough to get the flyers together into a head, to be the head of a flying organization. My intentions were not at any time that it should be any part of the Ku-Klux Klan.
Mr. GARRETT. Now, how long have you known Mr. Simmons?
Mr. WRIGHT. I have never met Mr. Simmons, but I have been told a lot about him by Mr. Clarke, when I joined the klan in New York City.
Mr. GARRETT. Well, you had not known Mr. Simmons before you approached him, or the organization, on this subject?
Mr. WRIGHT. Well, it was simply when they asked for qualifications of what a man wished to do, and what was he best fitted for. I simply said I was very much interested in aeronautics, and that it was a splendid thing for the klan to have a chance for cooperation. That was when I joined.
Mr. GARRETT. Well, did you join——
Mr. WRIGHT (interposing). Yes, sir; I joined as an individual.
Mr. GARRETT. Well, did you join before or after you sought the cooperation of Col. Simmons?
Mr. WRIGHT. Before.
Mr. GARRETT. Before?
Mr. WRIGHT. Yes, sir.
Mr. GARRETT. And it was after you had become a klansman that you took up the matter of undertaking to develop an interest in the Air Service on the part of the klan?
Mr. WRIGHT. Yes, sir.

Mr. GARRETT. I see. Well, that is what I was anxious to get straight in my mind. I got the impression in some way this morning that it was preliminary to your joining that you had taken up that question with him.

Mr. WRIGHT. No, sir. I received a questionnaire just like anybody else did. I do not know just how it originally came to me; I suppose somebody, or some fraternal order, had sent in my name, and they sent me a blank which I filled out and sent to Atlanta. I did not hear anything more about it until a couple of months later when I received a wire to be at such-and-such a place to go over the matter with this party, who happened to be Mr. Hooper.

Mr. GARRETT. I got the impression from your testimony this morning—and I want to see if I am right about it. This committee is making these inquiries, of course, with a view of determining whether it is proper to authorize a congressional investigation of this matter, and you are the only person who has been a member of the klan who has been before the committee, and presumably you know more about it than anybody else here testifying. I got the impression that the principal reason why you thought there ought to be an investigation was on account of the financial end of it, as handled by Mr. Clarke and Mrs. Tyler?

Mr. WRIGHT. Not only the financial end, but the whole thing—the moral end of it. They are teaching one thing and practicing themselves an entirely different thing; they are preaching one doctrine and living another.

Mr. GARRETT. Now, do you mean that Clarke and Mrs. Tyler are doing that, or do you mean that the organization as an organization is doing that?

Mr. WRIGHT. The only people that I ever dealt with, or have received a commission from, or had any dealings with, financially or in any other way, were Mrs. Tyler and Edward Young Clarke. If there is another organization—which I suppose they cover up legally—I do not know; but I know that Col. Simmons never passed on anything officially that was given me; my instructions were always given by Mrs. Tyler or Mr. Clarke, and I was a klansman.

Mr. GARRETT. That does not quite answer my question. Do you mean that the whole klan should be investigated——

Mr. WRIGHT (interposing). No, sir; I mean the imperial palace should be investigated; the conditions of the finances in the klan. Mr. Clarke has been brought out only as imperial kleagle. Mr. Clarke is also klabee, or acting as such, and is the treasurer and the imperial klaliff, vice president, who, in the absence of the imperial wizard, as I understand, has full authority over the klan. I heard Mr. Furney brought out in the testimony here as being treasurer. When I was in Atlanta Mr. Furney was purely the bookkeeper; he was not an imperial officer in any way, shape, or form.

Mr. GARRETT. Well, has the organization no power within itself to investigate its officers?

Mr. WRIGHT. No, sir. The imperial wizard has appointed himself imperial wizard. He has organized the klan; he is that officer for life; it is not like any other fraternal orders, where a man is elected upon vote each year. There is nobody can oust him, that I know of, unless it is the men that he appoints; he appointed his own staff. Therefore, he is not going to appoint any staff that would oust him; that is certain.

Mr. GARRETT. Now, was the fact that he was imperial wizard for life known to you when you joined?

Mr. WRIGHT. No, sir; it was not.

Mr. GARRETT. Do you know whether it is known to the members?

Mr. WRIGHT. I thought it was like any other fraternal order, that the officers were elected each year.

Mr. GARRETT. You do not know whether it is known generally among those who have joined or not?

Mr. WRIGHT. I do not think it is; no, sir.

Mr. GARRETT. Well, I did not mean to say that I understood you to put the whole thing upon the financial side of it this morning, because there was another side. But that is one element, at least—the handling of the finances.

Mr. WRIGHT. Yes, sir.

Mr. GARRETT. And the finances are handled, according to your best belief, or according to such information as you have, by Clarke and Mrs. Tyler? That is, they control it?

Mr. WRIGHT. They control everything that is used in the field forces; the imperial treasury money—which I do not know how it is arranged, exactly. I know that Col. Simmons signs checks on one bank, and Clarke signs checks on others, and Mrs. Tyler.

Mr. GARRETT. Well, did you know anything about what was to become of the $10 that you paid down to this organization?

Mr. WRIGHT. Not when I joined; no, sir. I did not know that until I got to Atlanta. And there are very few people that did know that division.

Mr. GARRETT. Well, did you care anything about it?

Mr. WRIGHT. At that time?

Mr. GARRETT. Yes.

Mr. WRIGHT. Yes; I certainly did.

Mr. GARRETT. As to how it should be used?

Mr. WRIGHT. Why, certainly.

Mr. GARRETT. How did you expect it would be used?

Mr. WRIGHT. I expected it would be used for something except for the personal benefits of one or two members of the order—like the funds of any organization would be used, by vote of the men they elect in office, and not by an imperial dictator, who is self-appointed and supreme in command, and who appointed everybody under him. There is no way of getting at him or controlling him in any way, except by the men he appointed himself.

Mr. GARRETT. Now, the imperial wizard of this organization, as I understand, is Simmons?

Mr. WRIGHT. Yes, sir.

Mr. GARRETT. But you say that Clarke is really running the thing?

Mr. WRIGHT. I say that Mrs. Tyler is really running it, and that he is her mouthpiece. or he is the man that "wears the pants".and can have a rank in the klan.

Mr. GARRETT. Well, now, on the other phase that you spoke about this morning, I understood you to say that Clarke and Mrs. Tyler were sending treasonable matter through the mails?

Mr. WRIGHT. Yes. sir. I would be very glad to cover that evidence with documents at any time the committee wishes. I came here on a few hours' notice, but I can do that.

Mr. GARRETT. Do you think it would require a congressional investigation to ascertain that fact if such matter was sent through the mails openly?

Mr. WRIGHT. I think. sir, that when any one person, according to their own boasts. has gained control and a footing in this country, and by their own boasts have 700,000 men who have to do exactly as one man says, that they have no choice by vote to throw out of office—how it is done I do not know, but I certainly do think that it should be investigated, and investigated thoroughly. I know that the klansman who joins the order does so with all good purposes and knows absolutely nothing about the real conditions at the imperial palace.

Mr. GARRETT. Well, pardon me; it may be that that element might necessitate or render proper a congressional investigation. But my question was directed to the allegation which you made of treasonable matter being sent through the mails.

Mr. WRIGHT. Yes. sir.

Mr. GARRETT. If that is a fact, there is no necessity of a congressional investigation to develop that, is there?

Mr. WRIGHT. Well, that was something that—I would not——

Mr. GARRETT (interposing). There is a law against that now, is there not?

Mr. WRIGHT. Yes, sir.

Mr. GARRETT. And the Post Office Department has a very large number of men in there who can read and determine whether the matter is treasonable or not under the law as laid down for the department, can they not?

Mr. WRIGHT. Well, that is something that I could not answer, sir, not knowing enough about law to say what kind of an investigation it should be. I did not in any way suggest the investigation. I just simply told—my purpose was not for an investigation, but it was simply to tell the klansmen who had been duped into going into this order what was being done with their money and how they were being laughed at for being such fools. That was my idea, and pressure was being brought upon me, as I say, by people whom I knew and knew well that I should tell the men in the thing just what the conditions were.

Mr. GARRETT. How long were you a member of the order?

Mr. WRIGHT. I joined last February.

Mr. GARRETT. Was any attempt made while you were a member of it to influence your action as a citizen in any way?

Mr. WRIGHT. My action personal!v?

Mr. GARRETT. Yes; your vote, for instance?

Mr. WRIGHT. No, sir; there was not as to my vote.

Mr. GARRETT. Do you know of any instance in which any of your fellow klansmen were ever sought to be influenced by any of the officials of the organization in their votes as citizens?

Mr. WRIGHT. Do you mean by that could I prove my documentary evidence to that effect? No; I could not.

Mr. GARRETT. No; I mean do you know of it of your own personal knowledge?

Mr. WRIGHT. Oh, absolutely; I know the whole plan of the klan was simply to gain control of the country through the ballot.

Mr. POU. It must have been organized by the Republican Party, then. [Laughter.]

Mr. CAMPBELL. That is not the way we got the 7,000,000 majority.

Mr. GARRETT. Well, you say that was the purpose of the klan?

Mr. WRIGHT. Yes, sir.

Mr. GARRETT. Who informed you that that was the purpose of the klan?

Mr. WRIGHT. I was informed by the man in charge of my domain, Lloyd P. Hooper.

Mr. GARRETT. That it was the purpose to weld all of this organization into a body that would all vote one way?

Mr. WRIGHT. Whichever way the imperial wizard would instruct them; yes, sir. Not only by him, but by Mr. Clarke.

Mr. GARRETT. Did Mr. Clarke tell you that at the time you joined, or after you joined?

Mr. WRIGHT. Mr. Clarke—no; after I joined; he told that. Or, the first time I heard it, really, was when I had joined the order, and they asked us all to bring friends of ours in, to meet Hooper and Clarke. There was a man whom I was very closely associated with, and he was the editor of my magazine, Capt. Collins, Rowe R. Collins; he was with the New York American, and I thought that he would be a good man for the order. He went up with me and heard the tale that Clarke had to tell, and Mr. Hooper, and their plans, which they went into for the first time in my hearing, of how they were going to gain control of New York and put in their own men, and——

Mr. GARRETT (interposing). That they would put their own men in office?

Mr. WRIGHT. In office; yes, sir.

Mr. GARRETT. In political office?

Mr. WRIGHT. And Capt. Collins immediately refused to join the order or have anything to do with it. In other words, the preaching that Mr. Clarke brought to New York was this: That the klan would pretty soon be able to dictate everything in New York, and that it would not be a very warm place for any Jew, or Catholic, or foreign-born, or any man that did not live up to their doctrine. Now, that has been preached everywhere in the pulpits, and everywhere else in the South by their men; there is no question about that. I am sure they do not deny that.

Mr. GARRETT. You mean that in the pulpits of the South?——

Mr. WRIGHT (interposing). Yes, sir.

Mr. GARRETT. Ministers of the gospel have said—what, now?

Mr. WRIGHT. They have stated—the imperial chaplain of the order has stated in their public meetings that the klan—not necessarily the klan, but the men who were 100 per cent Americans—would dominate America and control it; and "100 per cent Americans," in the klan language, are klansmen.

Mr. GARRETT. But that is not what you said a moment ago, Mr. Wright. What you said a moment ago was that they told you that they had come into New York?

Mr. WRIGHT. Yes, sir.

Mr. GARRETT. And that they would gain political control of New York?

Mr. WRIGHT. Yes, sir.

Mr. GARRETT. And that the place would be too hot for the Catholics and Jews?

Mr. WRIGHT. Yes, sir.

Mr. GARRETT. And now you state that ministers of the gospel were stating that over the South. Now, do you repeat that?

Mr. WRIGHT. I did not mean in the pulpit; I mean in public addresses different people in the South at meetings which I have attended. I did not really mean the pulpit of the church; I meant simply public addresses.

Mr. GARRETT. Well, did he tell you up there at that meeting what they were going to do with the Catholics and the Jews?

Mr. WRIGHT. No, sir; I did not find that until Clarke got feeling unusually happy one day out at his estate and boasted of his whole plans to Mr. Paydon, who was connected with me in the Knights of the Air, and myself.

Mr. GARRETT. And he told you then what he was going to do with them?

Mr. WRIGHT. He told us how he was going to control the country, and everything else; all of these details that I have written out. As I uderstand, one of the newspapers has announced a series of articles by Mr. Paydon. I have not seen him since I left the South; but I am sure it would be easy to get hold of him to corroborate any of the statements that I have made, for he was with me all the time when these statements were made.

Mr. GARRETT. I believe that is all.

Mr. RODENBERG. Let me ask you a question: This morning did I understand you correctly to say that you had visited that estate in Atlanta occupied by Mr. Clarke and Mrs. Tyler?

Mr. WRIGHT. Yes, sir.

Mr. RODENBERG. Where is that estate located? How far from the city?

Mr. WRIGHT. It is about a 20-minute ride by the automobile road out on Peach Tree Boulevard, off of Peach Tree Street; I could not tell you the exact location.

Mr. RODENBERG. How much of an estate is it?

Mr. WRIGHT. I could not say how many acres, but it is a pretty large estate.

Mr. RODENBERG. What would you estimate the value of the estate to be? Mr. Williamson said a few moments ago that he could not find any such estate; but you were there personally?

Mr. WRIGHT. I was there personally, and I am sure——

Mr. RODENBERG (interposing). Have you any idea of the value of it?

Mr. WRIGHT. I should say the estate was easily worth, at the very least, between $75,000 and $100,000.

Mr. RODENBERG. And it is in the name of Mr. Clarke and Mrs. Tyler?

Mr. WRIGHT. Well, there is a very peculiar thing. When I reached Atlanta Mr. Clarke told me he wanted me to be prepared and to be sure to come out Sunday to his country home. So I was very much delighted to go out there.

I went out, and upon arriving I found Mrs. Tyler in possession of the household. Of course, I was very much surprised, because I had only met her semiofficially at that time.

Mr. RODENBERG. This is a residence, a large residence?

Mr. WRIGHT. A residence. They have plenty of servants. It is very easy to prove that. I say I can very easily prove it by witnesses who were out there with me. I have been out there several times since. The next day Mrs. Tyler called me as de, and she says, " You know, Mr. Clarke doesn't get along very well with his wife, and he, is a very sick and lonely man, and I have been letting him have a room out at my estate." So Mr. Clarke claimed the estate and so did Mrs. Tyler. I do not know who owned it.

Mr. RODENBERG. What time of year did Mr. Clarke unfold this political scheme to you?

Mr. WRIGHT. When I got down there at Atlanta in May, right after the convention.

Mr. RODENBERG. He did not tell you that in New York?

Mr. WRIGHT. No, sir. The only thing he told me in the presence of Capt. Collins, was that he was going to control New York, and that was enough to keep me out. I went down to Atlanta on the 6th of May. In the meantime I went right ahead with my own business in the East. I did not go South.

Mr. RODENBERG. From the 6th of May until the middle of September you were with them?

Mr. WRIGHT. Oh, no. I stayed down there. I was simply a member, resigning from all offices.

Mr. RODENBERG. You did not do any work after the 6th of May?

Mr. WRIGHT. For a month or more following that.

Mr. RODENBERG. You did work awhile after learning the political scheme?

Mr. WRIGHT. Yes. As I say, I had to get out of it as easily as I could.

Mr. RODENBERG. The point I was getting at is: You did work awhile after finding out what the political scheme was?

Mr. WRIGHT. Oh, yes. Yes, sir.

Mr. GARRETT. Where is the location of that mansion you were telling about? Do you know?

Mr. WRIGHT. It is 20 minutes' ride. Anybody in Atlanta can tell you that. I am not acquainted with Atlanta. I was not there long enough. It is right out on the outskirts. I was told that the reason they moved out there was because a vigilance committee had waited on them in the city and they had to find quarters that were not so open in the city.

(Thereupon, at 4.55 o'clock p. m., the committee adjourned until Wednesday, October 12, 1921, at 10.30 o'clock a. m.)

COMMITTEE ON RULES,
HOUSE OF REPRESENTATIVES,
Wednesday, October 12, 1921.

The committee met at 10.30 o'clock a. m., Hon. Philip P. Campbell (chairman) presiding.

Mr. CAMPBELL. Mr. Trotter, are you ready to proceed?

Mr. TROTTER. Yes, sir.

STATEMENT OF MR. WILLIAM M. TROTTER, OF BOSTON, MASS.

Mr. CAMPBELL. Mr. Trotter, where do you reside?

Mr. TROTTER. In Boston.

Mr. Chairman, I am speaking in behalf of the National Equal Rights League of Colored Americans. The league petitions in behalf of this resolution for an investigation. It holds that the Ku-Klux Klan by its own announced purposes and pronouncements, by its known acts, by its methods of procedure, by its regalia, etc., is a private, unofficial organization which interferes with the actions and activities and personal liberty of persons and citizens, most of whom are outside of its own membership, millions of them being ineligible to membership because of the rightful unchanging conditions of race and religion; and that it interferes with the actions of citizens by a method of coercion, through the agencies of terror and of corporal punishment. The league claims this interference and attempt to exercise functions of government because the self-announced purposes, in general, are to protect the weak from the brutality of the strong, to punish evildoers and lawbreakers and, in a sense, those who have been unapprehended, untried, unconvicted by the constituted authorities, and by the well-known facts that occur in the exercise of its functions; also, by the general announced purposes of the protection of womanhood and the maintenance of white supremacy in all things—matters that come under the Government. The method of coercion is shown by usually sending out threatening, warning notices to persons to cease doing things that they are doing or to do things that they are not doing. The agency of the terror is shown by the very name of the organization, avowedly perpetuating the greatest and most historic terror organization that this country has ever known, so terrible that Congress authorized the use of the Army and the Navy to prevent it. The terror is shown also by the methods of secrecy and of operation in the dark, and especially by the very regalia, the hooded gown, which not only does inspire terror but which to the promoters of the organization has a special beneficent value, and, Mr. Chairman, the corporal punishment is well known through these matters of tarring and feathering individuals which have been exploited in the public press and not denied.

Now, Mr. Chairman, the National Equal Rights League feels that a private, unofficial organization interfering with the actions and activities and the personal liberty of citizens along these lines, and seeking to exercise the functions that properly belong to the Government, and using coercion and terror and corporal punishment, and excluding millions of citizens, and basing its activities upon prejudice of race and religion is a real menace to the sense of personal security and the peace of mind of millions of citizens who are barred and banned; that it is a menace to the constitutional rights, especially the right of franchise of those who are barred and banned. It is a menace to life and limb to those who are barred and banned and their friends, and it is a menace to equality of rights and opportunity to those who are barred and banned, and a menace to the peace of the country in widening any breach that may exist between the various races, and disturbing what harmony of races we have.

We hold that any private organization of this sort and genus is something that menaces the peace of the land. We hold it is unAmerican; it is undemocratic; it is entirely inconsistent with free institutions; it is really an attempt to set up a superstate, private and invisible, objection to which was one of the chief reasons why this country did not agree to the world peace compact at Versailles.

We hold, Mr. Chairman, that at this particular time when our President is seeking to lead the world in a movement for world peace through world disarmament and is bringing the nations of the world to this very capital upon the matter of world peace, that this country can not afford to have notoriously in its own domain any such government-usurping organization, based openly upon prejudice against religious elements, based openly upon the suppression of another loyal race element, an invisible superstate seeking to bring about dissension rather than peace.

Mr. Chairman, we hold that any such organization—this or any other organization of a similar kind—ought to be illegal in the United States of America, and we favor this investigation oecause we hope it will lead to its suppression, either by present law or by the passage of a law that will make illegal private, unofficial organizations which undertake to exercise the functions of government.

I might read, Mr. Chairman, just one pronouncement by the imperial wizard, published in Nation and never denied, that might give you the reason why we are here with the Jew and the Irish and the foreigner, asking for this investigation. It reads as follows, Mr. Chairman:

" We exclude Jews because they do not believe in the Christian religion. We exclude Catholics because they owe allegiance to an institution that is foreign to the Government of the United States. Any native-born American who is a member of the English church or any other foreign church is barred. To assure the supremacy of the white race we believe in the exclusion of the yellow race and in the disfranchisement of the Negro. It was God's act to make the white race superior to all others. By some scheme of Providence the Negro was created as a serf. We harbor no race prejudice. The Negro never had and has not to-day a better friend than the Ku-Klux Klan. The law-abiding negro who knows his place has nothing to fear from us. We do not act until called upon."

And they do not say by whom called upon, but listen, please:

" But if needed, we have a great, invisible, and mysterious force that will strike terror intő the hearts of the lawbreakers."

Mr. Chairman, we have petitioned the Members of. Congress for a law to make illegal any private organization based upon race prejudice that seeks to exercise the functions of the Government, and with your permission I would like to call a few witnesses to amplify what I have said in objection to this organization, and I will first call upon the Rev. S. E. J. Watson, of Chicago, the chairman of our national executive committee, who will speak upon the menace to the peace of mind and sense of security of those who are barred and banned from the organization.

STATEMENT OF REV. S. E. J. WATSON, OF CHICAGO, ILL.

Mr. WATSON. Mr. Chairman, we are pleading, as has just been said, because of the influence that this organization is having on the morale of our people throughout the country, and it is proving a hindrance to their progress, as evidence already brought forward has shown that our people are included in the various races against whom this organization will operate. We do not complain of our race, and if I may be permitted, I will say that if given equal opportunity and privileges, knowing my people as I do, I would rather be a Negro to-day living in the United States of America than to be the king of any empire to which I might be called, for no man has a greater opportunity to serve humanity than a true-hearted man in the midst of our people, and these 11,000,000 of our people are discouraged and threatened in their home life and possessions and are now feeling discouraged to the point that the morale is really lowered, for many are driven in the night from possessions that they have been accumulating since the days of slavery, and made to leave them; and we can produce evidence and statements from some who were driven to the effect that men recognized in the mob that drove them met them elsewhere in the city and offered them their railroad fare and a small sum of dollars for their possessions and asked them to leave on the first train. Any organization destined to so terrorize the citizenship of the country and disturb their peaceful home relations is certainly, as we contend, a menace to the progress of that part of American citizenship, and if you will permit us also to advise, the thing at which this organization strikes, the desire for social equality on the part of this race, is, in our estimation, entirely unwarranted. Equality is made to mean, however, as we understand it by this organization, that when we seek to make our homes sanitary and beautiful, we are striving to take what does not belong to our race, and we feel that even for an organization to express fear admits in itself that there is danger, and they are conceding themselves the very thing that they propose to fight.

To add to the present discouragements of our race, the new idea of the Ku-Klux Klan, bringing with it all the memories that our fathers have told us of this organization or an organization by this name in bygone days, is creating such an unrest among our people that we are asking that the matter be investigated so as to give rest to this part of our citizenship.

We contend further that the time has come when this race which has striven to prove loyal should be given some encouragement by the people of this Nation to go forward in their striving for progress.

This invisible empire, if it thinks that there is a people in this country who need it to carry them to places where they can not go without it, we declare to you we do not need it to hinder us or prevent us from reaching heights where will and work might take us; and not desiring to take up your time, we simply come to plead that this matter be investigated thoroughly, so that it may not prove a hindrance and a menace to a struggling people who have proven themselves loyal to every call and stand yet ready to do the same again.

Mr. TROTTER. I will next call upon Rev. David Simpson Klugh, of Boston, a member of our executive committee, who will speak on the menace to the safety of life and limb for those banned and their friends.

STATEMENT OF REV. DAVID SIMPSON KLUGH, OF BOSTON, MASS.

Mr. KLUGH. Mr. Chairman and honorable committee, I live in Boston, Mass., but I am a southerner. I was born in South Carolina, educated in Georgia, and lived there the most of my life. I love the South. I love its people. I love all the people of the South, and I only wish that they loved me as I love them, and if they did, or showed it in their love, I would never be in Massachusetts to-day. I would be in the South.

Now, I think the Ku-Klux Klan organization ought to be investigated for the following reasons: First of all, an organization which is reputed in the country and published in the public press to say and do things that it is reputed this organization is saying and doing ought to be investigated to ascertain whether or not those things are true. If it is not true, the organization ought to be vindicated, and if it is true, it should be condemned, and there is no way to find that out without a thorough investigation.

I noted that your honor, in speaking in opening this hearing, laid stress on the fact of overt acts of violence attributed to this organization; that that was one of the things you wanted to find out, whether or not this organization was guilty of overt acts of violence against the rights and against the peace and dignity of the Nation or the laws of the Nation.

Now, I will submit a few cases that have been reported in the public press, and I have never seen them denied.

First of all, I will call attention to what was reputed to have been said by the imperial wizard in an address in Mississippi, June 8, 1921. This was reported in the Atlanta Constitution, that the imperial wizard, Col. Simmons, is reported to have said that what the Confederate soldiers——

Mr. TROTTER (interposing). Mr. Chairman, I would like to ask the Rev. Klugh not to read any pronouncement, but just confine it to the matter of cases. I would ask particularly that he would not read the declaration by Col. Simmons. It is the wish of the chairman, and we agreed to be brief.

Mr. KLUGH. Well, what I was going to say was simply this—I will be as brief as I can, but I think a man ought to have time to present his case.

Mr. CAMPBELL. Yes.

Mr. KLUGH. There is nothing to fear if you tell the truth and let everything be square and open, and that is what I mean.

Mr. CAMPBELL. You may proceed.

Mr. KLUGH. If Col. Simmons said this and meant it, it means a whole lot to the country; not only to me but the whole country.

Mr. FESS. Let him read it.

Mr. KLUGH. Thank you. He is reputed to have said that what the Confederate soldiers lost on the battle field was won back for the South and for white civilization by those same soldiers in the guise of the Ku-Klux Klan. Now, when I read that I could feel that it meant nothing else than this, that it meant if the South or any part of the country had failed to carry out a scheme and failed to subject certain citizens to eternal slavery—I saw nothing else but that that it could mean. If it was said and does not mean that, that ought to be known.

Mr. GARRETT. Of course, you knew that that was not correct, if it was stated, did you not; that nobody had been reduced to slavery by any action since the war?

Mr. KLUGH. What I took it to mean was they were organizing and that that was the purpose; that it was not yet consummated, but was to be consummated by the organization which was being organized throughout the country.

Mr. GARRETT. The statement which you read there, was that an organization subsequent to the war had won what the Confederate soldiers lost on the field of battle. It was the past that was referred to, as I gathered from your reading.

Mr. KLUGH. No; this organization that is organizing is for that purpose. That is the meaning I got from it, that it was for that purpose; not the old organization which was examined and put out of business in 1871; not that organization, but the new organization which was being formed, of which he was the imperial wizard. That is the understanding I, got from it.

Now, coming to the acts of violence, it is reported that one July Perry, a colored man, was lynched in Florida and that subsequently five others were burned, all growing out of the refusal to permit Perry to vote at Ocoee, Fla., November 2, 1920; that the massacre was preceded three days before by a public parade in Florida's metropolis of an organization calling itself the Ku-Klux Klan with hooded robes and masks to conceal the personal identity of the members, a body declaring for white supremacy.

If that is not true, it ought to be known. If it is true, it should also be known, and we claim that this is an act of violence and it is attributed to the Ku-Klux Klan. If it is not true, we ought to know it, and no man should be branded for such lawless action as that, because the colored people love the South and we love the country and love you, and we should.

We realize that in our numerical strength in this country, in our financial ability, in our voting ability, if we had any, we could never on the present hypothesis do what is sometimes attributed to my people, or have the aspiration to do what is sometimes attributed to my people. I know them well. It is not the purpose, and never has been, for the colored man to dominate the white man or to dominate the country. We know that it is a physical impossibility. It is our purpose to live in peace and in friendship. It is our purpose to take advantage of the civilization that you have made, and it is the highest ambition of many colored people to copy after the good things of the white people, and I am sorry sometimes they copy too many of the bad things. We want that opportunity and we feel that the Ku-Klux Klan is a menace to us, as has been said, and that it carries out its plan of prejudice by violence—these overt acts of violence, and, if you please, gentlemen, it does not stop with us, as we can further show that it is attributed or alleged that the Ku-Klux Klan will vent its spite upon any man who seems to be friendly to us in certain sections of the country.

It is reported that the Rev. Philip S. Irwin, a white archdeacon of the English Episcopal Church, was whipped and tarred and feathered near Miami, Fla., and warned to leave the town or he would be lynched, and the only offense that he was guilty of was trying to give colored citizens good information as a preacher and as a parish of the church; in other words, he was their pastor and spiritual adviser.

Now, these instances might be multiplied, but I do not feel it is necessary, because I want to be brief, but I will call your attention to one more incident, which we regard as violence and an overt act against the good citizens of our country. A certain bellboy in Texas, who was reported simply to be friendly, and I think we all should be friendly—that is, should have friendship—and the paper said that he was friendly, was not only whipped almost to the point of death but was branded on his forehead by "K. K. K.," and that boy wears that brand to-day.

Now. If the Ku-Klux Klan are not guilty of such violent acts, it ought to be known. This organization should not be branded with such overt acts of violence against any group of citizens if it is not guilty, and if it is not guilty it ought to be known, and the only way to know it is to have an investigation.

Mr. CAMPBELL. Is it alleged that that was done by masked men?

Mr. KLUGH. It is alleged that he was whipped, yes; by masked people, as I understood it.

Mr. CAMPBELL. And branded?

Mr. KLUGH. And was branded with that brand right on his forehead. If he had been tried for any act of lawlessness whatsoever—we want the law enforced. We do not want bad people in our country, and if he was not living according to the law he should have been tried by law and punished by law, not by the Ku-Klux Klan. We believe in law and order. We believe in supporting our Government. We believe in supporting you, and we do not believe that any organization should exist, whether secret or otherwise, that takes the place of the law of the land.

I shall not multiply these. There are some 60 cases that could be reported, but I am sure that before this honorable committee it is not necessary to go into all that, but simply to show that there is room for procedure on the ground of these reported acts of violence, overt acts of violence, and attributed to the Ku-Klux Klan. Gentlemen, I thank you for the time you have given me. These papers may be submitted. You may have them; I do not need them.

Mr. POU. Was this photograph of the boy, Alexander Johnson, taken after the mutilation or branding took place?

Mr. KLUGH. I beg your pardon.

Mr. POU. I say, is this a genuine photograph of Alexander Johnson?

Mr. KLUGH. Yes.

Mr. POU. I do not see anything about this except just this photograph.

Mr. KLUGH. It is reported in another paper. That is simply his picture, but the report is somewhere else.

Mr. TROTTER. That is just his picture, and it was taken from life after the act was committed. The instance itself we did not bring.

Mr. KLUGH. Right under that mark [indicating] you will see that something is said about it. These papers may be left for the committee to look at.

Mr. GARRETT. You had better identify those papers by name.

Mr. KLUGH. These are copies; these are clippings from southern papers and reprinted in the Guardian; the Boston Guardian clipped them.

Mr. POU. Will you read what you have in mind? I do not see——

Mr. TROTTER (interposing). Mr. Member, it is not there; the instance itself is not there, but simply the picture.

Mr. KLUGH. Is not this the case that happened at Daceyville, Tex.?

Mr. TROTTER. No. It is simply the picture, and the instance we did not happen to bring with us. It was reported in the Associated Press and sent throughout the country.

Mr. RODENBERG. I read the story at the time; I remember reading it.

Mr. TROTTER. It was widely published. I am the editor of that paper, and I sent for a photograph of the boy after he had been branded and made a cut of it and put it in the paper.

Mr. GARRETT. It was alleged that he was too friendly with a white woman.

Mr. TROTTER. That was the allegation, that he was friendly with a white woman, and this private organization undertook to punish him for it before he had been arrested or tried or anything of the kind. Now, Mr. Chairman, I would like to call upon Rev. N. A. N. Shaw, of Boston, to protest against the klan as a menace to the harmony of the various elements of the country and peace of the land. Mr. Shaw is the national president of the Equal Rights League.

STATEMENT OF REV. N. A. N. SHAW.

Mr. SHAW. Mr. Chairman, I simply want to call attention to what I consider an overt act on the part of Mr. Paydon, the goblin in charge of the New England territory. His name was referred to in the testimony given here yesterday as being a partner of Mr. Wright, and as prince of the air, or something. In explaining the klan in Boston a couple of days ago he said that if the Jews and the Catholics really knew the true purport of the klan they would not object to it because the negro problem demands the union of all white peoples to suppress them and to maintain white supremacy.

Now, the true purport of the klan seems to strike at the very heart of this race that we represent. There seem to be ameliorating circumstances with respect to the other groups that are excluded—that is, at certain stages; that has been amply hinted at at this hearing, that there are certain stages—according to Mr. Wright's testimony—where certain people can be elevated to certain ranks but at no time and at no stage can Negroes be admitted at all, and according to this goblin the real point, the real thing, is to annihilate Negroes as American citizens. That, of course, makes it very much our concern. If in the last analysis this organization is to disable, disfranchise, and annihilate the group that is known as colored Americans, then colored Americans can not help but naturally come to this committee and ask seriously and earnestly that this klan, with this avowed end and purpose, be investigated. As American citizens, about eleven millions of us, we would like to know just what is the true purport of this klan and how it proposes to operate to th's end. Of course, we have a number of specific instances of overt acts of violence tending to show the direction of the operation and the mode of operation, terrorizing, for instance, after the old fashion of the ancient Ku-Klux Klan and keeping colored American citizens away from the polls, driving them from their homes and all of those things. But according to this goblin these are only preliminary, because with all these things the real purpose is not understood, according to Mr. Paydon, by either Jews or Catholics.

We contend that any such statement, backed by the regular established procedure that has gone on and that is going on at the present time, makes 11,000,000 American citizens nervous, anxious, fearful, and unsettled, and the first law of nature asserts itself, the desire for protection, self-defense. I would never look at a young man like Mr. Wright, who testified here, if I met him on the street of any city, and imagine that he was a member of an organization that went masked in the dark to perpetrate murder and all kinds of lawlessness. I make this statement to show you that not a single man in this room is safe, because Mr. Wright looks as civilized and as intelligent as any man upon this committee, and if he is a klansman we can only be sure that colored men are not klansmen and we can not tell what man is a klansman, and your law makes it perfectly justifiable that homicide be committed when any man thinks he is in danger. And if the committee takes into consideration that one point, namely, the great jeopardy in which every white man is placed by the doctrines of this klan, by the actions of this klan, by the night parading under the mask and in the dark, with so much power that they can enter an American city, apparently in consort with the authorities, so that as they march and give their signal that city is thrown into absolute darkness and no light is seen anywhere, and who then is safe? And so I have come, representing the Equal Rights League of America, asking that a thorough investigation be made. It seems imperative; it seems inevitable; it seems necessary, for the very essence of the self protection of every man in the country, that this hatred and this antipathy and this race suspicion be clarified, so that men may understand that they can, with their families, live in America in security. Nothing in the history of the country has aimed a more deadly blow at the very foundations of our institutions as this klan, and it has set itself against a loyal, law-abiding, faithful set of American citizens who for 250 years and more have proved their loyalty beyond a question.

Those citizens have been driven to feel that here is a man, holding some high and exalted office in an organization that is country wide, calling upon every element, except this one element, to unite their forces in order to annihilate them, to suppress them, and to do them injustice of every kind. And we appeal to that thing in which we eternally believe, the conscience of this great Government and this Nation, and ask that you investigate, to the very last degree and fullest extent, an organization that is so notorious, an organization that is so barbarous, an organization that defies law and order and disgraces any civilized people. I thank you.

Mr. TROTTER. Mr. Wolff, secretary of the Boston branch of the National Equal Rights League, would like to say a word.

STATEMENT OF MR. ALBERT G. WOLFF.

Mr. WOLFF. I had told Mr. Trotter, in charge of the proceedings, that it might not be necessary to call upon me because Dr. Shaw had concluded about everything necessary to be said at this time, and so I am just going to say one word. I am secretary of the Boston branch of the National Equal Rights League, and I am a colored man, as you can see, but my activities are along patriotic lines and they are not confined alone to activities among the colored people. I am a colored man and I am proud of it, but I am first of all an American citizen. I am State counsellor of the Sons of Veterans of Massachusetts, a State organization, although I am a colored citizen. During the World War I made efforts to taken an active part in that struggle, but I was prevented from doing so. and yet I gave of my time, unstintingly, to stimulate the enlistment of soldiers and I served upon the legal advisory board and did all I could. that was possible, free gratis, to win the war and to uphold the interests of the United States in that great struggle.

So, in view of those facts, gentlemen, I come here to-day to urge strongly an investigation of this organization which is, in reality, a substitution of the mob for the law. It is unlawful and ought to be investigated, and as a previous speaker has said, ought not only to be investigated, but steps should be taken to see to it that no similar organization is permitted to exist in these great United States of ours. As a previous speaker has just said, there is great unrest at the present time among the colored people of this country, but they are honest. they are fair. and they are waiting anxiously, eleven millions of colored people all over this country, to see what action this committee here at Washington is going to taken in this matter, and the sole purpose and object of those people is simply this: They are not looking for social equality or anything of that kind; their sole purpose is to secure the protection under the law which is guaranteed them by the Constitution. That is all I want to say at this time, gentlemen, and I thank you for the opportunity of appearing before you at this time.

Mr. TROTTER. Unless you desire to hear any more witnesses that is all, Mr. Chairman, and I thank you.

ADDITIONAL STATEMENT OF MR. O. B. WILLIAMSON.

Mr. CAMPBELL. Mr. Williamson, on yesterday you were asked about the home or the premises occupied by Mrs. Tyler. At the time you said you did not know where she lived in Atlanta. Have you any statement now with respect to her place of residence?

Mr. WILLIAMSON. I have a statement that was given me by Mr. Clarke showing that Mrs. Tyler some six or eight months before the klan was organized purchased a home on Howell Mill Road, paying $1,500 down and agreeing to pay $75 a month thereafter until the total purchase price had been paid; Mr. Clarke said that he thought the home was worth about $10,000, and that Mrs. Tyler had paid between $4,000 and $5,000 on this property, and that no part of the money had been taken from the treasury of the klan. That, in substance, is the statement.

Mr. RODENBERG. You never saw the home?

Mr. WILLIAMSON. No, sir; I never did.

Mr. FESS. When did you get that information?

Mr. WILLIAMSON. I got that in Atlanta.

Mr. FESS. When?

Mr. WILLIAMSON. On the 4th day of October.

Mr. FESS. Then you had it yesterday?

Mr. WILLIAMSON. Yes, sir. I might have misapprehended your inquiry, because I thought you had in mind the question of whether Mr. Clarke and Mrs. Tyler were living in some home in Atlanta. This, Mrs. Tyler explained to me, was a small home, and I did not think it worth while to go out and look into it.

Mr. CAMPBELL. Did you talk to Mrs. Tyler about the home?

Mr. WILLIAMSON. Yes; I showed Mrs. Tyler this statement and she said it was correct.

Mr. CAMPBELL. What led you to get that statement from Mr Clark?

Mr. WILLIAMSON. I was trying to find out whether any of the funds of the klan had been taken to pay for a home for any of the persons connected with the klan.

Mr. CAMPBELL. Did Mrs. Tyler say that she was residing in that home at this time?

Mr. WILLIAMSON. I believe she did say that.

Mr. RODENBERG. Mr. Williamson, you made no further effort to find out about that home; you simply took Mr. Clarke's statement, and that is all?

Mr. WILLIAMSON. And Mrs. Tyler's statement.

Mr. RODENBERG. You did not try to verify the accuracy of the statement?

Mr WILLIAMSON. No. I saw, of course, that none of the funds, as shown by the statement, had been taken for any such purpose, so I dropped that phase of the inquiry.

ADDITIONAL STATEMENT OF MR. C. ANDERSON WRIGHT.

Mr. CAMPBELL. I wish you would examine that paper with particular reference to the description of the house alleged to belong to Mrs. Tyler. Is that the house in which Mrs. Tyler lived when you saw her at her home in Atlanta?

Mr. WRIGHT. Yes, sir.

Mr. CAMPBELL. I think you said the home in which she lived was a much more pretentious home than this is purported to be. Is this a correct description of the house?

Mr. WRIGHT. Not by any means, sir.

Mr. CAMPBELL. What kind of a house does Mrs. Tyler live in?

Mr. WRIGHT. The house itself was originally not so elaborate, but it has been elaborated and built around. It is not only the house but the estate that is so beautiful and of such value. The house itself is now modern in every way, having all facilities, and the farm is equipped complete in every way for everything; everything is run either by electricity or machinery all throughout; they have their own waterworks and everything else on the place; it is a complete ranch, you might say, in every detail.

Mr. CAMPBELL. Is it a frame, brick, or stone house?

Mr. WRIGHT. It is a frame house, with a porch all around it, and then there are numerous other buildings on the grounds—servants' quarters, and stables, and all other things. Mr. Clarke said it cost him a good many thousand dollars to dam a part of the estate to let the springs flow into the lake.

Mr. CAMPBELL. How many acres are in the estate?

Mr. WRIGHT. I could not tell you that, but you can not see the end of it, by any means, when you are on the property. It is a very large estate.

Mr. CAMPBELL. You mean by that——

Mr. WRIGHT (interposing). That there are numerous acres.

Mr. CAMPBELL. One hundred acres?

Mr. WRIGHT. I would not say, because I do not know.

Mr. CAMPBELL. But you say you can not see the limit of the place?

Mr. WRIGHT. No; you can not see the limit of the property from the house; it is a very elegant estate. I do not mean by that that the home is so elaborate, but I know the home is worth a great deal more than that. The grounds themselves are right near Atlanta, and only being 20 minutes by automobile from Atlanta the estate is worth more than that.

Mr. CAMPBELL. How many rooms are in the house, if you know?

Mr. WRIGHT. I should say about 10.

Mr. CAMPBELL. Are there driveways around the place?

Mr. WRIGHT. All around; very elaborate driveways; and in the rear are garages for their fleet of automobiles; they have a whole fleet of cars.

Mr. CAMPBELL. How many cars have they?

Mr. WRIGHT. I know of seven they had when I was there, either belonging to Mrs. Tyler or Mr. Clarke or the Southern Publicity Association.

Mr. CAMPBELL. Do they keep all of these cars on these premises?

Mr. WRIGHT. They keep most of them there, but keep some of them in the garage in the city, at the Ansley Garage. I want you to understand this thing, that I do not know anything about who owns this property, and I am not claiming here that it was bought with klan funds; I am simply stating that it has all been improved. Whether it was purchased during the time that they have been receiving these tremendous profits from the klan and whether they were the profits that legally belonged to them or not I am not in a position to state.

Mr. CAMPBELL. You said that Clarke stated to you that it had cost him a great amount of money to improve the property.

Mr. WRIGHT. Yes, sir.

Mr. CAMPBELL. Did he state how much it cost him?

Mr. WRIGHT. He said thousands of dollars, and he had me out there one day and there was a whole gang of workmen changing the level and improving the lawns and places like that that they built in there, and he said the money was going out at a terrific rate and that it cost him thousands and thousands of dollars. The peculiar thing that struck me about the whole thing was that Clarke would tell me this was costing him all that and Mrs. Tyler would tell me it was costing her this.

Mr. GARRETT. How old a man is Mr. Clarke?

Mr. WRIGHT. I should judge he is about 35.

Mr. GARRETT. How long were you in this home?

Mr. WRIGHT. Why, I was out there with Mr. Clarke at numerous times; I drove out with him and talked over matters to get away from the office, and I was out there several Sundays for dinner.

Mr. GARRETT. Did you state yesterday just how long you were in Atlanta in connection with this organization?

Mr. WRIGHT. Approximately one month.

Mr. GARRETT. From May 6 to June?

Mr. WRIGHT. Well, from a little before May 6 until June.

Mr. GARRETT. Of this year?

Mr. WRIGHT. Yes, sir.

Mr. GARRETT. Did you visit any other cities of the country or any other section of the country in connection with this work?

Mr. WRIGHT. Yes, sir.

Mr. GARRETT. Where did you go?

Mr. WRIGHT. I visited Washington, New York, Indianapolis, Chicago, Springfield, Ill., and Minneapolis.

Mr. GARRETT. Did you go to Texas?

Mr. WRIGHT. No, sir.

Mr. GARRETT. I do not know whether I got the right impression yesterday or not, but did the articles that you referred to as having written appear in your publication—the Tail Spin?

Mr. WRIGHT. No, sir; they appeared in the Hearst publications, the New York American, and a great many other papers throughout the country.

Mr. GARRETT. What was the time of these articles?

Mr. WRIGHT. They started on the 15th of last month and appeared for 20 days thereafter each day.

Mr. GARRETT. The 15th of September?

Mr. WRIGHT. Yes, sir.

Mr. GARRETT. Did you write these articles voluntarily or were you——

Mr. WRIGHT (interposing). I wrote them voluntarily, yes, sir.

Mr. GARRETT. What I mean is, did you offer them to this publication, or did some one representing this publication call upon you?

Mr. WRIGHT. Some one representing the publication called upon me.

Mr. GARRETT. Do you know how they learned you were a member of the klan?

Mr. WRIGHT. Yesterday I explained that one of my best friends, Capt. Collins, who had been in the Hearst organization for a great many years and now is night manager of the Universal Service in New York, was with me at one time and he refused to join the klan, and when the other papers started coming out with all the facts, but were not written by any former klansman, he came to see me and asked me if I would consider writing some articles. The Universal Service and the International—I do not know about the International—interviewed me and several reporters at various times, and then one night got me out of bed at my home and said the managing editor of the American wished to see me, and I came down and I agreed to write these articles to the best of my ability, covering the facts and the documents I had in my possession.

Mr. GARRETT. Did you write them yourself?

Mr. WRIGHT. Yes, sir.

Mr. GARRETT. And they appeared just as you wrote them?

Mr. WRIGHT. Yes, sir.

Mr. GARRETT. Without being revised by anyone?

Mr. WRIGHT. Of course, there were lots of things taken out of them that they would not publish.

Mr. GARRETT. You received pay for them, I suppose?

Mr. WRIGHT. Yes, sir.

Mr. GARRETT. Do you object to stating what you received per article?

Mr. WRIGHT. I would object to it right now. I would not mind myself, but I do not know whether they would care to have it known. It was not enough to pay the debts that the klan had caused me to obligate myself for and to have to pay myself.

Mr. GARRETT. That is interesting. What debts had the klan caused you to obligate yourself for?

Mr. WRIGHT. The entire expenses of forming the Knights of the Air in Philadelphia, and travel expenses to various cities, my supposed drawing account which never materialized, and all these things which caused me not only undue embarrassment but also very near caused me serious criminal trouble, and I had to call upon every resource I possibly could to meet and pay them, amounting to hundreds of dollars, all of which I brought out in my articles.

Mr. GARRETT. Do you mean by that you had some trouble with checks of some sort?

Mr. WRIGHT. Yes, sir.

Mr. GARRETT. Checks you drew that were not honored?

Mr. WRIGHT. Yes, sir; checks and drafts.

Mr. GARRETT. About how many of those were there?

Mr. WRIGHT. I could not say approximately, but there were a great many.

Mr. GARRETT. Do you remember what cities or locations you had trouble in about these matters?

Mr. WRIGHT. Yes, sir.

Mr. GARRETT. Where were they?

Mr. WRIGHT. The cities were Philadelphia—well, there was really only Philadelphia where I had trouble, but there were many things I had to make good.

Mr. GARRETT. Did you have any trouble about any checks in St. Louis?

Mr. WRIGHT. No, sir.

Mr. GARRETT. Or Houston, Tex.?

Mr. WRIGHT. No, sir.

Mr. GARRETT. I believe you said you did not go to Texas in connection with the work?

Mr. WRIGHT. No, sir.

Mr. GARRETT. But you did mention St. Louis as one of the places you visited?

Mr. WRIGHT. I was in St. Louis but I did not have any trouble with checks.

Mr. GARRETT. Were there any checks or drafts drawn by you upon this organization that were honored?

Mr. WRIGHT. At the start; yes, sir. I was furnished, supposedly, with a secretary at Atlanta, a girl by the name of Miss Fowler, who was supposed to receive my drawing account, expenses, etc., and place them in the bank in Atlanta. I was taken to this bank, which was the klan bank, and introduced by Mr. Clarke.

Mr. GARRETT. Did you ever have any trouble about any checks outside of these checks?

Mr. WRIGHT. Nothing personal; no, sir.

Mr. GARRETT. Did you have any trouble with any police or other officials or with the courts in any way in any of these cities, other than that growing out of these checks?

Mr. WRIGHT. Yes, sir; I had trouble originally, but I, of course, made it good immediately. I was able to borrow the money and pay it up. There was no trial or anything like that.

Mr. GARRETT. How long did this continue—their not honoring your checks?

Mr. WRIGHT. About three weeks.

Mr. GARRETT. I believe you stated yesterday you were in the overseas service?

Mr. WRIGHT. Yes, sir.

Mr. GARRETT. And also in the service here during the war?

Mr. WRIGHT. Yes, sir.

Mr. GARRETT. How long were you in the overseas service, Major?

Mr. WRIGHT. I was simply on inspection work. I did no fighting or anything like that.

Mr. GARRETT. How long were on this inspection work?

Mr. WRIGHT. Possibly two months.

Mr. GARRETT. In France?

Mr. WRIGHT. In England, not in France.

Mr. CAMPBELL. Mr. Wright, tell the committee just how the difficulties you had with respect to these drafts and checks arose. Were you authorized to draw, or did you understand that you were authorized to draw, on the Ku-Klux Klan in Atlanta?

Mr. WRIGHT. Certainly. I was sent by official orders to these various places.

Mr. CAMPBELL. And you made drafts or checks upon——

Mr. WRIGHT (interposing). Upon Atlanta; yes, sir.

Mr. CAMPBELL. And these checks were not honored?

Mr. WRIGHT. They were not; no, sir.
Mr. CAMPBELL. At Atlanta?
Mr. WRIGHT. At Atlanta.
Mr. CAMPBELL. But were sent back to the bank——
Mr. WRIGHT. Where they were cashed.
Mr. CAMPBELL. They were sent back to the bank where they were cashed, and you were called upon to make them good?
Mr. WRIGHT. Yes, sir.
Mr. CAMPBELL. They were indorsed that you had no funds in the bank at Atlanta, or dishonored?
Mr. WRIGHT. They were dishonored; yes, sir.
Mr. POU. What was the amount of all of these repudiated checks?
Mr. WRIGHT. I could not say approximately, but I would be very glad to submit to you a full list of the whole thing. I have it in detail. It was a good many hundred dollars.
Mr. POU. You have some idea approximately, have you not?
Mr. WRIGHT. I should say around six or seven hundred dollars. That was just for those obligations, but there were many other things I had to pay.
Mr. POU. You had no trouble with any checks except checks drawn on the so-called Ku-Klux Klan bank in Atlanta?
Mr. WRIGHT. No, sir.
Mr. CAMPBELL. And you understood you were authorized to draw those checks?
Mr. WRIGHT. Absolutely. I can prove that without any question of doubt. There are now being filed suits against them to collect that money.
Mr. CAMPBELL. You are bringing suits now against——
Mr. WRIGHT (interposing). Yes, sir.
Mr. CAMPBELL. Against whom?
Mr. WRIGHT. Against Mr. Clarke and Mrs. Tyler.
Mr. POU. Unless you have some special reason for withholding the information, it seems to me that it might throw some light upon your activities if you would tell this committee how much you realized for these articles.
Mr. WRIGHT. Well, that I do not know. It depends on how much they receive for the syndication of them. I have not been settled with in the matter.
Mr. POU. You know how much you have been promised?
Mr. WRIGHT. I would be very glad—but I would have to ask the permission of the editors of the American if it would be all right to give that out or not. So far as I am concerned, I am perfectly willing to give it out.
Mr. POU. How much have you received up to this time?
Mr. WRIGHT. Well, I have drawn about $2,000.
Mr. POU. And there is more yet to come?
Mr. WRIGHT. Yes, sir.
Mr. POU. About how much more?
Mr. WRIGHT. As I say, I would not like to say unless it is all right to say. I would be very glad to testify at the proper time and lay all the data before you.
Mr. POU. Why should there be any concealment about it? Why should there be any objection?
Mr. WRIGHT. It depends on how many papers use them. These articles are still running in a great many papers, and they are still being purchased by a great many papers, and I do not know exactly what arrangements will be made about that, because the contract was originally made with only one paper, and since then papers all over the country have purchased the articles.
Mr. POU. Do you expect to receive as much as $5,000, all told?
Mr. WRIGHT. Yes, sir.
Mr. POU. That is the compensation you get for this expose?
Mr. WRIGHT. It is just based on space rates and how much is used of it.
Mr. POU. I want to ask this witness this question. You said here yesterday that you had violated the oath that you took.
Mr. WRIGHT. Yes, sir.
Mr. POU. What sort of an oath would you consider to be binding, Mr. Wright?
Mr. WRIGHT. I would consider any oath to be binding that was lived up to by the people who gave it to you, but when people have not lived up to their oath to you I do not consider the oath binding in any way, shape, or form, and I am very glad to say I have broken the oath, and I think by doing it I have done a public service.

Mr. Pou. You put your hand on the Holy Evangelists of Almighty God and took an oath you would keep certain things secret?

Mr. Wright. You mean on the Bible?

Mr. Pou. Yes.

Mr. Wright. No, sir.

Mr. Pou. What sort of an oath did you take, then?

Mr. Wright. The oath has been described in the press. It is not taken on the Bible. It is administered by a kleagle or any field man who gives it and read off from the oath of the order.

Mr. Pou. It must not be much of an oath then if the Bible is not used in connection with it.

Mr. Rodenberg. There was a copy of the oath here yesterday.

Mr. Pou. I am asking this witness about it. In taking an oath, as I understand it, a man puts his hand on the Bible.

Mr. Wright. You place your hand over your heart and raise the other hand.

Mr. Pou. Oh. that is it? That is the Ku-Klux Klan oath, is it?

Mr. Wright. Yes, sir.

Mr. Pou. The Bible was not used at all?

Mr. Wright. The Bible is used in the room; yes, sir. It is read. Two chapters are read from the Bible, certainly. but your hand is not placed on a Bible or anything like that as it is in a great many other oaths.

Mr. Campbell. I believe that is all, Mr. Wright. The proponents of the resolutions have not submitted any other names for the committee. The committee is now ready to hear Mr. Simmons.

Mr. Etheridge. Mr. Chairman, I want to ask the indulgence of the committee, if it is consistent with its plan, to adjourn at this hour for a short recess or until such time as the committee may determine on account of Col. Simmons's indisposition. He is seized with a kind of nausea and thinks he would be feeeling better at the afternoon session, and, while we are ready to go on if the committee insists, we would like to ask that indulgence.

Mr. Campbell. It is now 10 minutes after 12, and the committee will recess until 2 o'clock.

Mr. Etheridge. Just a moment, Mr. Chairman. It has been suggested, in order to conserve the time of the committee, that inasmuch as I have been asked to give short testimony before this committee that it might be given now.

Mr. Campbell. We could hear you now.

STATEMENT OF MR. PAUL S. ETHERIDGE, OF ATLANTA, GA.

Mr. Campbell. Give your name and place of residence.

Mr. Etheridge. Paul S. Etheridge, Atlanta, Ga.

Mr. Campbell. What is your business?

Mr. Etheridge. I am an attorney at law.

Mr. Campbell. Whom do you represent here?

Mr. Etheridge. I am here in company with Mr. Simmons and am one of the imperial officers of this organization.

Mr. Campbell. What is your designation as an officer of the organization?

Mr. Etheridge. They call me the supreme attorney. It is equivalent to general counsel.

It was not my purpose. gentlemen, to make any statement or to offer any testimony before this committee. but in the course of the hearing thus far there have been several allusions to matters transpiring in and around Atlanta. which is my home town, and concerning which I am personally familiar, and I deemed it proper to make certain statements which I think will serve in some measure to clear up some misinformation that this committee has received regarding these things which, as I say, have been alluded to. Pardon this statement. to begin with. As I have observed and listened to what has been brought out by the proponents of these resolutions the bulk of it is argumentative and opiniative, and I am strongly tempted to indulge in argument; but that is not my purpose. I merely want to give you a few facts which I noted down in the course of this investigation.

It was asserted here on yesterday by the witness, Mr. Wright, that Mrs. Tyler is in truth and in fact the official head of this organization and the power behind the throne, so to speak.

Gentlemen. I have been a member of the imperial body, which is equivalent to the board of directors, of this organization for something over four years, and almost during its entire existence. I think I have attended every meeting of that body and have been called into consultation by the officials and by the body itself at numerous and various times, and, while I am not personally familiar with all the details of the work of this organization in the field. I am fairly familiar with the workings of the imperal body at the home office. I wish to state that I never met Mrs. Tyler until July 4, 1921, at which time I was casually introduced to her at a Fourth of July celebration in the city of Atlanta, and was informed at the time, gentlemen, for the first time that she was connected with the propagation department of this organization. I have nothing whatever to say to her efficiency or her official position in reference to that department of this work, but with reference to the plans and policies and government and control of this organization, if she has ever had anything to do with it, it has been outside of and beyond my knowledge. Never at any time have I ever had any consultation with her or have I known of her being called into consultation or her opinions asked for or offered regarding the wo. ings of this organization.

This is digressing from that point, but I do wish to say something with reference to the home——

Mr. CAMPBELL [interposing]. Before you take that matter up, would Mrs. Tyler be eligible to a seat in the council?

Mr. ETHERIDGE. She would not, sir.

Mr. CAMPBELL. And could not, under any circumstances, meet with what you call the council?

Mr. ETHERIDGE. She could not, sir.

Mr. CAMPBELL. Not being eligible to membership?

Mr. ETHERIDGE. That is true.

Mr. CAMPBELL. So, if she exercised any influence of a superior character, it would be from the outside of the organization?

Mr. ETHERIDGE. Entirely.

Mr. CAMPBELL. And from that branch of it of which she is a member, the propagation department?

Mr. ETHERIDGE. Yes, sir.

Mr. CAMPBELL. Which is not necessarily a part of the organization?

Mr. ETHERIDGE. No, sir.

Mr. CAMPBELL. I wish you would tell the committee what this propagation department consists of.

Mr. ETHERIDGE. I will respectfully ask to obtain that information more fully from Col. Simmons. I will give you, in a general way, though, this much: I am only familiar with the contract under which that work is being carried on, and I believe that contract is here.

Mr. CAMPBELL. That contract is in the record; yes.

Mr. ETHERIDGE. That is in the name of Mr. Clarke—and by the way, I wish to say that I was fully aware of Mr. Clarke's connection with the matter from its inception, and, furthermore, that my personal acquaintance with Mr. Clarke extends back to my boyhood. Unless you wish to question me further about that——

Mr. CAMPBELL. No; you may proceed.

Mr. ETHERIDGE. With reference to this home that Mrs. Tyler is alleged to own or Mr. Clarke and Mrs. Tyler, I can give you no information about the ownership or the title to that property. I can tell you this, however, that I am familiar with the property and have been for a number of years. In Fulton County, Ga., I am the chairman of the commission of roads and revenues of that county. Atlanta is in Fulton County, Ga. My duties carry me out over the county on its public highways, and having occupied that position, not as chairman, but as a member of that commission for the past 3½ years, I am familiar with all portions of the county, and particularly with reference to the condition of the highways. Now, in reference to this particular property, I have known it for some years because it was owned by a young lawyer, a friend of mine in Atlanta by the name of Frank E. Radensleben. He has lived there for a number of years, and in connection with his law practice has conducted a small vegetable farm out on the Howell Mill Road. This is not one of the main thoroughfares of Fulton County, Ga. I learned about three months ago that Mrs. Tyler owned that property—or less than three months ago, to be exact it was the first Wednesday in August that I learned of it, in this way, and this explains my giving you the information that I am the chairman of the commission of roads and revenues of Fulton County. On that day, which is the regular monthly meeting of the commission, a delegation of citizens appeared before our body and petitioned us to make certain improvements upon the highway known as the Howell Mill Road. A number of citizens appeared and presented their petition, both men and women.

Among them was Mrs. Tyler, whom I had met on the Fourth of July prior to that date. After the meeting I asked Mrs. Tyler where she lived on that road, since she was in that delegation, and she told me that she had bought the Randensleben property. Gentlemen, that property consists of something like 20 acres of as poor land as we have in Fulton County. It is out in the woods, so to speak. There is a little elevation going out from Atlanta on the right and a cottage, and a very modest cottage, sits on the brow of the hill, and it is quite true you could not see the extent of the estate from there, because you could not see more than 100 yards or so in any direction from that cottage on account of its elevation. It is in the woods on the side of a hill. Between the cottage and the road is a small ravine, and Mr. Radensleben built a little rustic footbridge across that ravine, reaching over to his house. The cottage, I would say, consists—I have never been in it—of some six or seven rooms. I am familiar with values in that locality and in Fulton County pretty well. I own property in more than one location in Fulton County, in the city and in the suburbs and in the country. That property, gentlemen, is not worth over $10,000 or $12,000 at the outside, on the market or in the general course of conveying property in and around Atlanta, Ga.

Mr. CAMPBELL. Do you know whether or not it has been improved in the manner indicated by Mr. Wright a moment ago?

Mr. ETHERIDGE. I was by that property, sir, during the month of July. It was before I knew that Mrs. Tyler owned it, and I did not observe any changes there. The house sits something like 100 yards, perhaps, off the road on the elevation I spoke of. But I have always known the property as Frank Radensleben's home. I did not notice any changes going on there, sir, but I could not positively say about that.

Reference was made yesterday to a matter that happened in Atlanta in connection with the school board there, and the statement was made that a Miss Riordan had been discharged by the board of education, and I think the statement was that it was because she was a Catholic. One of your local papers stated yesterday that I am a member of the board of education of Fulton County; I mean, of the city of Atlanta. That is a mistake. I am in nowise connected with that board. I do know, personally, each member of the board of education of the city of Atlanta and am familiar with the action of the board—it was widely published—with reference to Miss Riordan; and, furthermore, I have discussed the matter with more than one member of that board.

For more than 20 years I have been familiar with the activities of that board and have been familiar with the school situation in the city of Atlanta, and anyone who is at all familiar with it knows there has been quite a bit of friction. It has been a matter of a great deal of complaint, and there has been more or less trouble between the teaching force and the board of education. Some of our people think there has been a lot of politics in the school department of our city government.

It is the practice of the board of education, and has been for a number of years, to elect—that is to say, to reelect in most instances—its teaching force each year. Teachers are not discharged. They are elected or not reelected. This board of education at this time failed to elect a number of teachers, and, particularly, the superintendent, W. F. Dykes, and there was considerable newspaper comment about the action of the board in regard to Prof. Dykes, the superintendent, who failed of reelection. Miss Riordan was among those who were not reelected. There were several others, and so far as I know those others were Protestants and not Catholics.

Mr. RODENBERG. Do you know how long Miss Riordan had been in the schools there?

Mr. ETHERIDGE. A number of years; she had been there a long time, and, so far as I know, was an efficient teacher; at least she had that reputation. I do know this to be a fact, though, gentlemen—whether it is true or not I do not know—the statement was on the part of members of the board of education that Miss Riordan was active in the organization of the teaching force, which was antagonistic to the board of education; that she was an organizer and, to a certain extent, an agitator in those matters that brought about friction between the board of education and the teaching force. I wish to make this statement, knowing the individual members of the board, that there was not a klansman among them.

I have one other matter that I wish to refer to, and that is what was termed here yesterday the Lakewood affair, in which some time in the early spring a man lost his life out near Lakewood Park. which is in the suburbs of the city and near my own home. It was stated yesterday that a man by the name of Pitts and a man by the name of Schute were involved in that affair. and that they were defended by one Capt. Coburn, who was the supreme attorney of this organization; and it was stated by another witness, Mr. Wright. as a matter of known fact, that this was a tragedy or affair in which the Ku-Klux Klan was involved. Now, this tragedy caused a great deal of newspaper comment and a great deal of stir in the community, as any tragedy of that kind naturally would, and I was interested in it as any other and every other person in the city was. I do not recall, gentlemen, having ever heard that transaction attributed to the activities of the Ku-Klux Klan except in this: The attorney who represented Mr. Thomas before the investigation held by the coroner, and who was connected with the matter in all of its legal phases, gave out to the press that his client had received certain Black-Hand letters, two in number, if I recall, signed, one of them, "The Eyes of a Thousand Real Men," and the other signed, "The One Thousand Eyes"—something to that effect—and there was from that source an intimation but never a direct charge and it received no credence, so far as I recall, either in the press or in the public comment, that the klan was in anywise involved in it. Now, the statement. I think, was made by Mr. Thomas, of the New York World. that the parties involved. Pitts and Schute, were indicted but the charges were withdrawn and they were not tried. That is an error. I know of my personal knowledge that they were both indicted and prosecuted and that the indictment was drawn and presented to the grand jury by the solicitor general, John A. Boykin. who is an acknowledged klansman, and that they were prosecuted before a jury in the criminal division of the superior court of Fulton County by Mr. Boykin. The jury acquitted. Now, the statement that Mr. Coburn. acting in this matter. was acting as the supreme attorney of the klan must be an error, for I occupied that position at that time and had for more than a year prior to that time, and I wish to state that at no time did the imperial body or the local klan consult me with reference to this Lakewood affair; I was never consulted about it. I was in court during the progress of the trial. and heard the testimony of all the witnesses, and know the outcome of the case. That. gentlemen. covers the matter.

Mr. CAMPBELL. Now. to refresh my own recollection, Pitts and Schute were indicted for abducting this man?

Mr. ETHERIDGE. No, sir: they were indicted on a charge of assault with intent to murder; they were indicted on that charge and they were tried on that charge.

Mr. CAMPBELL. Growing out of what state of facts?

Mr. ETHERIDGE. The fact that on a certain night, the date of which I can not recall. but early in the spring. they were known to have been in a party where a man by the name of J. C. Thomas killed a man and stated that he had been attacked by three men. Now. I heard this man Thomas's statement, or his testimony, in the trial of the Pitts and Schute cases. He did not state that he was carried out by these men and threatened with a beating or attempted to be tied to a tree: the evidence that he gave to the jury in that case, which is a matter of record in the courts there, as I recall it, was that he was carried out there and that these men jumped on him and attacked him with pistols or knives, and that he fought for his life. killed one of them and wounded another: and on his statement the bill of indictment was drawn. And in the trial of the case it may be interesting to know that this man Thomas was thoroughly impeached by the defense in that case. His record was put before the jury, and it was shown that he had served several sentences in the penitentiary and that he was absolutely unworthy of belief.

Mr. CAMPBELL. Was he tried for the murder of the man who was killed?

Mr. ETHERIDGE. No, sir; he never was.

Mr. CAMPBELL. Was the case presented to the grand jury?

Mr. ETHERIDGE. The case—of course. I do not know what took place before the grand jury, but I assume that the case in all of its phases was investigated by the grand jury and all available information placed before them.

Mr. CAMPBELL. And Thomas was not indicted?

Mr. ETHERIDGE. Thomas was not indicted. Now, one other thing I wish to say, and that is that, while I can not dispute the fact of those men being members of the Ku-Klux Klan, I wish to state that I am a member of the local klan at Atlanta, Ga., and there is only one there. If they or any of them are members, I did not know it.

Mr. RODENBERG. You would not personally know all the members, anyhow?

Mr. ETHERIDGE. No, sir; I would not. As I said. I can not say that they were not; but I never heard that charge made against either Pitts or Schute—that they were members of that klan.

Mr. CAMPBELL. Did the klan figure in the trial in any way?

Mr. ETHERIDGE. Not at all. The statement has been made that Capt. Coburn was supreme attorney and defended them. It is true that Capt. Coburn did defend those men but it is not true that he was supreme attorney of the klan.

Mr. RODENBERG. What was his official connection?

Mr. ETHERIDGE. None that I know of; at least, I did not know of any at that time. I understand that now he is connected with the propagation department somewhere in the West; that has been my information, but I can not give you any definite facts about that. I know Capt. Coburn and know him very well.

Mr. RODENBERG. Did he have any official connection with the klan at that time?

Mr. ETHERIDGE. Not that I know of, and I think not.

Mr. RODENBERG. Would you not know positively?

Mr. ETHERIDGE. If he was connected with the imperial body, I would; but if he was one of the subordinate members of the local organization, then possibly I would not.

Mr. CAMPBELL. Unless you have something further, that is all.

Mr. ETHERIDGE. No; I am through, unless you gentlemen have some further questions.

Mr. CAMPBELL. The committee will recess until 2.30 o'clock.

AFTER RECESS

The committee met pursuant to recess at 2.30 o'clock p. m.

Mr. GARRETT. Mr. Chairman, before you proceed with the regular order. I want to submit a request for unanimous consent or make a motion touching some evidence. Allusion was made, I may say, by way of preliminary statement, by one of the first speakers this morning to an episode alleged to have occurred in Florida, wherein a colored man. it was stated, was burned, growing out of an effort to exercise the right of franchise. I have learned since the recess for lunch was taken that all the facts in connection with that episode were developed before the Committee on Census of the House of Representatives at the last session of the Congress, in connection with what is known as the Tinkham resolution; that the facts, briefly, are that two colored men went to the place at some point there in Florida and offered to vote. It was found that they were not registered, as required under the laws of the State of Florida. They attempted to vote despite that, were in a disorderly condition, and an officer of the law attempted to quiet them. and one of these colored men shot and killed this officer. A fight then occurred, in which perhaps one other white man was shot and both of these colored men killed. It was a shooting scrape, a general fight. wherein the officer was killed, and there was no burning about it. Those facts, as I understand, were all developed before the committee. and I wish to ask unanimous consent that the clerk of this committee may obtain, if possible, the evidence taken before the Committee on the Census and incorporate it in our record, so that this committee can use it in connection with its consideration of these resolutions.

Mr. CAMPBELL. If there is no objection that may be done. [After a pause.] That will be done if the testimony can be secured.

(In pursuance of Mr. Garrett's request, the clerk of the committee procured the testimony of Representative Clark and Representative Sears, both of Florida, given before the Committee on the Census January 5, 1921. which committee at that time had under consideration measures for the apportionment of Representatives. The testimony relative to the incident in question is as follows:)

Mr. LARSEN. What is the approximate vote of that county?

Mr. CLARK. About 1,800. Now, I want to call your attention to the Ocoee situation, down in Orange County, where it was said that so many of those Negroes were killed, beat up, run out of town, and everything else. This man White states as a matter of fact that a Negro by the name of Norman attempted to vote and that a row started. He stated that the Negro was a qualified voter. That is in the record. He stated it positively. Here is a telegram from the supervisor of registration of Orange County, who certified to the list of qualified voters. Here is what Mr. Bliss, supervisor of registration, states in a telegram addressed to myself:

ORLANDO, FLA., *January 4, 1921.*

Hon. FRANK CLARK,
     Member of Congress, Washington, D. C.:

M. N. Norman, colored, 48 years old, had only reg'stered in September last; had lived many years in Orange County; had only paid 1919 poll tax, and consequently was not a qualified elector.

E. R. BLISS,
     Superintendent of Registration, Orange County, Fla.

I want to read you a letter from Joseph H. Jones, State's attorney for the seventeenth judicial circuit, at Orlando, a man who stands as high as any citizen in Florida. He is a gentleman of the very highest character. Here is what he says:

"After the Ocoee affair I had a session of the grand jury, and had before that body 21 witnesses. The jury was a very high-class one and the witnesses were examined at great length and particularly. I will by next mail send you a copy of the presentments of the jury"——

Mr. HERSEY. What is this affair?

Mr. CLARK. This is where they claim a lot of those Negroes were killed, near Orlando.

Mr. BARBOUR. And that houses were burned, and so on.

Mr. CLARK. Mr. Jones states in this letter, the portion I just read, that he would send the presentments of the grand jury. I should like to file that with the committee when it gets here. I will read the balance of this letter. [Reading:]

"I gave my special attention to this matter, remaining on the ground nearly all night and back there the next morning early, remaining all day and into the night, until matters had become quiet.

"I saw only three dead Negroes and two whites at Ocoee. Perry (colored) was hung at Orlando, making four Negroes and two whites, as the result of the affair.

"I think it probable two other Negroes were killed.

"I saw that the three Negroes mentioned above received decent and proper burial in good coffins, and I even assisted personally in their burial in the colored cemetery at Ocoee.

"If I can be of any service to you, command me.

"With my personal regards and best wishes for the new year,

"Very truly, yours,

"JOSEPH H. JONES."

Mr. Jones means that in the utmost good faith. He is, of course, a law-abiding citizen and is the State's attorney there. What he means by saying that he personally assisted in their burial is that among the real people of that section there is no such feeling as has been stated here.

Mr. BEE. Let me ask you, Is it not true that this trouble at Ocoee occurred after the polls were closed?

Mr. CLARK. I think so.

Mr. BEE. After the election was over?

Mr. CLARK. Oh, yes; after the election was over, but it was caused by this man insisting that he was going to vote anyhow when he was not a qualified voter.

Mr. BEE. But it did not interfere with the election?

Mr. CLARK. Not at all; it occurred afterwards.

GRAND JURY GIVES REPORT OCOEE TROUBLE.

At 4 p. m. yesterday the grand jury impaneled on Monday by Judge Andrews concluded its report, which was as follows:

To the Hon. Charles O. Andrews, judge of the seventeenth judicial circuit, State of Florida:

We, the grand jury called by your honor to conduct an inquiry into the trouble at Ocoee, November 2, 1920, when two white men and three Negroes were killed, have carried on a rigid and searching investigation. Twenty-one witnesses have appeared before us and have been examined at length.

We have found that the State's attorney, Hon. Jos. H. Jones; the officers of the law, Sheriff Frank Gordon and his deputies; the chief of police of Orlando, E. D. Vestel, and his officers; the members of Orlando Memorial Post, No. 9, American Legion, together with other ex-service men; and the leading citizens of Ocoee, Winter Garden, Orlando, and near-by towns have performed their full duty in maintaining law and order, and, after the brief outburst of passion over the killing of the two white men, admirably succeeded in the execution of their obligations as loyal American citizens.

We find no evidence against anyone or any group of individuals as to who perpetrated the fatalities. In the death of the two white men, Elmer McDaniels and Lee Borgard, and the death of July Perry, a Negro, we accept the coroner's verdict. We exonerate Perry's widow and daughter, now in custody at Tampa, Fla., and recommend their release.

We are in full accord with your impressive words delivered to this jury previous to our deliberations. We believe that Orange County citizens in producing immediate order out of chaos at Ocoee have maintained the honor of their county and State. Judgment and sanity, law and order, peacefulness and sobriety actuate the people of Orange County at all times and in the most trying circumstances, and these people are determined that justice shall be done and that the prestige of the courts shall be increased to the highest possible standard, and that we go on record as being opposed to mob rule and deplore all semblance to lynch law but do firmly stand for law and order.

N. P. YOWELL, *Foreman.*
W. M. GLENN, *Secretary.*

ORLANDO, FLA., *November 30, 1920.*

The jurors inspected the interior of the courthouse and came to the conclusion that the county clerk's and tax collector's offices should be enlarged, and that the building should be heated by a central plant.

Those on the jury were H. D. Cox, A. R. Hewitt, B. T. Boyd, Thomas Etty, R. G. Hansel, W. M. Glenn, S. G. Harper, E. Doyle, N. P. Yowell, A. G. Branham, A. Belknap, C. H. Hill, H L. Beeman, E. H. Allen, A. Hanson, John Ammon, Thomas Walsh, and T. M. Arnold.

Witnesses were: E. D. Vestel, Frank Hogan, W. S. Jones, T. P. Smith, Preston Ayers, C. A. Boyer, J. I. Whitty, Clyde Pounds, Sam T. Salisbury, J. D. McMillan, B. D. Bennett, J. A. Hodnett, E. R. Hanner, R. P. Neeley, colored, Frank Gordon, W. C. Wilson, S. J. Strozier, Capt. B. M. Sims, N. N. Jensen, and A. B. Waites.

The grand jury was an especially good one, embracing citizens of the highest standing in this county.

The witnesses were as follows: E. D. Vestel, chief of police of Orlando; Frank Hogan, sergeant of police of Orlando, now chief deputy sheriff, Orange County; W. S. Jones, carpenter; T. P. Smith, policeman; Preston Ayers, formerly captain in World War and now commissioner, city of Orlando commission government; C. A. Boyer, attorney, lieutenant of home guards, in charge of detail sent to keep order on night of the affair; J. I. Witty, deputy sheriff at Ocoee; Clyde Pounds, deputy sheriff at Ocoee; Sam T. Salisbury, formerly in American Expeditionary Forces and formerly chief police of Orlando; J. D. McMillan, cashier Bank of Winter Garden; B. D. Bennett, orange grower and a leading citizen; J. A. Hodnett, merchant, Winter Garden, and formerly marshal of Winter Garden; E. R. Hanner, contractor, of Hanner Bros., Orlando, Fla.; R. P. Neely, orange grower and farmer (colored); Frank Gordon, sheriff Orange County; W. C. Wilson, business man, of Winter Garden, and justice of peace of that portion of the county; G. J. Strozier, merchant and formerly representative, Legislature of Florida; Capt. B. M. Sims, orange grower, real estate, and leading citizen; N. N. Jensen, cashier Bank of Ocoee; A. B. Waites, laborer.

(COPY EXHIBIT D.)

ORLANDO, FLA., *January 4, 1921.*

Hon. FRANK CLARK,
House of Representatives, Washington, D. C.

DEAR MR. CLARK: I am inclosing copy of presentments of the grand jury in the Ocoee affair; also list of witnesses before that body, giving their occupation and standing in the county.

I also send list of the grand jurors, many of whom you personally know, namely, N. P. Yowell, leading dry-goods merchant between Jacksonville and Tampa; A. G. Branham, formerly commissioner city of Orlando; W. M. Glenn, editor and proprietor of Sentinel; Harry L. Beeman, owner of the 'San Juan Hotel, and a leading citizen, etc.

The colored man who precipitated the trouble was not a qualified voter, Mose Norman by name.

If there is any other information I can give or anything further in which I may be of service, please let me know.

I was called out of town on an inquest—accidental drowning—hence delay in forwarding this copy of the presentments.

With best wishes,

Very truly, yours,

JOSEPH H. JONES.

Mr. SEARS. I was in Orlando on the day of election and at least a hundred men and women were in line at the polls waiting to vote—that is, colored people, as also were many white citizens of that county—and they had had no trouble. The negroes had voted all during the day. And when I went home no trouble had occurred at Ocoee. As I understand, this negro who caused trouble had been drinking. He went to the polls and started a row, and then went back to his home to arm himself. Again, I do not want to mislead the committee, but my recollection is that Ocoee is largely a German-American settlement, and the rest of them are northerners and southerners. Where they made their mistake was in permitting that negro to go back home to arm himself.

I only referred to that briefly when it was brought up a moment ago by a member of the committee. I have no intention of bringing out any new issues. I started to say, as I understand it. the killing was done after the polls closed. Two white men were first killed. That was the information given to me after the killing, and it simply raised a riot, but it had nothing to do with the election. Men, both white and black, were wrought up, and you could not stop it until it fought its way out. These negroes simply armed themselves and went into a house. The sheriff and his deputies tried to make arrests, when two of the deputies were killed, and from that time the other killings began. As I say, it had nothing at all to do with the election.

Mr. TAGUE. Mr. Chairman, may I ask if the proponents' case has been closed? My reason for asking is this: This is the greatest Jewish feast and holiday, Yom Kippur, and therefore none of them are present to present their side of the case. If they wish to be heard, may I ask that they be heard at a later time?

Mr. CAMPBELL. Oh, yes; this will not be concluded until those who desire to be heard have an opportunity.

Mr. UPSHAW. Mr. Chairman——

Mr. CAMPBELL. Congressman Upshaw.

STATEMENT OF HON. W. D. UPSHAW, A REPRESENTATIVE IN CONGRESS FROM THE STATE OF GEORGIA.

Mr. UPSHAW. Mr. Chairman, ever since I have been in Congress I have made it a rule, along with my other colleagues, to show every possible courtesy to my constituents when they come to Washington. Regardless of creed or station, I go with them to that department or that committee and introduce them where they have business.

It is my official duty as well as my personal pleasure to present to this committee one of my prominent constituents.

I do not know what Col. William Joseph Simmons is going to say to this committee, but, knowing his sterling character as I do, I am prepared——

Mr. RODENBERG (interposing). Mr. Chairman, that is not necessary. He does not need a formal introduction to the committee.

Mr. UPSHAW. May I say, Mr. Chairman, that I have a resolution (H. J. Res. 201) before this committee, and that in lieu of speaking to that resolution, and I intend to refer to it, I am speaking now. I ask the privilege of proceeding for about a moment.

Mr. CAMPBELL. Proceed.

Mr. Upshaw. Knowing his sterling character, as I do, I am prepared to underwrite his every utterance as the truth of an honest, patriotic man. I do not know "what all" Col. Simmons has been doing behind closed doors, but I do know that, as a sturdy and inspiring personality, as a heroic veteran of the Spanish-American War, as an honored Knight Templar and member of something like a dozen other honored and well-known fraternities, as a consecrated churchman, and a God-fearing citizen, he is as incapable of an unworthy, unpatriotic motive, word or deed, as the chairman of this committee, the Speaker of the House of Representatives, or the President of the United States.

I have known this good man to use his great influence to stop an incipient race riot. I have known him to dispense benevolence to a Negro educational institution. I have known him to prevent Negroes from being mobbed for crime, even as they were recently mobbed for no crime by white men in Omaha, in Chicago, in Indiana, and even here in the Nation's capital.

Not for one minute would I stand for personal or organized wrongdoing by any man or any friend. More than any other Congressman, because of my relationship to this district, I want to know the light and I want the world to know the light and I want the country to know the light concerning this ororganization and other secret organizations whose deeds are questioned by many and whose memberships are limited by race, creed, or color.

I have the privilege, gentlemen of the committee, of presenting to you my long-time, personal friend and constituent, Col. William Joseph Simmons.

STATEMENT OF MR. WILLIAM JOSEPH SIMMONS, OF ATLANTA, GA.

Mr. Simmons. Mr. Chairman and gentlemen of the committee——

Mr. Campbell (interposing). Col. Simmons, I hardly think it necessary that I should say so to you, but I deem it probably important to say that anything you may say here, voluntarily or under examination by members of the committee, may be used by the authorities in any action that might result in the courts. I simply make this statement out of abundance of caution. I assume that, perhaps, your attorney has advised you that any statement you may make may be used by the Government, if they should find it proper or expedient to bring any action.

Mr. Simmons. I thank you, sir.

If you will allow me just a few remarks before going into the matter, in justice to your committee, I want to state that I am a sick man; have been confined to my bed for two weeks and left my bed to come up here. I have been out of bed only three days and in that time have undergone the hardest travel and have been in bed most of the time since I got here. I may not look sick. My sickness is not expressed in my face. I belong to the Irish race, and I believe if I was dead, I would be a handsome corps. I have suffered with an attack of tonsillitis combined with laryngitis, which developed into bronchitis with threatened pneumonia. So it looks like I have had all the "chitises."

My name is William Joseph Simmons, residing in Atlanta, Ga. They call me "Colonel," largely out of respect. Every lawyer in Georgia is called "Colonel," so they thought that I was as good as a lawyer, so they call me that. However, since that matter has been called into question, I am a veteran of the Spanish-American War. I am a past commander of my Spanish-American war veterans' post. I am a past national aid-de-camp of the Spanish-American War Veterans' Association and also a past provisional division commander. I was at one time the senior colonel in command of five regiments and colonel of my own regiment of the uniform rank of the Woodmen of the World, and I was known as "Colonel." I have used that title on certain literature of the klan for the reason that there are three other "W. J. Simmonses" in Atlanta, and for some time our mail got confused. It is merely a designation. They accord it to me as an honor and I appreciate it, but at no time and in no place have I arrogated to myself the fact that I was a colonel of the Army. I served there, but I was under a colonel and I found out how the colonels do.

As a brief introduction, please, I am a churchman and proud of it. I hold a distinction which I suppose few men hold, and that is I am a member of two churches—the Congregational Church and a full-fledged associate member of the Missionary Baptist Church, given me as an honor. I am a member of a number of fraternal orders—the Masons, Royal Arch Masons, the Great Order of Knight Templars, and then I have these affiliations that I have gone into, about 12 or 15 in number, in my lifetime, seemingly have passed the committees and have been active in the work. In fact, I have been a fraternalist ever since I was in the academy school way back yonder, and I believe in fraternal orders and fraternal relationships among men, in a fraternity of nations, so that all people might know something of the great doctrines—the fatherhood of God and the brotherhood of man.

Before proceeding, if you will permit me, please, Mr. Chairman, I wish to tender my deep and heartfelt thanks to the fairness and squareness and manifest honesty of a large number or a large portion of the press and to tender my thanks and appreciation to the picture men that shot me all over this room yesterday morning and shot me out on the streets. When I got through I felt like I was half shot.

Mr. Chairman, owing to my physical condition, I want to crave, sir, the patience of your committee in going through this statement. I will state to you frankly that at any time, under the strain of talking, I am liable to have a coughing spell that may result in a vomiting spell, which has been with me now for over 10 days. So if I get in one of those conditions, I very respectfully request that you will have just a short adjournment until I can get through with those paroxysms and get back on the job; and to this end I have prepared here as a part of my utterances this statement in written form, and after reading this I wish to then take up certain exhibits that I will mention in here, and after carefully reviewing those exhibits, as carefully as time will permit, then I will have a few closing remarks, after which I then hold myself subject to the questions of your honorable committee, and will attempt to give you the truth, the actual truth, under God, as I know it, from all the information I have.

I appreciate the opportunity of appearing before this committee and respectfully ask that I be allowed to make my formal statement, prepared seriously and carefully and with only a desire of setting forth exact facts, without interruption. After this statement is presented to your honorable body I will be glad to answer any questions asked, if possible. I also request, if it pleases you, Mr. Chairman, that I be sworn, so that this statement and my entire testimony be under oath.

Mr. CAMPBELL. Neither the chairman nor any other member of this committee is authorized to administer oaths.

Mr. SIMMONS. Very well; I would request it, if it was within your power to do so.

Mr. CAMPBELL. It is not.

Mr. SIMMONS. Then I will proceed, Mr. Chairman, with the same consciousness of truth in making my statement as if I were under oath.

Twenty years ago I received the inspiration to establish a fraternal, patriotic, secret order for the purpose of memorializing the great heroes of our national history, inculcating and teaching practical fraternity among men, to teach and encourage a fervent, practical patriotism toward our country, and to destroy from the hearts of men the Mason and Dixon line and build thereupon a great American solidarity and a distinctive national conscience which our country sorely stands in need of.

At that time I was a mere young man and knew that my youth and immature thought would not permit me to successfully launch the movement, so I kept my own counsel all through 15 subsequent years, working, thinking, and preparing my head and heart for the task of creating this institution for the interest of our common country and for the promotion of real brotherhood among men. To this work and to this end I dedicated my life and all my energies, after being thoroughly convinced that there was a place for such a fraternal order and that the order could and would fill that place.

It was in the month of October, 1915, that I decided to launch the movement. I mentioned to many of my friends what I had in mind and heart and as a result a meeting was held which was attended by 34 splendid citizens of the State of Georgia. As a result of this meeting, after I had briefly outlined to these men the purpose of this meeting, application for charter to the State of Georgia was made, which application was signed by every man present. The charter was granted and the same was issued December 4, 1915, signed by the Honorable Philip Cook, then secretary of State. In the months following, in the progress of our plans, we decided to have a charter from the Superior Court of Fulton County, Ga. I here introduce, marked "Exhibit A," certified copy of that charter. Application was made, according to law, and the corporation was created and classified as a standard, fraternal, elemosynary society, like unto the order of Masons, Knights of Pythias, Odd Fellows, Elks, and other institutions of like nature and provides that the organization shall be national in its scope.

This charter from the Superior Court was issued and duly registered July 1, 1916, and on the 4th day of the same month, after the incorporators had met in a body and accepted the charter and proclaimed me the official head of the order, we then proceeded with the work of the organization, which work has been continuous through all the hardships incident to our progress from that day unto this, and I here introduce, marked "Exhibit A-2," the charter issued to each klan, which shows the sole purpose of that local klan.

You will please permit me to refer to myself in connection with this movement because I am the founder of the institution. For three years the work was a tremendous struggle, made more arduous by a traitor in our ranks who held under me a position of trust, who embezzled all of our accumulated funds in the summer of 1916 and went off and attempted to organize a counterfeit order. The treasonous conduct of this man left me penniless, with large accumulated debts against the order. I was advised to give it up by many, but I felt and knew that my honor was at stake. I would not quit the organization in that hour of adversity, for to do so would have been both cowardly and unjust, because the different concerns to whom we owed money would have lost every dollar we owed them. I felt myself personally responsible, even though this was a corporation and under the law I was not personally liable. I had respect to the sacred principles of moral honor. I was forced to mortgage my home in order to get money with which to carry on the fight against this traitor's counterfeit order and also to assist in the work we had to do.

During all this time of dread and darkness I virtually stood alone, but remaining true to the dictates of unsullied honor, I steered the infant organization through dangerous channels and finally succeeded in making good in the payment of all debts and starting the institution about a year ago upon a nationwide expansion.

Through the dark hours of struggle and bitter sacrifice incident to the launching of this movement, for over nine long months I had an average of one meal a day. I have fought a good fight, I have truly kept the faith, and God permitting me, Mr. Chairman, I shall finish my course, with love toward all, with malice toward none. I shall pursue the right as God shall give me a vision of the right.

If the Knights of the Ku-Klux Klan has been a lawless organization, as has been charged, it would not have shown the remarkable growth it has, for in the klan is as fine a body of representative citizens as there is in the United States. In each community where there is a klan will be found members from the leading citizens, men who stand at the forefront in their cities. These men would not stand for lawlessness.

It has been charged that the klan is a gigantic swindle, run solely to enrich a few of the inside ring. I, as the executive head of the klan, have received during the past six years altogether approximately $12,000, an average of $2,000 per year. I can not be in any wise accurate in these figures, because I have not run it up, but I may state just here that for two or three years I received not a penny, only what I could get out and do myself. I have also a home, purchased by klan members, but not by the klan, but by voluntary subscriptions of 25 cents and 50 cents and a dollar. This home is not completely paid for, and I knew nothing of this until it was given to me as a complete surprise as a birthday remembrance on the 6th day of last May by members of the klan from every section of the country.

And I may add just here, from what has been presented for my information regarding the home in which I now reside, that property is in the hands of a board of trustees who are looking after it; and they told me, "When we get the home paid for then the deed will be made to you; but we do not want you to bother with that until it is all paid for." A board of trustees is handling that home.

The secretary, treasurer, and other officials of the klan receive salaries lower than they would receive from business institutions for their ability and for the work that each of them does. I introduce here, marked "Exhibit B," the pay roll and salaries paid and the expenses of the klan.

If the klan was seeking to enrich a few insiders the money would go into our pockets. Instead, we are spending the surplus money of the klan in the education of young men and women who are the very foundation of the Nation. This money is being spent in the further building and enlargement of Lanier

University, Atlanta, Ga. We have spent and are spending on Lanier University the sum of $150,000. That amount, Mr. Chairman, covers the indebtedness of the institution that we expect to meet and the improvements we expect to make there in the next year or so.

I herewith introduce, marked "Exhibit C," for the permanent records of this committee the entire record and expenses pertaining to Lanier University; also, the entire receipts and expenditures of the klan.

The university is not sectarian; it does not teach nor even touch the Knights of the Ku-Klux Klan; I mean, in its teaching. The only two courses that are compulsory, in addition to the standard collegiate curriculum, is a course in the fundamentals of our civilization, which are the tenets of the Christian religion, using the Holy Bible as a basic textbook. The other course is teaching and inculcating the fundamentals of pure Americanism and the development of correct American citizenship, a course that is now being worked out using the Constitution of the United States, the Declaration of Independence, and commentaries and Supreme Court decisions that will be helpful in such a course.

Those are the two distinctive features of that university, and they will be made a part of its regular curriculum. Many of the faculty and trustees are not even members of the klan. It is to be a great American educational institution. I here introduce, marked "Exhibit D," the list of trustees and members of the faculty. They are among the leaders in educational work in the South, and are men and women who could not be misled nor who would prostitute their calling as teachers of the young men and women of America, nor would they be connected with an institution or organization that was even faintly tinged with what has been charged against the klan.

The charge has been made that Mr. Edward Young Clarke and Mrs. Elizabeth Tyler, who have charge of the propagation work for the klan, have received for this work from five to twenty-five millions of dollars. The contract of the klan with Mr. Clarke and the complete financial statement regarding it, to the best of my knowledge, are here introduced and marked "Exhibit E." Under this contract the per capita cost of the propagation work for the klan is much lower than many fraternal and other organizations pay for similar work. Mr. Clarke and his organization have conducted many successful undertakings. When I say Mr. Clarke and his organization, I mean the organization he had in publicity work before he became connected with the klan. Mr. Clarke had charge in the South of two campaigns for funds for the Salvation Army and a Y. M. C. A. and Red Cross drive for the same purpose, and Mrs. Elizabeth Tyler was engaged in all those drives and in similar work. She held a position with Mr. Clarke in the Southern Publicity Association. and, as I understand, she was the secretary and treasurer of that organization. The Salvation Army presented to Mr. Clarke a gold watch as an appreciation of his faithful work. The klan contract is with Mr. Clarke, Mrs. Tyler being his first assistant and having no official connection with the klan. She is a splendid business woman. and she is employed there to look after the work of that office, just as stenographers and other assistants are employed. There are two other men employed in the executive work of that branch.

When the klan as a fraternal order could not be hurt by being attacked. a personal character attack was made against Mr. Clarke and Mrs. Tyler, but no statements made in these attacks have been proven. The klan is at present conducting a searching investigation of these character attacks, and when all facts are in our possession the klan will officially issue a statement regarding them and give the exact truth. When these charges were first made the resignations of Mr. Clarke and Mrs. Tyler were voluntarily placed in my hands, the resignations not being acted on until such time as we had full opportunity for mature and careful consideration of all facts before us and until the investigation was completed.

During my association, and the association of other officials of the klan, with Mr. Clarke and Mrs. Tyler their conduct and character have been of the highest.

The life, character, and record of every official of the klan has been searched by those attacking us, but nothing has been found against any of us that would stand the acid test of court proof or of proof before this committee.

The charge even has been made and published against me that I was an imposter and fraud, in that I had posed as a veteran of the Spanish-American War when I had not even served as a soldier in that war. The same patriotism and love of country inspired me in founding the Knights of the Ku-Klux Klan that inspired me as a youth of 18 to volunteer in the First Regiment Alabama Volunteers, Company B, and to serve through the Spanish-American War as a private, receiving at its close an honorable discharge. The untruthfulness of this charge against me is in line with all the other slanderous charges against the klan.

The charge has been made that the klan takes the law into its own hands; that it terrorizes private citizens in many communities by lawless acts against person and property. These charges are untrue. I state, Mr. Chairman, that klans can not take action on anything outside of their lodge rooms or ceremonial duties unless they have an order, so to speak, written and signed by myself. That is a law in the klan to keep anyone within our membership from doing things—in other words, holding them in control—that contravene the law. Before God and this honorable committee, I have never authorized nor signed any kind of instructions that could in any way be construed as a violation of the law or to be carried out in violation of the law of my country.

There have been only a few instances where lawless acts have been alleged against individual members of the klan. You will notice I say "alleged," and there is a possibility that if individual members of the klan have committed acts of lawlessness that those same men were members of other fraternal orders, and should the other fraternal orders be condemned? No. In these instances the charter in that community was revoked or suspended, although the acts of the individual members were not the acts of the klan as a body and were condemned by all those disbanded klan members. The charter was revoked or suspended, as we have no room in our organization for those who take the law into their own hands, because to do so violates a most solemn oath. Individual members of other organizations have committed and been charged with outrages and crimes, but that does not condemn the whole order, as an order, of lawlessness.

Just here I will call attention to this particular point—and I am stating to you, Mr. Chairman, the very best knowledge and information I have and in all truth. There was an instance that occurred in Pensacola, Fla., where three men were reported to have donned white vestments and gone into a Greek café, handed the proprietor of that café an envelope that was sealed, and said, "You beat it," walked on out, calmly went up the street, and disappeared. As soon as that information was brought to my knowledge I immediately suspended the charter at Pensacola, Fla., for the purpose of making an impartial and unbiased investigation. It never was established that these men were actually members of the klan, and therefore I gave instructions for the restoration of the charter, having the promise of the officials of that klan that they would use every effort to find out who was illegally counterfeiting or imitating the costume of this organization. Perchance some of the robes had been stolen from the room in which we met with other lodges and where we had our regalia. Those men should be brought to the bar of justice by the proper authorities.

In Mobile, Ala., the charter of the klan was revoked. The law had not been violated, but a very silly, uncalled-for, and ridiculous thing occurred, prompted by one man who was a member of the klan. The klan knew nothing about it. The exalted cyclops and his terrors, or subordinate officers, knew nothing of it. The then secretary of that particular klan thought he had the authority of Napoleon Bonaparte in his day, so he went out and had printed some little posters, about half as big as that page [indicating], with all sorts of warnings to bootleggers, chicken thieves, crap shooters, and everybody else in that community. He was going to have a clean town, and he had signed at the bottom of it, or printed there, "Knights of the Ku-Klux Klan." It was a silly act, perpetrated by a man who did not have sense enough to be in this organization, and for that that charter was revoked, so that the members could make a careful search, and later on we would reorganize with men who were men. That was done to clarify the matter.

Another instance that has been conspicuously portrayed upon the pages of the newspapers in this country—possibly amplified and enlarged to make good, sensational reading,—is the Beaumont, Tex., affair. Information, sir, in my possession, as it has been given to me by the highest and most respected citizens of that town, is that the men, from the knowledge and information they could gather, who did that work or committed that crime were not of the klan. The klan did not do it. There may have been in that number of possibly half a hundred men some members of the klan, but information was given to me, from the information they could gather, that possibly nearly half of that number of men were members of other fraternal orders, and from all the information I could gather, after careful investigation, it seemed that that act was committed as a result of the emotions of an enraged community. I note that it is said that an explanation was given to the newspapers bearing the seal of the klan. Information came to me from the officer who is charged with the keeping of the seal or is the custodian of the seal—he is the secretary of the local organization—and he swore to me that about three days before this thing occurred the seal was stolen and the circumstance was this: He had his office jointly with the secretary of the Grotto, which, in a way, is a Masonic organization. The seal was kept in a safe, and he had occasion to use it late one evening and was called out of the office after using it and set it up on top of the safe, expecting to be back in a few minutes, but he was detained and forgot about the seal until the next morning, if my memory holds good, and when he had occasion to use it he found it was gone. After a most diligent search he could not locate it and reported the theft of the seal to the chief of police and to the sheriff of the county. The next he knew of that seal or imprint of that seal—whether it was a real imprint or an imitation, I do not know—was when a communication was sent to the newspapers bearing the seal, but that communication in the newspapers was typewritten, and my information is that the newspaper men who received this communication said that a Mexican brought this paper to them. That is a brief statement of the Beaumont affair, and although I have searched diligently and carefully I have not yet any evidence that will stand in any court of law showing that the Knights of the Ku-Klux Klan in Beaumont, Tex., perpetrated that wrong. As the question has been raised in the papers, I can only say—and I say it in all justice to the victim, whom I understand was Dr. Paul, in justice to him and to the American public—that from the information I have it seems that the people of that town felt that they were warranted in doing what they did do.

I will pass on with this paper, and I will come back and further review the different points in my offhand remarks, but I want to state this to you, Mr. Chairman, if you please: Possessing the authority and power I do in the government and regulation of this organization, that whenever a man presumes to take the law into his own hands and to commit a misdeed against his fellow citizens, that man, under our regulations, by that act is automatically out of this organization. That is understood by all the members who come into this organization. In such cases, if I had any evidence that the legal authorities of the law needed to punish the guilty, I have done all I could to assist and have never yet refused. God knows that I would never attempt, nor have I ever attempted, to shield a criminal in the commission of crime.

I introduce here, marked Exhibit F, the notice of a reward for the capture of those posting a notice signed "K. K. K." in a South Carolina town, and attention is called to the fact that the reward is larger for a klan member guilty of this than a nonmember. For three years a standing reward has been advertised for any person who uses the name of this order without authority or using its name or costume for any purpose which contravenes the law of the land, a $500 reward. We try to keep enough money on hand to pay that reward if it should be justly claimed.

The klan does not countenance nor will it tolerate any lawless acts by its members. Instead we teach respect for the law, love of country, and a closer fellowship of service. I here introduce, marked Exhibit G, and will read later, the ritual, oath, and other secret books and works of the klan. In the oath attention is called to the section where all klan members swear to uphold and respect the law of the United States, the State, county, and city where the members live. No man who would break his solemn oath by taking the law into his own hands is worthy of membership in any organization or worthy to be a citizen of our glorious country.

The charge has also been made that the klan as an organization gives an opportunity for evil-minded persons to threaten others, to satisfy their private grudges, and to commit outrages, using the klan as a cloak. This charge is absurd on its face when an examination of the records for the past 10 years will show that there were as many of these so-called outrages committed before the klan was organized as since its organization.

Mr. Chairman, much has been said in the papers in the last few months about outrages being committed by masked men. My opinion is that there are possibly 1,000 different kinds of masks made, and it seems that when people see these inflammatory articles about masked men they think of the Ku-Klux

Klan. If some masked highwayman should hold a man up on the streets of Washington and rob him of 30 cents the papers here would say, "The Ku-Klux is busy in Washington," because of the mask. This is witnessed by the night riding of Kentucky and the many cases in all sections of the United States where individuals were lynched, whipped, and otherwise maltreated. It is also witnessed by the recent civil war in West Virginia. The klan has, however, been blamed by those attacking it with committing all these crimes, and we are expecting daily to be blamed for the West Virginia situation, although this was brought on by the union mine workers insisting that all sections should be unionized, even though the men engaged in the peaceful pursuit of their work and happiness desired only to be let alone. Does the West Virginia condition convict the entire United Mine Workers of America with being a lawless organization? It does not. In their desperation to destroy the klan those attacking us have charged us with everything from high prices to the spread of the boll weevil.

I noticed some time ago that the klan was charged with outrages, or, rather, an outrage against a Negro in Arkansas, and I state to you as an honorable man that that particular outrage occurred in Arkansas 18 months before we had one member in Arkansas.

It has been charged that this organization incites to riot. Can that charge be substantiated? No; because no man can place his finger on any spot on the map of the United States in which a klan has been organized and well established where there has ever been a riot, racial or otherwise, and in every town where riots have occurred there is no klan there or was not there at the time of the riots.

The charge has also been made that the klan is organized for the purpose of assisting the enforcement of the law. Nothing to substantiate this charge has been produced, and there is no room in the United States for any organization organized for any such purpose. The law is supreme, and if we were organized for any such absurd purpose the klan would not have lived a year and could not have grown as it has.

The charge is made that we are organized to preach and teach religious intolerance, and especially that we are anti-Roman Catholic, anti-Jew, and anti-Negro. The conduct of the klan proves this absolutely untrue. Many alleged outrages have been attributed to the klan, but none of these were against Roman Catholics, Jews, and Negroes per se, and none were committed by the klan. It is indeed strange that if we organized to persecute the Roman Catholics, Jews, and Negroes that nothing has been done against them. In the United States the question is not and should never be whether a citizen is a Protestant, a Roman Catholic, a Jew, or a Negro, but whether he is a loyal American.

Since the fight against the klan we have been offered and urged to use, by those who are anti-Roman Catholic and not members of the klan, possibly the greatest existing mass of data and material against the Roman Catholics and Knights of Columbus. In this material, so we are told, there are affidavits and other personal testimony attributing to the Roman Catholics and Knights of Columbus in America more outrages and crimes than the klan has ever been charged with. Included in these charges against the Roman Catholics and Knights of Columbus are murder, whipping, tar and feathers, and crimes of all natures.

If the klan was anti-Roman Catholic we would have certainly used the material offered us, but the offer was received, although those making it are anxious that this evidence be presented to Congress. If the klan is to secure members on an anti-Roman Catholic, anti-Jew, and anti-Negro appeal, we do not want such members, and have never secured them in this way. Discussions involving any man's religious beliefs are never allowed in a meeting of the klan. If it ever occurs and the fact is made known to the proper officials of the klan, those who indulge in it, even the presiding officers who permit it, are rigidly penalized.

It has been charged that the klan is a hideous, oath-bound organization of dark practices and secrets. If we were such an organization would I have even thought of filing our ritual and the constitution of the klan in the Copyright Office of the Library of Congress, so that all could read who cared to do so? You will not find in the Copyright Office the ritual and secrets of many organizations. Mr. Chairman, if we had been organized for all this mischief, we would not have had to incorporate this organization and file our constitution, laws, and ritual in Congress. No band of outlaws ever did anything like that, and we would not have done it if we had been organized for all this mischief. The very fact that the Kloran, as we call it, is over here in your Library of Congress, and has been there for approximately five years, where all who cared could read it, and that was proclaimed, under decree, as the official ritual of the organization, is evidence within itself that the purpose of this movement is right. All of our work will stand the clear light of an impartial investigation, and although all papers printing the World stories have openly violated the copyright laws, we have not as yet objected to this violation, as the documents stolen and printed without permission clearly show on their face that there is nothing in them except a love of country and a pure Americanism.

In this connection, Mr. Chairman, permit me to say—and I intended to make this statement before I started—that we are not here to interfere in any way, by lobbying or otherwise, with the carrying forward of the resolutions which your honorable committee has under consideration. Some distinguished gentlemen yesterday—several of them met me—I have met so many folks and good-looking folks that I can not remember names—and said, "How many witnesses are you going to put before the committee?" I said, "I am the only one." It would not have been necessary to have asked for it, but if I had merely hinted it, sir, I could have had 500 as stalwart citizens as there are in America to stand before your honorable committee and give you testimony that will corroborate every statement I make. I am not here to railroad, or lobby, or make any big showing; I am here from a sick bed, because, in justice to your committee, you are entitled to know the truth on both sides.

We have also been charged with making a special effort to secure members of the klan among the law-enforcing officials of each town where there is a klan in an effort to seduce them from enforcing the law or to wink at violations by the klan. Mr. Chairman, that is a tremendous indictment against the honor of American citizenship. Any man who has been elected by the people to serve in an office of public trust, who, on entering that office, takes a solemn oath to discharge his duty as an officer of the law, and who can be hoodwinked and who can be seduced by any fraternal order, by any church, or by any force on the face of the earth, is unworthy to make one track in the soil or sand of America. Those making these charges do not know the character of men in the United States that compose our law-enforcement machinery or they would know that these men can not be seduced by any secret organization to let slip their oath of office. In Atlanta, the home of the klan, after searching investigation by the World and other papers, it was found that only three officials in the county belonged to the klan, and a small number of the council, although many of those interviewed said they would like to belong to the klan, as they knew many citizens of Atlanta of the highest type who were members.

It has been charged that the klan is organized for the purpose of intimidating the Negroes in the South. It may surprise this committee to learn that the growth of the klan in the North and East has been much larger than in the South. As I say, it has been charged that the klan is organized for the purpose of intimidating the Negroes in the South. Mr. Chairman, I brand that charge as absolutely untrue. I am a southern man, a native of Alabama. I was born among, reared among, and associated with Negroes all my life. I have played with them in the yard of the old home; I have gone fishing with them in the old mountain streams; I have hunted with them; I have worked with them in the fields and in the shops, and I have worked over them. My mind goes back to my fourteenth and fifteenth years. Every Sunday morning I had my class of Negro children and many old Negro men; I taught them their A, B, C's, and taught them how to write. I have spent hours on Sunday mornings writing the love letters of the Negro men to their sweethearts and reading those that came back and carried on the correspondence. I have always been the friend of the Negro, and this committee o. its most searching investigation can go back to the old town of Harpersville, Shelby County, Ala., and ask those old Negroes something about Joe Simmons. They will tell you. It is my desire as a man, and the desire of this great institution that has been maliciously attacked, as soon as we can get the organization crystallized and solidified, to inaugurate movements and to assist in work that can not be other than conducive to the best interests of the Negroes in the South. Right here I recall one noted Negro, I. N. Fitzpatrick, bishop of the African Methodist Episcopal Church South. He is a personal friend of mine and I appreciate his friendship.

He has called on me at my home and at my office. Four or five years ago I talked with the bishop about this movement and I have, although not with me but in my possession at home. a beautiful letter from him which concludes by praying God's blessings upon the klan and upon its official head.

It was charged and sent broadcast over the United States that the Masonic bodies of Missouri had condemned the klan. This charge is false. I spoke three weeks ago to a gathering of over 3,500 in Shrine Temple Moola, at St. Louis, and the statement that the Knights of the Ku-Klux Klan had been condemned by the Masonic bodies of Missouri has been strongly denied.

The klan has been charged with inciting to riot. It is a proven fact that in no city where there was a klan has a race riot occurred. When the race riots occurred in Washington, Chicago, East St. Louis, and Oklahoma there was no klan in these cities, although it is equally strange that the World and the Hearst papers have not charged us with the responsibility of these riots. even though at the time they occurred we had no members in these cities.

It has been charged that some of our officials have weird oriental titles, and that we are for this reason undermining the democracy of America. That charge is almost too silly to pay any attention to. It is laughable when it is remembered that many secret orders in America have even more high-sounding titles than exist in the klan. For instance, imperial potentate, or, as an old German used to call it, "pot-entate": imperial prince; supreme chancellor; grand sire of the world—he is the granddaddy of the whole business, you know; grand exalted ruler; great Incohonee; supreme monarch; grand master; great grand master; sovereign grand commander; grand gu gu; general dissimoot of the Military Order of the Serpents—and you veterans of the Spanish War know what that fellow is—and many others too numerous to mention.

The fight being conducted against the klan is similar to the fight over 15 years ago on the Masons, as the same charges were made against them and the same effort to destroy them was made as is made to-day against the Knights of the Ku-Klux Klan, this fight on the Masons even resulting in the formation of an anti-Masonic political party.

The attacks against the klan were originated and started by the New York World, which is owned or controlled by a Jew, Mr. Pulitzer, whose main purpose is circulation and revenue. The circulation manager of this paper stated to one of the newspaper trade publications, the editor and publisher of New York which published this statement. that the Ku-Klux attacks had added a hundred thousand circulation to the World and additional advertising.

The World, according to their own statement. spent over four months, with unlimited resources at their command, in an investigation of the Knights of the Ku-Klux Klan, using trained investigators, newspaper men, and covering every section of the country. In the face of this careful investigation the World has not been able to prove anything detrimental to the klan except their own colored views of unfounded rumor and expressing the attitude of its Jewish ownership.

The World saw that the klan was the fastest growing purely Protestant, non-political organization in the United States. The World knew that when you strike at a man's religious and fraternal organizations you are striking at the very fiber of his being and that then all political affiliations and party lines are forgotten.

The World is the stronghold of the Democratic newspapers and the Democratic Party. and it has been said by those in a position to know that if the World could, by shrewd propaganda and untruthful slanders, force a Republican Congress and administration to throttle or destroy a purely local American Protestant fraternal organization, as is the Ku-Klux Klan, that its hundreds of thousands of members, friends. and those who think as does the klan, would at the polls three years from now forget party lines and preference and vote the Democratic ticket.

Hearst's New York papers have also attacked the klan, not from their usual and often repeated motive of being the only savior of the country, but purely from a motive of circulation, as some of those connected with the Hearst organization said that their circulation fell as that of the World grew on account of the Ku-Klux stories, and therefore Hearst must start a so-called expose of the Ku-Klux Klan, and you gentlemen know something of that expose.

Just as Judas Iscariot betrayed Jesus Christ for 30 pieces of silver, so there was found by the Hearst papers a man, C. Anderson Wright, a former klansman. who for money betrayed his oath. My information is that the Hearst papers paid this man $5,000 cash and $100 a week as long as he worked on the

stories, and also agreed to protect him from any damage suits and other legal
actions resulting from his libelous stories. All of the stories purporting to
come from the pen of Mr. C. Anderson Wright are false from start to finish
and most ridiculous in the character of their contents.

The Hearst papers have charged the klan with being un-American. This
charge is a travesty when it is remembered that during the war, and even
after the United States entered the World War, the Hearst papers were, on
account of their pro-Germanism, looked on askance by the great majority of
the American people. The name "Hearst" was by the New York Tribune
newspaper pictured on the billboards as a snake coiled in the American flag.
The assassination of the immortal McKinley is not yet forgotten, with which
the Hearst papers were charged as being responsible by the'r articles, editorials,
and propaganda. It is public knowledge that the British Government during
the World War barred the Hearst papers and the Hearst news service from
England on account of their pro-Germanism.

We have been charged with operating as our official organ the Searchlight,
now a daily paper published in Atlanta, Ga., and in this paper it is charged
have appeared articles tending to incite religious prejudice and intolerance, one
in particular by Mr. Carl F. Hutchison. The Ku-Klux Klan does not own the
Searchlight, never has put a dollar in it, has no control over it, nor is this paper
its official or even semiofficial organ. Not be'ng a molder of publ'c opinion,
but a chronicler of public opinion, it prints articles from anyone. This paper
has from time to time written articles regarding the klan, as have other publications. It is the official organ for the State of Georgia of the Junior Order of
American Mechanics, one of the greatest fraternal organizations, but we have
not seen any attempt to attack this order on account of the Searchlight editorials and articles, though the Junior Order name stands at the masthead. Mr.
Carl F. Hutch'son, whose art cles were objected to by the Hearst papers and
the World, and who had this matter laid before the postal authorit:es, is not
even a member of the Knights of the Ku-Klux Klan.

The Ku-Klux Klan is not a political organ'zation, nor does it seek politcal
power, although this has been charged aga'nst us.

In spite of the fact that bills introduced in Congress providing for an investigation of the Knights of the Ku-Klux Klan have been introduced by Roman
Catholic Members of the House, we favor the passage of such a resolution, but
demur to the wording in so far as attacks against the klan are concerned. In
fact, the very bitterness of the wording of some of these resolutions shows the
apparent motive back of their introduction in the House.

I would also like to introduce here, marked "Exhibit H," for the permanent
records of this committee, the copy of a telegram sent to every Member of the
House and Senate urging that they vote for an investigation of the klan.

A congressional investigation committee has a wide scope and broader powers
than any other body, much broader than a grand jury or the courts, and for this
reason we seek such an investigation, so that the truth may be proven and the
klan officially cleared from the lying slanders and charges made against it. We
further know that a congress:onal investigation will be impartial.

The Ku-Klux Klan, through me, also telegraphed to the President and Attorney General Daugherty asking for a Federal probe by the Department of Justice.
I introduce here copies of these telegrams, marked "Exhibit I."

We know that the Department of Justice has a wide authority and many
sources of information at its command and are satisfied that their investigation
also will be impartial, and are glad that this investigation is now proceeding
under the direction of Hon. William J. Burns who, although a Catholic, we
know and are convinced will not let his religious beliefs swerve him in the
slightest degree from justice.

I am not here to oppose the resolution of a congressional investigation of the
Knights of the Ku-Klux Klan, but to plead that such an investigation be made,
as when the investigation is finished it will set at rest for all time the charges
against the klan, and the klan and othe'' organizations in America will then
stand out in their true light.

When the World and Hearst attacked the klan we voluntarily went to the
Department of Justice and to the Post Office Department and offered them all
our books, records, files, and every bit of information they might desire, and
our entire records are open to th's committee. If we had been a lawless organization would we have done that? No, sir. We would have tucked our great,
long-forked tails, folded our horns, and gone to the high timber. We would
never have thought of it. "He that hath light within his own clear breast may

sit in the midst of night and enjoy bright day," and, Mr. Chairman, in our breasts we have that holy light that will illumine our pathway, though we are surrounded by the dismal darkness of Pluto's wild domains, in every kind of an investigation that is to be made by the authorities of my Government.

The klan would appreciate the opportunity of presenting to a congressional investigation committee at least a thousand witnesses from every section of the United States, especially from the North and East. These witnesses will be the most representative in their community, men who are known and respected for the things they have lived for and done in their cities. These men will tell the committee what the klan stands for, what it has done in building better citizenship and what it has done in matters of charity, etc. I can not state here that we have paid out vast sums of money and done great and wonderful things yet, because, remember, sir, this organization was in its swaddling clothes 18 months ago, and for the last 12 or 18 months it has just gotten old enough to be able to run around a little.

I here introduce, marked "Exhibit J," copy of news story from one of the Houston, Tex., papers, the original paper being on file in Atlanta. In the story it is shown that Mr. Jack Ralston, an electrician, was accidentally killed in the performance of his duties and that within 24 hours after his death the Houston klan placed in the hands of his widow the sum of $1,000 to take care of the temporary needs of the family.

In this connection let me say that we are doing all we can to give practical expression to that principle of ours of benevolence. We are doing to-day work of that nature in supporting widows and orphans and assisting in their support in many places.

When the Memphis, Tenn., explosion occurred the klan that day gave $500 to the Negroes who were injured. No longer than last Christmas we made possible the Christmas celebration of the old slaves in Atlanta by our contributions. I was informed by the Negro preacher that they could not have had the Christmas dinner and celebration if it had not been for our contribution. I was cordially invited out to meet the old darkies and address them, but I could not go on account of previous engagements. I can tell of scores of instances of our practical benevolence, freely given in the interest of humanity, but it is in nowise the policy of myself or the order to advertise its charitable works, for those things we hold as our duty since we are the recipients of countless blessings from the great God.

We would also like to present to the congressional investigation committee the sheriffs and other officials of many towns to tell of the klan and its loyalty and respect for the law.

Standing here in the presence of God, before this committee of one of the greatest law making and deliberative bodies in the world, and standing in the shadow of the Capitol of our great Nation, I say to you, gentlemen, that if the Ku-Klux Klan was guilty of a hundredth part of the charges that have been made against us, I would from this room send a telegram calling together the grand concilium for the purpose of forever disbanding the klan in every section of the United States.

I ask your indulgence while I read the various exhibits previously referred to, as in them are various points that I would like the opportunity of personally pointing out. After they are read I will be glad to answer any questions that your honorable committee may desire to ask, if it is within my power to do so.

(Thereupon, the committee adjourned, to meet Thursday, October 13, 1921, at 10.30 o'clock a. m.)

COMMITTEE ON RULES,
HOUSE OF REPRESENTATIVES,
Thursday, October 13, 1921.

The committee met at 10.30 o'clock a. m., Hon. Philip P. Campbell (chairman) presiding.

Mr. CAMPBELL. Col. Simmons, are you ready to resume?

Mr. SIMMONS. Yes, sir.

Mr. CAMPBELL. We will hear you further.

STATEMENT OF MR. WILLIAM JOSEPH SIMMONS—Resumed.

Mr. SIMMONS. Mr. Chairman and gentlemen of the committee, I wish to correct an impression made yesterday in the testimony of Mr. C. Anderson Wright regarding checks; that is, fraudulent checks. The impression seemed to have been made that the trouble he had had, if my information is correct, on four different occasions where he had trouble with the authorities of the law, possibly resulting in arrests—that these were drafts on the Knights of the Ku-Klux Klan that were not honored. It seems that he has made a strenuous effort to get out from under by these accusations, and not only accusations, but these instances where he has had trouble, by making the impression upon your honorable committee and the people of this Nation that the trouble was attributable to drafts that he made on the Knights of the Ku-Klux Klan, which drafts were not honored. Mr. Chairman. I have never authorized any man going into the field to make a draft upon the Knights of the Ku-Klux Klan ; never.

Mr. RODENBERG. Did Mr. Clarke give this authority or authorize him to do that? That is the statement he made—that Mr. Clarke was the one who authorized him to draw them.

Mr. SIMMONS. Well, now. I am speaking to the general impression. My information is, in all sincerity, gentlemen, that the checks which he had trouble with were his personal checks. Now, of course, Mr. Clarke—and I will explain the propagation department to you gentlemen, when I get to it in my run of exhibits—if Mr. Clarke, by any arrangements of any particular nature with Mr. Wright, failed to pay certain checks, from my actual and absolute knowledge on that I could not say, but I know this, all other business transactions with which I am familiar and in which Mr. Clarke had a part with all other field men, every check that has been sent out by Mr. Clarke has been paid.

Mr. RODENBERG. But you have no absolute personal knowledge as to whether or not Mr. Clarke authorized this young man to draw against the treasury?

Mr. SIMMONS. No; not as a proposition or agreement between Mr. Clarke and this man.

Mr. RODENBERG. You do not know about that positively?

Mr. SIMMONS. No; but as far as the orders are concerned. I can state this, Mr. Chairman. From my knowledge of Mr. Clarke's dealings with field men in all instances I have never had one word of complaint. I have not had even one word of complaint from Mr. Wright as to checks not being paid, or that he was stranded and needed funds. If this be the fact, as he states—if his word is altogether the truth—he could have easily written me and the matter would have been immediately straightened out. I make that statement for the purpose of clearing up any wrong impressions.

Now, I have the information which would lead me to believe that the statements of Mr. Wright in trying to create this information were not altogether true regarding certain dealings while he was in Houston, Tex., prior to the time he became connected with this organization, and I have been informed that a Houston, Tex., paper quite recently has published something to this effect, and gave a list of the "bum" checks. That is rather a slang word, but it expresses the idea. Now, this is regarding Mr. Wright before he became connected with the organization, and I have heard of things of this nature at other places, namely, in St. Louis, and by a gentleman in Chicago.

Now, I make this statement simply to correct the impression which was made that this trouble could be attributed to the fact that this organization had failed to protect its honor in the meeting of a draft or check upon it.

Mr. RODENBERG. Let me understand you correctly. Do you mean to say that Mr. Wright had issued fraudulent checks before he became connected with the klan?

Mr. SIMMONS. That is my impression, sir.

Mr. RODENBERG. Do you not investigate the character of a man before you give him employment in your klan?

Mr. SIMMONS. Yes, sir; but I did not know about this until after he had been appointed.

Mr. RODENBERG. Do you not take the trouble to find out something about a man before you give him an official connection with your order?

Mr. SIMMONS. Well, sir. there are a lot of things in a man's life that do not come out, and a little later in my testimony I will touch on that point under certain notations I have here.

Before going into a consideration of the various exhibits. Mr. Chairman, I wish to make the statement that the evidence so far that has been presented before your honorable committee by the proponents of these resolutions and the witnesses before your committee consist of inferences, rumors, and opinions; in other words, largely hearsay and deductions resulting in personal opinions from a hearsay basis.

I am here. as I stated yesterday, to present to your honorable committee facts as I honestly and conscientiously know them. I have no malice toward anyone. I am not here to ridicule anyone as myself and this organization has been ridiculed unjustly in certain of the newspapers. I do not resort to ridicule as an instrument to carry any point. I have always tried to be—and it is a characteristic of this organization—square and fair, because in the record of one's life, in all those things that go to make up the sum total of human life on earth, we must ultimately one of these days stand before a great tribunal, and before that Judge we must give an account. Having respect to this, I seek to live and to conduct myself as a man in all things that touch the interest of my fellow man, and my prayer and my most strenuous effort in this organization has been to transmit this conviction to the organization and to every member of it.

Sometimes. Mr. Chairman, if you please, a man who is endeavoring hard to play an honest game feels the lash and sting of unjust and unwarranted ridicule, especially when that comes from a source that he is powerless to answer back. Let that be as it may. I have drunk deep of the bitter cup of Gethsemane. In my strenuous effort to stand true to the standard of what is regarded by all men with proper perceptions the standard of unsullied honor I have been made to suffer unjustly for those things I have conscientiously endeavored to do which I knew were for the best interests of my fellows.

Now, Mr. Chairman, to you and to your honorable committee and to the great American people I am dealing in these exhibits, especially those particular exhibits that affect the internal workings of our organization, in actual facts.

There is one other point I wish to state in these preliminary remarks before I get to the exhibits which was presented to your honorable committee by one of the proponents—I do not remember now just who it was—in a very scathing and uncultured manner, that this organization had grown so powerful, or words to this effect, and was of such a criminal nature that it even would go into the courthouses of our country and tear the records from the books, Mr. Chairman, this is not true; this is not true. No person by any authority of this organization has ever done a thing like that. That charge within itself is extremely ridiculous and does not comport with the dignity and integrity of the man who made it. A reference was made to the mutilation. I might say, of certain court records in Atlanta. I can not just now give you names of men who talked with me in Atlanta about the disappearance of these court records, because, as you understand, for the past two or three weeks I have been sick in bed; but information has been given to me, and I have been informed that it is somewhat current in Atlanta, Ga., that right recently when certain court records were missed those records, or else a verbatim copy of those records, were seen in the possession of representatives of the New York World. An effort is being made to attach this crime against recorded justice to this organization. Sir, I would not believe there was a man in America who would so far forget himself as a man to attempt tactics like that.

Mr. Chairman and gentlemen of the committee, I will now take up for your consideration the exhibits referred to on yesterday.

First, I present for your consideration Exhibit A, which is the charter of the Knights of the Ku-Klux Klan from the Superior Court of Fulton County, Ga., which instrument created this organization a legal entity and gave it authority and permission to start on its way. It has been stated here by some one that this organization is a private organization. I judge that statement was made for the purpose of creating the impression that it had no legal status and was not recognized as such. This, sir, is a copy of this organization's charter from the superior court, bearing the imprint of the seal of the superior court and signed by Hon. Arnold Broyles, clerk of the Superior Court of Fulton County, Ga.

There are certain points in this that I especially want to call to your attention, and then, if your honorable committee desires, it shall be placed in your hands. This charter sets forth the fact that the purpose and object of said corporation—that is, Knights of the Ku-Klux Klan—is to be purely benevolent and eleemosynary; that there shall be no capital stock or profit or gain to the members thereof.

Paragraph 4:

" 4. The petitioners desire that the society shall have the power to confer an initiative degree ritualism, fraternal and secret obligations, words, grip, signs, and ceremonies under which there shall be united only white male persons of sound health, good morals, and high character; and further desire such rights, powers, and privileges as are now extended to the Independent Order of Odd Fellows, Free and Accepted Order of Masons, Knights of Pythias, et al, under and by virtue of the laws of the State of Georgia.

"8. Petitioners desire that they shall have the right to adopt a constitution and by-laws and elect the first kloncilium (supreme executive committee), which shall possess all the powers of the 'imperial klonvokation' (supreme legislative body) until the first organization and meeting of that body, and shall fix the number, title, and terms of officers composing said 'kloncilium' (supreme legislative committee).

"9. Petitioners desire the right to own separate unto itself and to control the sale of all paraphernalia, regalia, stationery, jewelry, and such other materials needed by the subordinate branches of the order for the proper conduct of their business; the right to publish a fraternal magazine and such other literature as is needed in the conduct of the business of the order; the right to buy, hold, and sell real estate and personal property suitable to the purpose of the said corporation; to sell, exchange, or sublease the same or any part thereof; to mortgage or create liens thereon; to borrow money and secure the payment thereof by mortgage or deed of trust and to appoint trustees in connection therewith; to execute promissory notes; to have and to use a common seal; to sue and be sued; to plead and be impleaded; to do and perform all these things and exercise all those rights which under the laws of Georgia are conferred upon societies or orders of like character."

I wish to make, sir, a brief comment here upon that paragraph. It has reference to our control of our paraphernalia, and so on. I was responsible for that particular paragraph being inserted in our petition for a charter, and that fact is evidence to you gentlemen and to the world that there certainly was not any mercenary motive in my mind or heart in the creation of this institution, because the designing of this paraphernalia, the preparation of its rituals, and all those things is a product of my own head and hand, and I could have said to these incorporators, "Gentlemen, you will adopt this as your official regalia and ritual, and you may use it provided you pay me a royalty thereon, for it is my own work;" but I can say to you, Mr. Chairman and gentlemen of your honorable committee, God will bear me witness that I have never in all these six years ever had one iota of a mercenary or a commercial thought to flit through my mind and heart with reference to this organization—never.

At one time there was a man associated with me, back in the very beginning or very shortly after the beginning, a man who got a commercialized or mercenary vision of this thing; a man much older than myself, who had been a successful organizer for other fraternal orders. Repeatedly he would come into my office and tell me of the great money-making possibilities provided certain plans that he had worked out should be authorized and enforced, and pleaded with me to authorize them and let him enforce them, finally stating that he could guarantee a cold $1,000,000 to myself and to himself if those plans were carried out. I never had such a feeling to come over me in my life.

Now, Mr. Chairman——

Mr. RODENBERG (interposing). Would you object to stating who that man was?

Mr. SIMMONS. J. B. Frost—Jonathan B. Frost. one of the men whose name appears here as one of the petitioners in this charter.

Mr. Chairman, I would not stand before you and pose as an angel, nor before the world, because I am conscious of the fact that I am not growing any wings. Sir, I have nothing back there but a pair of shoulder blades, and they are under the skin, but I can be and am sincere and honest in some things, at least. When that man made that statement to me I told him I did not know but what some day this organization might become a commercialized institution, but W. J. Simmons would be dead and 3 feet under the ground before any man could pull it. I meant what I said then. I mean what I say now—that no man, to my knowledge, as long as I lived and had the power, could prostitute this movement to a grafting game.

He jumped to his feet and said, "You do not mean to call me—with an oath—a grafter?" I said, "No, sir; I do not; but your plan smacks of it, and I will destroy this organization now, what little we have, before that shall be done."

Some time after that, sir. he stated to me that if I would appoint him and six men whom he should name as imperial officers he would see to it that $30,000 was put on a table in my room within 24 hours. He said, "I do not ask you for any underwriting; just give me your word and it will be done. You do not have to make these appointments until that money is put on the table." I told him then and there I did not know so much about myself as to whether I could be bought or not, but no man could buy this organization and prostitute it for grafting and commercial purposes.

Then I had this language inserted in our application so that this order—not W. J. Simmons or somebody else—but this order should control its paraphernalia, its regalia, its jewelry, and these other things, because I had had somewhat of an insight into the paraphernalia business, where great corporations of the United States had made their millions out of paraphernalia of secret orders, and if that be true, why would it not be a good idea from a business standpoint and for the organization's interest that the organization should have control and have its own stuff manufactured? In addition to that, it was a protection against counterfeit organizations manufacturing imitative costumes, and so on, and trying to counterfeit this organization, which I learned about afterwards, and we have had to deal with three or four attempts to form counterfeit organizations or imitations. This is a protection. It simply protects us, so that if any man should get in position so that he was using an imitation of our stuff or of our regalia I could easily have a check on him to see whether he was entitled to have it and use it or not.

This charter from the superior court under which we are now operating and have operated for these years is evidence conclusive that the Knights of the Ku-Klux Klan is a legal entity, and if it had not been, Mr. Chairman, I never would have put on paper and sent through the United States mails the words "Knights of the Klu-Klux Klan, Incorporated." This is a corporation granted under the code of the State of Georgia, and it is to be national in its scope.

There, sir, you have Exhibit A, the charter granted by the superior court of Fulton County, Ga.

Mr. Chairman and gentlemen of the committee, I now present to you Exhibit A-2, which is the charter issued by the Knights of the Ku-Klux Klan to its local or subordinate lodges.

This is a specimen copy. Of course it is not filled in with the names, but is a specimen copy. There is the charter of the local organizations. I introduce this for the purpose of acquainting your honorable committee with the powers and prerogatives of local organizations, because you have been told, Mr. Chairman, that the exalted cyclops, or the president of the local klan, had full and monarchical powers and could do as he pleased. If he thought there was a man in the neighborhood that should be attended to all he had to do was simply to tell certain members of the klan to go do it and it was done. Sir, that testimony was given here before you or testimony of that character. I want to tell you, Mr. Chairman, that that testimony is false, and the man who gave it knew it was false. The exalted cyclops is truly the president of the local organization and is required to preside over its meetings and direct its activities according to fixed laws and the constitution of our order. There is nothing in that testimony that is based upon facts. You gentlemen on the committee, if perchance you are members of any fraternal orders, know what the charter of the local organization means and stands for, and the purpose of it. It is the same in this. It reads here:

"To all who read and respect these lines, greeting: Whereas the imperial wizard hath received a petition from the following-named citizens of the invisible empire."

Then there is a blank.

"Praying for themselves and others and their successors to be instituted a klan of the order under the name and number of ——, Klan No. —, realm of ——, and same to be located at ——, in the county of ——, State of ——, United States of America, and they having given assurance of their fidelity to the order and their competency to render the service required, and their ready willingness to take upon themselves and their successors the responsibilities thereof, and their serious determined purpose to rightly use and not abuse the powers, privileges, and prerogatives conferred on them as such, and be faithful and true in all things committed to them.

"Now, know ye that I, the imperial wizard "—

And so on.

"By authority in me vested, do issue this charter to the aforesaid petitioners."

72359—21——6

And so on. Now, then, Mr. Chairman, it goes on to say:
" The said klan is hereby authorized and empowered to do and to perform all such acts and things as are prescribed by the kloran."
That is our ritual, which is in the exhibits.
" Laws, imperial decrees, edicts, mandates, and usages of the order, and to enjoy all the rights, privileges, and prerogatives authorized by the constitution thereof; and klansmen are strictly enjoined to valiantly preserve and persistently practice the principles of a pure patriotism, honor, klanishness, and white supremacy, ever keeping in mind and heart the sacred sentiment, peculiar purpose, manly mission, and lofty ideals and objects of the order, a devoted loyalty to their emperor, the imperial wizard, a steadfast obedience to the constitution of the order, a faithful keeping of their oath of allegiance, and a constant unwavering fidelity to every interest of the invisible empire, to the end that the progress, power, purpose, and influence of klankraft be properly promoted, the knowledge of the faithful, self-sacrificing service, and noble achievements of our fathers be not lost to posterity, and all those things for which our beloved order is founded to do and to perform, and to protect, preserve, and perpetuate, be diligently done and scrupulously maintained, and that they be blameless in preserving the grace, dignity, and intent of this charter forever.
" I solemnly charge you to hold fast to the dauntless faith of our fathers and to keep their spotless memory secure and unstained, and true to the traditions of our valiant sires, meet every behest of duty, in all the relationships of life and living, promptly and properly, without fault, without fail, without fear, and without reproach."
Now, then, as a guaranty that the authority of the local organization shall not be misused, that is, purposely or repeatedly, this clause is presented for your consideration:
" The imperial wizard has and holds the full and unchallengable authority, right, and power to suspend or revoke this charter, and to annul all the rights, prerogatives and immunities conferred hereby, for the neglect or the refusal on the part of the said klan to conform to and comply with the kloran, constitution, laws, imperial decrees, edicts, mandates, rulings, and instructions, or its failure to respect the usages of the order, as proclaimed by and maintained under the imperial authority of same."
This is accepted by the local organization on motion or vote that is certified to by the exalted cyclops, who is elected at the head of the klan at the time the klan is chartered. That is accepted on the conditions as stipulated on its face, and there is nothing therein contained that gives the exalted cyclops or any klansman the privilege of being or even suggests the opportunity to be as we have been accused of being. I judge, Mr. Chairman, that you have not a copy of this charter among your papers in this hearing, and I gladly submit it to you, with the seal of the order attached.
Mr. Chairman and gentlemen of the committee, before passing from that and taking up the others, there is information that you are entitled to in that connection. It has been charged in certain newspapers that I hold an iron rod over the members of this organization and can do with them and by them just as I pleased; that I hold imperial powers. That, like the other accusations, is also untrue.
Mr. RODENBERG. You are elected for life, are you not?
Mr. SIMMONS. I will get to that, if you please, when I get to the constitution and laws. If I forget it when I run over them I wish you would call my attention to that. Here is a peculiar feature about the Ku-Klux Klan, gentlemen. It is an infant organization, and if any person on earth should have the control of the conduct and the nourishing of the baby, the mother of the baby should have that right. Are the parents imperialistic in their control of the children of their own creation? This institution was of my own conception and those splendid gentlemen associated with me as incorporators and imperial officers. Every year when we had a meeting of our imperial concilium, or executive committee, and the work gone into, they gladly yielded of their own accord and encouraged me in the development of the work. They felt, having their various business interests and not having studied and planned this proposition as I had, that I was superior to any of them in competency to work out the plans and further the creation of this child, so to speak, and whatever powers I have are in no wise imperialistic, according to the impression that certain newspapers have tried to create. I do not hold such powers. I have a constitution—or the order has a constitution—and laws that lay down regulations. But I do not hold this power, and if you will examine the character of

all fraternal orders you will find that the grand master or the great incohonee or supreme chancellor or the sovereign supreme commander, or whoever is at the head of the organization, has the power to issue edicts, decrees, and things of that nature for the protection, for the preservation, for the propagation and proper functioning of the organization all down the line.

The authority I hold in this organization may possibly be compared with the authority of a general in an army. I use that as an illustration. He can issue his orders down the line and those orders must be obeyed, but that general can not issue an order in violation of the regulations and rules of war. He can not do it. He would be court-martialed if he did. That general can not say to one of his subordinate officials, "Take that boy from that company out here and shoot him." He can not do that, unless there be reasons for it and those reasons set forth in a military court. But within those army regulations he is the general in command, because he is responsible for the successes of that army. I give that information to you for your benefit. The American people have had held up before them glaring word pictures in various newspapers as to the great imperial wizard. They have referred to and ridiculed the title "wizard" and have pictured him as sitting away down there in Georgia, in a million-and-a-half-dollar palace, on an exalted throne, and that hundreds of American citizens, who have forgotten the dignity of their American citizenship, were bowing and scraping before that wizard, and that the wizard was sitting there on his throne, as the picture would go, with horns and a spike-headed tail holding an iron rod in his hand and driving American citizens to do his bidding and to do his law. Mr. Chairman, that is the impression that has gone out by reason of this newspaper scandal and sensation, and that impression is unjust, without foundation, and I do not believe honestly in my heart that the papers which sent that out believed it themselves. Mr. Chairman, if to-morrow morning our great President Harding should resign and all the functioning faculties of our great American Government would become instantly paralytic, and if the American people should rise up and proclaim me the monarch of America, I would die before I would accept it. God knows my heart, and to you gentlemen I am true. My disposition from boyhood up has been tinged with a distinctive streak of timidity, and I have never had any desire to rule or to govern, and I have never gone into the head chair of any fraternal order, of the various fraternal orders of which I am a member, to preside over the deliberations of their meetings without a vivid consciousness of my unworthiness for the place and my desire to be down the line sitting in the chairs with the other fellows.

My position in this order is a position of necessity. If I be the founder of it—I repeat the illustration, if I be the mother, so to speak, of this institution—where can there be any extreme or unreasonable imperialistic powers in the authority of the mother over her own child? Is the judge on your bench, in the courts of your land, imperialistic when that judge can speak and it is done; when he can say to a sheriff, "Arrest that man for contempt of court," or this, that, and the other? It is within his prerogatives, and it is done. In giving his charge to the jury he can enunciate his opinions and his conclusions, and in giving them the jury takes them as law from the bench. Is that judge imperialistic, monarchial? It may be, yes; but the position he holds is for the purpose of seeing that justice is done. But that judge, with all the authority he has in the trial of that case, can not break the laws that control his conduct.

Some of the ridicule that has been poured out to the American people is so ridiculous that it exposes the fallacy of all of it. Only yesterday I read in the paper, sir, that I appeared before your honorable committee with a great diamond sticking in my tie. That is no diamond; that is an imperial stone.

Now, Mr. Chairman, I get to Exhibit B.

Mr. CAMPBELL. We have a great deal to do, and if you can give us the facts and submit the exhibits with a brief explanation I am sure it will serve your purpose and ours.

Mr. SIMMONS. Very good. I am glad you called my attention to it, because it will certainly serve my purpose. This is Exhibit B. I want to state to you, Mr. Chairman, in all honesty and frankness, that I have these exhibits here, gotten out from the office, regarding the financial affairs. Understand, sir, that I was for the last two weeks at home and I was sick in bed, and for a time prior to that I was off on trips, as I am away a great deal of the time. I made a trip into the middle north in the interest of encouraging and instructing the members of this organization, and I have not had any occasion, getting up out of my bed to come here, to go back and check over and altogether verify these particular exhibits or to see about the typographical errors. We detected one here yesterday, I believe it was, with reference to a date; it should have read 1920, and it read 1921. This has reference to monthly salaries; that is, salaries stipulated as such and not amo nts of commission made. From the 1st of August, 1921, the salary of the imperial wizard is fixed at $1,000 a month. That was at the last meeting of our supreme executive committee, so called. Before that time, beginning, I judge, about a year ago, it was agreed upon that it should be $100 a week.

Mr. Pou. How many members of the executive committee were at the meeting which fixed the $1,000 a month salary?

Mr. SIMMONS. I will get to that a little later, but will answer your question now. The total number of imperial officers that constitute this so-called supreme executive committee, which is the authoritative body until the general klonvokation is called and organized, is 16 in number.

Mr. RODENBERG. Is that committee elected or selected?

Mr. SIMMONS. In the development of the organization—you see, the organization is now in a formative state, and under the charter the imperial officers are selected until the imperial klonvokation—which will be the supreme legislative body—is called and organized.

Mr. RODENBERG. Selected by whom?

Mr. SIMMONS. Selected by myself.

Mr. RODENBERG. You selected the executive committee?

Mr. SIMMONS. Yes, sir. I get men who are available and men who are competent to discharge such duties.

Mr. RODENBERG. You have had no election up to this time?

Mr. SIMMONS. No; the imperial klonvokation has not been called, but I am going to call that for Thanksgiving Day of this year.

Mr. RODENBERG. For the purpose of electing an executive committee?

Mr. SIMMONS. Yes; in other words, the organization will pass out of its provisional state into its permanent form, and that is provided for in our constitution, which you gentlemen can see and read.

Mr. FESS. Do you prefer not to be interrupted?

Mr. SIMMONS. Well, yes, sir; but, of course, I am not going to object to questions.

Mr. FESS. I have some questions I want to ask.

Mr. Pou. I think we have treated the colonel very courteously. We have refrained from asking him questions for quite a while, and I am sure he will not object.

Mr. SIMMONS. Not at all.

Mr. FESS. Was there any provision for back pay?

Mr. SIMMONS. Yes, sir. I am glad you asked that question, because in the questioning of the gentlemen there it had slipped my mind. At the last meeting of the imperial concilium—in fact, for the last three or four years—every year it would meet the question would be brought up by some one to fix some kind of a compensation, as they called it, for the services of the imperial wizard. The organization was not in a financial condition to take on anything like that as a compensation for services rendered, and I would not permit the passage of a resolution along that line. I told the gentlemen that when the time arrived that the order was able, then the order could do as it wished in those matters; and if they wanted to make some expression—I would not accept it as compensation— but if it would come to me as an expression of appreciation for the back services I had rendered, without compensation specified, of course, I would accept it. But I hold myself and my pocketbook always subject to the needs of the organization.

This last meeting of the imperial concilium was called in the latter part of July, and we had to have an adjourned session in August to complete the business, or we had to go into August with it, and they then fixed a sum as an expression of appreciation for my services, going back to the five years past, or, rather, the six years since it started in December, 1915, and that sum was to be a sum of money amounting to $5,000 a year for five years, to be paid at whatever time the organization could pay it without affecting its funds for the other work of a general nature.

Mr. FESS. $25,000 in all?

Mr. SIMMONS. Yes, sir; for five years. Of that I have received one payment, and that was just a few weeks ago. I have received only one payment.

Now, the imper al kligrapp, who is the supreme secretary, and who is one of the businest men in America, draws a salary of $300 per month. The imperial klabee, or the supreme treasurer, who is Dr. H. C. Montgomery, of Atlanta, an optician, and not Mr. H. H. Furney, as was stated yesterday, receives a salary of $300 per month. Mr. Furney is cashier and head bookkeeper, and, of course, has to do with the details of the office work. As I have said, the imperial klabee, or treasurer, receives $300 per month, and the cashier and head book-keeper receives the same amount. The chief of the department of investigation, as we call it, receives $500 per month. That is a gentleman whose work it is to investigate carefully the reports and work of the kleagles and organizers. In other words, he is a general auditor to check up the work of the organization. His work entails a great deal of travel and, as I have said, he draws a salary of $500 per month. Stenographers are paid at the rate of from $15 to $30 per week. Field men in the character of lecturers, klorenic teachers, and charter deliverers and special investigators are paid at the rate of from $50 to $75 per week, plus their traveling expenses, such as railroad fare and hotel bills. The average expense account of these men is from $35 to $50 per week. This is Exhibit B, which I submit for the record.

(Exhibit B appears elsewhere in this record.)

Mr. SNELL. Were all of the 15 members of the executive committee present when your salary or compensation was fixed?

Mr. SIMMONS. No, sir. I have not seen the minutes since they were recorded; but, if my memory holds good, there were 14 present. Now, the constitution prescribes that 6 members of the imperial concilium shall constitute a quorum, the imperial wizard being present. There were 14 present. We had a resignation from that board.

Next, gentlemen of the committee, is Exhibit C, which is one of the financial statements, a copy of which you have before your committee for consideration.

Mr. FESS. Before you leave the financial department, how many field men have you?

Mr. SIMMONS. The field men of the organization work and function with the department of propagation, and I will get to that before the end of my remarks, or at the conclusion. Having been down sick most of the time for the last two months, I can not state accurately how many field men we have.

Mr. FESS. Are they all on salary?

Mr. SIMMONS. No, sir; every man is employed on a commission basis. The men classified as field men are lecturers and ritualistic teachers.

Mr. FESS. How many are there?

Mr. SIMMONS. I would say that there are possibly 18 or 20 of that character. I can not be positive about that, because that is a matter under the propagation department.

In this Exhibit C, a copy of which you have before you, you will see clearly the totals under the different items. You have a copy of Exhibit C, which was submitted through the department to you. That is one of the financial balance sheets as of October 1, 1921, of the Knights of the Ku-Klux Klan general funds.

(Exhibit C appears elsewhere in this record.)

Mr. SIMMONS. Exhibit D has reference to Lanier University, its faculty and board of trustees, as they have been selected. Possibly by this time those gentlemen whom I say have been selected have been elected under the arrangement by which the old board of trustees was to elect these gentlemen and then to automatically resign. That arrangement has been brought about by this time.

Mr. FESS. Would that place the control of the university through this board in your klan?

Mr. SIMMONS. No, sir; it would not, because a great number of these gentlemen here are not even members of the klan. Lanier University is an educational institution to be fostered by our organization, or the Ku-Klux Klan, until it can become self-sustaining and can take care of itself. It is a great institution that we are seeking to build along certain lines, as I said yesterday in the remarks I made. In its faculty are Dr. E. C. James, doctor of literature, who is one of the professors that has joined the university; Rev. J. H. Boldridge, A. M., D. D., LL. D.——

Mr. SNELL (interposing). Suppose you just file that statement. I do not think that it will be necessary to read all of those names.

Mr. SIMMONS. That will suit me.

(Exhibit D appears elsewhere in this record.)

Mr. POU. Can you give us an idea of the number on the faculty?

Mr. SIMMONS. There are other professors.

Mr. SNELL. Suppose you give us the number.

Mr. SIMMONS. There are nine here.

Mr. RODENBERG. What is the enrollment?

Mr. SIMMONS. I can not state that. We are just opened for matriculation, or they were just opening when I left Atlanta, and I can not state positively how many have been enrolled.

Mr. FESS. What is the curriculum?

Mr. SIMMONS. It is a standard curriculum. It is a member of some organization, and the curriculum is standard.

Now, Exhibit E gives the contract between the Knights of the Ku-Klux Klan (Inc.) and Edward Young Clarke, who is at the head of and and in control of the propagation department. Would you like for me to read that contract?

Mr. SNELL. If you would explain in a few words what the contract is, it would be better.

Mr. SIMMONS. I will make this statement to you, that the contract that is now in effect between this organization and Mr. Clarke is a business contract. The purpose of this contract was to secure him to head the propagating organization—that is, to take up that line of work for the extension of the organization. There is a guaranty that that work shall be done properly, according to the requirements and regulations of the order. It is like any other contract of a business nature, and can be canceled by either party for cause. If there should be a cause, it would be canceled.

Now, this contract allows Mr. Clarke compensation on a commission basis, you might say. He draws no salary from the organization, but he is paid or reimbursed for his services and for the services of that department. It is a contract that allows Mr. Clarke to retain for his department or for that department of the work compensation on the basis of 80 per cent. In other words, he is allowed to retain $8 out of the $10 donation or initiation fee. Now, gentlemen of the committee, that is not an enormous commission. Before I took this matter up with Mr. Clarke I talked with three gentlemen who had been connected with organization work for fraternal orders, and they told me this: "Col. Simmons, your initiation fee is not big enough." They told me, "If I were doing this work, I would have to have every penny of the $10 in order to guarantee me proper compensation and the money that I would have to advance in organizing the organization machinery and going through with it."

Mr. FESS. Do you not think that a commission of 80 per cent is inordinate?

Mr. SIMMONS. In a commercial way, yes, sir; although I have received something like that in other things when I was on the road with propositions of a business nature. If you are familiar with the organization and development of fraternal orders and have made a study of that subject, you will see that this is not inordinate. I was with a fraternal order or a fraternal insurance order with an initiation fee of $5, and I got all of that as my commission, together with a bonus of $3 from the headquarters. That was the contract I had.

Mr. FESS. I do not know anything about that phase of it.

Mr. SIMMONS. From my knowledge of fraternal orders, I do not consider that at all excessive.

Senator WATSON of Georgia. Mr. Chairman, would a Senator be allowed to ask the witness a question?

Mr. CAMPBELL. We have not had anyone from the outside asking questions.

Senator WATSON of Georgia. I am not on the outside, but I am on the inside. I am very much inside, and I will stay inside, too.

Mr. CAMPBELL. We have not permitted anyone not members of the committee to ask questions.

Senator WATSON of Georgia. I am asking now if you will permit me to ask him a question? I do not see why you should not permit me to do so, if you want a fair investigation.

Mr. CAMPBELL. We might have that request from everybody in the room.

Senator WATSON of Georgia. Everybody in this room is not a United States Senator. This man comes from my State, and I am going to see that he has fair play, too.

Mr. CAMPBELL. Has anyone asserted that he has not received fair treatment?

Senator WATSON of Georgia. I am simply asking if I may ask him a question.

Mr. CAMPBELL. I think, Senator, that you might ask him a question, so that we may get rid of the matter.

Senator WATSON of Georgia. I want to treat your committee with all respect, and I will treat it with all respect, but I think that a Senator might ask a question of one of his constituents.

Mr. CAMPBELL. You may proceed. You do not need to insist upon your rights, Senator.

Senator WATSON of Georgia. I will not claim any rights of a Senator here, but I will when this matter comes to the Senate.

Mr. CAMPBELL. You may ask your question.

Senator WATSON of Georgia. I was going to ask my constituent, with whom I am very slightly acquainted, and to whose order I do not belong, but which I intend to defend from any unjust attacks from anybody, if he did not know that both the House and the Senate here within the last few weeks have been creating offices by the dozen and by the score that carried salaries all the way from $15,000 to $35,000 as retainers for lawyers who are to be paid special fees for services rendered after these retainers have been paid, and that these fees of $35,000 come out of these taxpayers?

Mr. SIMMONS. I did not know that.

Mr. CAMPBELL. You may proceed, Col. Simmons.

Mr. SIMMONS. I will submit Exhibit E for the record.

(Exhibit E appears elsewhere in this record.)

Mr. SIMMONS. Mr. Chairman and gentlemen of the committee, I would respectfully request the opportunity to go through this phase of the matter now, and I will touch upon it in my recapitulation. I want to touch upon this particular thing, because it has been made so conspicuous here in these hearings that somebody was going to get immensely rich out of the Ku-Klux Klan; $2 of each $10 received as initiation fee or donation—and it is a donation—goes into the general fund of the order; the other $8 goes as a commission to Mr. Clarke, who is at the head of that department. When Mr. Clarke signed this contract, he made the statement just prior to signing it, " Mr. Simmons, it is going to cost a large sum of money to organize or create an organization force. We have no machinery of that nature, and I have got to find men. We will have to spend a lot of time in finding men, and this machinery must be constructed, and it will cost something." The truth of that statement is borne out by the fact, according to my information, that he put $7,000 of his own money into it and borrowed $5,000 more before he got the machinery constructed to begin the work. There is an agreement that if there is a failure on his part, or if he can not make good, he will have no recourse against the order or against myself. In other words, the money that he has advanced in this work would be a loss to him.

Mr. SNELL. How many members have come in in the last 16 months?

Mr. SIMMONS. I was informed from the records on the day I left, as has been brought out here, that there were about 85,000 members. That was the information I received at that time.

Mr. SNELL. How many members have you in the order at the present time?

Mr. SIMMONS. I would state that to you only approximately. I think, gentlemen, that you can readily see that I am not in a position to give exact figures, because I have been away on trips.

Mr. SNELL. Well, up to the time you left.

Mr. SIMMONS. I will give it approximately. My information is that we have in the neighborhood of about from 90,000 to 95,000 members. The statement here quoting Mr. Clarke as saying there were 126,000 members, I think, is incorrect and is in excess of the real number.

Mr. RODENBERG. If my memory serves me correctly, I read in a Chicago newspaper at the time you were in Chicago, but I am not quite clear as to whether or not it was an interview or was supposed to be an extract from one of your addresses, a statement in which you were said to have said that the order had a membership of 750,000.

Mr. SIMMONS. No, sir; I have never made any such statement in my life, because it is untrue.

Mr. RODENBERG. You say you have about 90,000 or 95,000 members?

Mr. SIMMONS. That is my idea of it, or that is approximately the number. Frequently people may ask me how many members we have, and I may say, " We have 1,000,000, but that is said more in jest. That statement is false, like a good many other things that have been printed. Under this contract with Mr. Clarke he must pay all of the expenses of that department. He must pay his field men, and it has been brought out here that the kleagles get $4 for each man brought in. I used to get $8 from another organization years ago. One dollar goes to the State organizer or head of the State, 50 cents goes to the grand goblin, or head of the domain, leaving $2.50 to Mr. Clarke, the imperial kleagle. Out of that $2.50 Mr. Clarke must pay the assistants in his office, including his stenographers, the printing for that department, and all of the other bills incident to the proper functioning of that department. Whatever is left is his compensation for his services.

I might state just here, and I may have occasion to refer to it in my general recapitulation, that Mrs. Tyler is in nowise connected with this order other than as Mr. Clarke's first assistant, or as his business manager in the propagation department. Now, just what contract or arrangement Mr. Clarke made with Mrs. Tyler for that work I do not know. What he pays to the stenographers or to the men working as executives in the propagation department I do not know. Those are contracts that have been made between himself and those whom he has employed in the department. That is his work. This contract that he has with the order is a contract to do a certain piece of work. If he makes good, the contract holds, but if he does not make good, then he is off and another man takes his place, just as in all other matters of business management. None of those fees are excessive. You will find attached to the contract a statement headed "Balance sheet consolidated Knights of the Ku-Klux Klan (Inc.), propagation funds, general fund, October 1, 1921." This shows that it is a business proposition.

I will say this, Mr. Chairman and gentlemen of the committee, that under that contract Mr. Clarke can not go contrary to the rules and regulations, or, in other words, contrary to the governing authority of this order. If anything is done by himself or is authorized by him in the propagation department that is not authorized by this order, it is not a matter of this order. He can not do as he pleases, or chase the imperial wizard around the imperial palace like a dog would a cat.

Exhibit F has reference to the position that this order takes to protect itself against unscrupulous imitators of any and every nature, as, for instance, posting notices signed "K. K. K.," and that sort of nonsensical and disgusting conduct. This statement is reproduced from the local paper of Florence, S. C.

Mr. CAMPBELL. I suggest that you place that statement in the record.

Mr. SIMMONS. All right.

(Exhibit F appears elsewhere in this record.)

Mr. SIMMONS. I wish to state that that is in keeping with the statement I made yesterday. For years we have had a standing offer of a reward of $500 for the arrest of any man illegally using this name.

Now, I submit to you as Exhibit G these pamphlets and documents, and I will refer to them as briefly as possible and pass them to you. This is the "A, B, C," known as the general prospectus of the order. Now, I have marked here an index on the front page referring to the special points so as to facilitate your committee in looking through the documents for matter regarding the character of the organization, and I would respectfully request, in view of the slanders that have been published, that your honorable committee particularly study those passages that have been marked.

Next, I submit the constitution and laws of the Knights of the Ku-Klux Klan, or the governing rules and regulations.

Mr. RODENBERG. You might answer now that question I propounded awhile ago as to your own tenure of office.

Mr. SIMMONS. I will touch upon certain things leading to that particular article. It has been stated that there were no laws that would control the Ku-Klux Klan in America, and that they defied all law, would go into the courthouse and destroy records, etc. Mr. Chairman, that is not true. There is a law that forbids a klansman to violate the law, because he solemnly swears obedience to the law, and no klansman can violate the law and be a man. In a few minutes I want to present to you the ritual of the Ku-Klux Klan, and I shall crave permission to call your attention to a few points in there that have been wrongly stated in the press. Before doing that, however, you might say, "If you expose to us your ritual, will you not be violating your oath?" I can state to you, in reply to that, in the interest of this organization, that at the call of this honorable committee of the Congress of our Government, while seeking this information to help you in your just deliberations, that can be done. and I refer you to section 14, article 9, of the constitution and laws of the order, which provides——

"Whenever a question of paramount importance to the interest, well-being, or prosperity of this order arises, not provided for in this constitution, he [the imperial wizard] shall have full power and authority to determine such question, and his decision shall be final."

We have made no provision in this constitution for a hearing before the congressional Rules Committee, and, therefore what I do here is not covered by the constitution. Mr. Chairman, I have come to the point where I believe that for the interest and prosperity of this organization and for the interest of the American people a question has arisen not provided for in this constitution, and I stand before you to exercise my imperial prerogative and determine that question, and my answer shall be final. In doing that I am going to present to you and to your honorable committee the ritual of this organization, together with the oath, and I shall discuss that briefly so that you may go into them and analyze them. On page 6 you will find the Ku-Klux kreed, and I wish you would read that carefully, because that is an epitome of our belief. On page 8, in article 2, you will find the objects and purpose, and I have marked sections 1 and 3. Article 3 relates to the territorial jurisdiction, assemblies, etc. Mr. Chairman, I would like to read two or three of these sections, because I believe they are of paramount importance; and even though suffering as I am I am willing to go through the exertion necessary to do this. I do that in order that you may have before your committee statements to assist you in interpeting this matter. A great deal has been said here about the objects and purposes of this order, and I will read these extracts to you:

" SECTION 1. The objects of this order shall be to unite only white male persons, native-born Gentile citizens of the United States of America, who owe no allegiance of any nature or degree to any foreign Government, nation, institution, sect, ruler, person, or people; whose morals are good; whose reputations and vocations are respectable; whose habits are exemplary; who are of sound minds; and at or above the age of 18 years, under a common oath into a common brotherhood of strict regulations for the purpose of cultivating and promoting real patriotism toward our civil government; to practice an honorable clannishness toward each other; to exemplify a practical benevolence; to shield the sanctity of the home and the chastity of womanhood; to forever maintain white supremacy; to teach and faithfully inculcate a high spiritual philosophy through an exalted ritualism, and by a practical devotedness to conserve, protect, and maintain the distinctive institutions, rights, privileges, principles, traditions, and ideals of a pure Americanism."

Mr. Chairman, how can any man presume to state to the world, in newspapers or otherwise, that this is an un-American or an anti-American organization? In one place there the statement is made, " To forever maintain white supremacy." That is being taken as an indication that the organization has for its mission the practice of violence and injustice toward other races and colors. That is not so. The supremacy of the white man means the supremacy of the white man's mind as evidenced by the achievements of our civilization. That is the supremacy that is taught by the klan, its object being to preserve the dignity and achievements of the white race in justice, fairness, and equity toward all of the human family.

Mr. RODENBERG. How would you maintain white supremacy, or what means would you adopt in maintaining it?

Mr. SIMMONS. That is simply the enunciation of a principle. Now, in the application of any principle no one can tell just how the principle can be applied, but, as you can see from the connection there, it would be in keeping with our ideals and institutions. It would be in keeping with the principles of Americanism, or, in other words, it would be done in a patriotic and just way.

Mr. RODENBERG. Would it be left to the local klan to adopt such methods as they thought fit for the maintenance of white supremacy?

Mr. SIMMONS. No, sir; methods of that nature would be handled by the governing authority of the organization. It is not, as has been published to the world, a matter of race hatred, but it is simply the principle of race pride, which we accord to all races, but which we have the right to assert in the enunciation of that principle with regard to our own race. You have never heard me, Mr. Chairman and gentlemen of the committee, enunciate one word marked by race hatred, nor have I sent out any such statement.

Mr. FESS. The first Ku-Klux Klan, or order of the Ku-Klux Klan, operated back in Civil War times, when the invisible empire had some historical significance and when its object was more or less in question. The purpose of it, as understood throughout the country, was rather racial, and the investigation that followed later and the act on of the Government all involved considerable mystery about the Ku-Klux Klan. Now, the revival of that name attached to any order in which you use the term "white supremacy" naturally makes one go back to that day. Is the purpose of this order anything like that of the invisible empire back in Civil War times?

Mr. SIMMONS. You mean in its operations and in its modus operandi?

Mr. FESS. Yes.

Mr. SIMMONS. No, sir; we have no conditions existing now that would justify such a modus operandi. This is purely a fraternal and patriotic organization, and is in no sense a regulative or corrective organization.

These particular points to which I have asked your attention are marked, and I know that you gentlemen will carefully consider them. I wish to speak of them here because it has been charged that we are creating an invisible government, or a supergovernment, and are trying to get control of the affairs of the Government. Some superstitious person has certainly become scared at the whining of a cat. This phrase, "invisible empire," is merely a designation, memorial in its character, but it is simply a name applied to the universal jurisdiction of the organization. For instance, take one fraternal order that specifies its state jurisdiction as "grand domain," and so on. They all have these particular designations and have a right to adopt them. It is perfectly absurd for anybody to even think we are creating an invisible force to sneak around at night and commit acts of depredation or intimidation against people against whom we hold malice. That is extremely ridiculous and without any foundation. In spiritual application this invisible empire applies to the great invisible empire of the invisible God.

Article 4, section 1—I wish to read this and then I will pass on rapidly. This has reference to qualification for membership. It is a short paragraph:

"The qualification for membership in this order shall be as follows: An applicant must be a white, male, Gentile person, a native-born citizen of the United States of America, who owes no allegiance of any nature or degree whatsoever to any foreign government, nation, institution, sect, ruler, prince, potentate, people, or person "——

Mr. CAMPBELL (interposing). Did you not just read that, Colonel?

Mr. SIMMONS. No, sir; this is a little different from the other. This comes under the head of "membership."

"He must be at or above the age of 18 years, of sound mind, good character, of commendable reputation and respectable vocation, a believer in the tenets of the Christian religion, and whose allegiance, loyalty, and devotion to the Government of the United States of America in all things is unquestionable."

I can not see any anti-Americanism in that, and if it be pro-Americanism, which necessarily it has got to be if it is not anti-Americanism—if it be pro-Americanism, why should various religious creeds or devotees or people of various racial lines be uneasy and scared to death? If it is pro-Americanism, it is pro-Americanism.

Mr. POU. Would just one question disturb you, Colonel?

Mr. SIMMONS. No, sir; go right aread, sir.

Mr. POU. My Americanism teaches me not to despise any man because of his color or his race or his condition in life. Now, does not the very fact that by your constitution and by-laws you exclude certain large proportions of American citizenship—does or does not that of itself tend to teach a narrow Americanism rather than a broad Americanism? I would like to have your explanation of your constitution in this respect.

Mr. SIMMONS. No, sir. If your honor please, this is a standard fraternal order. Your question provokes an answer that I intended to take up in my closing talk, but I will take it up here in this connection. This is a fraternal order. Every fraternal order has a right to fix a standard for members.

Mr. POU. Surely; to receive and exclude whomsoever they please.

Mr. SIMMONS. Every man has a right to say who shall come into his home and enjoy the free hospitality of his home. The Knights of the Ku-Klux Klan exclude from its membership no man on account of religious creeds or alignments in his personal devotion to the great God. Is the Knights of the Ku-Klux Klan, may I raise the question, the only organization that has a restricted membership? Is not the great order of Knight Templars in Masonry an organization that has a restricted membership? Is not the great Junior Order of United American Mechanics an organization that has a restricted membership? Is not the organization of Knights of Columbus of America an organization that has a restricted membership so that no one but those who subscribe to the Catholic creed can be admitted? The great orders of the Jews in this country, do not they have a restricted membership, and no one can join those organizations unless they be devotedly of the Jewish faith.

Is the Christian Church in America an unjust and a bigoted organization because they will admit no one, whether it be Methodist, Baptist, Catholic, or Protestant, or any others, to the fellowship of their congregations unless that person subscribes to the tenets of the Christian religion? Gentlemen, this proposition has been flaunted across the pages of the newspapers of this country, and the bigotry in all this is in those movements behind the newspapers that have persecuted and are persecuting, by slanderous statements, an organization that in so far as a human organization can possibly be, is as pure in its intention as the drifted snows on the crest of the mountain tops; and I ask you, Mr. Chairman and gentlemen of your committee and all the American people, to lay aside all this dust and stir that has come up and all the sensation that has been created for the purpose of engendering and stirring up ill feeling, to see the facts in the case and let the jury of the great American public decide, and I will repose my case in that instance in the conscience and the unsullied honor and in the sober judgment of the American people.

Again let me repeat, there are many, many fraternal orders in this country that have and hold restricted memberships. Then why can not this organization, by its standard, be accorded the same privileges without any prejudice or without any vile accusation hurled against it? I can not see, in all sober justice.

The imperial kloncilium, my dear sir, you called attention to that a moment ago—article 6, section 1:

"The imperial kloncilium shall be the supreme advisory board of this order and shall be composed of all the imperial officers named in article 7 below.

"SEC. 2. The imperial kloncilium shall be the supreme court or tribunal of justice of this order and shall have full appellate jurisdiction and shall hear and determine all appeals of whatever nature presented to it from realm, provinces, klans, and from members of this order.

"SEC. 3. It shall have full power and authority, acting in the presence of the imperial wizard, to act in any and all matters until the imperial klonvokation is called into its initial session and duly organized, and in the interim thereafter. Any and all of its acts of a legislative nature shall become effective as law upon the ratification of same by the imperial wizard of this order."

The imperial klonvokation is the supreme legislative body, and in the interim——

Mr. RODENBERG (interposing). Every klan will have representation there?

Mr. SIMMONS. Yes, sir; that will be of a more representative nature; that is, every klan or every certain number of klans within a district. We do not want to have in that meeting too many representatives so as to make it too expensive; that is, we want to make our government as economical as possible; but it will be arranged on a representative basis. I get your point.

This goes on down and refers to the imperial officers and then refers to the imperial wizard, and section 2 of article 8 says:

"The imperial wizard shall hold office for life or during good behavior."

As long as the old horse is pulling well, it is no use to take him out of the harness when you have him harnessed up. He can not do you any harm.

Mr. RODENBERG. I had in mind that the title of emperor would carry with it life tenure.

Mr. SIMMONS. Yes, sir; but my friend, that title of emperor has to do only with a mere title, affecting the bridge work or the ceremonial work of the organization. It is ridiculous for intelligent newspapers and people to jump on that old word "emperor" and try to make a great show out of it. I can not understand that sometimes, but I am coming to this point:

"He may be removed for just cause"—it has been thrown over the United States and the hearts of good men and women have been stirred about the fact that he is there with an iron rod in his hand and no power under heaven can remove him.

"He may be removed for just cause by a unanimous vote of the imperial kloncilium, or after charges have been preferred and a trial upon a three-fourths vote of said body in session assembled."

Mr. Chairman, you see that this old wizard has got to be good if he wishes to be a wizard.

Then comes the article relating to duties, prerogatives, and so on, kleagles and giants, and regalia, costumes, and so on, and things of a different nature.

Mr. FESS. Who calls together the klonvokation or the kloncilium?

Mr. SIMMONS. The imperial kloncilium?

Mr. FESS. Yes; how do they get together?

Mr. SIMMONS. Well, it is just like being a committee or advisory board or just like your committee. The chairman calls it and the imperial wizard is the chairman of this advisory board and executive committee.

Mr. FESS. As I understand it, the imperial wizard creates the kloncilium until you get into working operation?

Mr. SIMMONS. Yes, sir; that is provided for.

Mr. FESS. Then, when will that klonvokation be called, and who calls it?

Mr. SIMMONS. You understand, Mr. Chairman and gentlemen of the committee, this organization is in the act of being born. You can not compare the actual working of this organization like you can these old fraternal orders that have been here for a hundred years. It is in a creative or creating state, and this method has been carefully adopted and worked out as the most practical and economical way of handling the organization until such time in the development of the organization as we can have a supreme body; in other words, until we have enough surplus money to call this body together in its initial session.

Mr. FESS. I understand that, but it appears to me that the imperial wizard is " it " and will be " it " until he decides not to be.

Mr. SIMMONS. No, sir; he will be " it " until he is thrown out by prostituting his character or for any just cause.

Mr. FESS. By whom?

Mr. SIMMONS. By the kloncilium, as specified in this law.

Mr. FESS. In a klonvokation; and who calls that?

Mr. SIMMONS. That klonvokation can be called, if it is for the trial of the imperial wizard, as to his character or his incompetency—it can be called by any person and be demanded.

Mr. FESS. Is not the kloncilium still under you?

Mr. SIMMONS. Yes, sir; it is now under me and of me. I am the chairman of it.

Mr. FESS. How long will that be; until you decide otherwise, is not that true?

Mr. SIMMONS. Until I decide what otherwise?

Mr. FESS. That it will not be under you. Are you not the whole thing?

Mr. SIMMONS. Oh, no; not altogether.

Mr. FESS. It strikes me you are.

Mr. SIMMONS. Yes, sir; that is true; but I judge that your conception of this thing is not clear, because you have possibly not had any experience with fraternal organizations and work. Now, sir, as I stated awhile ago, I had planned to call the imperial klonvokation this coming Thanksgiving Day in the development of things; and I can state to you this, sir, that in all the development of this work I am absolutely unselfish, unambitious, and sincere, and that that klonvokation shall be called at the very earliest possible moment.

Mr. CAMPBELL. After all, that is a matter in which the public has very little interest.

Mr. SIMMONS. None whatever.

Mr. CAMPBELL. That is a matter that concerns the members of the organization.

Mr. ETHERIDGE. Mr. Chairman, may I direct the colonel's attention to one point in the constitution which I think answers the question of the committee, and that is the provision in the constitution for the regular annual meeting of the governing body as provided in the constitution.

Mr. SIMMONS. Yes; they will find that in here.

Mr. CAMPBELL. That is not a matter of public concern.

Mr. FESS. Mr. Chairman, I think it is a matter of great public concern whether this organization is an organization with one man with supreme authority to do just as he pleases with it or whether the members of that organization have that authority; in other words, whether the membership is under him rather than him being under the membership. I think that has everything to do with it.

Mr. CAMPBELL. It is a matter in which the members have a very vital interest.

Mr. SIMMONS. Mr. Chairman, I have done my best to make that clear and when you get to this point in your studies of this matter, if you desire further light on it, I believe you will call upon me to get it, and you will get it, but let this thought stay in your minds in considering this, this organization has not yet perfected its governmental functions. It is approaching that stage but has not quite got to it. That is the point I wish to make. We have not perfected it. We are perfecting, but we have not yet perfected the governing or the character of that particular work and its functions, and how it shall function. We are simply constructing and developing and working on to it. These facts have been scattered out and the constitution and laws have been in the hands of the klan and the members and there has not been any objection from the inside so far that I know of, of any nature.

Now, the kloncilium meets every year in its regular annual sessions, as you will find in here, and we discuss things together. We are all together in that in order to get at the best methods and policies to pursue.

Now, I will call your attention to sections 25 and 26 of article 17. This is a point I want to get clearly before your committee because it is way down at the end of this and you might run over it:

"A klan, or a member of this order, must not use the official costume, or any part of same, of this order on any occasion or for any purpose other than in ceremony of this order, or in an official klavalkade—that is, a parade—under penalty of forfeiture of charter of the klan or of expulsion from this order of the member."

"SEC. 26. No klan, and no member of this order, shall use the name of this order or any part thereof for any purpose that contravenes in any manner the laws of the land, or in any manner that will in any way reflect, or probably reflect upon the reputation and good name of this order, or compromise, or injure this order, or any member of this order, in any way."

That is our law, and all true men in our klan have sworn to stand by this law. There are others, possibly, who would not, but then they are not true.

Now, Mr. Chairman, there is one more point I want to refer to and then I will pass this into your hands, and that is, "Offenses and penalties," under our laws, article 19, section 1. I am not going to read all of this but just particular points.

Mr. CAMPBELL. Would you just as soon suspend now and resume at 2 o'clock?

Mr. SIMMONS. Mr. Chairman, it will take me possibly five minutes to finish this part of the exhibit:

"Offenses against this order deserving penalty shall be: Treason against the United States of America."

The statement was made before your hearing, sir, that this organization had been guilty of sending matters of treason or sending treasonous matter through the mail. The first thing here is treason against the United States of America.

"Violating the oath of allegiance or any supplementary oaths or obligations thereto of this order; criminal act or acts proven; disregard of public decency"—gentlemen, these are the offenses deserving penalty—"disregard of public decency, disrespect for virtuous womanhood * * * excessive drunkenness in public places, drunkenness or drinking intoxicating liquors during a klonklave or on the premises thereof, or entering a klonklave in an intoxicated condition," and so on.

Then here is a grave offense against this order:

"Swearing allegiance to or otherwise becoming a citizen or subject of any nation, or subject of any nation, government, or institution of any nature or classification, or any ruler, potentate, prince, or person, or any cause whatsoever that is foreign to or is inimical to the Government of the United States of America and its established institutions, or aiding or abetting such a government, nation, institution, ruler, potentate, prince, or person against the interest, well-being, or dignity of the United States of America or the distinctive institutions of its government."

Gentlemen of the committee, how can any man speak the truth and say this is an un-American, anti-American, anarchistic crowd or gang? I have read you from the supreme law of the organization, and I respectfully submit for your careful consideration this constitution and laws of the order.

Mr. SNELL. We will now adjourn the hearing until 2 o'clock this afternoon.

AFTER RECESS.

Mr. CAMPBELL. Colonel, we will resume.

Mr. SIMMONS. Mr. Chairman and gentlemen of the committee, I want to assure you that I am going to be as hasty as possible, because I am suffering. Before taking up the other exhibits I wish to thank the committee for the fair and impartial manner of its hearing and its most kind consideration of me on account of my physical condition, for which, sir, I am profoundly grateful.

In answering Dr. Fess's question this morning, regarding the meeting of the grand klonklave and the governing body of the Ku-Kiux Klan, I desire to correct the impression that the committee may have received and to clearly bring out the fact that to-day, and as the klan has been operating during the past, the grand kloncilium is the governing body, is composed of 16 members from all sections of the United States—that is, from many of the States—and that this body meets at a regular date set forth in the constitution and does not meet only on call of the imperial wizard. It can also be called at any time by any member and the body can then remove the imperial wizard from office for cause. The impression was that this body could only be called to meet by me and that if I refused to call the meeting my tenure of office was for life.

The first grand kloncilium was appointed by me and other officials of the klan in consultation, and in an effort to get the best body of men that could be found. The next imperial kloncilium will probably be elected in November or December of this year, when the imperial klonvokation, the supreme legislative body, is called together in its initial session and organized.

The grand klonklave is entirely different from the grand kloncilium in that it has not yet met, as just stated. That is the supreme legislative body. The imperial klonvokation is composed of delegates elected from each klan or a district in the United States. These delegates are elected by the vote of the individual organizations.

The grand kloncilium in meeting, as the klan is at present being conducted, authorizes all expenditures of money, appropriations, etc. The kloncilium authorized the Lanier University matter, and no money is spent, outside of the regular expenses, without the authority of this body. I respectfully call your attention to the charter issued by the superior court of Fulton County, which authorizes the procedure we have followed.

Mr. Chairman and gentlemen of the committee, I will resume the exhibits, and this is the finish of Exhibit G. I desire to briefly call your attention to a few paragraphs, because a wrong impression has been given to the people by reports contained in the papers, which picked certain things out of this book but did not publish it all, as they should have done. This is a marked copy of our ritual and the pages are marked, to which you can refer.

A klonklave or meeting of a local organization has, at its opening, a devotional ceremony. I want to state to you, sir, that the opening of a meeting of a local organization, which is known as a klonklave, can not be opened in regular order unless the sacred altar is properly prepared. To properly prepare that sacred altar the flag of our country must be unfurled and placed at the altar. The altar is draped with the Stars and Stripes. Upon the altar is a vessel of water, which is the dedicating fluid, an unsheathed sword, which represents the ability of American citizens to strike in defense of the flag, and upon that altar, sir, is the Holy Bible, opened at the twelfth chapter of Romans. Every oath administered in that meeting is on the Holy Bible. Of course, when we have large classes coming in all can not actually touch it, but the Holy Bible is open upon the altar and the oath is administered on that sacred book.

I call your attention to the opening song, which breathes every sentiment of fraternity, of honor, love, justice, and sublime patriotism for our common country.

The newspapers published broadcast, with a strain of ridicule, the next to the last passage of our opening prayer, where it says:

" We invoke Thy blessings upon our emperor."

They did not publish, sir, in justice to this organization, the paragraph just above it, which I will read:

" God save our Nation! And help us to be a Nation worthy of existence on the earth. Keep ablaze in each klansman's heart the sacred fire of a devoted patriotism to our country and its Government."

Mr. Chairman, I do not believe there is another organization on earth, of a fraternal nature, that has those words and that sentiment expressed as forcibly as in the prayer of the Ku-Klux Klan. I wish to ask you to review this prayer when you have the time to take it up. It is especially marked.

In the closing ceremony the question is always asked:

" Faithful klaliff, what is the fourfold duty of a klansman? "

He answers:

"To worship God: be patriotic toward our country; be devoted and loyal to our klan and emperor, and to practice clannishness toward his fellow klansmen."

The faithful kludd is asked:

"How speaketh the oracles of our God?"

The answer is:

"Thou shalt worship the Lord thy God. Render unto the State the things which are the State's. Love the brotherhood; honor the king. Bear ye one another's burdens, and so fulfill the law of Christ."

These are quotations from the book. I call your attention to the coising klode or the closing song, and it reads:

"God of eternity
Guard, guide our great country,
Our homes and store.
Keep our great State to Thee,
Its people right and free;
In us Thy glory be
Forevermore."

There are other marked passages but I am hastening through as I am suffering with my throat. From page 25 permit me, sir, to read briefly that which appears under the title "Qualifying Interrogatories." These are read to the man in an outer anteroom when he is presenting himself there to be initiated and before he comes in:

"SIRS: The Knights of the Ku-Klux Klan, as a great and essentially a patriotic, fraternal, benevolent order, do not discriminate against a man on account of his religious or political creed, when same does not conflict with or antagonize the sacred rights and privileges guaranteed by our civil Government and Christian ideals and institutions.

"Therefore, to avoid any misunderstanding, and as evidence that we do not seek to impose unjustly the requirements of this order upon anyone who can not, on account of his religious or political scruples, voluntarily meet our requirements and faithfully practice our principles, and as proof that we respect all honest men in their sacred convictions, whether same are agreeable with our requirements or not, we require as an absolute necessity on the part of each of you an affirmative answer to each of the following questions:

"Is the motive prompting your ambition to be a klansman serious and unselfish?"

That is to ascertain whether a man comes there out of curiosity or is serious, and the questions must be answered with an emphatic "Yes."

"Are you absolutely opposed to and free of any allegiance of any nature to any cause, government, people, sect, or ruler that is foreign to the United States of America?

"Do you esteem the United States of America and its institutions above any other Government, civil, political, or ecclesiastical, in the whole world?

"Will you, without mental reservation, take a solemn oath to defend, preserve, and enforce same?

"Will you faithfully obey our constitution and laws and conform willingly to all our usages, requirements, and regulations?

"Can you be always depended on?

There are other questions, but those I call to your especial attention. If he gives an affirmative answer to these questions, then the ceremony proceeds; if not, we respectfully request that he retire and the donation he has made goes back to that man more freely than it came from him.

Mr. GARRETT. You say there are other questions?

Mr. SIMMONS. Yes. I can read them all, if you wish. There are 10 questions in all.

Mr. GARRETT. I think it might be well enough to read them.

Mr. SIMMONS. All?

Mr. GARRETT. All.

Mr. SIMMONS. Very well, sir. I will read every one of the 10, inclusive.

Mr. GARRETT. You have read four already.

Mr. SIMMONS. I will go back, because I do not want to skip any of them:

"Are you a native-born, white, gentile American citizen?"

In regard to that, Mr. Chairman, permit me to say that we will not accept in our order any man who can not meet our requirements.

Mr. RODENBERG. In other words, you mean by that you exclude the Jews?

Mr. SIMMONS. Yes; for the Jews do not believe in the tenets of a Christian organization, and we exclude them as other organizations exclude them. Another question that I went over:

"Do you believe in clannishness, and will you faithfully practice same toward klansmen?"

The oath, you will notice, says, "honorable clannishness." The definition of that word is simply practical fraternity; in other words, brotherhood.

"Do you believe in and will you faithfully strive for the eternal maintenance of white supremacy?"

That question was brought up this morning, and I gave an explanation of it. I believe those are all that I have overlooked; I have read the others. That is a preliminary. Here is a thing especially impressed upon a candidate before he enters the room:

"The distinguishing marks of a klansman are not found in the fiber of his garments or his social or financial standing but are spiritual, namely, a chivalric head, a compassionate heart, a prudent tongue, and a courageous will. All devoted to our country, our klan, our homes, and each other; these are the distinguishing marks of a klansman."

Again it reads:

"A klansman speaketh the truth in and from his heart. A lying scoundrel may wrap his disgraceful frame within the sacred folds of a klansman's robe and deceive the very elect, but only a klansman possesses a klansman's heart and a klansman's soul."

I call your attention to the prayer of the klan, which has been ridiculed in the press, a part of which I got several years ago from a clipping. I found afterwards that it was written by a man named Holland. It is paraphrased a little bit. It is Holland's famous poem, "God give us men," and we teach this wonderful poem to those who come into this organization. The words, "the invisible empire," are substituted for the words of Mr. Holland's poem, "a time like this." It reads:

"God give us men! The invisible empire demands strong
Minds, great hearts, true faith, and ready hands.
Men whom the lust of office does not kill;
Men whom the spoils of office can not buy;
Men who possess opinions and a will;
Men who have honor; men who will not lie;
Men who can stand before a demagogue
And damn his treacherous flatteries without winking!
Tall men, sun crowned, who live above the fog
In public duty and in private thinking;
For while the rabble, with their thumb-worn creeds,
Their large professions, and their little deeds,
Mingle in selfish strife, lo! freedom weeps,
Wrong rules the land, and waiting justice sleeps.
God give us men!"

That ends Mr. Holland's poem, and then I have added myself:

"Men who serve not for selfish booty,
But real men, courageous, who flinch not at duty;
Men of dependable character; men of sterling worth;
Then wrongs will be redressed, and right will rule the earth.
God give us men!"

Then the candidate who hears that prayer of the klan is asked this question:

"Sir, will you by your daily life as a klansman earnestly endeavor to be an answer to this prayer?"

He must answer in the affirmative or else he is turned back. Now, here is the charge to the candidate as he comes in, and, Mr. Chairman, I will just refer to this briefly. In other words, this is the charge that he is given, and we are now entering into what we are teaching in our secret meetings, so called, and every fraternal organization has a right to teach its principles to the members who come in.

When he is presented the question is asked:

"Is the motive prompting your presence here serious and unselfish?"

Then the charge:

" It is indeed refreshing to meet face to face with men (or a man) like you, who, actuated by manly motives, aspire to all things noble for yourselves and humanity.

" The luster of the holy light of chivalry has lost its former glory and is sadly dimmed by the choking dust of selfish, sordid gain.

" Real fraternity, by shameful neglect, has been starved until so weak her voice is lost in the courts of her own castle, and she passes unnoticed by her sworn subjects as she moves along the crowded streets and through the din of the market place. Man's valuation of man is by the standard of wealth and not worth; selfishness is the festive queen among human kind, and multitudes forget honor, justice, love, and God, and every religious conviction to do homage to her, and yet with the cruel heart of Jezebel she slaughters the souls of thousands of her devotees daily.

" The unsatiated thirst for gain is dethroning reason and judgment in the citadel of the human soul, and men, maddened thereby, forget their patriotic, domestic, and social obligations and duties and fiendishly fight for a place in the favor of the goddess of glittering gold; they starve their own souls and make sport of spiritual development."

The final charge by the chaplain is:

> " Men speak of love and live in hate,
> Men talk of faith and trust to fate,
> Oh, might men do the things they teach!
> Oh, might men live the life they preach!
> Then the throne of avarice would fall, and the clangor
> Of grim selfishness o'er the earth would cease;
> Love would tread out the baleful fire of anger,
> And in its ashes plant the lily of peace."

The final charge by the exalted cyclops is, in part:

" The prime purpose of this great order is to develop character "——

And here, Mr. Chairman, every man is acquainted with the purpose of this order:

" The prime purpose of this great order is to develop character, practice clannishness, to protect the home and the chastity of womanhood, and to exemplify a pure patriotism toward our glorious country.

" You as citizens of the invisible empire must be actively patriotic toward our country and constantly clannish toward klansmen socially, physically, morally, and vocationally; will you assume this obligation of citizenship?"

Then he is told that this is a serious undertaking, that we are not running a circus or clown playing, and at the windup of this charge he is informed of the fact that if he does not feel himself qualified to measure up to the ideals of this institution he is privileged to retire. He can walk out if he wishes. I want to state to you, sirs, that there are no means or methods resorted to by which any man who enters the portals of the invisible empire is intimidated; every man comes in in possession of all his natural faculties; he is not even blindfolded; he is not even intimidated in any way by grewsome scenes or spectacular exhibits; he comes voluntarily and as an American citizen and as a man in possession of all his faculties; and he takes the obligation of the klan in the presence of the holy Bible.

Mr. CAMPBELL. Do the members of the klan at that time wear the mask?

Mr. SIMMONS. Oh, yes; that is in the spectacular scene, you see, because he is a stranger and there is a stranger in their presence.

Now, I have gotten to the point where I am going to present the oath. I want to impress upon your minds that this oath is administered before the sacred altar at which there is unfurled and mounted the American flag; the altar is draped with the sacred, open Bible, the unsheathed sword, and the vessel of dedicating fluids, which is water, not from the Chattahoochee River, however, and it is not sent from there in sacred cans either.

Mr. GARRETT. Mr. Chairman, before the gentleman presents that, I ask unanimous consent that the committee stand in recess for five minutes.

(A recess was taken, after which the chairman said:)

Mr. CAMPBELL. Col. Simmons, after a brief consultation with the members of the committee, I simply want to say, on behalf of the committee, that we do not want you to feel that the committee requires you at this time to give this oath. We simply leave to you the question as to whether or not you shall give it.

Mr. SIMMONS. Mr. Chairman, I appreciate that courtesy on the part of your committee, and I am ready to submit this oath to your hands, sir.

Mr. CAMPBELL. You may proceed, then.

Mr. SIMMONS. I would like to read just the last part of it, which is of vital interest to the American people and which has not been called attention to in the press:

"I will be truly clannish toward klansmen in all things honorable."

Regarding the keeping of secrets of a klansman, as provided in this secret bond of klansmen, and as proved by this oath that this is not a treasonous organization or inimical to the Government of the United States, I wish to say that the secrets of a klansman are sacred except in four points: Any man who violates this oath, any man who commits treason against the United States of America, rape, and malicious murder. These are excepted. If I should commit an act of treason against this Government and should tell another member of this organization, it would be his bounden duty to turn me over to the authorities at the earliest possible date, or if I should commit any of these other things. Now, then, the last two paragraphs, in conclusion:

"I most solemnly assert and affirm that to the Government of the United States of America and any State thereof of which I may become a resident I sacredly swear an unqualified allegiance above any other and every kind of government in the whole world. I here and now pledge my life, my property, my vote, and my sacred honor to uphold its flag, its Constitution and constitutional laws, and will protect, defend, and enforce same unto death.

"I swear that I will most zealously and valiantly shield and preserve by any and all justifiable means and methods the sacred constitutional rights and privileges of free public schools, free speech, free press, separation of church and state, liberty, white supremacy, just laws, and the pursuit of happiness against any encroachment of any nature by any person or persons, political party or parties, religous sect or people, native, naturalized, or foreign of any race, color, creed, lineage, or tongue whatsoever.

"All to which I have sworn by this oath, I will seal with my blood, be Thou my witness, Almighty God."

In asking for a charter for this organization we specifically requested that this organization should have authority to administer an oath and that was granted. I tell you, Mr. Chairman, it would be hard for me to believe a man on any oath who, under the circumstances of his admission to the klan, without any intimidation but voluntarily, assumes that oath to his country, and to that which is right will violate it willfully and maliciously.

(The complete oath follows:)

(1)

You will place your left hand over your heart and raise your right hand to heaven.

OATH OF ALLEGIANCE.

SECTION 1. *Obedience.*—You will say "I," pronounce your full name, and repeat after me: "In the presence of God and man, most solemnly pledge, promise, and swear, unconditionally, that I will faithfully obey the constitution and laws and will willingly conform to all regulations, usages, and requirements of the * * * which do now exist or which may be hereafter enacted, and will render at all times loyal respect and steadfast support to the imperial authority of same, and will heartily heed all official mandates, decrees, edicts, rulings, and instructions of the I* W* thereof. I will yield prompt response to all summonses, I having knowledge of same, Providence alone preventing."

SEC. 2. *Secrecy.*—"I most solemnly swear that I will forever keep sacredly secret the signs, words, and grip, and any and all other matters and knowledge of the * * * regarding which a most rigid secrecy must be maintained, which may at any time be communicated to me, and will never divulge same nor even cause the same to be divulged to any person in the whole world unless I know positively that such person is a member of this order in good and regular standing, and not even then unless it be for the best interest of this order.

"I most sacredly vow and most positively swear that I will never yield to bribe, flattery, threats, passion, punishment, persecution, persuasion, nor any enticements whatever coming from or offered by any person or persons, male or female, for the purpose of obtaining from me a secret or secret information of the * * *. I will die rather than divulge same, so help me God. Amen!"

You will drop your hands.

Gentlemen (or sir), you will wait in patience and peace until you are informed of the decision of the E* C* and his * * * in klonklave assembled.

---

(2)

You will place your left hand over your heart and raise your right hand to heaven.

OATH OF ALLEGIANCE.

SEC. 3. *Fidelity.*—You will say "I," pronounce your full name, and repeat after me: "Before God and in the presence of these mysterious *smen, on my sacred honor do most solemnly and sincerely pledge, promise and swear, that I will diligently guard and faithfully foster every interest of the * * * and will maintain its social cast and dignity.

"I swear that I will never recommend any person for membership in this order whose mind is unsound or whose reputation I know to be bad or whose character is doubtful or whose loyalty to our country is in any way questionable.

"I swear that I will pay promptly all just and legal demands made upon me to defray the expenses of my * * * and this order when same are due or called for.

"I swear that I will protect the property of the * * * of any nature whatsoever, and if any should be intrusted to my keeping I will properly keep or rightly use same, and will freely and promptly surrender same on official demand; or if ever I am banished from or voluntarily discontinue my membership in this order.

"I swear that I will most determinedly maintain peace and harmony in all the deliberations of the gatherings or assemblies of the I* E* and of any subordinate jurisdiction or * * * thereof.

"I swear that I will most strenuously discourage selfishness and selfish political ambition on the part of myself or any *sman.

"I swear that I will never allow personal friendship, blood or family relationship, nor personal, political, or professional prejudice, malice, nor ill will to influence me in casting my vote for the election or rejection of an applicant for membership in this order, God being my helper. Amen!"

You will drop your hands.

---

(3)

You will place your left hand over your heart and raise your right hand to heaven.

OATH OF ALLEGIANCE.

SEC. 4. *ishness.*—You will say "I," pronounce your full name, and repeat after me "Most solemnly pledge, promise, and swear that I will never slander, defraud, deceive, or in any manner wrong the * * * a *sman nor a *sman's family, nor will I suffer the same to be done if I can prevent it.

"I swear that I will be faithful in defending and protecting the home, reputation, and physical and business interest of a *sman and that of a *sman's family.

"I swear that I will at any time without hesitating go to the assistance or rescue of a *sman in any way; at his call I will answer. I will be truly *ish toward *smen in all things honorable.

"I swear that I will never allow any animosity, friction, nor ill will to arise and remain between myself and a *sman, but will be constant in my efforts to promote real *ishness among the members of this order.

"I swear that I will keep secure to myself a secret of a *sman when same is committed to me in the sacred bond of *smanship, the crime of violating this solemn oath, treason against the United States of America, rape, and malicious murder alone excepted.

"I most solemnly assert and affirm that to the Government of the United States of America and any State thereof of which I may become a resident, I sacredly swear an unqualified allegiance above any other and every kind of government in the whole world. I here and now pledge my life, my property, my vote, and my sacred honor to uphold its flag, its Constitution and constitutional laws, and will protect, defend, and enforce same unto death.

"I swear that I will most zealously and valiantly shield and preserve by any and all justifiable means and methods the sacred constitutional rights and privileges of free public schools, free speech, free press, separation of church and state, liberty, white supremacy, just laws, and the pursuit of happiness against any encroachment of any nature by any person or persons, political party or parties, religious sect or people, native, naturalized, or foreign of any race, color, creed, lineage, or tongue whatsoever.

"All to which I have sworn by this oath, I will seal with my blood, be thou my witness, Almighty God. Amen!"

You will drop your hands.

Now, I am concluding this in just a moment. After the oath has been administered, there is the ceremony of dedication, and this question is asked:

"Sirs, have you assumed without mental reservation your oath of allegiance to the invisible empire?"

He answers, "Yes." Then this statement follows:

"Mortal man can not assume a more binding oath; character and courage alone will enable you to keep it. Always remember that to keep this oath means to you honor, happiness, and life; but to violate it means disgrace, dishonor, and death. May honor, happiness, and life be yours."

Mr. Chairman, just a word there: Is this the only organization of a fraternal nature that administers an oath? We are charged with being an oath-bound secret organization, and we have also been charged with pronouncing the penalty of death. Mr. Chairman, this word "death" in the dedication ceremonies refers to death to the invisible empire, or, in other words, complete expulsion forever from it. So far as he is a member of this organization, he is no more. That is what it means.

Mr. RODENBERG. It does not mean physical death?

Mr. SIMMONS. No, sir; not in any sense of the word, and it is ridiculous to presume that.

Now then, in the concluding part of this dedication ceremony this statement is made:

"As a klansman may your character be as transparent, your life purpose as powerful, your motive in all things as magnanimous and as pure, and your klanishness as real and as faithful as the manifold drops herein, and you a vital being as useful to humanity as is pure water to mankind."

Then follows the act of dedication under the fiery cross in these words:

"I dedicate you in body, in mind, in spirit, and in life to the holy service of our country, our klan, our homes, each other, and humanity."

To that end he is dedicated. Then, comes the dedicatory prayer, as follows:

"Now, Oh God! We, through Thy goodness, have here dedicated with thine own divine distilled fluid these manly men at the altar kneeling, who have been moved by worthy motives and impelled by noble impulses to turn from selfishness and fraternal alienation, and to espouse with body, mind, spirit, and life the holy service of our country, our klan, our home, and each other—we beseech Thee to dedicate them with the fullness of Thy spirit, keep him true to his sacred, solemn oath to our noble cause, to the glory of Thy great name. Amen!"

Then, at the final windup, this statement is made:

"My fellow klansman: The insignia or mark of a klansman is honor. All secrets and secret information of the Invisible Empire is committed to you on your honor. A klansman values honor more than life itself. Be true to honor, then to all the world you will be true. Always remember that an honorable secret committed is a thing sacred."

Mr. Chairman, I gladly commit to you one of the rituals of the Knights of the Ku-Klux Klan. I would like to state for your information, that the heavy-face type show the words that are said, and the light-face type indicate the words of instruction as to what is to be done. There is a document known as the Imperial Instructions, which, however, is incorporated in the oath. You will find in the oath, when you read it, an oath of obedience not only to the constitution and laws of the Knights of the Ku-Klux Klan, but to all imperial edicts, decrees, rulings, and instructions. This is supposed to be given to every man when he has been initiated. These are the imperial instructions. This is an official document bearing the signature of the imperial wizard, with the impress of the seal. The subject of this pamphlet is the practice of klanishness, and it tells the candidate what we mean by that. I want to commit this pamphlet to you for your careful perusal. It explains what we mean and what we teach and suggest regarding the practice of klanishness. Here permit me to call this to your attention by reading especially something about what we call in here Patriotic Klanishness. We teach—

"An unswerving allegiance to the principles of a pure Americanism as represented by the flag of our great Nation, namely: Liberty, justice, and truth. Real, true Americanism unadulterated, a dogged devotedness to our country, its Government, its ideals and institutions. To keep our Government forever free from the alien touch of foreign alliances and influences, that liberty's effulgent torch be not dimmed. By your vote as a citizen select only men of pure patriotic impulses to serve in positions of public trust. Vote not politics, but patriotism. Exercise your rights and prerogatives as a civil citizen for the best interest of your State and community and for the general public weal; the making of just and equitable laws and the righteous enforcement of same; bitterly oppose tyranny in any and every form and degree, and displace the corrupt politicians with dependable patriotic statesmen. 'He who saves his country saves all things, and all things saved bless him; but he who lets his country die lets all things die, and all things dying curse him.'"

I wish to commit this official document to you.

Here is a pamphlet of our literature from which I will not read any passage, because I have them marked. With it is a little pamphlet we send out entitled, "Americans, take heed!" This is a signed editorial feature of the April, 1920, issue of McClures' Magazine. I will not take the time to read it, but request that it be considered.

Mr. Chairman, that completes Exhibit G, referring to the documents and books of the organization. I now submit Exhibit H, which is a copy of the telegram sent to all Congressmen regarding the resolutions before Congress. With your permission I would like to read it.

Mr. CAMPBELL. That has been read by all the Members of Congress. It was printed in the newspapers.

Mr. SIMMONS. Then I will submit it.

(Exhibit H appears elsewhere in this record.)

Mr. SIMMONS. Exhibit I is a copy of the telegrams sent to our President and to the Attorney General.

(Exhibit I appears elsewhere in this record.)

Mr. GARRETT. Did you get any answer to those telegrams?

Mr. SIMMONS. Yes, sir; I had an answer to them a few days before I left Atlanta. I had an answer from Attorney General Daugherty, and I also received a letter from the secretary to the President acknowledging receipt of the telegram and promising his consideration of the same.

Mr. GARRETT. You say you had an answer to the telegram that you sent to the Attorney General?

Mr. SIMMONS. Yes, sir; I got a letter from the Attorney General acknowledging receipt of the telegram and stating that it would have due consideration.

Mr. GARRETT. That was the substance of his answer?

Mr. SIMMONS. Yes, sir; that was the substance of it. Of course I can not quote his letter.

Exhibit J is a verbatim copy, I am assured, of a news story from a Houston (Tex.) paper under date of September 29, 1921, the original paper being on file in Atlanta, Ga. This is a news story regarding the death of Jack Ralston, an electrician, and the payment to his widow of $1,000 by the local klan in line with our beneficent work.

(The exhibits submitted by Mr. Simmons are as follows:)

EXHIBIT A.

GEORGIA, FULTON COUNTY.

To THE SUPERIOR COURT OF SAID COUNTY:

The petition of W. J. Simmons, H. D. Shackelford, E. R. Clarkson, J. B. Frost, W. L. Smith, R. C. W. Ramspeck, G. D. Couch, L. M. Johnson, A. G. Dallas, W. E. Floding, W. C. Bennett, J. F. V. Saul, all of said State and county, respectfully shows:

1. That they desire for themselves, their associates, and successors to be incorporated in the State of Georgia for the period of 20 years, with the right of renewal; when and as provided by law, as a patriotic, secret, social, benevolent order, under the name and style of "Knights of the Ku-Klux Klan."

2. The purpose and object of said corporation is to be purely benevolent and eelemosynary, and there shall be no capital stock or profit or gain to the members thereof.

3. The principal office and place of business shall be in Fulton County, Ga., but petitioners desire that the corporation shall have the power to issue decrees, edicts, and certificates of organization to subordinate branches of the corporation in this or other States of the United States and elsewhere, whenever the same shall be deemed desirable in the conduct of its business.

4. The petitions desire that the society shall have the power to confer an initiative degree ritualism, fraternal and secret obligations, words, grip, signs, and ceremonies under which there shall be united only white male persons of sound health, good morals, and high character; and further desire such rights, powers, and privileges as are now extended to the Independent Order of Odd Fellows, Free and Accepted Order of Masons, Knights of Pythias, et al., under and by virtue of the laws of the State of Georgia.

5. Petitioners desire that there shall be a supreme legislative body in which shall be vested the power to adopt and amend constitutions and by-laws for the regulation of the general purpose and welfare of the order and of the subordinate branches of same.

6. Petitioners desire that the "Imperial Klonvokation" (supreme legislative body) be composed of the supreme officers and "kloppers" (delegates selected by the "klororo" State convention) of the several "realms" (subordinate jurisdiction); and of such other persons as the constitution and by-laws of the society may provide.

7. Petitioners desire that the business of the society shall be under the control of the "Imperial Wizard" (president), who shall be amenable in his official administration to the "Imperial Kloncilium" (supreme executive committee), a majority of whom shall have authority to act and a two-thirds majority power to veto the official acts of the "Imperial Wizard" (president) in the matters pertaining to the general welfare of the society; and to contract with other members of the society for the purpose of promoting and conducting its interests and general welfare in any way, manner, or method he may deem proper for the society's progress and stability, subject to the restrictions of the power of the "Imperial Wizard" (president) as is heretofore set forth in this paragraph.

8. Petitioners desire that they shall have the right to adopt a constitution and by-laws and elect the first Kloncilium (supreme executive committee), which shall possess all the powers of the "Imperial Klonvokation" (supreme legislative body) until the first organization and meeting of that body, and shall fix the number, title, and terms of officers composing said "Kloncilium" (supreme legislative committee).

9. Petitioners desire the right to own separate unto itself and to control the sale of all paraphernalia, regalia, stationery, jewelry, and such other materials needed by the subordinate branches of the order for the proper conduct of their business; the right to publish a fraternal magazine and such other literature as is needed in the conduct of the business of the order; the right to buy, hold, and sell real estate and personal property suitable to the purpose of the said corporation; to sell, exchange, or sublease the same or any part thereof; to mortgage or create liens thereon; to borrow money and secure the payment thereof by mortgage or deed of trust and to appoint trustees in connection therewith; to execute promissory notes; to have and to use a common seal; to sue and be sued; to plead and be impleaded; to do and perform all these things and exercise all those rights which under the laws of Georgia are conferred upon societies or orders of like character.

10. Wherefore petitioners pray an order incorporating them, their associates and successors, under the name and style aforesaid with all the powers and privileges necessary to the extension of the order or the conduct of the business and purposes of orders of like nature.

And your petitioner will ever pray.

E. R. CLARKSON,
B. H. SULLIVAN,
Petitioners' Attorneys.

Filed in office this the 26th day of April, 1916.

ARNOLD BROYLES, *Clerk.*

GEORGIA, FULTON COUNTY.

In the superior court of said county, ——— term, 1916.

Whereas W. J. Simmons, H. D. Shackelford, E. R. Clarkson, J. B. Frost, W. L. Smith, R. C. W. Ramspeck, G. D. Couch, L. M. Johnson, A. G. Dallas, W. E. Floding, W. C. Bennett, J. F. V. Saul, having filed in the office of the clerk of the superior court of said county their petition seeking the formation of a corporation to be known as the Knights of the Ku-Klux Klan, a purely benevolent and eleemosynary society, having no capital stock, for the purpose of conducting a patriotic, secret, social, benevolent order, and having complied with the statutes in such cases made and provided, and upon the hearing of said petition the court being satisfied that the application is legitimately within the purview and intention of the Civil Code of 1910 and laws amendatory thereof, it is hereby ordered and declared that said application is granted, and the above-named petitioners and their successors are hereby incorporated under the said name and style of the " Knights of the Ku-Klux Klan " for and during the period of 20 years, with the privilege of renewal at the expiration of that time according to the provisions and of the laws of this States, and said corporators and their successors are hereby clothed with all the rights, privileges, and powers mentioned in said petition and made subject to all the restrictions and liabilities fixed by law.

This 1st day July, 1916.

J. T. PENDLETON,
Judge Superior Court Fulton County, Ga.

———

STATE OF GEORGIA, County of Fulton, ss:

I, Arnold Broyles, clerk of the superior court of Fulton County, Ga., do hereby certify that the within and foregoing is a true and correct copy of charter of Knights of the Ku-Klux Klan, with order of court granting same, as appear on file and recorded in charter book No. 12, page 495, of the records of Fulton County, Ga.

Witness my hand and seal of office this the 11th day of February, 1921.

[SEAL.]   ARNOLD BROYLES,

Clerk Superior Court Fulton County, Ga.

———

EXHIBIT A–2.

[Specimen copy of charter.]

L'envoi: To the lovers of peace and order, peace and justice, we send greeting, and to the shades of the valiant, venerated dead we gratefully and affectionately dedicate the Knights of the Ku-Klux Klan. Amen.

IMPERIAL PALACE, INVISIBLE EMPIRE, KNIGHTS OF THE KU-KLUX KLAN (INC.).

To all who read and respect these lines, greeting:

Whereas the imperial wizard hath received a petition from the following-named citizens of the invisible empire, ———, et al., praying for themselves and others and their successors to be instituted a klan of the order under the name and number of ——— Klan No. ———, realm of ———, and same to be located at ———, in the county of ———, State of ———, United States of America, and they having given assurance of their fidelity to the order and their competency to render the service required, and their ready willingness to take upon themselves and their successors the responsibilities thereof, and their serious, determined purpose to rightly use and not abuse the powers, privileges, and prerogatives conferred on them as such, and be faithful and true in all things committed to them.

Now know ye that I, the imperial wizard, emperor of the invisible empire, Knights of the Ku-Klux Klan, on this the ——— day of the ——— month of the year of our Lord 19———, and on the ——— day of the ——— week of the ——— month of the year of the klan ———, and in the ——— cycle of the third reign of our reincarnation, by authority in me vested do issue this charter to the aforesaid petitioners, their associates and successors, under the name and number aforesaid from the day and date hereon, and same is effective from the date of its acceptance by said klan as certified below.

The said klan is hereby authorized and empowered to do and to perform all such acts and things as are prescribed by the kloran, laws, imperial decrees, edicts, mandates, and usages of the order, and to enjoy all the rights, privileges, and prerogatives authorized by the constitution thereof; and klansmen are strictly enjoined to valiantly preserve and persistently practice the principles of a pure patriotism, honor, klanishness, and white supremacy, ever keeping in mind and heart the sacred sentiment, peculiar purpose, manly mission, and lofty ideals and objects of the order, a devoted loyalty to their emperor, the imperial wizard, a steadfast obedience to the constitution of the order, a faithful keeping of their oath of allegiance, and a constant, unwavering fidelity to every interest of the invisible empire, to the end that the progress, power, purpose, and influence of klankraft be properly promoted, the knowledge of the faithful, self-sacrificing service and noble achievements of our fathers be not lost to posterity, and all those things for which our beloved order is founded to do and to perform, and to protect, preserve, and perpetuate, be diligently done and scrupulously maintained, and that they be blameless in preserving the grace, dignity, and intent of this charter forever.

I solemnly charge you to hold fast to the dauntless faith of our fathers and to keep their spotless memory secure and unstained and true to the traditions of our valiant sires, meet every behest of duty in all the relationships of life and living promptly and properly, without fault, without fail, without fear, and without reproach.

The imperial wizard has and holds the full and unchallengeable authority, right, and power to suspend or revoke this charter and to annul all the rights, prerogatives, and immunities conferred hereby for the neglect or the refusal on the part of the said klan to conform to and comply with the kloran, constitution, laws, imperial decrees, edicts, mandates, rulings, and instructions, or its failure to respect the usages of the order as proclaimed by and maintained under the imperial authority of same.

In testimony whereof I, the imperial wizard, emperor of the invisible empire, Knights of the Ku-Klux Klan, do hereunto affix the great imperial seal of the invisible empire and hereunto set my hand and seal, and same duly attested— "Non silba sed anthar."

Done in the aulic of his majesty in the imperial palace, in the imperial city of Atlanta, Commonwealth of Georgia, United States of America, on the day and date above written.

By his majesty:

[SEAL.]

WILLIAM JOSEPH SIMMONS,
Imperial Wizard, Emperor of the Invisible Empire,
Knights of the Ku-Klux Klan.

Attest:

L. D. WADE, *Imperial Kligrapp.*

CERTIFICATE OF ACCEPTANCE.

This certifies that above charter was read to and unanimously accepted by above-named klan on the —— day of ——, 19—.

(Signed)

—————————————————
(Exalted Cyclops.)

Witness:

—————————————————

CERTIFICATE OF DELIVERY.

This certifies that the charter from which this is detached was read to and unanimously accepted by —— Klan, No. ——, realm of ——, located in the city of ——, county of ——, State of ——, on the —— day of ——, 19—, AK. ——.

The following-named exalted cyclops and terrors were duly elected and installed:

E. C. ——. Address, ——.

Klaliff, ——; klokard, ——; kludd, ——, kligrapp, ——. Address, ——.

Klabee, ——; kladd, ——; klarogo, ——; klexter, ——; klokann, ——; night hawk, ——. Number of charter members, ——. Number of charter petitioners, ——.

Signed:

———— ————,
Kleagle in Charge.

Exhibit B.

Monthly salaries.

Imperial wizard, dating from August 1, 1921, only_____ $1,000
Imperial kligrapp_____ 300
Imperial klabee _____ 300
Cashier and head bookkeeper_____ 300
Chief department of investigation_____ 500

Stenographers are paid at the rate of from $15 to $30 per week.

Field men in the capacity of lecturers, kloranic teachers, and charter deliverers and special investigators are paid at the rate of from $50 to $75 per week, plus their traveling expenses, such as railroad fare and hotel bills. The average expense account of these men is from $35 to $50 per week.

Exhibit C.

Balance sheet as of October 1, 1921. Knights of the Ku-Klux Klan general fund, from June 15, 1921, to October 1, 1921.

[All records previous to June 15, 1920, are in memorandum form, no books to that time being opened. These records will be properly booked when turned over to accounting department: same are held by Col. W. J. Simmons, and due to ill health and urgent business he has been unable to attend to this duty.]

The approximate amount involved in the above is: Receipts, $151,088.72; disbursements, $102,503.53; bank balance, $48,585.19.

	Receipts.	Expenditures.
Traveling expense	$507.78	
Miscellaneous expense	95.25	
Office expense	345.44	
Field work salaries	5.00	
Postage	233.02	
Furniture and equipment	9,855.29	
Speakings and specials	88.00	
Office supplies	2,600.79	
W. J. Simmons, salary	5,000.00	
Advertising	13,431.29	
Publicity	6,526.01	
New klan commissions	3,134.00	
Imperial kloncilium expense	805.26	
Legal service	2,438.78	
May celebration	446.82	
Washington bureau		$10.10
Reserve fund account		21,996.65
Building repairs	3,446.80	
Printing	17,962.04	
Property improving expense	1,875.40	
W. J. Simmons, special account		547.35
Bond sale expense	1,394.20	
Propagation fund account		14,359.45
Kostumes account	13,079.05	
Klan supplies account	15,372.40	
Accounts receivable, klan		9,254.32
Accounts payable		35,727.73
Bond premiums, klan		1,257.30
Klan klectokens		21,200.00
Klan dues		7,268.85
Kleagles kostume account	828.90	
Interest and exchange	300.91	
Express freight drayage	95.04	
Gold bond account		773.51
Bills receivable	4,480.10	
Bond retirement	1,104.00	
Lanier University	22,474.32	
Insurance account	509.15	
Accounts receivable, miscellaneous	8,793.71	
Book bank statement		24,833.49
Total	137,228.75	137,228.75
Bank account as shown by books		24,833.49
Reserve fund credit		21,996.65
Bank balance upon opening books	48,585.19	
Approximate bank balance Oct. 1		1,755.05
	48,585.19	48,585.19

Assets and liabilities of the Knights of the Ku-Klux Klan, Oct. 1, 1921.

	Assets.	Liabilities.
Furniture and equipment	$9, 855. 29	
W. J. Simmons, special		$547. 35
Propagation fund account		14, 359. 45
Accounts receivable, klan accounts		9, 254. 32
Accounts payable		35, 727. 73
Bond premiums		1, 257. 30
Simmons home fund	3, 000. 00	
Bills receivable	4, 480. 10	
Accounts receivable, miscellaneous	5, 793. 71	
Lanier University	22, 474. 32	
Bank balance (see memorandum schedule No. 1)	1, 755. 05	
Total	47, 358. 47	61, 146. 15
Approximate furniture and fixtures not shown on books	8, 000. 00	
Liabilities above assets	5, 787. 68	
Total	61, 146. 15	61, 146. 15
20-year gold bonds amounting to		18, 000. 00
Due from all klans reports covering third quarter of 1921 from dues and klecrokens which should run approximately	50, 000. 00	

NOTE.—Explanation: Klan accounts receivable show as a liability due to the fact that kostumes and supplies are paid for when ordered and merchandise is in process of manufacture and has not been shipped.

Balance sheet as of Oct. 1, 1921, Knights of the Ku-Klux Klan propagation fund from June 1, 1920, to Oct. 1, 1921.

	Disbursements.	Receipts.		Disbursements.	Receipts.
Propagation commissions, 85,126 at $2		$170, 252. 00	New York bureau	$1, 031. 84	
Fieldwork salaries	$19, 356. 70		Knights of the air	2, 778. 66	
Office salaries	17, 891. 12		Printing	1, 317. 50	
Traveling expense	24, 631. 91		Auto account	1, 468. 08	
Miscellaneous expense	3, 754. 23		Interest and exchange	3. 40	
Office expense	2, 531. 82		Employees' bond premium		$1, 180. 67
Building and grounds expense	920. 00		Express, freight, and drayage	1, 778. 64	
Office rent	2, 175. 00		Imperial palace property	10, 000. 00	
Typewriter-furniture rent	258. 00		Insurance account	262. 85	
Telephone-telegraph account	5, 347. 05		W. J. Simmons, special account	186. 50	
Postage	1, 540. 53		Improvements to property	15. 00	
Furniture equipment	4, 631. 07		Department of investigation	823. 57	
Speakings and specials	6, 681. 35		Atlanta klan	3, 050. 94	
Office supplies	1, 167. 10		Simmons home fund	3, 000. 00	
Multigraphing	613. 23		National motor specialty corporation	600. 00	
W. J. Simmons, salary	7, 600. 00		Accounts receivable	8, 403. 96	
Advertising	329. 43		Cash on hand	500. 00	
Publicity	4, 718. 56		Bank balance	3, 873. 68	
Klan proper—account	14, 459. 45			171, 432. 67	171, 432. 67
Legal service	2, 334. 91				
May celebration	5, 102. 32				
Washington bureau	6, 395. 87				

Assets and liabilities, Oct. 1, 1921, Knights of the Ku-Klux Klan.

Propagation fund.	Assets.	Liabilities.
Assets:		
Furniture and equipment	$4, 631. 07	
Klan proper account	14, 459. 45	
Auto account	1, 468. 08	
Imperial palace property	10, 000. 00	
Atlanta Klan	3, 050. 94	
Simmons Home fund	3, 000. 00	
Revolving fund (cash on hand)	500. 00	
Bank balance	3, 873. 68	
Accounts receivable (list attached)	8, 403. 96	
Liabilities: Employees' bond premiums		$1, 180. 67
	49, 387. 18	1, 180. 67
Assets above liabilities		48, 206. 51
	49, 387. 18	49, 387. 18

Accounts receivable, propagation fund, Knights of the Ku-Klux Klan.

W. S. Coburn	$600. 00	Carl F. Hutchinson	$100. 00
Homer Pitts	200. 00	C. W. Allen	100. 00
J. C. Nolan	100. 00	G. R. Sparks	100. 00
T. J. McKinnon	25. 00	Thomas E. Scott	702. 00
A. J. Padon, jr	360. 00	N. B. Forrest	1, 000. 00
G. L. Williams	17. 50	F. J. Marshburn	50. 00
Paul N. Autrey	50. 00	B. H. Sullivan	300. 00
H. B. Cobb	1, 189. 46	J. A. Murdock	150. 00
W. M. McRae	150. 00	W. B. Gresham	60. 00
W. R. Mountcastle	50. 00	A. J. Grant	45. 00
D. E. Newton	100. 00	A. D. Ellis	1, 000.00
J. O. Wood	500. 00		
C. L. Davis	25. 00	Total	8, 403. 96
C. A. Ridley	1, 530. 00		

EXHIBIT D.

FACULTY LANIER UNIVERSITY.

Dr. E. C. James, Litt. D.; Rev. J. H. Boldridge, A. M., D. D., LL. D.; Dr. Byron W. Collier; J. D. Bradley, A. M., LL. D.; Prof. Kurt Mueller; Mrs. I. F. O'Neil; Miss Louise Morgan; Mrs. E. C. James; Nathan Bedford Forest, secretary and business manager.

The following gentlemen have been selected to constitute the board of trustees of the Lanier University, Atlanta, Ga., for the ensuing year, together with others to be announced later:

John Galen Locke, M. D., Denver, Colo.; Robert A. Gunn, Chicago, Ill.; Frank Starr, Chicago, Ill.; C. L. Herrod, Columbus, Ohio; Arthur T. Abernathy, D. D., Cincinnati, Ohio; Gen. A. B. Booth, New Orleans, La.; Rev. A. D. Ellis, D. D., Beaumont, Tex.; Rev. W. J. Mahoney, D. D., Gulfport, Miss.; Hon. Thomas J. Shirley, Birmingham, Ala.; Hon. F. C. Handy, Raleigh, N. C.; Rev. A. W. Lamar, D! D., Ellijay, Ga.; Thomas E. Green, M. D., Chatsworth, Ga.; William Simmons, LL. D., Atlanta, Ga.; Hon. J. I. Lowry, Atlanta, Ga.; A. D. McWilson, Atlanta, Ga.; Harry C. Montgomery, Atlanta, Ga.; Hon. Paul S. Etheridge, Atlanta, Ga.; Hon. Frank Hooper, Atlanta, Ga.; Rev. Caleb A. Ridley, D. D., Atlanta, Ga.; Rev. Robert L. Bell, D. D., Atlanta, Ga.; Nathan Bedford Forest, Atlanta, Ga.; Marion T. Benson, M. D. Atlanta, Ga.

[Lanier University bulletin announcements for the year 1921–22.]

LANIER UNIVERSITY.

Officers of administration.—Col. William Joseph Simmons, LL. D., president; Gen. Nathan Bedford Forrest, secretary and general manager; Edward Carroll James, Litt. D., dean; Mrs. Edward C. James, dean of girls.

Reorganization.—Lanier University has recently passed into new hands and has been completely reorganized. The new management has assumed the financial obligations of the institution, taken possession of the property, and arranged for the opening of the school on September 29, 1921.

Extensive work in renovation of the buildings and improvements in buildings and grounds is now going on. New and improved equipment will be placed in the dormitories, classrooms, laboratories, dining room, and culinary department.

The grounds are being graded. Walks and driveways are to be built. The entire plant will be transformed, and it will present a very attractive appearance at the time of the opening.

The name.—Lanier University was named for Sidney Lanier, the illustrious poet. Thus we would build a monument to him who, above all others, interpreted not only the soul of the South, but of the Nation, and gave to all thinking men a new vision of our needs and possibilities. Sidney Lanier was a seer. He had the gentleness of a woman and the courage of a Norse hero. Sidney Lanier never lowered his verse to sectionalism. He was always for America and for humanity. For this reason his name and ideals are to be immortalized in Lanier University, an all-American institution of learning.

Location.—The university grounds, consisting of 40 acres, are located on the northeastern side of Atlanta, just off the extension of Highland Avenue, in the Druid Hills section.

Atlanta.—Atlanta is a great educational center. It is also a center of commercial, social, and religious matters. Contact with the city is a stimulus and an inspiration to students.

Atlanta is the great railroad center of the Southeast, therefore it is easily reached from all directions. The elevation is over 1,000 feet above sea level, and the climate is ideal for a school.

Coeducational.—The university is open in all departments to both sexes. Full college courses are offered in every department, and the usual degrees are conferred.

Preparatory department.—The preparatory department is maintained for the benefit of boys and girls who are not ready for college.

The faculty.—Great care has been exercised in assembling a faculty of trained, experienced, successful teachers, each of whom is the embodiment of scholarship. Recognizing the fact that knowledge is not the only necessary qualification of teachers, the management has taken into account the personality of the members of the faculty. As the scope of work enlarges with the development of the plans of the university, other able teachers will be added to the corps of professors and instructors.

The scope of study.—The university includes the following departments: Liberal arts (full collegiate courses); fine arts (music, art, dramatic art); home economics; commerce (bookkeeping, accounting, shorthand, typewriting, commercial law, etc.); law; pharmacy; correspondence courses; preparatory department (the four years of high school).

College entrance.—1. For entrance without conditions all students must offer 15 units from an accepted school, according to the usual standard of valuation.

2. Any student who is admitted to the regular college classes of the university must present the following: Three units in English, two units in mathematics, two in languages other than English. The other nine units are elective. Consult the following list.

The 15 units may be selected from the following list:

Composition and rhetoric, 1½; English literature, 1½; algebra to quadratics, 1; algebra through the binomial theorem, ½; plane geometry, 1; solid geometry, ½; Latin grammar and composition, 1; Caesar, four books, 1; Cicero, 6 orations, 1; Vergil, six books, 1; Greek, 1, 2, or 3; German, 1, 2, or 3; French, 1, 2, or 3; Spanish, 1; ancient history, 1; mediaeval and modern history, 1; English history, 1; American history, 1; civil government, ½ or 1; physiography, ½ or 1; physiology, ½; physics, 1; chemistry, 1; botany, ½ or 1; zoology, ½ or 1; agriculture, 1 or 2; manual training, 1 or 2; commercial arithmetic, ½; commercial geography, ½.

Lanier University provides for an unusually wide, attractive, and useful system of electives. Modern education demands this practical plan. Lanier does not force all its students into one mold. The program meets the educational need of each and every student.

Lanier University wishes to prepare each and every student for some profession or calling. We desire that our graduates shall be thorough and efficient. We urge graduation with the B. A. or B. S. degree. Those who take either course are urged to choose electives in some of the practical schools of the university. This will give them preparation for a profession. In other words, young men and women may take the B. A. or B. S. degree course and their elective work in the school of pharmacy, law, accountancy, bookkeeping, expression, Biblical literature, education, or other schools and be ready for positions when they graduate.

By following our program students may save time in equipping themselves for their various callings in life. For example: A student wishes to practice pharmacy as a life calling; he also wishes to graduate from the university with the B. A. or B. S. degree. Instead of taking separately the four-year college course and the two-year pharmacy course, which would require six years, we allow the student to take the two courses together and graduate at the end of the four years from both schools. This may be carried out in all of the departments of the university.

Requirements for the degree of bachelor of arts or bachelor of science.—1. It will be noticed that the scheme given below is a combination of election by groups and election by subjects.

2. Attention is called to the fact that 67 hours of work in recitation or the equivalent will be required for the B. A. degree. Of this number subjects may be elected covering 19 hours, and of the latter number subjects may be elected in music or in art covering six hours.

The following subjects are required of all students who become candidates for the B. A. degree. Those who ask for the B. S. degree will substitute science for Latin:

Freshman:	Hours.
Bible	2
English	3
Latin	3
Mathematics	3
French, German, Spanish, Greek [1]	3
History	3
Biography	1
Total	**18**

Sophomore:	
Bible	2
English	3
History IV	3
Physics, chemistry, or biology [2]	3
Laboratory	2
Modern language or Greek	3
Elective	3
Total	**19**

Junior:	Hours.
Bible	1
Psychology and moral philosophy	3
Economics, sociology, and political science	3
Electives	8
Total	**15**

Senior:	
Bible	1
Ethics and Christianity	3
History	3
Elective	8
Total	**15**

NOTE.—It will be observed that electives may be selected from different schools upon the approval of the dean and credit committee, as follows: Pharmacy, Biblical literature, education, law, commercial education, domestic science, expression, music, art. Literary courses as outlined in the catalogue.

Extension courses.—The stress of modern life and the vicissitudes of fortune prevent thousands from availing themselves of instruction in college. The extension courses of Lanier University are intended for men and women who can not attend as resident students.

The extension department of Lanier University is based upon the principle that every individual is entitled to a chance for an education and training. If one can not come to the university, then we are prepared to go to that individual.

In the extension department Lanier University seeks to reach anyone anywhere who desires broader knowledge or more thorough scholarship.

Lanier University ideals.—There are many kinds of schools, ranging all the way from the kindergarten to the university. Not so long ago many of these had apparently no distinctive features, their objects being simply the acquisition of knowledge of some subjects. Of course, the professors were striving always to have on hand a sufficient supply to fill the students' minds or overawe them with its profundity.

A change has come about, and now almost every school has its peculiar advantages or specialties to set forth by advertising and other means in order to entice patronage.

Lanier University has its distinctive features, which it presents for the consideration of the people of the country. It will lay more than the usual stress on these two ideas especially:

1. The inculcation and practice of the tenets of the Christian religion as they are accepted by our evangelical denominations, without regard to sectarian alignments.

2. The teaching and application of the principles of purest American citizenship, using as a basis the Constitution of our great national Commonwealth and the Declaration of American Independence.

These two ideas will stand out in all the instruction in this university, every subject having its relationship to them made plain. Christianity has a vital relation to all true knowledge and to education of the highest and truest type. All of the subjects taught in the university have their bearing, either directly

---

[1] History or physics required when modern language is offered for entrance credits.
[2] When not offered for entrance special arrangement must be made for chemistry and physics.

ɔr indirectly, on the development of the purest citizenship. Our American civilization is a Christian civilization, and the Lanier University recognizes and emphasizes this fact in all departments and work.

Some scientists profess to believe that science is out of accord with the Bible and likewise out of harmony with the tenets of the Christian religion. We teach that true science is harmonious with the statements and revelations of the Scriptures and with the teachings of Jesus Christ, the Son of God.

The history of the world is strewn with the wrecks of nations that forgot God and neglected the fundamentals of citizenship on which the stability of the State depends.

Many of the textbooks and much of the teaching of the present in our schools are tainted with false science and unwholesome humanitarianism, leading ultimately to a corrupt and degenerate citizenship.

Lanier University is committed with all earnestness to the development of Christian citizenship of the highest type.

If you desire education on the principles and under the influences set forth above, then, of all schools, Lanier University offers you the opportunity.

The future of Lanier University.—Lanier University is national in scope. The future is full of hope for the largest development. Plans are forming for the erection of substantial stone buildings with every modern improvement and adapted for the accommodation of the hundreds of students who will within a year come from all sections of the Nation.

Owing to the delay in establishing the school under the new management and the limited accommodations at present, no extensive efforts will be made to secure a large attendance for the coming year. We wish to do thoroughly all that we do. A number of applications have been awaiting these announcements.

All applications should now be filed without further delay.

Letters about business matters should be directed to Gen. Nathan B. Forrest, Secretary of the University, 501 Flatiron Building, Atlanta, Ga.

Letters and inquiries about credits, entrance, and courses of study should be directed to Dr. Edward C. James, Dean, 501 Flatiron Building, Atlanta, Ga. After September 29, 1900 Highland Avenue.

Fees.

	Per quarter.	Per session.
Literary tuition (subfreshman)	$35.00	$105.00
Literary tuition (university)	40.00	120.00
Piano, director		129.00
(a) With director, private lessons, two per week, 30 minutes each	43.00	129.00
(b) With director, private lessons, two per week, 20 minutes each	30.00	90.00
(c) With director, class lessons, three in class, 60 minutes to the class	30.00	90.00
(d) With director, classes for very advanced students	33.33	100.00
Piano, assistant	27.50	82.50
Violin, director	43.00	129.00
Voice, director	40.00	120.00
Pipe organ	40.00	120.00
Harmony	10.00	30.00
Analysis	10.00	30.00
Normal, full course	10.00	15.00
Combination course for diploma students:		
Harmony, counterpoint, analysis, normal	25.00	75.00
Use of piano 2 hours daily, per year	7.50	22.50
Use of piano, each extra hour, per year		5.00
History of music, full course		15.00
Domestic science	25.00	75.00
Domestic art	10.00	30.00
Expression	33.33	100.00
Pharmacy	33.33	100.00
Laboratory, fees, chemistry, and physics, each		10.00
Library fee		2.00
Law	33.33	100.00
Diploma fee		10.00
Certificate fee		5.00
Board, per quarter	80.00	240.00
Room rent, each student (2 to room)	20.00	60.00

Graduate school according to course or subject taken.

Terms of payment.—Fifty per cent of tuition and board for the year must be paid in advance or satisfactory arrangement made with the secretary at the opening of the session, and the balance on February 1.

The students registering in the extension department of Lanier University are earnestly urged to make the tuition fee complete at the time of enrollment if possible. The instruction in these courses is presented at such a reasonable figure that we ask for this cooperation from our students.

If there are students who are unable to do this, however, we will permit them to make their payments under the following plan: One-third of the fee at registration; one-third of the fee within 60 days of registration; one-third of the fee within 90 days of registration.

Exhibit E.

OFFICIAL DOCUMENT—IMPERIAL KLEAGLE'S CONTRACT.

State of Georgia, *County of Fulton:*

This agreement, made and entered into on this the 7th day of June, A. D. 1920, by and between the Knights of the Ku-Klux Klan, a corporation of said county, acting by its imperial wizard (president), W. J. Simmons, party of the first part, and Edward Young Clarke, of said county, party of the second part.

Witnesseth, that the said party of the second part hereto having, by virtue of this agreement, been appointed imperial kleagle (general superintendent of the organization department) of said first party, and it being desirable that the details of his rights, privileges, powers, duties, responsibilities, and compensation, etc., in addition to that laid down in the constitution and laws of the said corporation be definitely fixed:

Therefore, it is agreed by the said parties hereto that this contract shall continue so long as it is mutually agreeable; that it shall remain of force and may be canceled by either party hereto without previous notice of any intention to do so.

It is agreed that said second party may employ, subject to the approval and appointment of the said imperial wizard (president) of the corporation aforesaid, and subject to the right and power of said imperial wizard (president) to revoke all such appointments, such assistant organizers as he (the said second party) may deem necessary in order to properly carry out the plans for the propagation and extension of said corporation; provided, that such persons so appointed or employed be members of the said corporation in good and regular standing prior to their appointment, and that they maintain their good standing therein as an essential condition on which their appointment is made.

It is agreed that in all things the said second party shall be subordinate to the said imperial wizard (president), and shall attempt no plans or methods of work without the consent or approval of the said imperial wizard.

It is agreed that the said second party shall receive as in full compensation and expenses of himself and his duly appointed and commissioned subordinate organizers the sum of $8 for each and every new member brought into the said corporation by himself and his assistant subordinate organizers, and in addition to the $8 he shall receive $2 for each new member added to all klans organized by himself or his subordinate organizers within a period of six months after the date of the charter of all such klans organized by himself and his subordinate organizers.

It is agreed that no expense or debts shall be made or incurred by the said Edward Young Clarke or his subordinate organizers, and no obligation entered into with any firm, company, corporation, or person for which the said first party hereto or the said imperial wizard (president) shall be bound to make any outlay of or expenditure of money, unless there be a specific approval of the particular item or items of all such expenditures, prior to the incurring of same, by the said imperial wizard (president) of the said corporation.

It is agreed that the said second party shall advance, from time to time, as may be necessary the office rent and all other expenses incident to the proper conduct and furnishing of the main office of the aforesaid corporation, and in addition thereto a sum of not less than $75 per week and traveling expenses of the said imperial wizard (president) of the aforesaid corporation, reimbursing himself for such expenditures or advancements out of the $2 due by him to the aforesaid corporation on account of each member received into the aforesaid corporation by him and his duly appointed and commissioned subordinate organizers.

Duly executed in duplicate in the city of Atlanta, Ga., on the day and date above written.

[SEAL.]   KNIGHTS OF THE KU-KLUX KLAN (INC.),
         BY W. J. SIMMONS, *Imperial Wizard (President)*.
         EDWARD YOUNG CLARKE.

I certify that the above and foregoing is a true and correct copy of the contract existing between the Knights of the Ku-Klux Klan (Inc.), and E. Y. Clarke. This the 8th day of October, 1921.

         WILLIAM JOSEPH SIMMONS,
         Imperial Wizard (President),
         Knights of the Ku-Klux Klan.

Attest:

         L. D. WADE,
         Imperial Kligrapp (Secretary).

Balance sheet, consolidated, Knights of the Ku-Klux Klan (Inc.)—Propagation fund, general fund—Oct. 1, 1921.

	Disbursements.	Receipts.
Propagation commissions, 85,126 members, at $2		$170,252.00
Traveling expense	$25,139.69	
Miscellaneous expense	3,849.48	
Office expense	2,877.26	
Field work salaries	19,361.70	
Office salaries	17,891.12	
Postage	1,773.55	
Furniture and equipment	14,486.36	
Speakings and specials	6,769.35	
Office supplies	3,767.89	
W. J. Simmons, salary	12,600.00	
Advertising	13,760.72	
Publicity	11,244.57	
Klan commissions—Propagation department	3,134.00	
Imperial kloncilium expense	805.26	
Legal service	4,773.69	
May celebration	5,549.14	
Washington bureau	6,395.87	10.00
Reserve fund account		21,996.65
Repairs to building	3,446.80	
Printing	19,279.94	
Property improvement	1,890.40	
W. J. Simmons, special account	186.50	547.35
Bond sale expense	1,394.20	
Propagation fund account	14,459.45	14,359.45
Kostumes account	13,079.05	
Klan supplies account	15,372.40	
Klan account receivable		9,254.32
Accounts payable		35,727.73
Klan bond premiums		1,257.30
Klan klectokons		21,200.00
Klan dues		7,268.85
Kleagles kostumes account	828.90	
Interest and exchange	304.31	
Express, freight, and drayage	1,873.68	
Gold bond account		773.51
Bills receivable	4,480.10	
Bond retirement	1,104.00	
Lanier University	22,474.32	
Insurance account	770.00	
Accounts receivable	17,197.67	
Buildings and ground expense	820.00	
Office rent	2,175.00	
Typewriter and furniture rent	258.00	
Telephone and telegraph account	5,347.05	
Multigraphing	613.33	
New York bureau	1,031.84	
Knights of the air	3,778.66	
Auto account	1,468.08	

Balance sheet, consolidated, Knights of the Ku-Klux Klan, etc.—Continued.

	Disbursements.	Receipts.
Employees bond premiums		$1,180.67
Imperial palace property	$10,000.00	
Department of investigation	823.57	
Atlanta klan	3,050.94	
Simmons home fund	3,000.00	
National Motor Specialty Corporation	600.00	
Cash on hand	500.00	
Bank accounts	3,873.68	24,833.49
Total	308,661.42	308,661.42

Consolidated assets liabilities, Knights of the Ku-Klux Klan—Propagation fund, general fund—Oct. 1, 1921.

	Assets.	Liabilities.
Furniture equipment	$14,486.36	
Propagation fund	14,459.45	$14,359.45
W. J. Simmons, special account	186.50	547.35
Auto account	1,468.08	
Imperial palace property	10,000.00	
Atlanta klan	3,050.94	
Simmons home fund	6,000.00	
Accounts receivable	14,197.67	
Revolving fund, cash on hand	500.00	
Bank balance (propagation fund)	3,873.68	
Bank balance (general fund. Fee schedule No. 1)	1,755.05	
Employees bond premiums		1,180.67
Klan accounts receivable		9,254.32
Accounts payable		35,727.73
Klan bond premiums		1,257.30
Bills receivable	4,480.10	
Lanier University	22,474.32	
Approximate furniture and fixtures, not booked	8,000.00	
Total	104,932.15	62,326.82
Assets above liabilities		42,605.33
Grand total	104,932.15	104,932.15

EXHIBIT F.

[Reproduced from the local paper of Florence, S. C.]

KU-KLUX KLAN DID NOT POST NOTICE—OFFER REWARD FOR IDENTITY OF PERSON USING "K. K. K." SIGN.

FLORENCE, S. C., *October 31.*

Officials of the Florence klan of the Ku-Klux declared that they had no knowledge of the sign posted on the door of Mike Shia, warning that individual that "this is the last time."

A similar notice was found posted on the door of Shia on the morning after the initial appearance of the Ku-Klux Klan on the streets of the city. The klan was not responsible for that notice, either, according to the officials.

"Inasmuch as the klan has been charged with this performance," said the officials, "and some one has used the K. K. K. sign by which the organization is generally known, we are willing to offer, and do offer, a reward of $100 for any information leading to his arrest and conviction. If it be found that the person who posted these signs is a member of the organization, we offer a larger reward for proof leading to arrest and conviction."

Officials of the local klan were very much put out when they learned the sign had been posted on Shia's door. They desire to impress upon the public that they were not concerned in it.

EXHIBIT G.

KLORAN—KNIGHTS OF THE KU-KLUX KLAN.

*　　　*　　　*　　　*　　　*　　　*　　　*

KLOKARD. Your excellency, the sacred altar of the klan is prepared; the fiery cross illumines the klavern.

E. C. Faithful Klokard, why the fiery cross?

KLOKARD. Sir, it is the emblem of that sincere, unselfish devotedness of all klansmen to the sacred purpose and principles we have espoused.

E. C. My terrors and klansmen, what means the fiery cross?

ALL. We serve and sacrifice for the right.

E. C. Klansmen all: You will gather for our opening devotions.

*　　　*　　　*　　　*　　　*　　　*　　　*

(The stanzas are sung to the tune of From Greenland's Icy Mountains and the chorus, Home, Sweet Home.)

I.

We meet with cordial greetings
In this our sacred cave
To pledge anew our compact
With hearts sincere and brave;
A band of faithful klansmen,
Knights of the K. K. K.,
We all will stand together
Forever and for aye.

CHORUS.

Home, home, country and home,
Klansmen we'll live and die
For our country and home.

II.

Here honor, love, and justice
Must actuate us all;
Before our sturdy phalanx
All hate and strife shall fall.
In unison we'll labor
Wherever we may roam
To shield a klansman's welfare,
His country, name, and home.

After singing, the Kludd at the sacred altar leads in the following prayer: (All must stand steady with heads reverently bowed.)

Our Father and our God, we, as klansmen, acknowledge our dependence upon Thee and Thy lovingkindness toward us; may our gratitude be full and constant and inspire us to walk in Thy ways.

Give us to know that each klansman by the process of thought and conduct determines his own destiny, good or bad: May he forsake the bad and choose and strive for the good. remembering always that the living Christ is a klansman's criterion of character.

Keep us in the blissful bonds of fraternal union, of clannish fidelity one toward another and of a devoted loyalty to this, our great institution. Give us to know that the crowning glory of a klansman is to serve. Harmonize our souls with the sacred principles and purposes of our noble order that we may keep our sacred oath inviolate, as Thou art our witness.

Bless those absent from our gathering at this time; Thy peace be in their hearts and homes.

God save our Nation! And help us to be a Nation worthy of existence on the earth. Keep ablaze in each klansman's heart the sacred fire of a devoted patriotism to our country and its Government.

We invoke Thy blessing upon our emperor, the imperial wizard, and his official family in the administrations of the affairs pertaining to the government of the invisible empire. Grant him wisdom and grace; and may each klansman's heart and soul be inclined toward him in loving loyalty and unwavering devotion.

Oh, God! For Thy glory and our good we humbly ask these things in the name of Him who taught us to serve and sacrifice for the right. Amen! (All say "Amen!")

CLOSING CEREMONY, KNIGHTS OF THE KU-KLUX KLAN.

The order of business having been finished, the E. C. will arise, give one rap with his gavel and say:

"My terrors and klansmen, the sacred purpose of the gathing of the klan at this time has been fulfilled; the deliberations of this klonklave have ended."

E. C. Faithful Klaliff: What is the fourfold duty of a klansman?

The klaliff will arise and say:

"To worship God; be partiotic toward our country; be devoted and loyal to our klan and emperor, and to practice clannishness toward his fellow klansfen." (And remains standing.)

E. C. Faithful Kludd: "How speaketh the oracles of our God?"

The kludd will arise and say:

"Thou shalt worship the Lord thy God. Render unto the state the things which are the state's. Love the brotherhood: honor the king. Bear ye one another's burdens, and so fulfill the law of Christ." (And remains standing.)

E. C. Faithful Klokard: "What does a klansman value more than life?"

The klokard will arise and say:

"Honor to a klansman is more than life." (And remains standing.)

* * * * * * *

[Tune, America.]

God of Eternity
Guard, guide our great country,
Our homes and store.
Keep our great state to Thee,
Its people right and free.
In us Thy glory be,
Forevermore.

After the singing all look toward the mounted flag and will gtnh and then stand with bowed heads; the kludd standing at the sacred altar will pronounce the following benediction:

THE BENEDICTION.

May the blessings of our God wait upon thee and the sun of glory shine around thy head; may the gates of plenty, honor, and happiness be always open to thee and thine, so far as they will not rob thee of eternal joys.

May no strife disturb thy days, nor sorrow distress thy nights, and when death shall summons thy departure may the Saviour's blood have washed thee from all impurities, perfected thy initiation, and thus prepared, enter thou into the empire invisible and repose thy soul in perpetual peace.

Amen! (All say, "Amen.")

* * * * * * *

QUALIFYING INTERROGATORIES.

The klokard will first ask each candidate his name and then speak to the candidates in the outer den as follows:

SIRS: The Knights of the Ku-Klux Klan, as a great and essentially a patriotic, fraternal, benevolent order, does not discriminate against a man on account of his religious or political creed, when same does not conflict with or antagonize the sacred rights and privileges guaranteed by our civil government and Christian ideals and institutions.

Therefore, to avoid any misunderstanding and as evidence that we do not seek to impose unjustly the requirements of this order upon anyone who can not,

on account of his religious or political scruples, voluntarily meet our requirements and faithfully practice our principles, and as proof that we respect all
honest men in their sacred convictions, whether same are agreeable with our
requirements or not, we require as an absolute necessity on the part of each
of you an affirmative answer to each of the following questions:
Each of the following questions must be answered by (each of) you with an
emphatic " Yes."
First. Is the motive prompting your ambition to be a klansman serious and
unselfish?
Second. Are you a native-born white, Gentile American citizen?
Third. Are you absolutely opposed to and free of any allegiance of any
nature to any cause, Government, people, sect, or ruler that is foreign to the
United States of America?
Fourth. Do you believe in the tenets of the Christian religion?
Fifth. Do you esteem the United States of America and its institutions above
any other Government, civil, political, or ecclesiastical, in the whole world?
Sixth. Will you, without mental reservation, take a solemn oath to defend,
preserve, and enforce same?
Seventh. Do you believe in clannishness and will you faithfully practice same
towards klansmen?
Eighth. Do you believe in and will you faithfully strive for the eternal main-
tenance of white supremacy?
Ninth. Will you faithfully obey our constitution and laws, and conform
willingly to all our usages, requirements, and regulations?
Tenth. Can you be always depended on?

*   *   *   *   *   *   *

KLADD. The distinguishing marks of a klansman are not found in the fiber
of his garments or his social or financial standing, but are spiritual; namely,
a chivalric head, a compassionate heart, a prudent tongue, and a courageous
will. All devoted to our country, our klan, our homes, and each other: these
are the distinguishing marks of a klansman, oh, faithful klexter! And these
men claim the marks.
KLEXTER. What if one of your party should prove himself a traitor?
KLADD. He would be immediately banished in disgrace from the invisible
empire without fear or favor, conscience would tenaciously torment him, re-
morse would repeatedly revile him, and direful things would befall him.
KLEXTER. Do they (or does he) know all this?
KLADD. All this he (or they) now know. He (or they) has (or have) heard,
and they must heed.
KLEXTER. Faithful kladd, you speak the truth.
KLADD. Faithful klexter, a klansman speaketh the truth in and from his
heart. A lying scoundrel may wrap his disgraceful frame within the sacred
folds of a klansman's robe and deceive the very elect, but only a klansman
possesses a klansman's heart and a klansman's soul.
KLOKARD:

God give us men! The invisible empire demands strong
Minds, great hearts, true faith, and ready hands.
Men whom the lust of office does not kill;
Men whom the spoils of office can not buy;
Men who possess opinions and a will:
Men who have honor; men who will not lie;
Men who can stand before a demagogue
And damn his treacherous flatteries without winking!
Tall men, sun-crowned, who live above the fog
In public duty and in private thinking;
For while the rabble, with their thumb-worn creeds,
Their large professions and their little deeds,
Mingle in selfish strife, Lo! freedom weeps,
Wrong rules the land, and waiting justice sleeps.
God give us men!
Men who serve not for selfish booty,
But real men, courageous, who flinch not at duty;
Men of dependable character; men of sterling worth;
Then wrongs will be redressed, and right will rule the earth;
God give us men!

After a pause, the klarogo faces the candidates and says:
" SIRS: Will you (or each of you) by your daily life as klansmen earnestly endeavor to be an answer to this prayer?"

* * * * * * *

The exalted cyclops will arise and address the candidates as follows:
" Sirs, is the motive prompting your presence here serious and unselfish?
" It is indeed refreshing to meet face to face with men (or a man) like you, who, actuated by manly motives, aspire to all things noble for yourselves and humanity.
" The luster of the holy light of chivalry has lost its former glory and is sadly dimmed by the choking dust of selfish, sordid gain. Pass on!"
The exalted cyclops will resume his seat, and the kladd will face his party toward the nighthawk and advance behind the nighthawk until he hears the signal of allw from the klokard. On hearing the signal from the klokard the nighthawk stops and stands steady; the kladd will also stop his party immediately in front of the klokard's station and face them to the klokard's station and answer the signal by the same. On receiving the answer, the klokard will arise and address the party as follows:
" Real fraternity, by shameful neglect, has been starved until so weak her voice is lost in the courts of her own castle, and she passes unnoticed by her sworn subjects as she moves along the crowded streets and through the din of the market place. Man's valuation of man is by the standard of wealth and not worth: selfishness is the festive queen among humankind, and multitudes forget honor, justice, love, and God and every religious conviction to do homage to her; and yet, with the cruel heart of Jezebel, she slaughters the souls of thousands of her devotees daily. Pass on!"
The klokard will resume his seat, and the kladd will face his party as before and advance behind the nighthawk until he hears the signal of allw from the klaliff. On hearing the signal of the klaliff the nighthawk stops and stands steady; the kladd will also stop his party immediately in front of the klaliff's station, facing them to the klaliff, and answer the signal by the same. On receiving the answer, the klaliff will arise and address the party as follows:
" The unsatiated thirst for gain is dethroning reason and judgment in the citadel of the human soul, and men maddened thereby forget their patriotic, domestic, and social obligations and duties and fiendishly fight for a place in the favor of the goddess of glittering gold; they starve their own souls and make sport of spiritual development. Pass on!"
The klaliff will resume his seat, and the kladd will face his party as before and advance behind the nighthawk until he hears the signal of allw from the kludd. On hearing the signal of the kludd, the nighthawk stops and stands steady; the kladd will also stop his party immediately in front of the kludd's station, facing them to the kludd, and then answers the signal by the same. On receiving the answer, the kludd will arise and address the party as follows:

> " Men speak of love and live in hate,
> Men talk of faith and trust to fate,
> Oh, might men do the things they teach!
> Oh, might men live the life they preach!
> Then the throne of avarice would fall, and the clangor
> Of grim Selfishness o'er the earth would cease;
> Love would tread out the baleful fire of anger,
> And in its ashes plant the lily of peace.
> Pass on!"

The kludd will resume his seat, and the kladd will face his party as before and advance behind the nighthawk until he hears the signal of allw from the exalted cyclops. On hearing the signal of the exalted cyclops, the nighthawk stops and goes to and takes position at the sacred altar; the kladd will also stop his party immediately in front of the exalted cyclops's station, facing them to the exalted cyclops, and then answer the signal with the same. On receiving the answer, the exalted cyclops will arise and address the party as follows:
" Sirs, we congratulate you on your manly decision to forsake the world of selfishness and fraternal alienation and emigrate to the delectable bounds of the invisible empire and become loyal citizens of the same. The prime purpose of this great order is to develop character, practice clannishness, to protect the home and the chastity of womanhood, and to exemplify a pure patriotism toward our glorious country.

" You as citizens of the invisible empire must be actively patriotic toward our country and constantly clannish toward klansmen socially, physically, morally, and vocationally ; will you assume this obligation of citizenship?

" You must unflinchingly conform to our requirements, regulations, and usages in every detail and prove yourselves worthy to have and to hold the honors we bestow; do you freely and faithfully assume to do this?

" Sirs, if you have any doubt as to your ability to qualify, either in body or character, as citizens of the invisible empire, you now have an opportunity to retire from this place with the good will of the klan to attend you; for I warn you now if you falter or fail at this time or in the future as a klansman, in klonklave or in life, you will be banished from citizenship in the invisible empire without fear or favor.

" This is a serious undertaking; we are not here to make sport of you nor indulge in the silly frivolity of circus clowns. Be you well assured that ' he that putteth his hands to the plow and looketh back is not fit for the kingdom of heaven ' or worthy of the high honor of citizenship in the invisible empire, or the fervent fellowship of klansmen. Don't deceive yourselves; you can not deceive us, and we will not be mocked. Do you wish to retire?"

E. C. Faithful kladd, you will direct the way for these worthy aliens to the sacred altar of the empire of chivalry, honor, industry, and love, in order that they may make further progress toward attaining citizenship in the invisible empire, Knights of the Ku-Klux Klan.

   *   *   *   *   *   *   *

DEDICATION.

The E. C. addresses the candidates as follows :

" Sirs, have (each of) you assumed without mental reservation your oath of allegiance to the invisible empire? Mortal man can not assume a more binding oath ; character and courage alone will enable you to keep it. Always remember that to keep this oath means to you honor, happiness, and life; but to violate it means disgrace, dishonor, and death. May honor, happiness, and life be yours."

   *   *   *   *   *   *   *

(Then he holds up the vessel from the sacred altar, containing the dedication fluid, and addresses the candidates as follows:)

" With this transparent, life-giving, powerful, God-given fluid, more precious and far more significant than all the sacred oils of the ancients, I set you (or each of you) apart from the men of your daily association to the great and honorable task you have voluntarily allotted yourselves as citizens of the invisible empire, Knights of the Ku-Klux Klan.

"As a klansman may your character be as transparent, your life purpose as powerful, your motive in all things as magnanimous and as pure, and your clannishness as real and as faithful as the manifold drops herein, and you a vital being as useful to humanity as is pure water to mankind.

" You will kneel upon your right knee."

Just here the following stanza must be sung in a low, soft, but distinct tone, preferably by a quartet:

[Tune, Just As I Am Without One Plea.]

To Thee, oh, God ! I call to Thee—
True to my oath, oh, help me be!
I've pledged my love, my blood, my all;
Oh, give me grace that I not fall.

   *   *   *   *   *   *   *

E. C. Sirs, ' Neath the uplifted fiery cross which by its holy light looks down upon you to bless with its sacred traditions of the past I dedicate you in body, in mind, in spirit, and in life to the holy service of our country, our klan, our homes, each other, and humanity.

   *   *   *   *   *   *   *

DEDICATORY PRAYER.

God of all, author of all good, Thou who didst create man and so proposed that man should fill a distinct place and perform a specific work in the economy of Thy good government, Thou has revealed Thyself and Thy purpose to man, and by this revelation we have learned our place and our work. Therefore we have solemnly dedicated ourselves as klansmen to that sublime work harmonic with Thy will and purpose in our creation.

Now, oh, God, we, through Thy goodness, have here dedicated with Thine own divinely distilled fluid these manly men at the altar kneeling, who have been moved by worthy motives and impelled by noble impulses to turn from selfishness and fraternal alienation and to espouse with body, mind, spirit, and life the holy service of our country, our klan, our home, and each other. We beseech Thee to dedicate them with the fulness of Thy spirit, keep him (or each of them) true to his (or their) sacred, solemn oath to our noble cause, to the glory of Thy great name.   Amen.   (All say " amen.")

    *   *   *   *   *   *   *

THE KLONVERSATION.

    *   *   *   *   *   *   *

After the instructions have been given the klokard will say:

" The kladd will now conduct you to the exalted cyclops, where you will receive from him the CS and PW, the sacred symbol and imperial instructions, to which give earnest heed."

The kladd conducts the party to the station of the E. C. and says:

" Your excellency, these klansmen (or this klansman), having been instructed in the way of the klavern, now awaits to receive from you the CS and PW, the sacred symbol of the klan and imperial instructions."

E. C. will arise and say:

" My fellow klansman (or klansmen) the insignia or mark of a klansman is honor.   All secrets and secret information of the invisible empire is committed to you on your honor.   A klansman values honor more than life itself. Be true to honor, then to all the world you will be true.   Always remember that an honorable secret committed is a thing sacred.

" I am about to commit to you three vital secrets of the invisible empire— the CS and PW and the sacred symbol, the mioak.   Do you swear to forever hold them in sacred, secret reverence, even unto death?

" The CS and PW enables you to meet with and enjoy the feellowship of klansmen in klonklave assembled.

" For the present and until changed the CS is —— and the PW is ——.

" The mioak, the sacred symbol of the klan, is that (he explains what it is) by which klansmen recognize each other without word, sound, or sign.

" I now present you with the material insignia of a klansmen, the sacred symbol of the plan, by name the mioak.   Be faithful in its wearing.   It must be morn on your person where it may be readily seen.   Tell no person in the whole world what it is, its meaning and significance, even by hint or insinuation, as it is a positive secret of the plan.   Don't fail to recognize it by whomsoever 'it is worthily worn; always appreciate its sacred significance and be true to same.   As a test of your honor I invest you with this symbol and commit to you its sacred secret."

He pins on the breast of the new klansman the insignia and explains its symbolic meaning.

" You will now receive imperial instructions.   Carefully preserve and seriously study this document and give earnest heed to same, for on the practice of its teachings in your daily life depends your future advancement."

" You (or each of you) now are instructed klansmen, possessing all the rights, privileges, and protection as such will take your place with klansmen in the sacred fellowship of the invisible empire."

The E. C. will then give two raps with his gavel, take his seat and proceed with the other business.

THE IMPERIAL PROCLAMATION.

To all nations, people, tribes, and tongues, and to the lovers of law and order, peace and justice, of the whole earth, greeting:

I, and the citizens of the invisible empire through me, proclaim to you as follows:

We, the members of this order, desiring to promote real patriotism toward our civil Government; honorable peace among men and nations; protection for and happiness in the homes of our people; love, real brotherhood, mirth, and manhood among ourselves, and liberty, justice, and fraternity among all mankind; and believing we can best accomplish these noble purposes through the channel of a high-class mystic, social, patriotic, benevolent association, having a perfected lodge system with an exalted, ritualistic form of work and an effective form of government, not for selfish profit but for the mutual betterment, benefit, and protection of all our oath-bound associates, their welfare, physically, socially, morally, and vocationally, and their loved ones, do proclaim to the whole world that we are dedicated to the sublime and pleasant duty of providing generous aid, tender sympathy, and fraternal assistance in the effulgence of the light of life and amid the sable shadows of death, amid fortune and misfortune, and to the exalted privilege of demonstrating the practical utility of the great, yet most neglected, doctrine of the fatherhood of God and the brotherhood of man as a vital force in the lives and affairs of men.

In this we invite all men who can qualify to become citizens of the invisible empire to approach the portal of our beneficent domain and join us in our noble work of extending its boundaries; in disseminating the gospel of "klankraft," thereby encouraging, conserving, protecting, and making vital the fraternal human relationship in the practice of a wholesome clannishness; to share with us the glory of performing the sacred duty of protecting womanhood; to maintain forever white supremacy in all things; to commemorate the holy and chivalric achievements of our fathers; to safeguard the sacred rights, exalted privileges, and distinctive institutions of our civil Government; to bless mankind, and to keep eternally ablaze the sacred fire of a fervent devotion to a pure Americanism.

The invisible empire is founded on sterling character and immutable principles based upon a most sacred sentiment and cemented by noble purposes; it is promoted by a sincere, unselfish devotion of the souls of manly men, and is managed and governed by the consecrated intelligence of thoughtful brains. It is the soul of chivalry and virtue's impenetrable shield—the devout impulse of an unconquered race.

Done in the aulic of his majesty, the imperial wizard and emperor of the invisible empire, Knights of the Ku-Klux Klan, in the imperial palace, in the imperial city of Atlanta, Commonwealth of Georgia, United States of America, this the 4th day of July, A. D. 1916 Anno Klan L.

Signed by his majesty,

[SEAL.]   WILLIAM JOSEPH SIMMONS,
                                                      Imperial Wizard.

  •   •   •   •   •   •   •

A SACRED DUTY—A PRECIOUS PRIVILEGE.

A true American can not give a higher and more sincere expression of appreciation of and gratitude for what was accomplished by our fathers in the defense of home and the sacred rights of our people than by becoming a "citizen of the invisible empire, Knights of the Ku-Klux Klan." He can not align himself with any institution that will mean so much for himself, his home, and his country as this great order.

It stands for America first—first in thought, first in affections, and first in the galaxy of nations. The Stars and Stripes forever above all other and every kind of government in the whole world.

Benevolence—in thought, word, and deed based upon justice and practically applied to all. To right the wrong; to succor the weak and unfortunate; to help the worthy and to relieve the distressed.

Clannishness—real fraternity practically applied—standing by and sticking to each other in all things honorable. Encouraging, protecting, cultivating, and exemplifying the real "fraternal human relationship" to shield and enhance each other's happiness and welfare. A devoted, unfailing loyalty to the principles, mission, and purposes of the order in promoting the highest and best interest of the community, State, and Nation.

What it is: It is a standard fraternal order enforcing fraternal conduct, and not merely a "social association." It is a duly incorporated, legally recognized institution, honest in purpose, noble in sentiment and practical in results that commands the hearty respect of all respectable people throughout the Nation. It is not encouraging nor condoning any propaganda of religious intolerance nor racial prejudice. It is an association of real men who believe in being something, in doing things worth while, and who are in all things 100 per cent pure American. Yet it is vastly more than merely a social fraternal order.

Its initial purpose: An enduring monument to the valor and patriotic achievements of the Ku-Klux Klan. That this monument be not embodied in cold, emotionless stone, but in living, pulsating human hearts and active human brains, and find a useful expression in the nobility of the character of real manly men; this is the only memorial that will adequately befit the memory of the valiant Ku-Klux Klan.

Its lineage: The most sublime lineage in history, commemorating and perpetuating, as its does the most dauntless organization known to man.

Its secret: Sacred guardianship to the most sacred cause.

Its courage: The soul of chivalry and virtue's impenetrable shield. The impulse of an unconquered race.

Its teachings: To inculcate the sacred principles and noble ideals of the world's greatest order of chivalry; and direct the way of the initiate through the veil of mystic philosophy into the empire invisible.

Its character: The noblest concepts of manhood idealized in thought and materialized in practice in all the relationships of life—mystery and action, mastery and achievement.

Its ritualism is vastly different from anything in the whole universe of fraternal ritualism. It is altogther original, weird, mystical, and of a high class, leading up through four degrees. Dignity and decency are its marked features. It unfolds a spiritual philosophy that has to do with the very fundamentals of life and living, here and hereafter. He who explores the dismal depths of the mystic cave and from thence attains the lofty heights of superior knighthood may sit among the gods in the empire invisible.

Its patriotism: An uncompromising standard of pure Americanism untrammeled by alien influences and free from the entanglements of foreign alliances. Proclaiming the brotherhood of nations but wedding none, thereby unyielding in the dignity of our own independence and forever faultless in our freedom.

Its mission: Duty—without fault, without fail,- without fear, and without reproach.

Its society: The practical fraternal fellowship of men whose standard is worth not wealth; characeter, not cash; courageous manhood based upon honor untarnished by the touch of hypocrisy or the veneering of society's selfish social valuations.

Its place: In the heart of every "true American," alongside of every other fraternal order, and in its original casting, unique mannerism, sacred sentiment, noble purpose, and peculiar mysticism it is separate and apart from any and all and peerless in its distinctive peculiarities.

Its fraternity: Not merely reciting in ceremony pretty, time-worn platitudes on brotherly love, but to enforce a fraternal practice of clannishness, thereby making devotion to its standard worth while. "The glory of a klansman is to serve."

Its origin: This great institution, as a patriotic, ritualistic fraternal order, is no hastily "jumped-up" affair. It has been in the making for the past 20 years. It is a product of deliberate thought. The one man (William Joseph Simmons) who is responsible for it conceived the idea 20 years ago. For 14 years he thought, studied, and worked to prepare himself for its launching. He had dedicated his life to this noble cause. He kept his own counsel during these years and in the silent recesses of his soul he thought out the great plan. During the early days of October, 1915, he mentioned his ambition to some friends, among whom were three men who were bona fide members of the original klan when it disbanded. They most heartily cooperated with him. Having met with such encouragement, he invited several of his friends to a meeting on the night of October 26, 1915, at which time he unfolded his plans, and as a result all present, 34 in number, signed a petition for a charter. The petition was accepted and on Thanksgiving night, 1915, when were seen emerging from the shadows and gathering around the spring at the base of Stone Mountain (the world's greatest rock, near Atlanta, Ga.) and from thence repaired to the mountain top and there, under a blazing fiery cross, they took the oath of allegiance to the invisible empire, Knights of the Ku-Klux Klan. The charter was issued by the State of Georgia, December 4, 1915, and signed by Hon. Philip Cook, secretary of state. In the development of the order a petition was made to the superior court, Fulton County Ga., for a special charter, and said charter was issued July 1, 1916. The imperial wizard issued his imperial proclamation July 4, 1916.

And thus on the mountain top that night at the midnight hour while men braved the surging blasts of wild wintry mountain winds and endured a temperature far below freezing, bathed in the sacred glow of the fiery cross, the invisible empire was called from its slumber of half a century to take up a new task and fulfill a new mission for humanity's good and to call back to mortal habitation the good angel of practical fraternity among men.

PREREQUISITES TO CITIZENSHIP IN THE INVISIBLE EMPIRE.

This order is founded upon dependable character. It is not an ultra-exclusive institution, but its membership is composed of " picked " men.

No man is wanted in this order who hasn't manhood enough to assume a real oath with serious purpose to keep the same inviolate.

No man is wanted in this order who will not or can not swear an unqualified allegiance to the Government of the United States of America, its flag, and its Constitution.

No man is wanted in this order who does not esteem the Government of the United States above any other government, civil, political, or ecclesiastical, in the whole world.

No man is wanted in this order who can not practice real fraternity toward each and every one of his oath-bound associates.

Only native born American citizens who believe in the tenets of the Christian religion and owe no allegiance of any degree or nature to any foreign Government, nation, political institution, sect, people, or person, are eligible.

DEGREE FEES.

Membership in this order can not be bought; it is given as a reward for service unselfishly rendered. If you really believe in the order, and will practice its principles, and conform to its regulations and usages and contribute the sum of $10 toward its propagation and can otherwise qualify then membership is awarded you' upon this service rendered and pledged of future fidelity to the institution. This is not a selfish, mercenary, commercialized proposition. but the direct opposite.

THE KU-KLUX KREED.

We, the order of the Knights of the Ku-Klux Klan, reverentially acknowledge the majesty and supremacy of the Divine Being, and recognize the goodness and providence of the same.

We recognize our relation to the Government of the United States of America, the supremacy of its Constitution, the Union of States thereunder, and the constitutional laws thereof, and we shall be ever devoted to the sublime principles of a pure Americanism and valiant in the defense of its ideals and institutions.

We avow the distinction between the races of mankind as same has been decreed by the Creator, and we shall ever be true to the faithful maintenance of White Supremacy and will strenously oppose any compromise thereof in any and all things.

We appreciate the intrinsic value of a real practical fraternal relationship among men of kindred thought, purpose, and ideals and the infinite benefits accruable therefrom, and we shall faithfully devote ourselves to the practice of an honorable clanishness that the life and living of each may be a constant blessing to others.

" Non silba sed anthar."—Original creed revised.

*   *   *   *   *   *   *

OBJECTS AND PURPOSE.

ARTICLE II.

SECTION 1. The objects of this order shall be to unite only white male persons, native-born gentile citizens of the United States of America, who owe no allegiance of any nature or degree to any foreign Government, nation, institution, sect, ruler, person, or people; whose morals are good; whose reputations and vocations are respectable; whose habits are exemplary; who are of sound minds and at or above the age of 18 years, under a common oath into a common brotherhood of strict regulations for the purpose of cultivating and promoting real patriotism toward our civil Government; to practice an honorable clannishness toward each other; to exemplify a practical benevolence; to shield the sancity of the home and the chastity of womanhood: to forever maintain white supremacy; to teach and faithfully inculcate a high spiritual philosophy through an exalted ritualism, and by a practical devotedness to conserve, protect, and maintain the distinctive institutions, rights, privileges, principles, traditions, and ideals of a pure Americanism.

    *   *   *   *   *

SEC. 3. This order is an institution of chivalry, humanity, justice, and patriotism; embodying in its genius and principles all that is chivalric in conduct, noble in sentiment, generous in manhood, and patriotic in purpose; its peculiar objects being: First, to protect the weak, the innocent, and the defenseless from the indignities, wrongs, and outrages of the lawless, the violent, and the brutal; to relieve the injured and the oppressed; to succor the suffering and unfortunate, especially widows and orphans. Second, to protect and defend the Constitution of the United States of America and all laws passed in conformity thereto, and to protect the States and the people thereof from all invasion of their rights thereunder from any source whatsoever. Third, to aid and assist in the execution of all constitutional laws, and to preserve the honor and dignity of the State by opposing tyranny in any and every form or degree attempted from any and every source whatsoever by a fearless and faithful administration of justice, and to promptly and properly meet every behest of duty without fear and without reproach.

TERRITORIAL JURISDICTIONS, ASSEMBLIES, ETC.

ARTICLE III.

SEC. 1. *The invisible empire.*—The phrase "invisible empire" in a material sense denotes the universal geographical jurisdiction of this order and it shall embrace the whole world. The convention of the invisible empire shall be known as the imperial klonvokation. The phrase "invisible empire" in a spiritual sense denotes or applies to all the secrets and secret knowledge and information, secret work and working and things of this order, and to all that has been, to all that now is, and to all that is to be, the past, the present, and the future, yesterday, to-day, and forever; the dead of yesterday, the living of to-day, and the contemplated of to-morrow of the life that now is and of that which is to come.

    *   *   *   *   *   *

MEMBERSHIP.

ARTICLE IV.

SECTION 1. The qualification for membership in this order shall be as follows: An applicant must be white male gentile person, a native-born citizen of the United States of America, who owes no allegiance of any nature or degree whatsoever to any foreign Government, nation, institution, sect, ruler, prince, potentate, people, or person; he must be at or above the age of 18 years, of sound mind, good character, of commendable reputation, and respectable vocation, a believer in the tenets of the Christian religion, and whose allegiance, loyalty, and devotion to the Government of the United States of America in all things is unquestionable.

    *   *   *   *   *   *

KLANS.

ARTICLE XVII.

    *   *   *   *   *   *

SEC. 25. A klan, or a member of this order, must not use the official costume or any part of same of the order on any occasion, or for any purpose other than in ceremony of this order, or in an official klavalkade (parade) under penalty of forfeiture of charter of the klan or expulsion from this order of the member.

SEC. 26. No klan and no member of this order shall use the name of this order or any part thereof for any purpose that contravenes in any manner the laws of the land, or in any manner that will in any way reflect, or probably reflect, upon the reputation and good name of this order, or compromise or injure this order or any member of this order in any way.

* * * * * * *

OFFENSES AND PENALTIES.

ARTICLE XIX.

SECTION 1. Offenses against this order deserving penalties shall be: Treason against the United States of America; violating the oath of allegiance or any supplementary oaths or obligations thereto of this order; criminal act or acts proven; disregard of public decency; disrespect for virtuous womanhood; betraying or violating a sacred trust of a klansman; a purposely violation of this constitution and the laws of this order, or the by-laws of a klan of this order; excessive drunkenness in public places, drunkenness or drinking intoxicating liquors during a klonklave or on the premises thereof, or entering a klonklave in an intoxicated condition; the frequent use of profane language or vulgarity during a klonklave, or in an assembly of klansmen just prior thereto; conspiring against the interest and prosperity of this order or any klansman in any way, or being a party thereto, or being a party to any move, conspiracy, or organization whose existence or purpose is antagonistic or injurious to or is an imitation or counterfeit of this order, or whose name, style, or title is a colarable imitation of the name of this order; swearing allegiance to or otherwise becoming a citizen or subject of any nation, government, or institution of any nature or classification, or any ruler, potentate, prince, or person, or any cause whatsoever that is foreign to or is inimical to the Government of the United States of America and its established institution, or aiding or abetting such a government, nation, institution, ruler, potentate, prince, or person against the interest, well being, or dignity of the United States of America or the distinctive institutions of its Government.

* * * * * * *

THE PRACTICE OF KLANISHNESS.

* * * * * * *

(1) *Patriotic klanishness.*—An unswerving allegiance to the principles of a pure Americanism as represented by the flag of our great Nation, namely, liberty, justice, and truth. Real, true Americanism unadulterated; a dogged devotedness to our country, its government, its ideals, and its institutions. To keep our Government forever free from the alien touch of foreign alliances and influences that liberty's effulgent torch be not dimmed. By your vote as a citizen select only men of pure patriotic impulses to serve in positions of public trust. Vote not politics but patriotism. Exercise your rights and prerogatives as a civil citizen for the best interest of your state and community and for the general public weal; the making of just and equitable laws and the righteous enforcement of same; bitterly oppose tyranny in any and every form and degree, and displace the corrupt politicians with dependable patriotic statesmen: " He who saves his country saves all things and all things saved bless him; but he who lets his country die lets all things die and all things dying curse him."

* * * * * * *

THE KU-KLUX KLAN YESTERDAY, TO-DAY, AND FOREVER.

The purpose of the modern Ku-Klux Klan is to inculcate the sacred principles and noble ideals of chivalry, the development of character, the protection of the home and the chastity of womanhood, the exemplification of a pure and practical patriotism toward our glorious country, the preservation of American ideals and institutions and the maintenance of white supremacy.

* * * * * * *

While membership in the Ku-Klux Klan is open only to white American citizens, the organization wages war on no individual or organization, regardless of race. color, or creed. It takes no part as an organization in any political or religious controversy. and it concedes the right of every man to think, vote, and worship God as he pleases.

Among the principles for which this organization stands, in addition to those already enumerated, are: Suppression of graft by public officeholders; preventing the causes of mob violence and lynchings; preventing unwarranted strikes by foreign agitators; sensible and patriotic immigration laws,; sovereignty of State rights under the Constitution; separation of church and state; and freedom of speech and press, a freedom of such that does not strike at or imperil our Government or the cherished institutions of our people.

If there be any white American citizen who owes allegiance to no flag but the Star Spangled Banner and who can not subscribe to and support these principles let him forever hold his peace, for he is basely unworthy of the great flag and its Government that guarantees to him life, liberty, and the pursuit of happiness. That person who actively opposes these great principles is a dangerous ingredient in the body politic of our country and an enemy to the weal of our National Commonwealth.

   *   *   *   *   *   *   *

The Anglo-Saxon race, the only race that has ever proved its ability and supremacy and demonstrated its determination to progress under any and all conditions and handicaps. owes its high place in the world to-day to the fact that this spirit has been kept alive from the foundation of the world and has never lagged in any land or clime.

And if the Anglo-Saxon race is to maintain its prestige. if it is to continue as the leader in the affairs of the world and to fulfill its sacred mission it must maintain and jealously guard its purity, its power, and its dignity; and while it should aid and encourage to the limit of its abilty all men of whatever race or creed, it must forever maintain its own peculiar identity as the Anglo-Saxon race and preserve the integrity of its civilization, for the shores of time hold the shipwreck of all the mongrel civilization of the past which is evidence that in keeping with the laws of creative justice nature has decreed that mixed civilizations, together with governments of mixed races, are doomed to destruction and oblivion.

From the past the voice of the great Lincoln must be heard:

"There are physical differences .between the races which would forever forbid them living together on terms of political and social equality."

The imperative call of higher justice to the real patriots of our Nation is:

"In the name of our valiant and venerated dead and in due respect to their stainless memory and in the interest of peace and security of all peoples now living and for the sake of all those yet to be. keep Anglo-Saxon American civilization, institutions, politics. and society pure. and thereby, since we have received this sacred heritage. transmit it with clean hands and pure hearts to generations yet unborn. thereby keeping faith with the mind. soul, and purpose of our valiant sires and transmit our name into the future without dishonor and without disgrace.

"Let the solemn behest of higher duty be promptly and properly met in all the relationships of life and living without fault, without fail, without fear, and without reproach, now and forevermore."

The Ku Klux may be antagonized and forced to fight many battles, but perish? Never! To destroy it is an impossibility. for it belongs in essence to the realms spiritual. It is unshaken by unjust criticisms, no power can thwart it in its onward conquest of right; it courts not the plaudits of the populace, nor is it swerved from its course by the libel of its foes. Attuned with Deity, functioning only for all humanity's good, misjudged by ignorance. misunderstood by many, slandered by prejudice, sweeping on under the divine leadership of Deity, it never falters and will never fail.

The spirit of the Ku-Klux Klan still lives, and should live, a priceless heritage to be sacredly treasured by all those who love our country, regardless of section, and are proud of its sacred traditions. That this spirit may live always to warm the hearts of manly men, unify them by the force of a holy clannishness, to assuage the billowing tide of a fraternal alienation that surges in human breasts, and inspire them to achieve the highest and noblest in the defense of our country, our homes, humanity, and each other is the paramount ideal of the Knights of the Ku-Klux Klan.

When the baleful blast of reconstruction's storm was o'er,
The valiant, chivalric Ku Klux rode no more.
But ride on and on, thou spirit of that mystic klan,
In your noble mission for humanity's good;
Until the clannish tie of klankraft binds man to man
For our country, our homes, and womanhood.

   *   *   *   *   *   *   *

AMERICANS, TAKE HEED!

SCUM O' THE MELTING POT.

[By Herbert Kaufman. Signed editorial feature, April, 1920, issue McClure's Magazine.]

The Declaration of Independence, the Constitution, and the Gettysburg Address are descendants of the Magna Charta—supreme symbols of Anglo-Saxon souls striving for freedom, justice, and humanity. Anglo-Saxons established this Nation, wrote its code, and sent their sons into the wilderness to gather fresh stars for the flag.

Anglo-Saxon purpose cowed the intervening wastes, discovered world granaries beneath the prairies, scaled the grim western hills and unmasked Eldorado, questioned sullen deserts until they answered with gardens, and finished on the Pacific the great adventure begun at Plymouth Rock.

Then, when the last taunting horizon had been met and vanquished, when axe and rifle had won an empire, when scattered settlements were beaded on threads of steel, and a safe highway through opportunity had been paved in their generous blood, the pioneers, the risk takers tossed their port keys into the ocean and invited all creation to come at leisure and share a " sure thing."

The making of America is fundamentally an Anglo-Saxon achievement. Anglo-Saxon brains have guided the course of the Republic. Our ideals are Anglo-Saxon, our social traditions, our standards of honor, our quality of imagination, and our indomitability.

But Anglo-Saxon opinion is a fast diminishing force in national determinations. Strange shoddy has lately crept in the loom on which we weave our destiny ; intermarriage is steadily diluting the foundation strain, and if we continue to hold gates and veins wide open Anglo-Saxon conscience will soon cease to captain our genius.

It would slander a vast body of loyal citizens not to admit the devoted service of all who fought for us, wrought with us, valiantly supported the country in every crisis. Yet a review of the past 50 years disclose that each successive tide of immigrants has displayed less and less sympathy with our institutions, is more confirmed in its racial solidarity, more resistant to environment and assimilation.

Ominous statistics proclaim the persistent development of a parasite mass within our domain—our political system is clogged with foreign bodies which stubbornly refuse to be absorbed, and means must be found to meet the menace. We have taken unto ourselves a Trojan horse crowded with ignorance, illiteracy, and envy. We have Hessianized our essential enterprises until alien workers predominate the basic industries of the country and hold further progress at their regardless mercy.

Provocateurs of revenge and anarchy—opportunists and demagogues—are already forging their strength into a weapon that bodes democracy ill.

Reckless State laws admit them to local elections without process of naturalization, and inadequate naturalization tests put votes into their hands before we fairly get English into their heads.

The will of America is not calling land over for strikes ; the fist of America is not brandishing I. W. W bombs ; the choice of America is not sophisticating Congress and legislatures with snide statesmanship.

Nay ; the voice of America is being slowly drowned in jargon voices crying hate between labor and capital, hate between blindness and vision, hate between culture and coarseness, hate between law and license, even hate between the Anglo-Saxon peoples.

On to the melting pot and clean it o' this scum !

EXHIBIT H.

COPY OF TELEGRAM SENT TO ALL MEMBERS OF CONGRESS.

ATLANTA, GA., *September 30, 1921.*

There has been introduced in Congress a bill by Hon. Peter F. Tague, of Massachusetts, providing for a congressional investigation of the Knights of the Ku-Klux Klan; a similar bill has also been introduced by Hon. T. J. Ryan, of New York.

The Ku-Klux Klan desires that a bill providing for a congressional investigation pass the House, and has therefore to-day telegraphed every Member of the House asking his vote in favor of an investigation bill, our telegram being as follows:

"The Knights of the Ku-Klux Klan, through me, the founder and chief executive, respectfully asks and would appreciate your vote in favor of the passage of the bill introduced in Congress September 21, 1921, by Hon. Peter F. Tague providing for a congressional investigation of the Ku-Klux Klan.

"We demur to the wording of this bill in so far as charges against the klan are concerned, but we unreservedly agree with the purpose of the bill or any other resolution that will provide for and assure a congressional investigation of the Knights of the Ku-Klux Klan.

"We know that such an investigation will be impartial, and when completed the klan will be fully exonerated from all charges and slanders made against it.

"We would appreciate the opportunity of providing by documentary evidence and unimpeachable witnesses the factors back of the attacks against the klan, and also providing the absolute unreliability and untruthfulness of men launching signed newspaper articles in Washington and elsewhere against the klan.

"From our knowledge of the klan, its membership and activities, we know that the investigation will officially reveal that the klan was founded only on the principles of democracy, does not countenance religious or racial prejudice, and seeks only to bind together men for mutual service, and is inspired by love of justice, respect for the law, and a deep faith in the glorious future of the American people."

I have also telegraphed President Harding and Attorney General Daugherty respectfully asking an investigation of the klan by the Department of Justice.

Respectfully,

WILLIAM J. SIMMONS.

EXHIBIT I.

COPY OF TELEGRAM SENT TO PRESIDENT HARDING.

ATLANTA, GA., *September 28, 1921.*

President WARREN G. HARDING,
The White House, Washington, D. C.

SIR: The Knights of the Ku-Klux Klan respectively ask that an investigation of the klan by the Federal authorities be made.

We plead for and would welcome such an investigation, and can appeal to you the Chief Magistrate of the greatest Republic the world has ever seen, with clean hands, a clear conscience, and with a knowledge that after such an investigation is completed the Knights of the Ku-Klux Klan will stand out in the white light of vindication from charges made against it.

The klan was founded on the bedrock principles of democracy and patriotism. It seeks only to bring together in a confraternity men actuated by love of justice and a deep faith in the glorious future of the American people.

The klan is not a political organization to foster religious or racial intolerance. We affirm with millions of Americans that all men should have the right to vote and worship as they please, so long as they please not to attack or undermine the great principles upon which the United States were founded.

Our creed is simply an affirmation that the American Commonwealth was founded by the western races and is the highest expression of Protestant civilization. We seek only to keep our ancient faith and racial integrity and to encourage our members to better citizenship.

We have the same right that small minorities in our body politic have so long exercised. The Knights of Columbus, certain Jewish alliance, and foreign associations have organized and functioned for the purpose of inoculating in their members peculiar religious or racial loyalties.

We have the right to organize for the purpose of fostering in our memories the principles where America will stand or fall, the love of race and country, and a belief in the broad protestantism upon which our Nation was founded, the absolute separation of church and State, these things being the ancient landmarks of our Anglo-Saxon civilization in American institutions.

As founder and chief officer of the Knights of the Ku-Klux Klan I have been inspired by the same devotion of country that at the outbreak of the Spanish-American War caused me, a youth of 18, to enter the ranks in the First Regiment Alabama Volunteers, Company B, and to continue in the ranks for the duration of the war, receiving at its end an honorable discharge.

Respectfully,

WILLIAM J. SIMMONS.

COPY OF TELEGRAM SENT TO ATTORNEY GENERAL DAUGHERTY.

ATLANTA, GA., *September 28, 1921.*

Attorney General DAUGHERTY,
Washington, D. C.

SIR: The Knights of the Ku-Klux Klan, through me, the head of the order, respectfully requests that you order a complete and thorough investigation by the Department of Justice of the klan, its organization, purposes, and activities.

We pledge you the assistance of all officials and members of the klan in this investigation. Our records, books, files, etc., are at your disposal.

If any so-called outrages, as charged by a small partisan press, have been committed by members of the Ku-Klux Klan we will render every possible assistance to the Department of Justice in tracing down these alleged outrages and will be glad to fix the guilt on any man or men, members of the klan or not, who are cowardly enough to by threats, intimidation, or bodily force take the law into their own hands.

Our information proves that these alleged crimes have been committed by nonmembers of the klan to satisfy private grudges and in many instances by others with an ulterior motive to serve. The records for the past 10 years will show that there were as many or more similar crimes of this nature committed before the Knights of the Ku-Klux Klan was organized as since its organization, as is witnessed by night riding in many States.

The Knights of the Ku-Klux Klan is a purely fraternal order, founded on the bedrock principles of the Constitution of the United States. We do not teach nor practice class hatred, religious intolerance, or racial prejudice, disregard of the law, or the enforcement of the law by the individual.

We do teach and practice unselfish devotion to our country, to strengthen our membership in patriotic citizenship, and we exalt the fundamentals of our Anglo-Saxon civilization in order that the ideals and institutions of pure Americanism may be kept secure.

Respectfully,

WILLIAM J. SIMMONS.

EXHIBIT J.

[News story from Houston, Tex., paper under date of Sept. 29, 1921; original paper on file in Atlanta, Ga.]

JACK RALSTON DIES OF INJURIES—KLAN BEFRIENDS WIDOW—FUNERAL OF ACCIDENT VICTIM WILL BE HELD TO-DAY—KU-KLUX SENDS $1,000 IN BILLS—MRS. RALSTON SURPRISED AND PROUD TO LEARN HUSBAND WAS A KLANSMAN.

When the lights flickered on Wednesday night and went out for a large portion of the residence section of Houston there was darkness for a few hours for the many. For one, however, the lights will not come on again. That one was Jack Ralston, electrician, 1310 Lamar Avenue. Thursday morning he succumbed to injuries received as he worked high in the air Wednesday evening endeavoring to keep the lights trimmed and burning in the thousands of homes. As he worked, an overloaded circuit near by let go. There was a blinding flash of flame as the large copper cables fused and parted. Ralston was blinded and burned and knocked from his precarious perch 30 feet in the air to the ground. He was rushed to a hospital after two other workers had been injured in rescue work, but his wounds were so serious that he passed out in the early hours before daylight Thursday morning. And with his passing came darkness into a home, for Jack Ralston was happily married. He is survived by a widow and his mother.

FUNERAL SERVICES TO-DAY.

Funeral services under the auspices of the electrical workers' union will be held from the residence of his sister-in-law, Mrs. O. L. Verhelle, 1705 Capitol Avenue, directed by the Fogle-West Undertaking Co., Friday afternoon at 5 o'clock. Burial will be in Evergreen Cemetery, with Rev. T. J. Windham officiating.

The pallbearers will be: S. R. Bertron, jr., J. T. Dodds, W. A. McDonald, J. R. Beatty, J. A. McReynolds, D. E. Bostick, J. P. Wilson, and S. R. Smith. Active: D. E. Shown, G. H. McArthur, L. M. Kays, A. C. Anderson, H. Haberlic, and John Griffin.

L. M. Maxwell, who was working with Ralston when the accident occurred, is still at the Baptist sanitarium, where it was reported Thursday afternoon that he was in no immediate danger.

RAY OF SUNLIGHT ENTERS.

Soon after the grind of business began in Houston Thursday morning a little ray of sunlight crept into the Ralston home to dispel some of the darkness of death. As she sat with her sorrow Mrs. Ralston was visited, shortly before 10 o'clock, by a sympathetic friend. That friend, she soon discovered, was a fraternal brother of her husband. He brought with him twenty $50 bills and he handed them over to her, telling her that he had secured them from the bank within 10 minutes after it opened, and had gone direct to her with them. The money represented insurance carried by her husband in one of the lodges.

"Later he told me," said Mrs. Ralston, "that he was from the Ku-Klux Klan, and that Jack was also a member of the klan and that it was klan insurance he was giving me. He gave twenty $50 bills.

"I never knew until this morning that Jack was a klansman. He spoke of it sometimes and praised it highly, and I held the same views that he did, but I never knew he was a member. But if he should have told me, I would have gone to my grave before I would have told anyone.

"WILL CHERISH MEMBERSHIP CARD.

"I often saw his membership cards but never suspected what they were. One looked like a meal ticket, and I said to him one day, 'Jack, you have a meal ticket and I fix you lunch every day.' He said, 'Yes, I know, but I buy an extra meal every once in a while.' The other one is a pretty little black and white card. He told me that it was his union card. I shall keep both of them always.

"Two nights every week he always went out. He told me that he was attending the unions. I asked him why there were two meetings, and he told me that one was the inner meeting. All the while he was attending the klan meeting."

N. T. Starr, who was burned about the face and arms when he went to the rescue of Maxwell, other than suffering intense pain Thursday, was reported to be in no danger.

Mr. SIMMONS. Now, Mr. Chairman, I have finished with the exhibits, and for a few moments I would crave the indulgence of this committee to make a few closing remarks in the way of a recapitulation of what we have gone over. I assure you, sirs, that I will be as brief as possible, because I am suffering.

Mr. Chairman and gentlemen of the committee, I am the imperial wizard of the Knights of the Ku-Klux Klan and the supreme executive official of the same. I exercise only those rights and prerogatives that are given me by the constitution and laws of the organization and by the charter issued by the court creating the organization as a legal entity. If I have erred in any of these things, it has not been intentional nor with any purpose of misstatement.

Going back now—and I am going to be brief—it has been conspicuously presented to your honorable body that one Mrs. Elizabeth Tyler is the supreme boss of the whole business. I want to state to you, Mr. Chairman and gentlemen of the committee, that that is an absurd untruth. Mrs. Tyler is simply employed in the propagation department as the chief assistant to Mr. Clarke in that work. So far as I am concerned, I will say with reference to the gentlemen who testified and to the others who have been down there investigating, that at the time they were there I was either away or in bed sick, and, of course, they did not see much of me. Mrs. Elizabeth Tyler is not my boss, and I am not a figurehead. The only head I have is a red head, and I have never been bossed by but two women in my life, my mother and my wife. I explained to you this morning as best I could the workings of the propagation department, with Mr. Clarke and his organization under a contract conducting the propagation organization.

All of the fraternal orders of which I have any knowledge, with the exception of one or two, have used and resorted to the same methods. If you will go back and study the records of the fraternal orders, especially in recent years, you will find that they have had propagation forces and workers. I want to state here most emphatically, in the presence and fear of God, that the Ku-Klux Klan has been maligned and held up to the world as an anti-Catholic organization. It has been alleged that it is an anti-Catholic organization, but, Mr. Chairman, it certainly is not. I have never joined any so-called anti-Catholic organizations.

Mr. RODENBERG. This does not permit Catholics to become members.

Mr. SIMMONS. That is true, but neither does the Knights of Columbus permit Protestants to become members of that order. That is fair play each way, and we ask for no rights and privileges that other American citizens can not exercise for themselves. We simply ask for the rights and privileges accorded other American citizens. We question no man's patriotism because he is a Catholic or belongs to any other denomination, but this is simply a Protestant institution. I know, Mr. Chairman, that there are many good men in this country that are not permitted under our regulations to join. Four years ago I had a mighty good man who was anxious to join this order, and he told me he would give $50 to join it. I said to him, "You can not join." He said, "What is the matter with me?" I said, "Not a thing; you are a splendid high-class Christian gentleman." He was a teacher in a Sunday school, but he was a preacher of the Presbyterian Church in England, and that was a foreign institution to the Presbyterian Church in America.

There is nothing in that that anybody can take offense at. God knows that I studied this for 20 years, and I have never had any motive along that line. We antagonize no man's religion or creed so long as that creed is in accord with the Constitution of the United States. It has been charged here that certain organizers of the Ku-Klux Klan have been making headway in obtaining members by the circulation of anti-Catholic literature. I will say to you in all frankness that there was only one instance, according to my recollection, where a kleagle circulated or attempted to circulate anti-Catholic literature, and within less than a week, or as soon as I could get to that man, he was forever discharged from our work, and for that reason. We are not anti-Catholic. I say that to my Catholic friends, and I have lots of them. We are simply a Protestant order. If a Catholic can fulfill the requirements of the order he will be welcomed to our borders, and we say that to all. Some time ago it was published around that we were anticapitalist, but they could not get anywhere with that, and now they are trying to make it appear that we are antilabor, but we have nothing to do with those matters.

We are a fraternal order, but they say we are anti-Jew. No; we are not. I can count my Jewish friends by the score. We are not any more anti-Jew than they are anti-me in their own particular orders. If there is any Jew that can subscribe to the tenets of the Christian religion we will gladly welcome him in the faith. We will welcome him with open arms, but one of our requirements is that a man must be a believer in the tenets of the Christian religion. There are several fraternal orders in this country that have practically the same requirements that we have. We are not the only ones by any means. It has been charged that we are anti-Negro. No; we are not—most positively not. It seems that they predicate these statements upon the fact that Catholics, Jews, and Negroes do not come in, and that, therefore, we are antagonistic to them. Because the Negro can not come into this order does not mean that we are antagonistic to his interests or his highest well-being. There are scores of fraternal orders in this country that will not admit a Negro to membership. We are not the only one. It is charged that we are antiforeign born. No; we are not. One of our requirements is that a man must be a native-born American citizen. Now, why do we require that? Of course, I know and you know that there are thousands of foreign-born men in this country who are just as devoted to the Stars and Stripes as you and I are, but we had to draw the line somewhere. There are also thousands and thousands of foreign-born men in this country who, if they could get the opportunity, would snatch our flag from its staff and grind it under their heels. We do not want to take any chances, and we drew the line there rather than attempt to pick out and discriminate among individuals.

For that reason we drew the line and required that a man must be a native-born American citizen to become a member. We are not the only organization that has that requirement. Some question has been raised in regard to the robes and parades. Our costume has been adopted, and that is one of the rights of this corporation. Every fraternal order has the right to adopt its paraphernalia. Our costume complete is simply a memorial to the greatest heroes in the world's history. A great deal has been said about the mask or masked men. Are we the only people that use a mask? If so, what about the Mardi Gras celebrations in this country, and what about the Halloween celebrations? There are other celebrations in which masks are used. Our mask and robe, I say before God, are as innocent as the breath of an angel. There has been a great deal of talk about parades for the purpose of intimidation. There has never been such a parade. Our parade usually comes off as an announcement to the public in our peculiar way that the klan in that locality has been fully organized. They are held on any other occasions of celebration, but it is never for any purposes of intimidation. We have joined hands with some other fraternal orders in great patriotic parades. We always join hands with them in such parades. That is simply a memorial; that is all. I want to state to you, sirs, that never have we paraded in any incorporated town without the knowledge and consent of the mayor of that town or the chief of police. In Atlanta, Ga., the home of this order since it has been functioning, neither the mayor of the city nor the chief of police has been a member of the klan, and the record will show that every time we have paraded in Atlanta we have always had a permit from the mayor or the police headquarters to do so, and oftentimes have had a police escort. We will not parade unless it is agreeable or unless we have a permit from the authorities of the law. When we get that authority to parade we have the right to parade.

Mr. CAMPBELL. I have refrained from asking you any questions during your statement, but I think it pertinent at this point to direct your attention to the conflict between the sheriff of a county in Texas and klansmen in which a riot occurred because the klansmen insisted upon parading. Will you explain how that parade was held in defiance of the officer?

Mr. SIMMONS. I will explain that to the best of my ability from the information that I had received through newspaper sources and other sources up to the time I left. That happened right recently, as you understand. The klan there wished to hold a parade and it had been advertised or a notice given of it, because the people were there on the streets to see it. When they were forming, the sheriff of the county, who I am informed made a trip of 40 miles across the country to stop it, came up in what seemed to be somewhat of an intoxicated condition. That is my information, that he seemed to be in a somewhat intoxicated condition. He went up and demanded that there should be no parade. According to my information, the men in charge of the parade, and they were among the best citizens of the town, told him that it was simply an innocent parade. I am informed that in a very positive way the sheriff said, "You will have no parade. I have got to know who is in that parade." According to my information, they asked him then if the men who were the bearers of the fiery cross should unmask would it be all right. He said, "Yes; that will be all right." Those two men unmasked and the parade started. They told the sheriff that they had permission from the mayor and the chief of police. They came on down the street, but before they had gone far, the sheriff, cutting across through an alleyway, came up again and demanded that the parade should be stopped and the paraders dispersed. It is my information that the man carrying the flag said, "Where this flag leads, klansmen follow." An attempt was made to snatch the flag out of this man's hands, and possibly some rough or profane words were used regarding the flag.

When he attempted to snatch the flag out of this man's hands, this man struck him with his fist, knocking him down. In knocking him down, the sheriff's pistol fell out of its holster. This man jumped up and drew a dirk knife, when somebody in the crowd picked up the sheriff's pistol and shot him just as he was trying to stick the knife in him. Then a general melee followed.

Mr. RODENBERG. Were there numerous shots fired in the crowd?

Mr. SIMMONS. I suppose so.

Mr. RODENBERG. Were the klansmen armed?

Mr. SIMMONS. Not to my knowledge; I have no information as to that.

Mr. CAMPBELL. Have you asked for or have you a report from the klan putting on that parade?

Mr. SIMMONS. No, sir; because I was sick in bed. That happened a few days ago, and I was in bed and not able to transact any business before coming up here.

Mr. ETHERIDGE. Mr. Chairman, may I answer that question, as a member of the imperial body? When Col. Simmons was sick and this matter occurred, there was a meeting called of the kloncilium, which is the governing body, and a demand made upon that local klan for a report. That report had not been received when I left Atlanta. I do not know that Col. Simmons had information of that action, because he was at home sick in bed.

Mr. CAMPBELL. Would a klansman be permitted to carry arms in a parade of that kind?

Mr. SIMMONS. No, sir; not if it was known. The rule applies there just like it does among citizens. Citizens are not permitted to carry concealed weapons, but oftentimes they do, sir. In fact, a klansman is not only not permitted to carry weapons, but he is not permitted to imbibe intoxicating liquors if he is going into a parade; and I have had many a man pulled out for that reason.

Now, Mr. Chairman, it has been alleged that this is a grafting, get-rich scheme. Just let me touch on that momentarily. Our initial admission fee is only the sum of $10. Mr. Chairman, I will say to you that I could make that $20 and it would not affect the increase of this organization 5 per cent. If it was a grasping game, why have we not made it just as big as we can? It is only $10, and all through this war period, when other fraternal orders were increasing their initial fees, we did not increase a penny.

If I remember correctly, the first three years, or possibly four years—I can not be sure about that—the initiation fee, by request of all the members we had in Atlanta, was reduced to $5 in order to start the movement. This $10 will cover two degrees in our work. Only the first degree has been communicated. Don't you know, sir—haven't you knowledge of many fraternal orders that charge more than $5 a degree? There are fraternal orders that charge $75 to $100 and $150 in which to be initiated. This is a very flimsy and foolish charge. Last winter and spring I received from all through the North and West—scores and scores, and I might say hundreds, of letters from men: " I believe in your organization; I can subscribe to your principles. Inclosed find $10, or a check for $10, or a money order; count me one of your members." In every instance, Mr. Chairman, in receiving that money through the mails we acknowledged receipt of the money and the letter and expressed our appreciation and wrote those men that we did not receive money in that way; that we would take their names, and whenever our organizer got in their community they would be called upon, and sent the money back to them. If we had been in a grafting game we could have legitimately kept that money.

Mr. POU. Have there been any complaints from the members of the organization against the officers on account of the gain that any of the officers have received?

Mr. SIMMONS. Absolutely none. I never heard of anything or any thought of that thing until the New York World said something about it. It seems that everybody is perfectly agreeable and well pleased except those who are on the outside. I have at different times given instructions that if any man was not pleased, or thought he had been in any way deceived, that his money should go back to him, even though he had taken the oath; and, to my knowledge, those instructions have been carried out. In this connection I would also like to state, Mr. Chairman, that there was presented here yesterday by Mr. Wright the statement that we receive enormous sums of money by supplying the lodges with furniture, and so on. We do not do anything of the kind, and he knows it There is an outfit, when a klan is chartered, that costs—I could not say just the exact amount, because material has been fluctuating so in price, but I would say a klan outfit, consisting of the altar furnishings and record books, costs about $25. That outfit is given to that klan when it is chartered without any cost whatever, and that is all that we furnish, and we do not sell any lodge furniture or things of that sort at enormous profit. Our books and records are open. Now, as to the manufacture of the robes: We control the manufacture of our paraphernalia, so that no outsiders can put up a counterfeit organization and counterfeit it. For the first three or four years, approximately, of our organization those robes were supplied at $3.75 an outfit, at actual cost, but the war came on and the price of cotton went up, and you know that cotton goods in places cost, possibly, more than silk. The cost of the robes went up. Mr. W. E. Flodding's concern was manufacturing the robes in Atlanta, and the prices went up so that he demanded $7.50 for the outfit, and I told him, "Mr. Flodding, we can not pay that," and Mr. Davis, of the Gate City Manufacturing Co., told me, "I think I can manufacture those robes at a less price," and he said, "You ought to have a margin to cover shipping, the express, and so on."

Many times we have had cartons or boxes of our robes lost in transit by the express company, especially during the war when there was so much traffic, and so I had to fix a price where we could be clear from a sensible business standpoint; in other words, a price that would cover the expense of getting out the robe and getting it to them and so on. So, owing to the high price of cotton and other material also, it was fixed at $6.50. Last spring I asked Mr. Davis if the price of the robes could be reduced, and he said, "Col. Simmons, the condition of the market is such I would not advise it. We do not know what it is going to be." He said, "I will tell you, though, if you say so, I will go to New York and find out if I can get any line on the future market of cotton goods." He did, and came back and said, "I would not advise it because, from all I can learn, by September the price of cotton goods is going to increase rapidly and you want to be safe on this."

Mr. GARRETT. May I ask you, has there been any gain to you or to the organization in profits made upon the costumes?

Mr. SIMMONS. Sir, there has been no gain to me. Wherever there is a surplus from the cost of getting that garment out and getting it to them and the price they pay, that has gone into the general funds of the organization. There were oftentimes, owing to the high prices, with a fixed price we were right up to it or, in other words, there was very little margin, if any, at all.

Mr. GARRETT. I believe Mr. Williamson testified that according to the investigation he had made the last contract which you have with the manufacturers of the paraphernalia, it cost you $4.50 or $4.60?

Mr. SIMMONS. Something like that; I do not remember now.

Mr. GARRETT. And that it was sold under that contract at six dollars and something?

Mr. SIMMONS. We have a fixed price for this reason: I thought, the 1st of July, about reducing the price. Then I was informed of the conditions of the market on materials and I thought it would create confusion if I reduced the price 50 cents and then again in 30 to 60 days would have to put it back up; but this profit is to be used in the general funds of the organization for the purpose of helping on the organization in the work we have to do.

Mr. GARRETT. Can you state to the committee what is the highest price that has been charged for one of these costumes?

Mr. SIMMONS. I think, sir, but I will not be sure about that on account of the fluctuation of prices, but I am reasonably sure that the highest price is $6.50. When this concern said they would have to have $7.50 to manufacture them and this other concern came up and said, "We can manufacture them cheaper than that, we think," of course we discontinued with the first firm and took up with the second one and we have been supplying them at $6.50.

Mr. GARRETT. Is there anything else except the costume utilized by the various klans that has been sold through the head lodge?

Mr. SIMMONS. Through the headquarters?

Mr. GARRETT. Yes.

Mr. SIMMONS. Well; yes, sir. For instance, the books, account books, and things of that nature. Of course, we control, or have ourselves the supplying of these things, stationery and matters of that kind are supplied through the general headquarters for the reason that we do not want our organizations all over the country going into any local print shops or places of that sort where our cuts would have to be scattered all over the country, so that we concentrate there.

Mr. GARRETT. Tell us about that. Tell us about the profits in those things.
Mr. SIMMONS. About three months ago, or, rather at the beginning of this fiscal year, July 1, the question was presented to me: What margin shall we ask on these various and sundry supplies; what margin shall we have over and above the actual cost? I made the statement to place the margin as low as possible, but to guarantee in the cost any loss or expense in transit or things of that sort, and I would judge from that it was fixed at about 10 per cent only.

Mr. GARRETT. If the lodge wished to purchase certain books that were required, they would purchase them through the central organization?

Mr. SIMMONS. Yes, sir; because we are the only ones that can supply them, of course.

Mr. GARRETT. And the central organization has a contract with some book-making concern to supply them?

Mr. SIMMONS. Well, sir it is not a contract. When we have printing to do we present the stuff, of course, and get prices on it, and, of course, as far as a contract is concerned, it is simply this: If we have half a dozen printing concerns, whichever one has the facilities to do the work right and at the lowest price gets it. It is not so much what you would call a contract, it is an agreement along that line.

Mr. GARRETT. Let us take, for instance, the charter which you exhibited here this morning and which is now a part of the committee's record. Is the local klan charged with the cost of that charter?

Mr. SIMMONS. No, sir; that charter and the outfit or paraphernalia that goes with it, as I stated a moment ago, is free. When they are ready to be chartered the charter is sent to them with what we call the klan paraphernalia; that is, the necessary paraphernalia for the functioning of the klan.

Mr. GARRETT. Do you make any profit out of that in any way?

Mr. SIMMONS. No, sir; not to my knowledge. There can be no profit, because that outfit is given free.

Mr. RODENBERG. The expense of that comes out of the $10 initiation fee?

Mr. SIMMONS. Yes; it comes out of that fee. The engrossing of the charter is free, and that charter is delivered free.

Mr. GARRETT. Was the statement of Mr. Williamson substantially accurate or accurate, in fact, as to the decision of this initial donation or fee or whatever it may be called?

Mr. SIMMONS. From the best I could understand Mr. Williamson from over here—and I could not understand him clearly—but to the best of my understanding what he said I think is approximately accurate. You can compare his statement with mine this morning as to the division of it.

Mr. GARRETT. Has there been within the thought of the responsible authorities of this organization the idea of having the so-called initiation charges designated as donations rather than fees for the purpose of preventing the Federal Government from receiving internal-revenue taxes upon the income of this organization as a corporation?

Mr. SIMMONS. Well, I will say to you in all honor and under God that that thought has never come into the mind of a single man; nothing of that nature, because that would not be just to our Government, and it would not be permitted.

Mr. RODENBERG. But you do not pay any income tax?

Mr. SIMMONS. I will get to that just in a few minutes, if you will pardon me, when I get to it in the regular sequence. Let me say this, so many of our great orders have become commercialized, in the creation of this institution we are steering it as far from any sentiment of commercialism as possible. This is really and truly a donation. One of the requirements for membership is that a man must be two things and do two things before he can be considered. He must be a native-born white American citizen at or above the age of 18 years, and so on. He must be a believer, so far as the light he has, in our purpose, work, and mission. He must do two things: He must make formal application or ask to come in himself either by signing an application for charter or else signing a regular application blank, and then he must render an unselfish service to our cause before he can be admitted.

Now, to make that apply to all and to all alike, and to be practical, that service rendered is expressed in his donation of $10. If a man's income is $5 a day, then he has contributed two days' unselfish service to the cause, and that is a donation, and accepted as such, and so specified in our laws and acknowledged as a donation to the propagating fund of the order, and when he signs his application and makes his donation the certificate certifying that he has made it is detached and given to him. Now, the party who received that $10, be it a kleagle or a member out yonder, the party who receives that $10 receives it in trust to be turned in to the organization. So that if a man, either a kleagle or an individual, should knock down that $10 or do away with it or appropriate it to himself, we have a check on him and can handle him for a misappropriation of it.

Mr. GARRETT. Was that provision in your regulations prior to the passage of the income and corporation tax law?

Mr. SIMMONS. Yes, sir; that has been a provision all the way through, from the very beginning.

Mr. RODENBERG. The income-tax law was not in operation long before this order started.

Mr. SIMMONS. Since you have asked that question, I will get to that point now. I was going to get to it any way, later, in reference to the income tax.

Mr. RODENBERG. I would like to get a specific answer, whether the imperial headquarters has at any time paid anything to the Federal Government in the shape of a tax on your per capita tax on the memberships, your profits on the regalia or your profits on the books that you furnish the local klans.

Mr. SIMMONS. I can state to you, sir, that we have not, and I wish to follow that statement by making this statement. When this law first took effect I went to the income-tax office in the Federal building in Atlanta and made inquiry as to whether this organization would come under that law or not, it being a fraternal, eleemosynary institution, and stated to the gentleman—that was whenever this law took effect, three or four years ago—and I stated to the gentleman that I wanted the information and if we came under that law we wanted to make provisions to meet the obligations of the Government, but if we did not, I wanted to know it. That gentleman informed me, "You do not come under this law," and that was the end of that conversation. He seemed to be very busy. I do not know who he was. That has been some time ago but the inquiry was made to that end and I was assured that the organization did not come under it. Now, if it does, then it is not a fault of mine or this organization, and if it can be shown that we are liable, we are ready to meet our obligations to the Government because we seek to meet them in all other things and we will not dodge them there. If it took every dollar in our treasury to meet obligations along that line, every dollar would go. We are honest there.

Now, while we are on the robe proposition, as best we can approximate it, only about 30 per cent of our membership has the regalia. It has been stated here that everybody is absolutely compelled to have it. They are urged to get it, but it is shown that only about 30 per cent of the entire membership has ever gotten the regalia.

Mr. GARRETT. By the way, is there any regulation as to where this regalia shall be kept?

Mr. SIMMONS. Oh, no, sir. That is left to the discretion and the good judgment of the local members. If you were a member and had lockers sufficient in the anterooms of the lodge room where you met, they could be kept there or you could carry it home with you. In other words, you are supposed to see that it is properly cared for, so that it is not in any way mutilated or soiled any more than could be helped. A good many of the organizations, I understand, have prepared lockers out in the anterooms and they are kept there; at others the members take them home with them and take care of them so that they will not be in any way misused.

Now, Mr. Chairman, there has been stated here something about the great imperial palace, and it has been advertised in the paper and spoken of as a million and a half dollar palace. We have not got anything like that. What has gone into it has been shown here in reference to the cost of that property. It is not yet all paid for, but even at that, are we the only institution that has got a great palace? The Scottish Rites in your town here have a magnificent temple which represents a splendid investment. The great order of the Nobles of the Mystic Shrine have their temples all over the country that represent millions, and other fraternal orders, too numerous to mention, have their headquarters buildings that cost large sums of money. So you see that allegation is futile.

Now, Mr. Chairman, it has been stated here repeatedly that this is an organization gotten together to terrorize, to scare people, bulldoze them, bluff them, and so on. All of those allegations, sir, are unfounded and untrue. If by our name—something was said a while ago or this morning about our name, Ku-Klux Klan; that the very name tended to terrorize, and so on. If that be true, sir, then, " Oh, shades of our colonial fathers, call out the Colonial Militia; the Red Men of America have organized to scalp every paleface on this continent." There are the Elks and the Moose and the Lions that are organized with those names. There is nothing in that. Shakespeare said there was nothing in a name. That name is a memorial.

Now, they talk about threatening letters, and, sir, hear me at this point. They talk about letters being sent out threatening people threatening them in life and limb, or with tar and feathers, and the destruction of their property, and all that sort of thing. That has been brought out here repeatedly. Does the Ku-Klux Klan do that? I say, by the authority of the Ku-Klux Klan, that is absolutely false. If the Ku-Klux Klan alone did that, why have I, as the imperial wizard, received hundreds of death letters in the past five months threatening my life in every conceivable way, cutting out in cardboard a representation of a coffin and inscribing thereon threatening and death-dealing sentences? Somebody else is sending out those letters besides the Ku-Klux Klan, for the klansman certainly would not threaten the life and shoot their wizard. I have got those letters, and many of them have been reported to the Post Office Department; numbers of them.

One other point, or just two further points, Mr. Chairman. Let me state to you this: No organization, no church, and no individual that is not on a sound financial basis commands the respect of the community. It was the purpose in the beginning of the creation of this organization to so fix it that the organization would be able to pay its obligations, and the surplus money over and above its obligations would be used for benevolent and educational purposes, and we worked out a plan so that the working operations will guarantee that the organization shall be sound financially. I noticed the other day that a gentleman sitting over there, in the questions of the committee, asked who worked out this system, whether it was the Ku-Klux Klan or some other organization way up in the Dakotas or in Wisconsin or somewhere, I do not just remember. The plan of the Ku-Klux Klan, sir, was worked out by myself something like 10 years ago, and it is virtually the same plan that I worked out when I was in the organization work of the Woodmen of the World, having organizers, district organizers, and State managers, and so on. It is a logical, sensible, businesslike plan, and it is effective when you have competent men to enforce it. We have borrowed nothing from anyone's organization, and we wanted to be a safe and sane organization financially.

Now, then one more point, Mr. Chairman, and I will have to close. I am sorry I am suffering as I am, but I can not help it. Julius Cæsar had his Brutus, Jesus Christ had his Judas, and our great and illustrious Washington had his Benedict Arnold. Sir, I can state to you that I can enter the fellowship of all three of those because I have suffered in my soul as a result of the treasonous and treacherous conduct of traitors. I refer to one in the beginning of my statement this morning. Right recently, those who have furnished material to the outside world and whose names have been put across the page, are one man by the name of Craven, of North Carolina; another man by the name of Fry, who hails from Tennessee; another man by the name of Wright, who hails, so far as I know, from New York. Mr. Craven was a disgruntled office seeker who tried to have me appoint him as State head of the State of North Carolina. When I had not made any appointments along that line, and had not gotten to that, I understood he was trying to get the appointment to use it for political purposes. The appointment was not made at the time he wanted it, and he sent threatening letters, and because he did not get it, or because he could not get that appointment he became a disgruntled office seeker in this order, and proved a traitor to his sacred trust. Mr. Fry, or Capt. Fry, as he is called, was in our field force. He also proved a traitor, and violated as solemn an oath as a man can take.

I will state to you, briefly, in closing, that Mr. Wright also took that oath, and in his own words he violated it for pay.

Now, this brings us to the point of the Knights of the Air, which has been brought out here, but has not been touched on by me, and then I have finished, sir. I have received some letters from Mr. Wright from his office in New York last winter.

Along in the latter part of the winter, I think—I can not be altogether accurate on that—he came down to Atlanta to see me. He said he was the head of the different flyers' clubs, and so on, and that the whole flying organization of flyers all over the United States was disjointed and disconnected in clubs here and there, and that the men were losing their ability by not being able to train and exercise themselves up in the air; that he had gotten together many of the flyers around New York and they discussed the matter, and the conclusion was that he would come to Atlanta to see me. He came down and asked my opinion, after giving me data as to the condition of the flying force and the vast sums of money that had been expended, and he said that since the war it had been going to rack and ruin. He told me that with just a few months out of an airplane, a flyer almost had to learn the whole thing over again. I said, "Maj. Wright, I am not a flyer; I know nothing about that, but it seems to me that if a great organization could be formed composed of flyers, mechanics, and citizens who are interested in aeronautics, to be a fraternal, high-class social organization and practical organization, combining those three things, and made up of flyers gotten together in this national organization, that then you could do something, and possibly you could have some influence in the interest of aeronautics under the slogan, 'American supremacy in the air.'" He seemed to be pleased at that suggestion; it was just one that I merely offered. He was around there for a few days and went back to New York. The next I saw of Mr. Wright was when he came to Atlanta with a stack of petitions; I do not how many there were, but several hundred, signed, or supposed to be, by very prominent men. At our May celebration, on the stage in an Atlanta theater, he stepped forward and made the statement that these petitions asked me to take the headship of this organization, to be known as the Knights of the Air, and to step forward and save the aeronautic interests of our American Nation.

I never had a thing in my life that impressed me like that, a call from the big men of this country and other men, experienced flyers, all calling me to help them and to lead the movement to save America's interest in the air. I agreed to accept, prompted purely by patriotic motives, because I knew it was going to be an awful burden on me to start the work, work out its ritual, and those things. Mr. Wright impressed me as a big, splendid looking fellow, and I thought he was sincere. He was wearing the uniform of a major in the Air Service and I delighted in his presence. God knows I want to do everything I can to make America the greatest nation on earth and to hold that greatness forever. But a telegram was received by one of the newspapers in Atlanta. On the first petition in that package was the signature of Gen. John J. Pershing. He told me that that signature was attached by Gen. Pershing in the Shrine Temple of Philadelphia in the presence of several hundred Shriners. A newspaper received a telegram stating that Gen. Pershing disclaimed and disavowed the signature. I do not know Gen. Pershing's signature. Another telegram was received, or the news got to the papers, that Gen. Menoher, I believe it is—I can not pronounce those names because I am an Irishman, you know. He also disavowed attaching his signature. So, Mr. Chairman and gentlemen of the committee, I began to have doubts about the signatures to those petitions, and that is the reason why the Knights of the Air has not yet developed, at least, that is one of the reasons; the other reason is that I have been so busy.

Mr. RODENBERG. Even after that, though, did you keep Mr. Wright on the pay roll? Was he still employed by the klan after you made this discovery?

Mr. SIMMONS. Understand me, please, that this came from a newspaper.

Mr. RODENBERG. But you said a moment ago that you yourself had a mental doubt about his integrity, but even after that you kept him on the pay roll.

Mr. SIMMONS. Mr. Wright was in the employ of Mr. Clarke in the propaganda department. We talked it over and I then said, "Now, Mr. Clarke, let us see if we can not clear this matter up and be satisfied in our minds." We were extremely busy at that time in our work, and I said, "This Knights of the Air business can wait."

Mr. RODENBERG. About when was this? When did this occur? When did you first get a doubt in your mind?

Mr. SIMMONS. It was a few days after the 6th of May, I should say, along about the middle of May. And then I said, "This Knights of the Air business can wait." Of course, after this newspaper information came to me there was an explanation offered to me by Maj. Wright. I told him the matter ought to be looked into and he said Gen. Pershing did not disavow signing that petition, but stated that he had refused to accept an office in this organization. I had no reason then to doubt Mr. Wright's statement but, of course, I had my eyes opened, and so I let it stand at that because I was so busy with other things.

So Mr. Wright was employed there; he was made a king kleagle ana made chief of staff of the Knights of the Air. He suggested that we should have the headquarters in Atlanta. Rooms were secured by Mr. Clarke, in Mr. Clarke's name, in the Hurt Building. The rooms were not to be lavishly furnished, but Mr. Clarke told me that Mr. Wright, without authority, went out and purchased something over $2.000 worth of furniture and equipment, and incurred that expense, but he said, " I will stand for it."

Mr. RODENBERG. Did you acquaint Mr. Clarke with the suspicions you began to entertain regarding Wright?

Mr. SIMMONS. I stated, " This looks rather strange, Mr. Clarke."

Mr. RODENBERG. Notwithstanding that Clarke gave him employment and made him one of the king kleagles?

Mr. SIMMONS. I said, " It looks very strange, but as we believe Mr. Wright is honest there must be a mistake somewhere; let us wait and not condemn until we are sure.

Mr. RODENBERG. Of course you could very easily have confirmed your suspicions by getting into communication directly with Gen. Pershing or Gen. Menoher?

Mr. SIMMONS. Yes; that is true.

Mr. RODENBERG. You did not do that?

Mr. SIMMONS. No; because at that time and following that I was down sick.

Mr. RODENBERG. Did Mr. Clarke seek to ascertain anything about it?

Mr. SIMMONS. I do not know.

Mr. RODENBERG. And he had control of the activities of Mr. Wright?

Mr. SIMMONS. I can not answer you about Mr. Clarke, but the fact is that in the progress of the thing I was told by Mr. Clarke that he had to get rid of Mr. Wright, and as a result he did.

Mr. RODENBERG. How long was this?

Mr. SIMMONS. Well, it must have been—I can not say definitely about those things, but possibly a month. He said, " I have him out on some work in Chicago, and after he does that I will have to dispose of him." That statement I make, Mr. Chairman, to the very best of my knowledge and belief, because those dates and things I can not be accurate about.

I wish to conclude by this statement: I have come before you without a delegation to back me up. I could have had hundreds of men; by merely hinting hundreds of men would have come. I have not come here with any purpose of lobbying or wire pulling; I have come here, as I shall stand before my God on the day of judgment, in justice to your committee, to get the truth as I know it, and I have tried to speak the truth as I knew it in all the statements I have made. I have this to say: I am ready to leave my case, so to speak, or our case, to the judgment of your committee, the Congress of our great Nation, or to the greatest citizenry on earth, the people of this Nation; and if this organization is unworthy to live let me know it, please, and I shall destroy it. If it is worthy to live, then we as an organization should be accorded our rights as we accord rights to all other organizations, of all races, to live and teach their doctrines to their members, and to go their way in peace and in justice to all mankind.

Again I want to express to you, Mr. Chairman, my deep gratitude and thanks for the courtesies you have extended to me. I want to say to all those men and women who have given assurance, with your permission, of their belief in me that they have my thanks, and I want to say to my persecutors and the persecutors of this organization in all honesty and sincerity, no matter to what creed or race you may belong in your persecutions, through the medium of the press or otherwise, that you do not know what you are doing. You are ignorant of the principles as were those who were ignorant of the character and work of the Christ. I can not better express myself than by saying to you who are persecutors of the klan and myself, " Father, forgive you, for you know not what you do," and " Father, forgive them, for they know not what they do."

Mr. Chairman, I am done. [Applause.]

Mr. CAMPBELL. Spectators will refrain from any such demonstrations as that in this room.

Mr. ETHERIDGE. Mr. Chairman, give us 5 or 10 minutes if the committee wishes to ask any other questions.

Mr. CAMPBELL. I have observed the request of Col. Simmons not to interrupt him and ask question during his statement, but now I am desirous of asking him some questions and I think other members are.

Mr. ETHERIDGE. I think he will be in shape to answer those questions.

Mr. CAMPBELL. Col. Simmons does not feel able to submit to an examination at this time. We will therefore adjourn until to-morrow morning, Friday, October 14, 1921, at 10.30 o'clock a. m., hoping that the colonel will at that time be able to appear.

(Thereupon the committee adjourned until to-morrow, Friday, October 14, 1921, at 10.30 o'clock a. m.)

———————

COMMITTEE ON RULES,
HOUSE OF REPRESENTATIVES,
Monday, October 17, 1921.

The committee met at 10.30 o'clock a. m., Hon. Philip P. Campbell (chairman), presiding.

Mr. CAMPBELL. Col. Simmons, the Chair is informed that you desire about 10 minutes in which to make an additional statement. You may proceed.

Mr. SIMMONS. Thank you, sir.

Mention was made when the New York World introduced through one of its official representatives, who was the first witness called by this committee, as to the World's painstaking, accurate, and correct investigation of the klan and myself, and that the various articles published in the New York World were correct facts. I desire to ask this committee, if any publication, such as the New York World, to be considered honest and honorable, irrespective of how the committee may desire to look at the matter, or are its news columns worthy of consideration, when this newspaper deliberately violates one of the best known laws of the United States Government, of which you gentlemen are its representatives? I refer to the fact of the New York World having such an utter contempt and disregard for the laws of the United States, as to deliberately infringe upon the copyright of the ritual and other documents of our organization. Were not these laws made by Congress? Is such a newspaper or its representatives who are willing to do this, and then appear before this committee and speak of the alleged unlawful acts of the organization I represent, to be believed? You gentlemen know that those who come into court must come with clean hands. Irrespective of every effort, neither the klan nor any of its officials have ever been proven guilty of anything before any court of the land and my accusers, by their own testimony, standing here before this committee, have been proven guilty of violating the laws of the United States Government.

Furthermore, the New York World, in its assumed mantle of purity of purpose, as the servant of the people, through its official representative before your committee, has stated that it believed it was the duty of the New York World as the people's servant to investigate this organization and expose its activities.

Gentlemen of this committee, if the New York World or its representatives could have been able to secure any proof that would stand in the courts—county, State, or Federal—you know that the New York World would have, by now, placed in the hands of the proper authorities such evidence which would have long before this resulted in the indictment or arrest of the guilty parties that the New York World had such evidence against.

It is my duty as the official head of this organization to the best of my ability to protect it and its members against such unjust attacks as made upon the organization by the New York World. Therefore, I desire to place before your committee positive proof that the New York World has a reputation for inaccuracy and opening up its columns for propaganda purposes. In substantiation of this accusation, I respectfully refer the chairman of this committee and its members to the official report and hearings of the Committee on Foreign Relations, United States Senate, investigation of Mexican affairs.

This testimony on page 774, given before the Senate committee mentioned hereinbefore, refers, and I quote literally from the testimony, as follows:

"An unscrupulous American by the name of Robert H. Murray, the correspondent in that city (Mexico) of the New York World and an interested propagandist of the Carranza government."

On page 830 of the same hearings before the United States Senate committee, refers again to Robert H. Murray of the New York World as one of the provokers of intervention.

I also desire to call to the attention of the chairman of this committee and its members the testimony before the same committee mentioned hereinbefore of the Hon. Henry Lane Wilson. Mr. Wilson for 17 years was in the diplomatic service of the United States Government. This distinguished gentleman was appointed minister to Chile in 1897 by President McKinley, minister to Greece and Belgium in 1905 by President Roosevelt, and ambassador to Turkey and Mexico in 1909 by President Taft. The testimony of Mr. Henry Lane Wilson refers to the time that he was United States ambassador to Mexico and appears on pages 2286, 2287, 2288, 2296 of the Senate hearings referred to.

In this testimony appears the following: Mr. Wilson being asked by Mr. Kearful, attorney for the Senate committee, as to the name of the American newspaper correspondent who had circulated throughout the United States false statements and information regarding Mr. Henry Lane Wilson and Mexican conditions existing at that time in Mexico. Mr. Wilson, in answer as to whom the newspaper correspondent was, said: "The inventor of these stories was an American newspaper man by the name of Robert H. Murray." Mr. Wilson, continuing, said that Mr. Murray was an utterly worthless man with enormous vanity, and on account of Mr. Murray's continuously circulating false statements and stories, and particularly on account of freightening the ladies of the American colony in Mexico by spreading a report on a night when there was an uprising and firing that the American Embassy had been attacked, which resulted in the bringing on of a very hysterical condition among the ladies of the American colony; for this and for sending out false information to the New York World Mr. Murray was ordered out of the embassy. Mr. Wilson, continuing, said, referring to Mr. Murray, that this gentleman was socially ostracized by the American colony in Mexico at that time. Mr. Wilson, continuing his testimony, said that Robert H. Murray deliberately garbled his stories to the New York World and that the American colony in Mexico later protested against such methods. The New York World also from many sources received information that it was printing garbled statements from its correspondent, Murray, yet for several years thereafter he was employed by the New York World. Ambassador Wilson then charged, as shown in his testimony on page 2288, that Mr. Murray of the New York World had taken from the confidential files of the United States Embassy, without his knowledge or consent, official records which were later published in the New York World. If a representative of the New York World did that in Mexico City, and Henry Lane Wilson swears that it was done, who then stole the court records at Atlanta that have been referred to in the testimony before this committee?

I also desire to introduce for the information of this committee, part 15 of the hearings before a subcommittee on Foreign Relations. Sixty-sixth Congress, investigation of Mexican affairs as substantiation of these statements regarding Mr. Murray and the New York World.

I also desire to show this committee, through its chairman, a booklet entitled, "Facts," submitted by the committee of the American colony in Mexico to President Wilson and Secretary Bryan relative to the Mexican situation and the record of the Hon. Henry Lane Wilson.

I desire to call to the attention of this committee the names of 14 well-known American citizens, whose names appear as members of the executive committee of the American colony. I respectfully refer the chairman of this committee and its members to pages 27, 28, 29, 30, 31, 32, and 34 of the booklet prepared by that committee entitled "Facts." One hundred and fifty or more representative citizens of the United States in Mexico and throughout the United States, above their names, under the heading Exhibit G in this booklet, refer to the false statements in the New York World regarding Henry Lane Wilson and conditions in Mexico.

I also call the attention of this committee to the fact that the sworn testimony before the Senate investigation committee charges that through its representative, Robert H. Murray, the New York World opened up its columns to propaganda in the interest of a Mexican President and known enemy of the United States, who has been proven to be guilty and fully responsible for the death of over 587 American citizens in Mexico and along the border; likewise guilty with his subordinates for the countless outrages and the repeated ravishings of many American women and girls in Mexico and along the border; and that the testimony of reliable witness before the Senate committee shows that the representative of the New York World is repeatedly charged with having garbled the information published in the columns of his paper.

When this committee considers the various resolutions before it in regard to its investigation of the klan and its officers I desire to respectfully call the attention of the committee to the following facts:

First, that the New York World has never proven that this organization or its officials have committed one unlawful act which has or could result in prosecution before the courts of this country.

Second, that in Newspaperdom, a weekly publication, published in New York City in the interests of the newspaper profession, that in its issue for the week of September 12 to 17 contained a news story to the effect that Mr. James McKerman, circulation manager of the New York World, had told Newspaperdom that since the world began its klan stories had increased its circulation over 100,000 copies per day and its Sunday circulation over 125,000 copies.

Also that the World had boasted of the fact that through its influence with Congress that to make their story stand up, they expected to put the klan out of business. I will prove this by the sworn testimony before the congressional investigation of the klan that I want.

The official representative of the New York World is here before your committee and he can not deny the fact that from a financial standpoint their attack on the klan by the New York World has been from a circulation and advertising standpoint one of the greatest financial opportunities that the New York World has ever had.

Ask him if it is not a fact that the New York World syndicated these stories and sold them to approximately 15 or 20 other newspapers and at prices ranging from $50 to $100 per paper.

The New York World has stated through its representative before this committee that its purpose in printing these stories was for the benefit of the people. If so, eventually the great American public will decide this matter. It, however, is a fact that it has been undoubtedly the most profitable venture from a newspaper standpoint for a real cash income that the New York World has ever had.

The New York World, in connection with other interested parties, have endeavored to make their so-called case against this organization stand up before your committee, so that your committee would render a report which they would consider favorable, and thus back up their stories.

According to the testimony, reliable witnesses under oath before a Senate investigating committee, including Henry Lane Wilson, have sworn in their testimony that knowingly time after time the columns of the World contained untrue news items and dispatches, and the testimony of other witnesses under oath show that a representative of the New York World was a propaganda agent for a country hostile to all interests of the United States.

Hearst, seeing the World each day in big handsful taking his circulation away from his favorite paper, the New York American, could stand it no longer, so he, for cash profits, also attacked the klan and dug up a discharged representative of Mr. Clarke's. Discharged for misrepresentation and for other acts which at the proper time he will have to answer for in the courts. The testimony of the United States Post Office inspector before this committee, I believe, has already proved to the committee that Mr. Wright's stories, as published in the Hearst papers, were not true. For instance, such statements from him as the klan having a $20,000,000 income, its so-called emperor living in a $1,000,000 palace, and such other ridiculous statements.

Mr. Chairman and gentlemen of this committee, the klan and its officials, including myself, have been charged in the articles printed by the New York World and the Hearst papers with almost every unlawful act known, none of which, however, has ever been proven as true, honest, or correct, and in the end all of their accusations in a congressional investigation that I want and demand will be shown to be positively false. The files of the Department of Justice have many reports from their investigators in regard to the activities of Hearst during the war with Germany. Call before your committee Chief Burns, of the Department of Justice, and ask him to produce for your committee the files of his department regarding Hearst.

Hearst has made his big effort to expose everything, false or true, regarding the klan or its officials. Nothing he can ever print, or any other newspaper, regarding its officials can ever be of shame to us. Can Hearst stand the same pitiless searchlight of publicity regarding his own private life that I have stood? No. Hearst has our complete record, and we also have his.

Our organization has been charged with spreading propaganda against the Catholic Church. This is as false as all other accusations. As a matter of fact, friends of mine over a year ago placed in my possession signed letters from high officials of the Catholic Church of the United States that positively prove their participation, financial and otherwise, via the revolutionary route, to overthrow the Mexican Government, which had been recognized by this country. If the klan had been at all interested in any way hurting or attempting to hurt the Catholic Church in this country it could have then, by these documents, done so. They have never yet been used by me or any one connected with the klan.

Before a congressional committee I will, if so ordered by such committee, place indisputable documentary proof before them which will prove these statements correct.

I particularly desire to impress on your committee this fact, that in the testimony of the representative of the New York World, false statements and charges were made against the klan and its officials. If the New York World, in the opinion of many thousands of Americans in Mexico and the United States, deliberately garbled and published false information, as some of these Americans swore was done, and if the New York World was a continuous distributor for several years of propaganda through its columns in the interests of the proven enemies of the United States, as sworn testimony before a Senate committee states they did, then what could our organization expect from this newspaper?

I also ask this committee to consider the efforts of G. Anderson Wright to make his stories which are published in the New York American stand up, and in doing so, I believe it proper for me to call to the attention of this committee the record of Mr. Wright. This committee should also consider the fact that various employees of the Hearst organization through Mr. Wright hope and expect to be financially benefited by assisting Mr. Wright in bracing up his stories in the Hearst papers so that same can not be contradicted and proven to be untrue as they are.

If I am within my rights, I respectfully ask this committee, so that all facts regarding Mr. Wright be shown, to secure from the War Department the official records of Mr. Wright's military service and that same be included as part of the permanent records of this committee. Also that this committee secure a certified copy of the bankruptcy proceedings in Houston, Tex., of Mr. Wright, and that certified copies of his police record and check transactions in Chicago and various other cities be secured from the proper officials in these cities, so that in this way it will be proven to the satisfaction of the committee that Mr. Wright's statements regarding his connections with various check transactions be proven.

I wish to notify the chairman of this committee that there are plans on foot at the present time whereby one of the representatives of the New York World is to be tarred and feathered in the name of the klan, and that this plan has been originated and its details worked out by representatives of the New York World so that it will appear that the klan did this in a spirit of revenge. Furthermore, through this plan the World hopes to be able to secure additional circulation and advertising for their paper in keeping alive this matter. The congressional investigating committee that I want to investigate the klan will receive the sworn proof of this plan of the representatives of the World to further try to discredit or harm the klan.

I also desire to call to the attention of the chairman and the members of this committee, likewise to enter a protest against the incident which occurred in this room on the afternoon of Thursday, October 13. As I have stated before, I came before you from a sick bed, after having been there for several weeks, and attempted to give all available information in my possession regarding the klan, myself, and other officials. I tried to do this although I was sick. This resulted in a partial collapse on my part and when same occurred a gentleman sitting at that table just a few feet away from me, whom I understand is Assistant United States Attorney General Crim, bounced to his feet and said, "For cheap theatrical effect, damn such a fakir, I have been expecting him for many minutes." And then went over and talked to the chairman of this committee who in turn, I am informed by Congressman Upshaw, who told me that the correspondent of a prominent southern newspaper had told him that Mr. Crim and Mr. Campbell, the chairman of this committee, had said that my collapse was a cheap theatrical attempt to gain sympathy.

Mr. Chairman and members of this committee, I am not seeking sympathy, only justice, and that all facts be brought out before your committee so that the congressional investigation which I desire will prove that all of these attacks on the klan are part of a conspiracy to put the klan out of business.

Mr. CAMPBELL. Mr. Simmons, let me say right here that if all the rest that you have detailed up to this time since you began this morning is as false and as utterly without foundation as the statement that Mr. Crim and I had that conversation, you have given us something this morning that is absolutely of no use to the committee.

Mr. SIMMONS. Mr. Chairman, I will state to you, sir——

Mr. CAMPBELL (continuing). The conversation you relate did not occur between a representative of the Attorney General's office and myself.

Mr. SIMMONS. Now, then, Mr. Chairman——

Mr. CAMPBELL (interposing). I made no such statement to anybody.

Mr. SIMMONS. I am glad you make that statement. I am stating that that has been reported, and I do not believe it.

Mr. RODENBERG. I do not think you should dignify a report of that kind by insulting the chairman of this committee.

Mr. SIMMONS. No, sir; and this being reported, I think it is well for the chairman to know it and for this committee.

Mr. CAMPBELL. I think, Col. Simmons, you have gone far enough with this kind of thing.

Mr. SIMMONS. I just have a certificate here to insert as to my condition, sir, and then I will conclude.

Mr. CAMPBELL. I have been absolutely fair to you.

Mr. SIMMONS. You have, sir, and I have stated that repeatedly.

Mr. CAMPBELL. I stated to those who assembled here Saturday morning and to the members of the press that I had a telephone message from your physician that you were unable to attend here.

Mr. SIMMONS. Yes, sir. This is a report, and I do not believe it.

Mr. CAMPBELL. Why is it inserted here, then?

Mr. SIMMONS. It is inserted so that I might not overlook bringing the matter to your attention—that I had heard of these reports.

Mr. CAMPBELL. You could have brought the matter to my attention and to the attention of the representative of the Attorney General's office without all this blare of trumpets.

Mr. SIMMONS. I have attempted no blare of trumpets, pardon me, sir. I was honestly trying to get this before you. I do not believe that this occurred.

Mr. CAMPBELL. If you think you have fairly brought the matter to the attention of the committee your judgment of fair procedure is very different from that of other men who have appeared before this committee in the last 10 years.

Mr. SIMMONS. Well, sir, it is an honest effort to bring this before you, sir.

Mr. CRIM. Mr. Chairman, my name has been mentioned, and I simply wish to say on the record that I have no reply whatever to make to it. I think your reply has covered it.

Mr. SIMMONS. Yes, sir. Now, gentlemen——

Mr. RODENBERG. What is the name of that correspondent who was responsible for this story? Who told Mr. Upshaw this?

Mr. SIMMONS. I have it that a correspondent of a prominent southern newspaper——

Mr. RODENBERG (interposing). What is his name?

Mr. SIMMONS. I do not know his name.

Mr. RODENBERG. We want the name of that correspondent.

Mr. UPSHAW. The correspondent of the New Orleans Item.

Mr. RODENBERG. What is his name?

Mr. UPSHAW. He is the man who represents the Item here. I do not know his name. May I state, Mr. Chairman——

Mr. CAMPBELL (interposing). No; we are not going into this matter any further.

Mr. POU. We might as well be fair to Mr. Simmons. I myself heard comments all over this room at several points when he had his collapse—that the collapse was a fake.

Mr. CAMPBELL. I heard that, but I made no such statement.

Mr. POU. I do not say the chairman did, but Col. Simmons might just as well have a square deal, and while I am here I shall insist that he receive a square deal. I am sure the chairman will see that this is done.

Mr. CAMPBELL. He has been getting it.

Mr. SIMMONS. Now, Mr. Chairman, my denial of this incident, as my honest belief, comes a little further down in this statement. I have it connected altogether here, and just for the continuity of this statement——

Mr. POU (interposing). It has been charged all over the press of the country that it was a stage play by Mr. Simmons, to collapse when he did, yet every man in the room who had two eyes in his head could see he was not a well man.

Mr. Simmons. I read and introduce for the information of the chairman and the members of this committee a certificate of Dr. William J. Manning, the physician who has attended me from Thursday afternoon, October 13. I understand that Dr. Manning is one of the most reputable and prominent physicians in Washington. He has called to see me twice each day since my collapse before your committee. I desire that Dr. Manning's certificate be made a part of the permanent record:

WASHINGTON, D. C., *October 17, 1921.*

Certification is made that Col. William Joseph Simmons has been under my professional care since Thursday, October 13, 1921.

I found the patient very much depressed as a result of an attack of acute bronchitis, coupled with laryingitis, together with bilateral tonsillitis. He was running a high temperature, and as a result of the infection was a very sick man and naturally much exhausted, his history showing that he left his home in Atlanta with the conditions named.

It became necessary the next day to absolutely prohibit any physical or mental action on his part, and the chairman of the Rules Committee before whom he was appearing was so informed.

The records of the city health office, as a result of two cultures taken, showed the infection to be the result of a most virulent germ, a streptococcus. He is still suffering to a considerable degree as a result of the poison given off in his system by the organism mentioned, and is far from being a well man. So strong was his mental make-up and determination to appear before the committee again, however, that the writer has reluctantly given his consent for Col. Simmons to appear before the committee to-day, October 17, 1921.

Very respectfully,

W. J. MANNING, M. D.

Mr. Simmons. Mr. Chairman and gentlemen of this committee, I appeared before you, a volunteer witness. I understood and still believe the purpose of this investigation was to be fair, impartial, and in every way just, and for the purpose of bringing out all information possible with an idea of justly deciding the matters that this committee was called into being for. Instead of that, I find an array before me of an Assistant United States Attorney General, the Chief of the Bureau of Investigation, Department of Justice, and several of his assistants who have been and are constantly in conference with the representatives of the World and Hearst papers and the members of this committee.

Have the Department of Justice and this committee, with all of their vast powers for securing information, made any effort to secure information or evidence that would in any way be favorable to the klan, its officials, or myself, or have they made efforts to disprove as correct or incorrect the evidence laid before this committee, or to prove the character of some of the witnesses who appeared before this committee as good or bad, as believable or unbelievable, as far as their testimony is concerned?

Some parts of this investigation are not what I would call exactly fair and somehow smack of persecution.

The Washington Times, a Hearst newspaper, on last Friday afternoon published as a news item a statement which they credited to the chairman of this committee, saying to me when I collapsed from exhaustion, "Please refrain from any such demonstration as that."

That is quoted from the paper. I would like to file——

Mr. CAMPBELL (interposing). May I say here that that statement appearing in the paper has been denied by the representatives of the paper here as being attributed to me. You will not find a correspondent for the Washington Times who will assume the responsibility for having written that.

Mr. SIMMONS. Yes, sir.

Mr. CAMPBELL. Everybody in the room knew I did not address that to you.

Mr. SIMMONS. Yes, sir.

Mr. CAMPBELL. There was attempted applause at the time you did fall forward on the table, and I said, "We will have no demonstration here."

Mr. SIMMONS. That simply goes to show. Mr. Chairman, that if they will misrepresent a statement of yours they will misrepresent other things.

I will conclude, Mr. Chairman and members of this committee.

I have voluntarily appeared before your committee and given as complete and as correct statements regarding the klan, its officials and myself, as I possibly could, and always to my best knowledge of the facts, and no matter how secret and sacred those facts have been, I have presented them to your committee. I am willing. anxious, and ready and desire to answer any and all questions that I possibly can that may be asked of me by your committee, so that any additional information you desire can be brought out.

It is only fair and proper to likewise bring out any and all facts and information pertaining to C. Anderson Wright and other witnesses who have appeared before this committee so that it may be shown as to whether their statements regarding themselves or other matters are correct or incorrect.

The committee should be willing, in its desire to conduct a fair and impartial investigation, to also do everything within its power to prove or disprove the records or character of the witnesses who have voluntarily appeared before them.

I respectfully ask that Mr. C. Anderson Wright be recalled as a witness before this committee and by you asked the following questions.

My purpose in having these questions asked of Mr. Wright is to prove to the satisfaction of this committee that Mr. Wright is not what he claims to be, and that his reputation for truth and veracity is bad; furthermore, that his personal and business record has been and is such as does not entitle him to be believed, as far as the testimony given by him is concerned. In substantiation of the statement made by me regarding this matter, I desire that the committee call before it one of its previous witnesses, Mr. William J. Burns, Chief of the Bureau of Investigation, United States Department of Justice, so that the committee can learn from Mr. Burns the knowledge that he and his department have of Mr. Wright.

"Are you originally from Houston, Tex.?

" Were you ever in business in Houston or any other Texas city?

" If so, what kind of business?

" Did or did not that business or any other business that you have ever been connected with go into bankruptcy?

" Have you ever taken advantage of the bankruptcy law in Texas or any other State as an individual or under your own name?

" If so, were or were not charges made that it was a fraudulent bankruptcy case?

" Have you ever been officially discharged as a bankrupt by the court which handled your bankruptcy case?

" Is or is it not a fact regarding to your ever having been arrested in Texas?

" Have you ever been in trouble of any kind in Texas as a result of various transactions pertaining to checks, notes, or drafts, or for any other reason?

" Please tell this committee what was the result of such troubles with the authorities.

" Did your trouble in Texas happen before you were ever connected with the klan or Mr. Clarke?

" Is or is it not a fact that you passed worthless checks on the Blackstone Hotel, also Congress Hotel, in Chicago, and that such checks were drawn and signed by you on a bank account that was in your own name, and that such bank account had nothing to do at all either with Mr. Clarke or the klan?

" Is it not also a fact that these checks were passed on the Blackstone, also Congress, Hotel, before you had any connection with Mr. Clarke or the klan?

" Is it not also a fact that long before you had any connection with the klan or Mr. Clarke that you have had trouble in other cities outside of Texas and Chicago with worthless checks and which resulted in you being arrested by the authorities?

" Is it not also a fact that you are known to both the Pinkerton Detective Agency and the Burns Detective Agency as having repeatedly passed checks and drafts on hotels and other public concerns, and that such checks and drafts proved to be worthless?

" Is it not also a fact that when such checks and drafts were passed by you they later proved to be worthless; that this happened before you had any connection with Mr. Clarke or the klan?

" This committee desires to know the names of the various cities that you have ever been arrested in, and if you were arrested, what for, and the dates of such arrests; also, what was the outcome of these arrests?

" The Washington Times of Friday, October 14, carried a story that you had made affidavit that the various references of Col. Simmons to your check transactions were not correct, and that you had entered suit through Congressman

Voigt against Mrs. Tyler and Mr. Clarke. Where is the affidavit you made, and who did you make it before?

"The committee desires a copy of this affidavit, bearing the date mentioned, to be filed for its permanent records. When did you file the suit that the Washington Times story said you did, and where was same filed?

"When did you employ Congressman Voigt as your attorney?

"The Washington Times has also published a statement credited to you to the fact that your various business troubles in Texas resulted in your being so involved as to cause the loss of your personal fortune of $75,000. Is it not a fact that you never had a personal fortune of $75,000, or any such sum?

"Where did you secure $75,000—from whom, how, and on what date?

"Testimony has been introduced before this committee that when you approached Col. Simmons with the idea of creating the Knights of the Air that you later presented to him in the presence of a large audience in a theater in Atlanta, Ga., petitions that were supposed to be signed by very prominent United States officials, Army and Navy officers, and citizens of the United States, among whom were Gen. Pershing; Gen. Menoher; Maj. Biddle, of Philadelphia; and other well-known citizens. Are you aware of the fact that on the original petitions you told Col. Simmons, and also the audience in the theater referred to in Atlanta, Ga., are the original signatures of the various gentlemen whose names appeared on these petitions, and that these gentlemen claim to have known nothing at all about having signed these petitions or the Knights of the Air, and that these petitions are now in the possession of the attorneys of Col. Simmons?

"Can you tell this committee who signed these petitions or what 'egal right you had to put the names of these gentlemen on these petitions; and are you aware of the fact that to do so is forgery of their names; likewise, the use of their names without their knowledge and consent is a criminal offense?

"In your previous testimony before this committee you stated that you were Maj. C. Anderson Wright; also a reserve officer with that title in the Army Reserve Corps of the United States. Did you enlist or were you drafted?

"What camps in the United States did you serve in, and what were the dates of such service in such camps?

"You have, in previous testimony, stated to this committee that you were an aviator in the United States Army during the European War. In what camp did you receive your air training?

"Give the committee the record of the different ranks held by you in the Army, whether private, noncommissioned officer, or commissioned officer?"

Mr. CAMPBELL. Would you just as soon submit those questions in writing? It would save us a great deal of time.

Mr. SIMMONS. There is just another page of them, sir, if you will allow me to read them. [Reading:]

"You stated that you served overseas. What date did you sail for overseas service, and with what organization, giving company, battalion, command, squadron, regiment, or brigade; and who were your unit commanding officers, such as major, colonel, or general?

"What ship did you sail on for overseas service, and from what port did such ship sail?

"Where did you land in Europe, and where did your overseas service take place—what country or city?

"How long were you overseas?

"When did you return to the United States, what date, and on what ship, and where did you land upon your return from overseas service in the United States?

"What date were you discharged from the United States Army and in what city?

"Have you ever served in the Army at any time or place? Is it not a fact that you were never a commissioned officer in the United States Army, and that the only air service you ever had was at Ellington Field, Tex., and that you were not even an instructor there but simply an enlisted man, and had no flying record, service, or experience, except to occasionally go out with a flying instructor?

"You have testified before this committee that the money you have received from the Hearst organization, and that which you still expect to receive for your articles in Hearst's, will total at least $5,000. Is it not also a fact that you, in connection with certain employees of Hearst's, have been and are engaged in preparing, or plan to prepare, a book to be published regarding the klan and its officers, and that from the sale of such a book you expect to receive as profit for your part anywhere from $5,000 to $10,000 or more?

"The committee desires to learn the names of Hearst's employees who are interested in the preparation of this book with you; also what part of the profits you are to receive for your share.

"Is it not a fact that you, in connection with Al Woods, of New York City, also various employees of Hearst's, have prepared and made arrangements, or have planned to have staged in New York City a show which has been built up around the klan, and that this show within the next few weeks will make its appearance in New York City, and that from the revenues from this show you expect for your part of the profits not less than $10,000?

"Also, is it not a fact that from the articles you told this committee were written by you for the Hearst papers, the book referred to, and the theatrical show referred to, that you said you would make at least $20,000 or $25,000 out of all this?

"Haven't you repeatedly written to the Bureau of Investigation of the United Strtes Department of Justice trying to secure from them letters in answer to yours, so that these letters could be used in your article; also in your book, or referred to in the theatrical enterprise, and that you also tried to be employed by the Department of Justice?

"Is it not also a fact that you have repeatedly tried to be employed by moving-picture concerns, that thus you further could commercialize your connection with the klan?

"In your previous testimony before this committee you have stated in answer to a direct question from a member of the committee that you, and you alone, wrote the klan articles that appeared in the New York American above your name as author of the same. And is not it a fact that you did not write these articles and that you are not capable of writing them, and that the articles, as a matter of fact, were written by Mr. Hammer, one of the regular staff of the New York American?

"When you appeared in Atlanta, Ga., and at the time you presented the petitions referred to hereinbefore to Col. Simmons on the stage of a theater, and in the presence of a large audience, presumably bearing the signatures of prominent Americans, asking Col. Simmons to head the Knights of the Air, is it not a fact that you appeared in the uniform of a major of the United States Army and that you had no right to appear in such uniform, due to the fact that you are not a major, either active or reserve, of the United States Army?

"Are you familiar with the laws of the United States in regard to any citizen or individual appearing in the uniform of the Army or Navy when such use of these uniforms are illegal, and that you could be arrested under Federal laws for the use of these uniforms, provided you are not legally entitled to use same?

"Will you explain to this committee why in your testimony, also in the newspaper article bearing your name as author, you stated that the klan had an income of $20,000,000 when, as a matter of fact, the official testimony of Mr. Williamson, post-office inspector, shows the income to be only a little over $1,000,000?

"How is it that all of the statements that you have made to this committee of millions of dollars of income and hundreds of thousands of members of the klan are entirely different from what Mr. Williamson has testified to? In other words, the testimony of Mr. Williamson and yourself is altogether different, as far as facts and figures are concerned."

Mr. Chairman, I will submit those questions to you.

Now, Mr. Chairman. I will just make this closing statement, that, if I am within my rights, I shall request, sir, if there is any further hearing, secret or otherwise, that our organization, through myself, will have given to it a transcript of the proceedings, so that we will be in a position to make any answer that should be made, in justice to our organization.

I bring before your committee the fact that I am not here—we are not here—to block the resolut'on of Mr. Tague, Mr. Ryan, or Mr. Somebody Else, regarding a congressional investigation. When the congressional investigation comes on, facts under oath shall be presented and the American people shall judge if this patriotic organization shall be crucified, and the American people shall see it, and they will not forget.

I am ready now, sir, to subject myself to any questions.

Mr. CAMPBELL. Do you desire to stand or have a seat?

Mr. SIMMONS. I will sit over here, sir.

Mr. CAMPBELL. I am desirous of securing some concrete information with respect to this organization. I think if we can have some short answers and short questions detailing matters that are of public interest it will be of service to the committee. First of all, when did you first originate the idea of creating this organization?

Mr. SIMMONS. Well, sir, I can not give you the exact date, but it was about 20 years ago.

Mr. CAMPBELL. Did you at that time decide upon the name and uniform of the Knights of the Ku-Klux Klan following the days of reconstruction?

Mr. SIMMONS. It was not a decision made at that time; I was merely a youth at that time.

Mr. CAMPBELL. Did you conceive of that idea at the time you conceived of the organization?

Mr. SIMMONS. Approximately so; along about that time.

Mr. CAMPBELL. The purpose was to perpetuate. I understood you to say, the memory of the original klansmen of the reconstruction period?

Mr. SIMMONS. You misunderstood me. The purpose was a memorial to the men that served in that organization, both North and South, and to perpetuate their spiritual purpose.

Mr. CAMPBELL. The organization was created about five years ago, I think you said?

Mr. SIMMONS. Well, sir, it was created under the law in the fall of 1915.

Mr. CAMPBELL. And from 1915 down to June 7, 1920, you raised and disbursed how much money in connection with the organization?

Mr. SIMMONS. I could not answer you definitely on that point, because I have not had an opportunity to go back over the records and verify the records, as most of them were lost in moving the offices about three years ago, and I have never had occasion to reconstruct them, but it is my purpose to do so.

Mr. CAMPBELL. Well, approximately how much money?

Mr. SIMMONS. We had a membership up to the spring of 1920, I would estimate roughly, of about four or five thousand members altogether.

Mr. CAMPBELL. You received for each member the sum of $10?

Mr. SIMMONS. No, sir. For the first three years, o· approximately three years, the fee was placed at $5, and as to severa! of the organizations—we did not have but a small number of organizations at that time—but on different occasions and during the war period and the stress of the times I gave dispensations that admitted to membership on the donation of $6.50, including the robe, or $7, somewhere about that amount, and the robe was included.

Mr. CAMPBELL. About how many members were admitted for less than $10?

Mr. SIMMONS. Well, it would be very difficult, sir, to answer that question, because of a lack of opportunity and not having an opportunity to investigate that.

Mr. CAMPBELL. Have you a record?

Mr. SIMMONS. We have memorandum records; yes, sir; but I have not had any occasion to refer to them.

Mr. CAMPBELL. Where is that record kept?

Mr. SIMMONS. That is in Atlanta.

Mr. CAMPBELL. Did the post-office inspector have access to that record?

Mr. SIMMONS. Well, now, I do not know, sir. I was sick in bed when the inspector was down there, and I told——

Mr. CAMPBELL (interposing). You offered here Exhibit C, in which it is estimated that during that period there was collected and disbursed $151,088.72. Who made that record?

Mr. SIMMONS. That exhibit was prepared in the office and, as I stated when we presented those exhibits, I had not had an opportunity, being sick at home, to go over them and to verify them with the records.

Mr. CAMPBELL. Under whose direction was the money collected during that period and disbursed?

Mr. SIMMONS. That is, prior to 1920?

Mr. CAMPBELL. Yes.

Mr. SIMMONS. Myself, sir, by action of the executive committee.

Mr. CAMPBELL. I see you have an item here of $13,431.29 for advertising. In what way was that advertising done?

Mr. SIMMONS. Well, the character of the advertising was through advertising in the newspapers and as part of the publicity work.

Mr. CAMPBELL. Is this a sample of the advertising [indicating]?
Mr. SIMMONS. That is one of our advertisements; yes, sir.
Mr. CAMPBELL. That full-page advertisement?
Mr. SIMMONS. Yes.
Mr. CAMPBELL. This was in the Chicago Daily Tribune of August 16, 1921. Were the advertisements, prior to the propagation organization under the direction of Mr. Clarke, similar to the advertisement that appears in this paper?
Mr. SIMMONS. No, sir; that is the only advertisement of that nature that we have ever gotten out. The advertisements that we used were simply display ads in the papers in the different towns where we were effecting an organization.
Mr. CAMPBELL. What was the nature of that display ad?
Mr. SIMMONS. How is that?
Mr. CAMPBELL. To whom did it appeal?
Mr. SIMMONS. It was an appeal to the general public, and it appealed to the best citizens of a town, judging by results.
Mr. CAMPBELL. But what did it say?
Mr. SIMMONS. Oh, I can not remember the wording of those ads that appeared back three or four years ago; it is an impossible thing, sir; it would be impossible for me to tell you that when I have not had an opportunity in two or three years to look at those ads.
Mr. CAMPBELL. Did you assume there, as you do in this ad, that it was necessary to have a voluntary organization to aid the governments of the cities, of the States, and of the Nation in the administration of the laws?
Mr. SIMMONS. Those ads back there were not as full as those; it was simply an announcement ad in a community, if we went into a community to form an organization, and it was placed in the different papers, stating the fact where any person interested could get in touch, at a post-office box or whatver address our man had.
Mr. CAMPBELL. What I am trying to get at is whether or not you assumed the necessity of the organization you were creating for the purpose of enforcing the law.
Mr. SIMMONS. We never assumed that, sir, for the purpose of enforcing the law. Our contention has been and our statement has been for patriotic citizens to help in all things in preserving the peace and security of the community, like law-and-order leagues have been organized all over this country by citizens.
Mr. CAMPBELL. Did you hold that forth in the appeals you published during the early days of the organization?
Mr. SIMMONS. No, sir; I did not, sir; it was not a feature of our work to do that.
Mr. CAMPBELL. Is it customary, in the organization of patriotic orders, to make display ads in the newspapers?
Mr. SIMMONS. Well, sir, there are quite a number of fraternal orders in this country, and in the creation of them——
Mr. CAMPBELL (interposing). They are insurance orders, however.
Mr. SIMMONS. Not altogether.
Mr. CAMPBELL. As distinguished from this organization, which is purely a benevolent and eleemosynary organization.
Mr. SIMMONS. Not altogether. I have seen ads of the Moose.
Mr. CAMPBELL. That is an insurance organization.
Mr. SIMMONS. Well, I did not know it was so classified. They have some little benefits——
Mr. CAMPBELL (interposing). I understand it is.
Mr. SIMMONS. But I do not think they issue a policy; not to my knowledge, at any rate.
Mr. CAMPBELL. Did the organization at that time make a special appeal to any particular branch or class of our citizens?
Mr. SIMMONS. No, sir; it did not, other than those that were really and truly patriotic and of high class in their standing in the community.
Mr. CAMPBELL. I will come to that later. The organization went rather slowly up until June, 1920, I understood you to say.
Mr. SIMMON. Yes, sir; very slowly.
Mr. CAMPBELL. Members came in at a very slow rate?
Mr. SIMMONS. Yes; there was no one working it but myself then.
Mr. CAMPBELL. You collected in four or five years $151,000?
Mr. SIMMONS. No, sir; pardon me, sir. That amount——

Mr. CAMPBELL (interposing). The record states that you collected $151,088.72.

Mr. SIMMONS. Yes, sir. That is either a typographical——

Mr. CAMPBELL (interposing). That is an exhibit that you have yourself made a part of your testimony.

Mr. SIMMONS. Yes, sir; but I stated that I had not had time to go over those figures and verify them. The amount of money detailed there is based upon a supposed membership up to that time, which membership was stated in excess of the facts.

Mr. CAMPBELL. Why do you refer to it as a supposed membership? Do you not have a record of your members?

Mr. SIMMONS. It is a supposed membership by the man who compiled that statement.

Mr. CAMPBELL. Did not the man who compiled this statement have access to your records?

Mr. SIMMONS. No, sir; not at the time he compiled that statement.

Mr. CAMPBELL. Have you a roster of your members?

Mr. SIMMONS. Yes, sir; not complete, however, but we have a roster going back to a certain date.

Mr. CAMPBELL. From the date of the organization?

Mr. SIMMONS. Not altogether from the date of the organization; no, sir.

Mr. CAMPBELL. How were the names of the members preserved in the archives of the order, that is, those who originally belonged to it?

Mr. SIMMONS. They were preserved in the records of the local organizations.

Mr. CAMPBELL. Are there local records?

Mr. SIMMONS. Yes, sir.

Mr. CAMPBELL. Are there local records kept of the members of the klan?

Mr. SIMMONS. Oh, yes, sir; as in any other fraternal order.

Mr. CAMPBELL. Do you have in Atlanta, the head of the klan, a record in which you keep the names of the members of the local klans?

Mr. SIMMONS. Not all the members of the local klans; we have a record of the officers.

Mr. CAMPBELL. Why not all?

Mr. SIMMONS. Well, it would be too voluminous to have files of that sort, and it is not necessary.

Mr. CAMPBELL. All klansmen are known to the community in which they live, are they?

Mr. SIMMONS. Well. in part they are; I can not answer that question, sir, all the way through, for I am not familiar with all the communities, but there are those that are known; they are known in part.

Mr. CAMPBELL. On the 15th of June you entered into a contract with Mr. Clarke.

Mr. SIMMONS. The 15th of June of what year?

Mr. CAMPBELL. Of 1920.

Mr. SIMMONS. Yes, sir; I believe that was the year.

Mr. CAMPBELL. Was that the date, or was it the 7th of June?

Mr. SIMMONS. Well, along in the first of June; I do not remember now, but it began in the month of June.

Mr. CAMPBELL. What had been Mr. Clarke's business up to the time you made this contract with him?

Mr. SIMMONS. He was the president of the Southern Publicity Association.

Mr. CAMPBELL. What were the activities of that association?

Mr. SIMMONS. Well, my knowledge of the activities of that association and their work was that they had been putting on different drives for the Armenian Relief, Y. M. C. A., the Red Cross, and the Salvation Army.

Mr. CAMPBELL. During the war?

Mr. SIMMONS. Yes, sir. Well, I did not know them during the war; I did not know of Mr. Clarke during the war.

Mr. CAMPBELL. Do they put on drives for the Salvation Army now?

Mr. SIMMONS. Well, I do not know about that; that is their affair, which I am not familiar with.

Mr. CAMPBELL. They are promoters or advertisers for any organization that desires to get its business before a community—is that it?

Mr. SIMMONS. Well, I should say it is, from the word "publicity." It is the Southern Publicity Association.

Mr. CAMPBELL. Your contract with Mr. Clarke called for propaganda work, or what is the name of this organization?

Mr. SIMMONS. You mean that department?

Mr. CAMPBELL. Yes.

Mr. SIMMONS. The propagation department—that is, to extend the organization.

Mr. CAMPBELL. Instead of propaganda?

Mr. SIMMONS. Yes, sir.

Mr. CAMPBELL. The contract with Mr. Clarke, made by you, was for what purpose?

Mr. SIMMONS. For the purpose of having charge and looking after the interests of the extension of the organization; of that work.

Mr. CAMPBELL. For the purpose of securing additional members?

Mr. SIMMONS. Yes, sir; and for enlarging the organization, of course.

Mr. CAMPBELL. The contract gave Mr. Clarke $8 out of every $10 that was secured from members?

Mr. SIMMONS. Yes.

Mr. CAMPBELL. $2 went into the klan's funds?

Mr. SIMMONS. Yes, sir; for the general expenses of the organization.

Mr. CAMPBELL. Clarke and his organization had absolute control over the $8 and you had absolute control over the $2?

Mr. SIMMONS. Yes, sir; under the contract.

Mr. CAMPBELL. All the money that was accumulated was divided up so that the Clarke organization, or propagation organization, had $8 out of each member and you or the klan had $2 out of each member?

Mr. SIMMONS. Yes.

Mr. CAMPBELL. Under that contract the membership at once began to multiply, and out of the $2 per member, the exhibit you have filed, or your statement, shows that $171,432.67 was turned over to you or to the klan—is that correct?

Mr. SIMMONS. I could not state the absolute correctness of that for the same reason I gave you a few minutes ago. Those figures I judge to be approximately correct, but being sick at home for two or three weeks before coming here I never had time to go over them and verify them or go through the records.

Mr. CAMPBELL. All of this money that has been paid out has been paid out under your check?

Mr. SIMMONS. What money do you speak of?

Mr. CAMPBELL. The $171,000.

Mr. SIMMONS. Whatever amount—I can not say it is $171,000, but whatever amount has accrued to the organization.

Mr. CAMPBELL. Well, this is the amount that——

Mr. SIMMONS (interposing). Whatever amount has accrued.

Mr. CAMPBELL. That is said to have accrued to the organization from June 1, 1920, to June 1, 1921.

Mr. SIMMONS. Now, not all of that money has been paid out under my check.

Mr. CAMPBELL. Who else had authority to check on this fund?

Mr. SIMMONS. Dr. H. C. Montgomery. He is the supreme treasurer of the klan.

Mr. CAMPBELL. But aside from yourself and Montgomery, did anybody else have authority to check on this fund?

Mr. SIMMONS. No, sir.

Mr. CAMPBELL. Or to use any of it?

Mr. SIMMONS. No, sir.

Mr. CAMPBELL. For private purposes?

Mr. SIMMONS. No, sir.

Mr. CAMPBELL. You and he alone had authority to disburse it?

Mr. SIMMONS. Yes.

Mr. CAMPBELL. You had authority to disburse that fund, whatever the amount was?

Mr. SIMMONS. Yes, sir.

Mr. CAMPBELL. Under the contract with Mr. Clarke it was his duty to do the advertising, secure the members, take his $8, and give you $2?

Mr. SIMMONS. That is the substance of the contract. In other words, he was to direct the promoting of the organization and pay all the expenses of that promoting, his field men, and his clerk hire, and things of that sort; the expenses in general of the work of his department.

Mr. CAMPBELL. Did you have anything to do with the field work after that?

Mr. SIMMONS. No; I had nothing to do with it.

Mr. CAMPBELL. That is, you did not pay for it, or anything like that, and did not direct the men who did the work?

Mr. SIMMONS. No, sir; I had no direction of the folks there, because Mr. Clarke was employed to look after that, that was his business, like you would employ a man to build a house for you.

Mr. CAMPBELL. I notice that the first item in the disbursement of this $171,432.76 is field-work salaries, $19,356.70.

Mr. SIMMONS. I can explain that item to you. That money covers work that does not come altogether under the one in control of the propagating work. For instance, that covers field men that we designate as field men who go out, but who are not organizers or solicitors. They are men who go out for the purpose of instructing and lecturing, or instructing members already gotten in along the line of rightly forming and crystallizing the organization.

Mr. CAMPBELL. That is an aid to or supplementary to Mr. Clarke's work?

Mr. SIMMONS. It is an aid in a way, and in a measure it is supplementary, too, but this is the work of the organization itself or of the klan itself. It is for the purpose of seeing that these local organizations are properly put in and instructed.

Mr. CAMPBELL. Were there any other lecturers used in connection with the field work, or with securing members, aside from these field men?

Mr. SIMMONS. Well, I can not recall just now, not having familiarized myself with that work during the last month or two.

Mr. CAMPBELL. How much is left in the treasury of this organization out of this $171,000?

Mr. SIMMONS. How much is left?

Mr. CAMPBELL. Yes.

Mr. SIMMONS. How much in money totals?

Mr. CAMPBELL. Yes.

Mr. SIMMONS. I can not definitely answer that question, because I have not, by reason of sickness, had access to those records or been in the office recently to know what money has been used in the promotion of the educational institution. I can not state the exact amount.

Mr. CAMPBELL. To whom was some of this $19,000 paid?

Mr. SIMMONS. What $19,000 is that?

Mr. CAMPBELL. For the field work.

Mr. SIMMONS. Well, we have a number of men that have been engaged in that work. We have had Mr. John Q. Nolan, and we have had——

Mr. CAMPBELL (interposing). What do you pay Mr. John Q. Nolan?

Mr. SIMMONS. I do not remember the amount paid Mr. Nolan. Those are details that I do not touch at all, but the work has been carried on there.

Mr. CAMPBELL. Under the constitution you are chargeable with the duty of a very accurate supervision of all the funds of the organization?

Mr. SIMMONS. Yes, sir.

Mr. CAMPBELL. Under the constitution that you submitted as a part of your statement.

Mr. SIMMONS. Yes, sir.

Mr. CAMPBELL. Then you spoke of the funds of the organiaztion coming within the scope of your authority.

Mr. SIMMONS. Yes, sir; I have general supervision of them. That is, reports are made to me.

Mr. CAMPBELL. You say you have no idea to whom all this money was paid, or how much was paid to individuals.

Mr. SIMMONS. Mr. Chairman, I did not say that I have no knowledge.

Mr. CAMPBELL. Then, give us what knowledge you have on that subject.

Mr. SIMMONS. I can not answer specifically and directly in giving the exact amount on account of absence from the city and because of sickness. For that reason I have not been able to do so and have had no occasion to check into those details. Every week a report comes in to me, but I have not been able to review those reports for several weeks, or the weekly reports. When I am well on the job there when reports come in I review them and file them away. I have had no opportunity to consult them lately so as to be able to give you the details of them.

Mr. CAMPBELL. In addition to the salaries, I notice that you had paid out $24,631.91 for traveling expenses. How many men have you to whom you pay traveling expenses?

Mr. SIMMONS. The number of men varies. They are employed, and then may be layed off or discharged. It would be rather hard for me to estimate the number of men we have right now. Sometimes a man is simply employed to make a specific trip, and he makes that trip and comes back. Then possibly, a little later, he is employed for another trip and back.

Mr. CAMPBELL. About how many men do you have on your roll that you use in that capacity?

Mr. SIMMONS. I would say that there are approximately in that capacity from 20 to 30, or that many that we have used in a year.

Mr. CAMPBELL. You still use them, notwithstanding your contract with Mr. Clarke?

Mr. SIMMONS. On this special lecturing work, as I said.

Mr. CAMPBELL. Do you go out yourself?

Mr. SIMMONS. Yes, sir; whenever it is possible to go.

Mr. CAMPBELL. To Chicago and St. Louis?

Mr. SIMMONS. Yes, sir; and to Houston, New Orleans, and other places—wherever they need me.

Mr. CAMPBELL. Your expenses are included in that $24,000?

Mr. SIMMONS. Yes, sir; my expenses are paid, of course, when I go on business in connection with the order.

Mr. CAMPBELL. You have a telephone bill here of $5,347.05. What was the occasion for such extensive telephoning?

Mr. SIMMONS. That runs through the year.

Mr. CAMPBELL. This is for——

Mr. SIMMONS (interposing). For two years.

Mr. CAMPBELL. It is from June 1, 1920, to October 1, 1921.

Mr. SIMMONS. Yes, sir. Well, those telephone bills are incident to the work. We have had to pay out more on items of that nature, or for telephone and telegraph service, by reason of the fact that men going into the field were engaged in new work, and oftentimes they would phone in to get information, and, of course, the telephone and telegraph bills were big. That is the occasion of that. It is on account of the number of new men out telephoning or telegraphing in to headquarters for information. They telephone or telegraph in for information, and, of course, whenever those things come in we always pay the bills.

Mr. CAMPBELL. Your own salary is now $1,000 per month?

Mr. SIMMONS: Commencing on the 1st of August.

Mr. CAMPBELL. It is $1,000 per month?

Mr. SIMMONS. Yes, sir.

Mr. CAMPBELL. Prior to that time how much was it?

Mr. SIMMONS. Commencing last fall, I do not remember now definitely when, but I will say a year ago, or a little over a year ago, it was not in excess of $100 per week, with expenses included.

Mr. CAMPBELL. Something has been said here about some back salary being paid.

Mr. SIMMONS. Yes, sir.

Mr. CAMPBELL. How much was that?

Mr. SIMMONS. The governing body, or the imperial councilium, passed a resolution at its last meeting, on the 1st of August of this year, to pay me a sum that would be equal to $5,000 per year for the past five years, whenever the organization was in a position to do so.

Mr. CAMPBELL. How much of that $25,000 has been paid?

Mr. SIMMONS. Only one $5,000, or one payment.

Mr. CAMPBELL. One payment of $5,000 has been made?

Mr. SIMMONS. Yes, sir.

Mr. CAMPBELL. Upon the suggestion of what particular klansman or officer was that payment made?

Mr. SIMMONS. Now, I might tell you the incident as it happened.

Mr. CAMPBELL. You were present?

Mr. SIMMONS. I was present during the deliberations up to that time, when I was courteously requested to step out of the room for a while.

Mr. CAMPBELL. Who requested you to step out?

Mr. SIMMONS. I do not remember who did it. There were 14 or 16 men present.

Mr. CAMPBELL. Was it Mr. Clarke?

Mr. SIMMONS. No more so than any other officer. I think it was Mr. Wade or possibly Mr. Etheridge. Both of them were sitting to my left. I retired immediately, and when they notified me to come back I came back, and they acquainted me with what had been done.

Mr. CAMPBELL. Are any of those men holding positions that are of pecuniary advantage to them?

Mr. Simmons. Well, I think only in the way of their compensation for their services to the organization.

Mr. Campbell. Each of them has a salary?

Mr. Simmons. No, sir; not each of them. Mr. Wade is the supreme secretary.

Mr. Campbell. He has a salary of how much?

Mr. Simmons. Of $300 per month.

Mr. Campbell. Mr. Clarke has a contract?

Mr. Simmons. Yes, sir; on a commission basis.

Mr. Campbell. That is making him some money?

Mr. Simmons. I do not know how much it is making him.

Mr. Campbell. You could discharge Wade or Clarke at any moment?

Mr. Simmons. For cause; yes, sir.

Mr. Campbell. The house in which you live is in Clarke's name?

Mr. Simmons. The actual transaction——

Mr. Campbell (interposing). That is so or it is not.

Mr. Simmons. There is a board of trustees that handles it. It is under the control of a board of trustees.

Mr. Campbell. But it is in Mr. Clarke's name?

Mr. Simmons. It is under the control of a board of trustees.

Mr. Campbell. Is the property in his name or not?

Mr. Simmons. Possibly it is, because he consummated the transaction. He said, "You go into the house and take charge of the house, and we will turn it over to you when it is paid for." The board of trustees holds the building in trust for me until it is paid for, at which time they will turn it over to me in fee simple.

Mr. Campbell. I have a memorandum here somewhere, or a record, that shows that out of the accumulated funds of Clarke there was $111,000 that he divided fifty-fifty between himself and Mrs. Tyler. Did that come to your attention?

Mr. Simmons. No, sir; I am not familiar with what contract or agreement Mr. Clarke has made with those who work under him in his department. That is a matter for Mr. Clarke, or his business. He has contracted to do this work on a commission basis, for a certain commission, and all of the expenses incident to the running of the business of that department must be borne by him.

Mr. Campbell. Has it occurred to you at any time since the running of the contract that you were paying out of the $2 fund money for advertising and for promoting membership, or for securing membership, practically 70 cents out of every dollar that you get out of the $2 in the interest of Mr. Clarke's contract?

Mr. Simmons. No, sir.

Mr. Campbell. That has not occurred to you?

Mr. Simmons. No, sir; it has not occurred to me. It has not been done in the interest of Mr. Clarke's contract.

Mr. Campbell. Has it ever occurred to you at any time that Mr. Clarke thought he had a very good thing that might at any time be terminated by you, and that it would not be a bad thing for him and those associated with him to increase your salary, pay you in back pay the sum of $25,000, and have the deed to the home in which you lived in his name? Has it ever occurred to you that it might have occurred to Clarke that it would be a good thing for him to do that?

Mr. Simmons. No, sir. Mr. Chairman, every year the imperial koncilium has met since the second year of the existence of the order——

Mr. Campbell (interposing). There has been no meeting since the contract was made, has there?

Mr. Simmons. Yes, sir; the last meeting was last August. Every year they have tried to pass a resolution allowing this compensation to me, but I would not let them do it, because the order was not in a position to fix that compensation.

Mr. Campbell. The Clarke contract could be terminated by you at any time?

Mr. Simmons. For cause; yes, sir.

Mr. Campbell. Has the suggestion ever entered your mind that perhaps Mr. Clarke and Mrs. Tyler did not have the high ideals with respect to this organization that you had?

Mr. Simmons. No, sir; I have no evidence of that at all, sir.

Mr. Campbell. Has it ever occurred to you at any time that they were using it as a money-making scheme?

Mr. SIMMONS. No, sir; it has not. I have no evidence that would justify any opinion on my part of that nature.

Mr. CAMPBELL. The fact that they have collected $225,568.84 in one year and divided it among themselves does not suggest to you that that is a pretty good thing for two persons, or a good deal of money for two persons to make in one year out of a benevolent organization?

Mr. SIMMONS. Well, sir, that might on its face appear to be a splendid sum of money, but out of that they have had to pay considerable expense.

Mr. CAMPBELL. But you have been paying out of the $2 that came to you money for expenses incurred in increasing the membership of the order?

Mr. SIMMONS. Yes, sir; that is true.

Mr. CAMPBELL. Have they been putting anything over on you, do you think?

Mr. SIMMONS. No, sir; I have not had any occasion to be suspicious of anything of that sort up to date. They have done a splendid piece of work, and they have been paid to do it upon a commission of 80 per cent. I have worked for other fraternal orders upon the basis of 100 per cent.

Mr. CAMPBELL. You had a contract with the klan originally before this contract was made with Mr. Clarke?

Mr. SIMMONS. No, sir.

Mr. CAMPBELL. For 80 per cent, did you not?

Mr. SIMMONS. No, sir; I have no contract per se along that line.

Mr. CAMPBELL. That was the amount you were to get, was it not?

Mr. SIMMONS. By consent of the meeting. We had a very small organization, and I had been looking after all those things alone. I had to live, and I had nothing to live on. They consented to this, or, rather, they insisted upon my doing that. For every member I got myself, I was to receive 80 per cent, but that applied only to those that I actually solicited myself.

Mr. CAMPBELL. In the year that you have had prosperity in the order, what assets can you show for the order at this time?

Mr. SIMMONS. The assets we can show would be the home or head office property that we have recently bought.

Mr. CAMPBELL. That is paid for?

Mr. SIMMONS. Not altogether.

Mr. CAMPBELL. How much has been paid on that property?

Mr. SIMMONS. From the estimates that have been made, they must have paid something like $20,000 or $30,000.

Mr. CAMPBELL. What fund is that being paid out of?

Mr. SIMMONS. Out of the general fund of the organization.

Mr. CAMPBELL. Made up of the $2?

Mr. SIMMONS. Yes, sir.

Mr. CAMPBELL. Are the payments made by your check or Mr. Montgomery's?

Mr. SIMMONS. On this home?

Mr. CAMPBELL. Yes.

Mr. SIMMONS. On the office building?

Mr. CAMPBELL. Yes.

Mr. SIMMONS. They are made both ways.

Mr. CAMPBELL. You do not know how much has ben paid?

Mr. SIMMONS. No, sir; not exactly. There has been some estimate made, and certain lots adjacent to this property have been bought since I have been out of the office sick.

Mr. CAMPBELL. We have heard frequent references to your being away on account of sickness. How much time during the last year have you been away from your duties on account of sickness?

Mr. SIMMONS. In the last year, I would estimate possibly as much as four months.

Mr. CAMPBELL. Four months out of the twelve?

Mr. SIMMONS. Yes, sir.

Mr. CAMPBELL. When did this illness take you from your duties in the office?

Mr. SIMMONS. At various times.

Mr. CAMPBELL. I mean whether in the early part of the year or the latter part of the year.

Mr. SIMMONS. I had one attack that came on last November.

Mr. CAMPBELL. But recently you have not been in the office or engaged in the work of the organization?

Mr. SIMMONS. Not in any detailed work on account of my sickness and sickness in my home, except to answer correspondence addressed to me personally and to have general supervision of the work.

Mr. CAMPBELL. What is the nature of the lecture that is delivered by the men that you send out for organization purposes?

Mr. SIMMONS. Those lecturers are sent out for the purpose of instructing in the ritualistic work.

Mr. CAMPBELL. The lectures are made in connection with the development of the local klans?

Mr. SIMMONS. Yes, sir; and in crystallizing the movement for the future.

Mr. CAMPBELL. You hold out to the public that it is a purely patriotic and benevolent organization?

Mr. SIMMONS. A fraternal organization.

Mr. CAMPBELL. You say a fraternal organization, but you do not mean by that that it has fraternal insurance?

Mr. SIMMONS. No, sir; it is not a commercialized organization.

Mr. CAMPBELL. You hold out that it is a fraternal or patriotic organization?

Mr. SIMMONS. As set forth in the charter by the courts.

Mr. CAMPBELL. But it has no business or mercenary interests to serve?

Mr. SIMMONS. Only in the promotion of its own work.

Mr. CAMPBELL. And you claim that it was organized for the purpose of establishing a memorial to the klansmen of the reconstruction period?

Mr. SIMMONS. That is one feature of it.

Mr. CAMPBELL. To aid in the enforcement of the law?

Mr. SIMMONS. As citizens to assist in the preservation of the peace and security of the community, and only as citizens.

Mr. CAMPBELL. And to elevate and purify given communities when they show tendencies toward depravity?

Mr. SIMMONS. That question does not really provoke an answer that would reveal the purposes of the organization.

Mr. CAMPBELL. I understood you to say those were the purposes, broadly speaking?

Mr. SIMMONS. Broadly stated; yes, sir. We teach respect for the law, of course, and the elevation of the community along moral lines, or anything that will tend toward decency.

Mr. CAMPBELL. Do you make any suggestions in those lectures of a racial nature or having reference to the religious convictions of citizens?

Mr. SIMMONS. I never have myself, and the instructions that those lecturers take out from me is to the contrary effect.

Mr. CAMPBELL. You have instructed your lecturers not to refer to racial or religious matters?

Mr. SIMMONS. Yes, sir; and to simply present the purposes of the institution. If some lecturer out yonder in the heat of his enthusiasm should go contrary to that, that is another matter.

Mr. CAMPBELL. I observe in the testimony given a few days ago by the post-office inspector that the weekly letter sent out from Atlanta, from the propagation department, gives detailed information in some instances as to just what would be a clever appeal to make to particular communities. Is that done with your knowledge and consent?

Mr. SIMMONS. No sir; and I am glad you referred to that, because that is one item that I want to cover. I forgot it the other evening.

Mr. CAMPBELL. That has been going on for a year, or since the contract was made with Mr. Clarke, has it not? That is, these letters have been sent out.

Mr. SIMMONS. I do not know just when the letters began going out. Mr. Clarke took the matter up with me about getting out weekly letters.

Mr. CAMPBELL. You heard the letter read that was sent to the klansmen or the Clarke workers who were out in the field getting members with respect to the membership of the chief of police of Norfolk?

Mr. SIMMONS. No, sir; I never knew anything of that letter.

Mr. CAMPBELL. You heard that letter read here?

Mr. SIMMONS. Yes, sir.

Mr. CAMPBELL. It was a very clever letter, designed to appeal to other chiefs of police to get help in the enforcement of the law, was it not?

Mr. SIMMONS. As I remember that letter, as read here. I would judge so.

Mr. CAMPBELL. Has it not occurred to you that this idealistic organization that you have given birth to and have fostered so long is now being used for mercenary purposes by very clever people or propagandists who know how to appeal to the people of this community or in that for membership?

Mr. SIMMONS. So far, I have not. Nothing has come to my view that would prompt me to have such an opinion.

Mr. CAMPBELL. The letters read here a few days ago did not strike you as being cleverly designed to appeal to the prejudices of the different communities, or as appealing in one community to those who had any antipathy against some condition of people, and to those in another community who may have antipathies in regard to another or different condition of people?

Mr. SIMMONS. I grant you that those letters as read were calculated to convey that idea.

Mr. CAMPBELL. But the fact does not make any impression upon you that the organization is being used for anything other than purely idealistic and highly commendable purposes?

Mr. SIMMONS. I made the statement here, when I heard those letters read, that they were a distinct surprise to me. I knew nothing of them. I thought it well to get out weekly letters, or letters of the character I testified about.

Mr. CAMPBELL. Were those letters sent out without your knowledge or consent?

Mr. SIMMONS. Those particular letters read I did not know about.

Mr. CAMPBELL. The chief of police of Norfolk denies absolutely that he is a member of the organization. What do you think of the use of your organization by people who resort to such methods in securing members by making appeals that are absolutely not true?

Mr. SIMMONS. You want to know what I think of it?

Mr. CAMPBELL. Yes. You told us what you thought of certain papers that were telling things that were not true, and I want to know what you think of Mrs. Tyler in connection with the same matter?

Mr. SIMMONS. I think it is unjust to the organization, and it is a matter that should have a very rigid investigation.

Mr. CAMPBELL. What do you think in connection with Mr. Clarke, who evidently is in partnership with Mrs. Tyler, or Mrs. Tyler is in partnership with him, sending out those letters?

Mr. SIMMONS. If any such things have been sent out, it has been done without my knowledge or consent, and it will be thoroughly investigated. If it is not right, we will right it. We stand for the right, and I do not countenance any such tactics.

Mr. CAMPBELL. The letters referred to have a tendency to deceive, have they not?

Mr. SIMMONS. If those letters have gone forth, they have deceived me as well as others.

Mr. CAMPBELL. And were sent out for the purpose of deceiving the public, were they not?

Mr. SIMMONS. Well, now, I could not tell you the purpose of their being sent out. It appears that way. It has that appearance, but as to the purpose, those who are the authors of those letters themselves would have to tell you their purpose.

Mr. CAMPBELL. The purpose was to get members?

Mr. SIMMONS. The purpose was in line with their propagating department.

Mr. CAMPBELL. The purpose was to get $8 for Clarke and Tyler and $2 for the organization?

Mr. SIMMONS. I would reasonably suppose that the purpose of those letters was in line with their propagating department.

Mr. CAMPBELL. And their work is to get members. Did Clarke talk over with you tl. nature of the information or material that would be contained in these letters that should be sent out?

Mr. SIMMONS. No, sir.

Mr. CAMPBELL. You never had any consultation with him in connection with what these letters should contain?

Mr. SIMMONS. No; that was left altogether with him after he came to me and was recommended——

Mr. CAMPBELL (interposing). Was Clarke a klansman prior to his entering into the contract?

Mr. SIMMONS. Just a short time. I never knew him until a few months before.

Mr. CAMPBELL. He became a klansman shortly before you made this contract with him?

Mr. SIMMONS. Yes, sir; if I remember distinctly, I believe he came into the organization in December or January before the contract in June.

Mr. CAMPBELL. You knew he had a contract with, or had in partnership with him, this Mrs. Tyler?

Mr. SIMMONS. I had met Mrs. Tyler, but up to that time as secretary and treasurer of the Southern publicity association. He had a good many men also connected with his work in his office force—stenographers, and so on.

Mr. CAMPBELL. Did you know or did you not know of the division, fifty-fifty, of the $111,000 between Clarke and Tyler?

Mr. SIMMONS. No, sir; I did not know anything about that.

Mr. CAMPBELL. You did not know they had made that much of a profit in this last year?

Mr. SIMMONS. No; I did not know they had that agreement among themselves. That was a matter between them, of course, and I knew nothing of that.

Mr. CAMPBELL. There would be considerable inducement to them to secure additional members and the establishment of different klans?

Mr. SIMMONS. Yes, sir.

Mr. CAMPBELL. Under their contract they secure $8—or how much do they secure from each member that joins a local klan after it has been established?

Mr. SIMMONS. That part of the contract calls for $2, I believe it is.

Mr. CAMPBELL. Two dollars to them?

Mr. SIMMONS. For a certain length of time, and was put in the contract for the reason that oftentimes——

Mr. CAMPBELL. Speak a little louder, please.

Mr. SIMMONS. I am doing that as much as I can, sir. When they establish a local organization quite a number of men whom they have secured or possibly interested do not get into the organization prior to the issuance of the charter, but come in afterwards, and that was put in there so they would get the benefit of the work they had done before in that way.

Mr. CAMPBELL. So they will have an income as long as these local klans secure members?

Mr. SIMMONS. No, sir.

Mr. CAMPBELL. Will they not?

Mr. SIMMONS. No, sir; I believe it is six months—either three or six months—after the klan is chartered.

Mr. CAMPBELL. There is an additional fee of 15 cents per member; who gets that?

Mr. SIMMONS. No: there is no additional fee, Mr. Chairman.

Mr. CAMPBELL. What is that?

Mr. SIMMONS. That is a per capita tax.

Mr. CAMPBELL. Who gets that?

Mr. SIMMONS. That goes into the organization. That comes from the chartered klans only, and that goes into the general treasury of the institution. It has been stated here——

Mr. CAMPBELL (interposing). That goes into a fund over which you have control?

Mr. SIMMONS. Yes; that is the general fund. It has been stated here that was $3 a year, but that is a mistake. It is 45 cents a quarter and the reports are made quarterly.

Mr. CAMPBELL. Do you have any balance sheet in your office showing these receipts and expenditures?

Mr. SIMMONS. Yes, sir; I have the reports come in each week. They are long sheets, going into the details, and are filed away.

Mr. CAMPBELL. And yet you have no general or specific information with respect to the manner in which the fund that has come to the klan has been expended within the last year?

Mr. SIMMONS. Oh, yes, sir; I have a general knowledge of the expenditures of the fund.

Mr. CAMPBELL. I have been trying to get some specific information about that.

Mr. SIMMONS. The money has been spent, of course I thought that could be easily presumed.

Mr. CAMPBELL. It has been spent; yes.

Mr. SIMMONS (continuing). In development of the organization.

Mr. CAMPBELL. That is, it has gone out of the klan treasury?

Mr. SIMMONS. For the purposes of the klan, such as we have had our office force, you know, and fixtures and equipment and the help to promote the organization and the different interests and work which the klan is doing.

Mr. CAMPBELL. These letters are sent through the mails that are sent out for the purpose of securing members?

Mr. SIMMONS. Letters like you refer to?

Mr. CAMPBELL. Yes.

Mr. SIMMONS. I could not say just how they are distributed, sometimes those letters, or rather I know of occasions where one of the division superintendents or grand goblins, you might say, may take a batch of those to distribute out to his field men as he comes in touch with them. The method of the distribution of those letters I do not know because it is a matter I know nothing about, only from weekly letters being published to the field men keeping them in touch with headquarters and with facts and information about our progress. That is the extent of it, and it is agreeable to me that such letters of a stimulating nature should be sent out. That is as far as I know about how they are distributed.

Mr. CAMPBELL. And whether that "stimulating nature" has stated the truth has not been a matter into which you have made any investigation up to this time?

Mr. SIMMONS. No; I have had no occasion to. I knew of nothing that required an investigation.

Mr. CAMPBELL. Your attention has now been called to the fact that the chief of police of Norfolk says that it is absolutely false that he is a member of the organization, while the letters sent out to the different klansmen——

Mr. RODENBERG (interposing). Mr. Chairman, I object to notes being handed to the witness while he is on the stand.

Mr. POU. Why?

Mr. RODENBERG. He is on the stand and outsiders need not prompt him about any question that comes from the committee.

Mr. POU. The gentleman who handed him the note announced that he came here as a friend of Col. Simmons. I do not see any cause for any criticism.

Mr. RODENBERG. Otherwise, we might as well allow him to prompt him on any matter that comes up.

Mr. POU. That has always been done. My friend has been here a long time and if there has ever been any criticism of that kind about a witness I have never heard it before.

Mr. RODENBERG. I do not know that it is permitted at all. I have never seen it done before.

(At the request of the chairman, the stenographer read the pending question as follows:)

"Mr. CAMPBELL. Your attention has now been called to the fact that the chief of police of Norfolk says that it is absolutely false that he is a member of the organization, while the letters sent out to the different klansmen"——

Mr. CAMPBELL (continuing). Stated that he was a member of the organization and gave rather a dramatic picture of his initiation and of how he thanked the klansmen after they had stood up, 300 of them, each one pledging his support in the enforcement of the law which had been violated, and no attention had been paid to the violation; do you recall that?

Mr. SIMMONS. Yes, sir.

Mr. CAMPBELL. Now, I want again to call your attention to the fact that that seems to be the creation of a statement that would have a tendency to appeal to certain communities and the officers in certain communities to create organizations of this kind, to elicit their support in their enforcement of certain laws. Do you say now that that matter is to have attention from the klan?

Mr. SIMMONS. Not only that, sir, but any other matter that is brought to my knowledge that is tinged with any coloring of not being fair and square. Now, Mr. Clarke and Mrs. Tyler may have been informed or told that this man was a member. I do not know about that or about the source of their information.

Mr. CAMPBELL. The details were graphically given.

Mr. SIMMONS. Yes; I remember here the statement being presented that this man had disavowed his membership in the organization. I know nothing about that. I only know we have an organization in Norfolk, but as to who is and who is not a member I could not tell you.

Mr. GARRETT. Mr. Chairman, for my information, those letters that were read here by Mr. Williamson and the circulars purported to quote from letters received from Mr. Clarke and Mrs. Tyler, did they not?

Mr. CAMPBELL. I think some of them did. I have not been able to turn to that letter this morning.

Mr. GARRETT. The statement that was sent out about the chief of police of Norfolk showed upon its face, did it not, that they had received that information by letter or something of the sort from some one in Norfolk?

Mr. CAMPBELL. I think that is true.

Mr. GARRETT. That, of course, might have a very material bearing upon this inquiry which the committee is making.

Mr. CAMPBELL. I can not turn to that now.

On another phase of this matter, now, you have stated that one of the purposes you had in mind was to solidify the union of our common country, to promote the general welfare of all the people of the United States, and add to the good feeling existing in the country. Has it occurred to you that the revival of the name and uniform and the mask of the Ku-Klux Klan would be an agency that would promote good feeling in the United States, in the North or even in the South?

Mr. SIMMONS. No, sir. It has occurred to me there would be people who would dislike and be naturally prejudiced against the organization as almost every organization has those who are prejudiced against it.

Mr. CAMPBELL. The original klan came in at a time when feeling following the war was running very high and a condition existed down South that seemed to the people of the South to require some very drastic organization among their people, and the organization was made so secret that one neighbor scarcely know that another neighbor belonged. That is true, is it not?

Mr. SIMMONS. That is my information.

Mr. CAMPBELL. And even the robes and the marks were held in such secrecy that after they were removed from the wearer they were not within reach of any other hand than the hand of the wearer or some immediate member of his family. That is true, is it not?

Mr. SIMMONS. That is my information regarding the old organiaztion.

Mr. CAMPBELL. Aside from the known purposes of the organization, the mask and the robe were used to terrorize people who did not come within the original scope of those who should be affected by it; that is true, is it not?

Mr. SIMMONS. That is a matter of history.

Mr. CAMPBELL. Many innocent, well-intentioned white men in the South were terrorized by that organization?

Mr. SIMMONS. I never heard of an instance, in my studies, where any innocent man was ever terrorized or anything perpetrated against an innocent person.

Mr. CAMPBELL. At least they had the presumption of innocence surrounding them because they had not been convicted of any crime or of any offense, nor even charged with any, and yet they were made the object of the attentions of these masked men; that is true, is it not?

Mr. SIMMONS. I could not answer that, sir.

Mr. CAMPBELL. And this was made possible because men appeared in the nighttime in these robes and masks; that is true, is it not?

Mr. SIMMONS. I might say that history records them having their parades and other public exhibitions.

Mr. CAMPBELL. And your high purpose in creating this organization at this time was for the purpose of establishing a memorial to the klansmen of that period?

Mr. SIMMONS. It was memorializing their spiritual purpose, Mr. Chairman, and the work they did to save the civilization of our country.

Mr. CAMPBELL. To take with this organization at this time into the memories of this body those things that to many of us appear might well be forgotten. Has it occurred to you that the crimes, some sixty-odd in number, that have been recently charged against the Knights of the Ku-Klux Klan have been made possible by the very masks or the type of the masks that were worn in the reconstruction period by the klansmen of that day?

Mr. SIMMONS. You say has it occurred to me?

Mr. CAMPBELL. Yes.

Mr. SIMMONS. No, sir; it has not occurred to me. There are no grounds for that.

Mr. CAMPBELL. Now, I am not saying these crimes have been committed by klansmen. It is just probable that crimes were committed in the reconstruction period by men who were not klansmen; but the very fact that there is a robe and a mask concealing the identity of the individual who organized the mob or the posse or the procession or whatever it may be, call it by any name that will take from it any odium that might attach to it, yet they are concealed from the public, their identity is not to be known, and they protect themselves even against the sheriff of the county with instruments of death.

Mr. SIMMONS. The same thing might apply, sir, to the Mardi Gras parade.

Mr. CAMPBELL. That is a frolic.

Mr. SIMMONS. That is true. It is innocent just the same as this.

Mr. CAMPBELL. It is an innocent frolic.

Mr. SIMMONS. So is ours an innocent memorial parade, sir.

Mr. CAMPBELL. Was the parade in the Texas city in which the sheriff was shot, and will probably die, an innocent frolic?

Mr. SIMMONS. It was not so much a frolic as an innocent parade, and the sheriff interfered, and my information is there that he exceeded his authority.

Mr. CAMPBELL. However that may be, he did interfere and the klansmen insisted upon their rights to the frolic and to parade notwithstanding his denial to them of their right.

Mr. SIMMONS. My information is they insisted after they had gotten permission from the mayor and the chief of police to have the parade, and after two men had lifted their masks, according to my information, one bearing the cross and one bearing the flag, and they asked him if it would be agreeable if those carrying the flag and the cross would reveal their identity.

Mr. CAMPBELL. And he decided they should not parade, but the parade continued. Do you not see a difference between that and the Mardi Gras that have Thursday night off and parade as a lot of reckless, harum-scarum people out on the street having a frolic?

Mr. SIMMONS. It is a question——

Mr. CAMPBELL (interposing). Are the purposes of the klan similar to the purposes of the frolic on Thursday night at Mardi Gras?

Mr. SIMMONS. We have our social features or social festivities growing out of these parades.

Mr. CAMPBELL. Are the parades staged recently in Texas of that nature— are they in the nature of a frolic?

Mr. SIMMONS. Not in the nature so much of a frolic but as a social exhibition. Our plan or custom—it is not a plan—has been that wherever a klan has been organized, the first announcement is that they will have a parade.

Mr. CAMPBELL. A week ago last Sunday in one of the churches of a prominent town in Oklahoma the minister was preaching the Gospel to the congregation when 200 klansmen in full uniform marched into the church, terrorizing, disturbing the audience; was that in the nature of one of the frolics?

Mr. SIMMONS. I do not know anything about that incident, sir. I do not suppose they terrorized them.

Mr. CAMPBELL. Oh, it is said that the audience was very much disturbed, and naturally would be.

Mr. SIMMONS. Of course, I am not acquainted with that incident at all. I suppose if they went in, the minister knew of their coming and had planned it.

Mr. CAMPBELL. He did not know they were coming.

Mr. SIMMONS. I do not know about that. I know if I was a minister of a church, nothing like that would be pulled if I did not know something about it.

Mr. CAMPBELL. You say nothing of that kind would be pulled, and yet the only way to have prevented it would have been to resort to violence right there and then.

Mr. SIMMONS. I say I would have had knowledge of it.

Mr. CAMPBELL. And the minister would probably have received the same treatment as the sheriff in Texas.

Mr. SIMMONS. No; from my knowledge of the character of the men, they are not out for anything like that, sir.

Mr. CAMPBELL. But this thing was staged in this Oklahoma town——

Mr. GARRETT (interposing). Was that the account in which it was stated that the leader of the marchers stopped in front of the minister and said to him, "We are behind you, 3,000 strong"?

Mr. CAMPBELL. Yes; "You are not with us but we are behind you, 3,000 strong," then silently marched out. That was at least a very unconventional thing to do; was it not, Colonel?

Mr. SIMMONS. I should think so, sir.

Mr. CAMPBELL. Does that come within the teachings of your order?

Mr. SIMMONS. No, sir.

Mr. CAMPBELL. Does it come within the privileges of klansmen?

Mr. SIMMONS. No, sir; not by authority of the organization.

Mr. CAMPBELL. Can you imagine unmasked men, 200 in number, on a quiet Sabbath morning, walking into a church during the time that the congregation is at its devotions and announcing to the minister, "You are not with us but we are with you, 3,000 strong," and then silently walking out—can you imagine unmasked men doing that?

Mr. SIMMONS. I do not know of my imagination along that line. I know nothing of conditions out there. I can only say this, sir, that those things are not authorized by this organization, and if that could be construed as a disturbance of public worship, then the people involved have recourse to law. If that was not agreeable to the community and they knew the spirit of it, that organization would have its charter revoked in 10 minutes.

Mr. CAMPBELL. I have here a press clipping from another town in Oklahoma giving the name of a barber, and it states that klansmen, masked, took him out into the woods, some 6 or 7 miles from the town, stripped him and lashed him; then bound and gagged him; then brought him back and threw him into the street, naked, in the city. Does that come within the purview of the work of the klansmen?

Mr. SIMMONS. Absolutely, it does not; and that is like many other press clippings that have been shot out through the press.

Mr. CAMPBELL. Can you conceive of klansmen unmasked doing that sort of thing?

Mr. SIMMONS. I can not conceive of klansmen doing it masked. They do not do business that way. That is not their work. There may be some individuals——

Mr. CAMPBELL (interposing). This is charged to them.

Mr. SIMMONS. Yes, sir. As I say, I do not know about individual conduct any more than in any other organization; but there is nothing in our law or in my authority that would justify any act that contravenes the law.

Mr. CAMPBELL. Fred A. Ziegler, the assistant manager of a hotel in a Texas town, was taken out and tarred and feathered by men wearing the klansman's mask and klansman's robe.

Mr. SIMMONS. That has simply been charged.

Mr. CAMPBELL. Yes. The fact that he was taken out and tarred and feathered is more than a charge; it is more than a charge that the men wore the klansman's mask. There is no dispute about that. But who was behind the mask is not known; that is the matter to which I am leading up. You appear a very fair, high-minded man. I have the same impression of you that the post-office inspectors and others who have been down there have, that you are a man of ideals. I am now about to ask you if, in the furtherance of the ideals that you have, you think it a good thing to keep up the custom of klansmen appearing in public parades wearing the mask and the robe and appearing as being authorized in any way to appear in public wearing these robes, and I ask you now if you think it a good policy to pursue that, in view of the fact that some sixty-odd overt acts of violation have been committed against the rights of citizens, presumably by an organization or alleged to be by an organization that has for its avowed object the suppression of all violence and the enforcement of all law; and they have been able to do it under the mask?

Mr. SIMMONS. These things, Mr. Chairman, have only been alleged. If facts were brought to my attention that one klansman had committed an act that violated the laws of his country, that man would not remain in the organization any longer than the fact of his vanishment could be——

Mr. CAMPBELL (interposing). But if he committed an offense in violation of the laws of the land or of the organization, it would not be known to you any more than to the officers, because he was under a mask, and the mask would protect him against you as well as against other members of the community.

Mr. SIMMONS. You say he would not be known. If any klansman can not identify another one, honestly—that is, if the man behind that mask can not be identified—that robe comes off of him.

Mr. CAMPBELL. I assume that there are methods between klansmen at that time or at certain times when they have means of identification.

Mr. SIMMONS. Yes, sir.

Mr. CAMPBELL. But if two or three klansmen go out and commit a crime and you are not there and other klansmen are not there and the mask is off the next day, how are you going to identify the men who did it?

Mr. SIMMONS. Because a member of the organization who violates the oath regarding respect for law and order, his act can not be condoned or covered by his relationship with the organization. It would be the sworn duty of other men who have knowledge of it to expose it; and the general character of the men in this organization, Mr. Chairman—that is, I mean the general character of those who have to do with the control of it—are not the character of men that commit crimes behind masks or without masks.

Mr. CAMPBELL. What have you to say about these 200 men that walked into that church a week ago last Sunday in Oklahoma?

Mr. SIMMONS. I have made my statement regarding that incident.

Mr. CAMPBELL. Are they men of the high ideals that you say are incapable of such an unconventionality as that, to say nothing about disturbing the peace?

Mr. SIMMONS. I have not any information on that incident, and I can not say whether those men were members of this oroganization or whether it was an organization of that town or not, or whether the men had counterfeited that costume. I have no information regarding that incident myself.

Mr. POU. Were the 200 men masked or unmasked?

Mr. CAMPBELL. They were masked, so the story stated. Now, getting to the Texas case—Beaumont, Tex. The local organization there assumed full responsibility under the seal of the klan for the outrage that was perpetrated. What have you to say about that?

Mr. SIMMONS. I haven't any knowledge that they have assumed that responsibility; I have only been told through the papers that they did.

Mr. CAMPBELL. Have you made any effort to ascertain whether or not that statement was true?

Mr. SIMMONS. Which statement—of the press?

Mr. CAMPBELL. That they assumed the responsibility, under the seal of the klan.

Mr. SIMMONS. Investigations are now under way but have not been completed.

Mr. CAMPBELL. Who is making those investigations?

Mr. SIMMONS. Members of the organization we have sent down there.

Mr. CAMPBELL. Sent down from——

Mr. SIMMONS (interposing). From Atlanta. We have sent two attorneys down there and another man to make that investigation, and reports have not been submitted as yet.

Mr. CAMPBELL. That outrage s alleged to have occurred some time ago. Have you any reports on it at all?

Mr. SIMMONS. I have information on it, but no full and complete report yet.

Mr. CAMPBELL. You simply have a report that investigators are down there and at work?

Mr. SIMMONS. I know invest gators went there, but they have not yet submitted a report on it.

Mr. CAMPBELL. Have they returned?

Mr. SIMMONS. They have returned; that is, to my knowledge one has returned; I do not know about the others.

Mr. CAMPBELL. Has he stated to you verbally what he found out with respect to the conditions there?

Mr. SIMMONS. No; not altogether; because those things are coming out in his report. But he told me, he says, "From all the evidence I could possibly find there 's nothing to show that the local organization had anything to do with it; that it was the action of an outraged community."

Mr. CAMPBELL. But the local klan assumed full responsibility for it.

Mr. SIMMONS. He denied that.

Mr. CAMPBELL. But that was published under the seal of the klan?

Mr. SIMMONS. Yes, s r; that was under the imprint of the seal or what looks like the seal of that klan, which was lost.

Mr. CAMPBELL. The seal of the klan was lost?

Mr. SIMMONS. Or stolen; yes, sir.

Mr. CAMPBELL. What efforts have been made to recover it?

Mr. SIMMONS. I do not know; but the fact of it being lost was reported to the sheriff and the chief of police.

Mr. CAMPBELL. Is that all?

Mr. SIMMONS. That is my information, as soon as the fact was discovered.

Mr. CAMPBELL. Is that all that has been done?

Mr. SIMMONS. Simply the loss reported. I have not been down there, sir. The matter was reported to the author ties and a search was to be made, and they have been endeavoring to locate it, if possible. I have not the details of that incident.

Mr. CAMPBELL. Well, would it not be important to secure the services of men who could ascertain whether or not so important a matter as the seal of the klan, a secret order that appears in public in parades, only under mask, was stolen and the seal recovered as soon as possible? Is it a matter that is of so little consequence to the klan in Atlanta that this seal is being permitted to remain in the hands of people unauthorized to have it or use it?

Mr. SIMMONS. Oh, no, sir. I just stated to you, sir, that the work was going on. We have recently gotten a man, who is trained in that kind of work, to see if he could locate it, and we are going to locate it if it can possibly be found.

Mr. CAMPBELL. That outrage could not have been perpetrated by klansmen or others if it were not for the use of this robe and mask, could it?

Mr. SIMMONS. Well, I think so. There have been occasions, long before the Knights of the Ku-Klux Klan came into existence, where numbers of men gathered and d d certain things.

Mr. CAMPBELL. But there would not be such a mystery about it, would there, if it were not for the robe and mask?

Mr. SIMMONS. I could not answer about that, sir. My information is that there was nothing of the robe or mask used on this occasion, that is, of this order. There may have been certain vestments there to use as a disguise, a pillowcase, a pillow slip, sheet, or something of that sort. My information is that possibly a large number of those men were members of other fraternal orders, and I do not see why you do not involve them.

Mr. CAMPBELL. They must have been members of the klan.

Mr. SIMMONS. I do not know; I have no information about that, but some of them possibly were.

Mr. CAMPBELL. Even if they were members of other organizations, would you excuse them on that ground, as the imperial wizard, for the outrage that was perpetrated there?

Mr. SIMMONS. I would excuse no man for committing wrong.

Mr. CAMPBELL. Then why do you suggest that they probably belonged to some other orders?

Mr. SIMMONS. Simply for this reason: If that was committed by a large number of men and it is reasonable to suppose those men are members of various fraternal orders as well as the klan, why attach it on the klan?

Mr. CAMPBELL. It was attached to the klan because the klan assumed, under the seal of the order, the full responsibility for it.

Mr. SIMMONS. From my information, sir, I disavow that, that assumption.

Mr. CAMPBELL. Well, they were wearing at least some of the costume of the klan, or the mask of the klan.

Mr. SIMMONS. They may have been wearing something that looked like it, and it may have been possible to have the costume, because those costumes are kept in the lockers of a lodge room, where there are hundreds of them, and where they are convenient for use in the inside ceremonial work.

Mr. CAMPBELL. I will next take up what is known as the Atlanta case, a case that occurred near the city of Atlanta. Did you make a thorough investigation of that with a view of ascertaining who the klansmen were, if they were klansmen, who were responsible for what was done there?

Mr. SIMMONS. The courts, in the trial of those cases, made a very thorough investigation, and the officers of the county and the police and detective forces were on the case, and it was a case in which the law had the case in its own hands.

Mr. CAMPBELL. Did you make any effort to ascertain whether or not klansmen were responsible for that?

Mr. SIMMONS. I made no effort at the time for the reason that I was in Florida sick, down sick.

Mr. CAMPBELL. Who was in charge of the klan in Atlanta? What is the name of the man in charge? Is it the grand——

Mr. SIMMONS (interposing). You mean, who was in charge in my absence?

Mr. CAMPBELL. Yes.

Mr. SIMMONS. The imperial klaliff, looking after the business affairs.

Mr. CAMPBELL. Who was that?

Mr. SIMMONS. Mr. Clarke was imperial klaliff at the time.

Mr. CAMPBELL. He was in charge during that time?

Mr. SIMMONS. Yes.

Mr. CAMPBELL. Do you know whether he made any effort to ascertain who the responsible persons were for that outrage?

Mr. SIMMONS. The information coming to me—all the information I had on it at the time was from the exalted cyclops of the local klan.

Mr. CAMPBELL. What did the exalted cyclops of the local klan do toward ascertaining who the perpetrators were?

Mr. SIMMONS. I do not know; I am not familiar with his work, because the information he got he turned in to the Solicitor General, but he told me that the klan had absolutely nothing to do with it in any way, because the young man that was killed was one of the best friends I had in Atlanta personally and was a member with me in several fraternal orders.

Mr. CAMPBELL. It is said that the klan paid the attorney who defended the man charged with this attempted murder.

Mr. SIMMONS. If he was I do not know anything about it, and I certainly would have known.

Mr. CAMPBELL. You would have known about it?

Mr. SIMMONS. Yes, sir.

Mr. CAMPBELL. Notwithstanding the fact that you were away?

Mr. SIMMONS. Why, certainly. In my absence nobody else has any authority to draw upon the funds of the klan at any time.

Mr. CAMPBELL. You have not been able to account for the expenditure of over $130,000 out of the general funds of the klan, saying that you did not know. Is it possible that this payment could have been made to this attorney without your knowledge?

Mr. SIMMONS. Not after the money got into my hands—money of the klan.

Mr. CAMPBELL. But this money has been paid out after it went into the klan: $137,228.75 has been paid out and you have been unable to identify or to detail much of the expenditure.

Mr. SIMMONS. No, sir; and for the reason I stated on the outset of this, that I have not had an opportunity to acquaint myself or go into the details of those figures. I would not attempt to answer directly when I could not do it without a knowledge of the details.

Mr. CAMPBELL. The attorney to whom this alleged payment was made out of klan funds for the defense of the man charged with that crime is now in the employ of the klan, I believe out on the Pacific coast.

Mr. SIMMONS. That is my understanding, sir; he is in the propagation department. I know the man, and he is seeking the climate of California; he is a lawyer, and until he can build up his law practice there he will look into our work and direct it.

Mr. CAMPBELL. I think you stated a few days ago, when detailing some of the work of the klan, that a sum of money had been paid to a bishop of the African Methodist Episcopal Church by the name of I. N. Fitzpatrick. How much money was paid by the klan to that bishop?

Mr. SIMMONS. Well, Mr. Chairman, that has been five or six years ago. He has been to see me several times, both in the office and at my home, and getting collections for different benevolent interests of his church and people, and that was simply a contribution, more in the way of a personal contribution, and it has been so long ago that I could not state about the amounts.

Mr. CAMPBELL. I have a letter here signed by a man who says he knows, and he says there is no such bishop in the African Methodist Episcopal Church as Bishop I. N. Fitzpatrick and that there never has been a bishop by that name in that church.

Mr. SIMMONS. Well, I judge that fellow knows. I am not familiar with all the officials of the Negro churches, but I met this man, I. N. Fitzpatrick, as a bishop; he told me himself that he was a bishop of that church and was employed by the British Government in its work among the Zulus, missionary work in South Africa. I have seen him in Atlanta, but I have not seen him in the last two years. He was there merely on a leave of absence and was going back, and I have a letter from him—not in my possession now. There are other darkies around there that know him, and the fact that he was a bishop has never been contradicted or denied, and knowing the quality of the man I had reason to believe that he had stated the truth regarding his official connection. Further than that I do not know.

Mr. CAMPBELL. The finances of the klan, prior to June 1, 1920, were practically under your control?

Mr. SIMMONS. Yes, sir.

Mr. CAMPBELL. It is estimated that $151,000 came into the klan during that time and you do not know how it went out.

Mr. SIMMONS. I do not know that that was the amount. That is away in excess.

Mr. CAMPBELL. That is what your books show.

Mr. SIMMONS. I know, but that is in excess, and I have a right to correct it. My knowledge is that that is considerably in excess, and if I have time to go over this——

Mr. CAMPBELL (interposing). In any event, you do not know where the money went?

Mr. SIMMONS. Oh, yes, sir; the money went into the work of developing the organization; we had paraphernalia to get, to purchase, and we had numbers of things, general expenses, including items incident to the development of the organization. That was all used in that way and for my own living expenses, which were modest, and which will be proved by every citizen in Atlanta who knows me.

Mr. CAMPBELL. $171,000 has been received by the klan since June 1, 1920; you now have $12,000 in the bank and about $2,000 worth of furniture, as well as an equity in your home. What was done with the rest of the money?

Mr. SIMMONS. The statement you are quoting from——

Mr. CAMPBELL (interposing). I am quoting from the statement you have submitted as a part of your testimony.

Mr. SIMMONS. You have given me an insight into a statement made prior to this year, and I did not have an opportunity to go over that.

Mr. CAMPBELL. No; that is this year.

Mr. SIMMONS. I know; this year.

Mr. CAMPBELL. This last question refers to the finances within the past year.

Mr. SIMMONS. I understand, but those figures regarding our equipment are away under what we have had to pay out for our equipment. I believe you said $2,000 there.

Mr. CAMPBELL. I am not talking about equipment; I am talking about your assets. You list as assets the amount that was paid on the home in which you live and you list as assets, I think, the payment to the Lanier University.

Mr. SIMMONS. Yes, sir.

Mr. CAMPBELL. Then there is $12,000 in the bank. Those are all the assets listed, I think.

Mr. SIMMONS. Well, all of them are not listed, because we have equipment there, safes and files.

Mr. CAMPBELL. When were they purchased?

Mr. SIMMONS. They have been purchased along from time to time, as we needed them in the increase of the business.

Mr. CAMPBELL. Were the safes and files purchased before or after June 1, 1920?

Mr. SIMMONS. One, if I remember distinctly, was purchased before, and the others have been purchased since; we bought those things as we needed them in the prosecution of the work in the office.

Mr. CAMPBELL. You have furniture and equipment here at $9,855. Is that correct or not?

Mr. SIMMONS. I could not say whether that is correct or not——

Mr. CAMPBELL (interposing). Why was it recorded with such accuracy if it is not correct?

Mr. SIMMONS. Well, now, I can not answer you, because I was not present at the compilation of those figures. I do not know what the equipment cost; I could not tell you what it cost. For instance, they would suggest to me, "We need another safe." I would say, "Well, you have got to have it now?" "Yes." "Well, get it." "Well, what shall we get?" "Get a good one." That is what happened if we needed filing cases or needed a typewriter or things of that sort, and I did not know about the detailed cost of those.

Mr. CAMPBELL. The money, at least, is not now in the treasury, and the only things you have listed here show, as I have indicated, that you have assets in the neighborhood of $40,000 as the result of an income of $171,000. They are round numbers.

Mr. SIMMONS. Well, if there is any inconsistency in the facts, it certainly will be attended to on those matters as soon as possible. I want to verify those figures personally. You want facts from me personally as I know them, and I am giving them to you.

Mr. CAMPBELL. And under the constitution and by-laws of the order you are made solely responsible for the finances and property of the organization, under section 6, as I recall?

Mr. SIMMONS. Now, with an opportunity I can be in possession of those facts that seem to be inconsistent. On my return to the office I can get you a correction or rectify the statement there.

Mr. CAMPBELL. Does the fact that there appears to be such a discrepancy between the assets and the liabilities lead you to believe that may be you have been used, as has been suggested here, as a man of high ideals who may not know very much about what is going on in the organization? That has been the charge.

Mr. SIMMONS. Well, that is an opinion expressed.

Mr. CAMPBELL. Does it appear to you now that there is any justification for arriving at that conclusion, in view of your statement here now that you do not know what has been done with the funds of the organization?

Mr. SIMMONS. My answer to that question, sir, would simply be it is impossible for any man heading a movement to be acquainted with and thoroughly understand all the details that are going on, no more than the president of a bank could understand all the detailed transactions of his bank. They have been intrusted to those who are employed by the bank.

Mr. CAMPBELL. Then it may be that persons in whom you have reposed the greatest confidence have taken advantage of your credulity and of your ideals and have used the organization and its funds in a way that would not meet with your approval if you knew the details of their activities and expenditures?

Mr. SIMMONS. If that were true, I certainly would like to know it.

Mr. CAMPBELL. Do you not think it worth while to ascertain and find out whether or not it is true?

Mr. SIMMONS. Well, that question, Mr. Chairman—pardon me—is rather irrelevant, because I am going to——

Mr. CAMPBELL. You are going to find out?

Mr. SIMMONS. I told you at the very outset that if there is any wrong it shall be righted.

Mr. CAMPBELL. And if improper publicity has been given for the purpose of securing members, if false statements have been made to the public or to any part of the public in any given communities in order to secure additional memberships, will that have your attention?

Mr. SIMMONS. Would you not construe that as being wrong?

Mr. CAMPBELL. I certainly would.

Mr. SIMMONS. Yes; and I have said that whatever is wrong will be put right.

Mr. CAMPBELL. Do you regard that as wrong?

Mr. SIMMONS. I do regard that as not at all in keeping with the ideals and purposes of this institution, and that would be wrong, of course, if not in accordance with the ideals and purposes of this order.

Mr. CAMPBELL. And if the mails have been used by those who have been securing large sums of money fraudulently you agree that that matter should have attention?

Mr. SIMMONS. It certainly will have. I do not take and I have never taken any position which would condone any man or any person in the violation of the laws of the land; I would not condone it; I would not condone the act.

Mr. CAMPBELL. As between one citizen and another interested in our common country and the welfare of our whole people, I again ask you if it has occurred to you during this inquiry, or at any time recently, that the mask of your organization and your regalia are now being used in such a way as to lead men to violate the rights of other men and violate the law? Has it occurred to you whether or not that is true?

Mr. SIMMONS. No, sir; and your question indicates it has not, because men behind masks have violated the law and committed crimes long before the Knights of the Ku Klux Klan came into existence and in sections of this country since it has, where no klan exists and no klansmen live.

Mr. CAMPBELL. Summarizing, it has been alleged that about 60 overt acts have been committed by men wearing the klansman's mask within the past year. Does it not look to you that that is a matter that should have the serious attention of a man who has the responsible position you hold in the organization that is charged with these offenses?

Mr. SIMMONS. If these allegations can be definitely established in a court having jurisdiction that fact will have my consideration, but a court of jurisdiction should act.

Mr. CAMPBELL. What do you mean by a court of jurisdiction?

Mr. SIMMONS. Well, whatever court that it will come into.

Mr. CAMPBELL. Do you mean that if those 200 men who entered that church in Oklahoma a week ago last Sunday should be arrested for disturbing the peace of that congregation and for the exceedingly unconventional manner in which they entered the church and departed from it, that then you would take some action with respect to the wearing of masks generally or merely with respect to the charter of that particular klan?

Mr. SIMMONS. That all depends upon the circumstances, sir. As to the regalia, as such, that is a matter for the supreme executive committee or governing body to attend to.

Mr. CAMPBELL. If the legislatures of the States should take notice of this excessive activity on the part of people in wearing klansmen's masks within the past year and should undertake to enact laws preventing members of any organization from appearing in public parades in masks, would you regard such laws as unfriendly to the Knights of the Ku Klux Klan?

Mr. SIMMONS. Well, sir, it seems that we have been accused of being the only organizations appearing in masks, and if that be the case it would convey the impression that such legislation was directly aimed against the klan

Mr. CAMPBELL. Do you think that such legislation, or the attempt at such legislation, would be unjustified on the part of the legislators in any of the States?

Mr. SIMMONS. In so far as crime being committed by the klan is concerned——

Mr. CAMPBELL (interposing). No; my question was, do you think that it would be an unfriendly act on the part of the Texas Legislature, for instance, to legislate against men wearing the klansman's mask in the State of Texas, in open parades on the streets in the cities of that State?

Mr. SIMMONS. Do you mean to say that if the States pass a law prohibiting the use of masks by fraternal organizations or any fraternal organization——

Mr. CAMPBELL (interposing). The use of klansman's mask, or any mask in public parades?

Mr. SIMMONS. If such a law were enacted, we would wholeheartedly respect that law.

Mr. CAMPBELL. Would you regard the legislators who passed such legislation as enemies of the klan?

Mr. SIMMONS. I can not answer that question, because I would not know the minds and hearts of the men who did it. You would have to first give me some basis.

Mr. CAMPBELL. Would you charge them with being un-American?

Mr. SIMMONS. No, sir; certainly not.

Mr. CAMPBELL. You claim to be the only 100 per cent American organization in existence, I believe?

Mr. SIMMONS. I am rather of the opinion that the word "only" could be left out of that statement.

Mr. CAMPBELL. I think that I have found it in some of your literature.

Mr. SIMMONS. That may possibly be. We know and everybody else knows, as a matter of common knowledge and intelligence, that there are in this country many patriotic organizations that are 100 per cent American.

Mr. CAMPBELL. I think you and I belong to such a one.

Mr. SIMMONS. Possibly so, but I have not seen any signs from you. Mr. Chairman, that particular point has been jumped on like a hungry chicken jumps on a June bug.

Mr. CAMPBELL. The fact, however, is that the mask worn by the klansman has been used to conceal those who had any purpose to serve, good or bad, and that they have been able to conceal their identity from the public, does not strike you as being a question that should have your attention as imperial wizard of the invisible empire, or that you should go into the question of whether or not it would promote the welfare of the invisible empire to remove the mask?

Mr. SIMMONS. I will state that there is a possible ground there, just as there are a good many other things that we now have under consideration in the development of this infant organization.

Mr. CAMPBELL. Men of such high and noble purposes as klansmen should not conceal their names from the public or their faces from the public. Do you not think that it would be a good thing to let the public know who these noble men are?

Mr. SIMMONS. Yes, sir, certainly; and at the proper time the public is going to know.

Mr. CAMPBELL. When are you planning that the public shall know who the klansmen are?

Mr. SIMMONS. That is in the development of our work. We are simply making the organization. We are perfecting it in its ritualistic casting, and, in a way, we are in a state of childhood. The matter of wearing the robe and mask is nothing more or less than a memorial, or it is done for monumental purposes.

(Thereupon the committee took a recess until 2.30 o'clock p. m.)

The committee resumed its session at 2.30 o'clock p. m.

Mr. CAMPBELL. Col. Simmons, I understood you to say in your statement that the Knights of the Ku-Klux Klan was neither anti-Jew, anti-Catholic, nor anti-Negro; is that correct?

Mr. SIMMONS. The Knights of the Ku-Klux Klan is not anti anything but wrong.

Mr. CAMPBELL. Your answer is——

Mr. SIMMONS (interposing). The Knights of the Ku-Klux Klan is not anti anything but wrong.

Mr. CAMPBELL. It makes no war on the Jewish race?

Mr. SIMMONS. No, sir.

Mr. CAMPBELL. Nor on the Catholics as a church?

Mr. SIMMONS. No, sir.

Mr. CAMPBELL. Nor on the Negroes as a race?

Mr. SIMMONS. No, sir.

Mr. CAMPBELL. You have selected a phrase from one of Paul's epistles as one of the fundamental principles of your order. Why was that particular phrase selected if you have no war that you are making on anything or anybody?

Mr. SIMMONS. I judge, sir, that you have reference to the first and second verses of the twelfth chapter of Romans.

Mr. GARRETT. You are perfectly familiar with that, Mr. Chairman?

Mr. SIMMONS. I can quote those verses.

Mr. CAMPBELL. Paul asks that the brethren dedicate themselves to this great ·cause, which is their reasonable service. What cause do you invite the people into in which they shall offer their bodies as a living sacrifice or themselves as a living sacrifice?

Mr. SIMMONS. That selection from the Holy Bible which we have designated as a scriptural charter is one in which the apostle calls upon all men, beseeching them to present their bodies as a living sacrifice, holy, clean, and acceptable unto God. "which is your reasonable service," and he adds:

"And be not fashioned according to this world, but be ye transformed by the renewing of your mind, that ye may prove what is the good and acceptable and perfect will of God."

Mr. CAMPBELL. What service are you inviting the brethren to?

Mr. SIMMONS. The service of the Lord of Hosts.

Mr. CAMPBELL. Was it necessary to organize the Ku-Klux Klan in order that men and women, or men of a particular class or condition, might be invited to that service? Are not the invitations that Paul gave to all men without regard to race, color, or condition in life?

Mr. SIMMONS. That may be true. The purpose of the use of these Scriptures is to reveal the moral teachings of the fraternity and to show that this organization in the genius of its soul is evangelical. It is for no other purpose than to show that it conforms to the teachings of the Bible, with special reference to the New Testament.

Mr. CAMPBELL. In that connection I hand you some matter that has come to me through the mail, and I ask you to examine it and see if it is in keeping with the high purposes to which you have just referred.

Mr. SIMMONS. Will you permit me time to read this?

Mr. CAMPBELL. Yes. I call your attention particularly to the notice that is given there.

Mr. SIMMONS. No, sir; that is in nowise in keeping with the purposes, principles, and teachings of our organization.

Mr. GARRETT. Hardly any of us know anything about that except the chairman and the witness.

Mr. CAMPBELL. The matter to which I have called the attention of the witness is this: A picture of what is supposed to be a flashlight of the Ku-Klux Klan in robes, together with some printed matter indicating that Negroes in a certain quarter had better look out. That is pasted on this piece of paper, and on the margin there is written "two weeks." On both sides of the printed matter there appears "Get out or take your medicine. Ku-Klux Klan."

Mr. POU. Did that come anonymously?

Mr. CAMPBELL. No, sir; it did not. It was handed to me by a Member of the House of Representatives. It was mailed to one of his constituents. For prudential reasons, he has cut out the name of the man to whom it was addressed.

Mr. Pou. Did it come to the Member anonymously?

Mr. Campbell. No; it was brought to the Member by the man to whom it was addressed.

Mr. Pou. But it was anonymous to the man who received it, was it not?

Mr. Campbell. It was signed "Ku-Klux Klan."

Mr. Pou. But in its initiative it was anonymous to the first man who received it?

Mr. Campbell. Yes; except it was signed "Ku-Klux Klan."

Mr. Garrett. Is that signature or title "Ku-Klux Klan" signed with a pen?

Mr. Campbell. No; it is signed in printing, along with the printed matter. I call your attention to that again for the purpose of impressing upon you the fact that the secrecy which surrounds the membership of your order makes it possible for nonmembers to send such letters as that through the mail.

Mr. Simmons. Mr. Chairman, the mask and secrecy of our organization is a matter of policy that does not affect the principle.

Mr. Campbell. Does it not affect the principle?

Mr. Simmons. No. sir; it can not affect the principle.

Mr. Campbell. Is it not now affecting the principle?

Mr. Simmons. I mean to say that nothing that is wrong can affect that which is right in principle.

Mr. Campbell. That is a beautiful theory, but in practice is it not now and has it not been within the past year affecting the high purposes of your organization?

Mr. Simmons. I can not answer that question, because I am not in possession of information on that point. The wrongs committed in the name of Christ have not affected the principles of the Christ, but they remain immutable.

Mr. Campbell. Of course, you are not inviting any comparisons there?

Mr. Simmons. No, sir; I use that as an illustration, or as a standard of righteousness.

Mr. Campbell. You referred this morning to Mr. Wright, who appeared here and stated that he was formerly a member of the klan. Among other questions that you have submitted for consideration to submit to him are questions relating to certain petitions for the establishment of an aerial empire.

Mr. Simmons. The Knights of the Air.

Mr. Campbell. To have dominion over what?

Mr. Simmons. Not to have dominion over anything.

Mr. Campbell. My recollection is that there was some very high-sounding and rather attract've title in addition to that of Knights of the Air.

Mr. Simmons. There may have been some designations there in the scope of the fraternal features 'to be attached to that organization. I do not remember, but I believe it was the purpose, although it has never been established. It was proposed that they call it the Invisible Planet. Knights of the Air was to be the name of the organization.

Mr. Campbell. Knights of the Air of the Invisible Planet?

Mr. Simmons. Or the Invisible Planet Knights of the Air. I am not clear about that.

Mr. Campbell. And Mr. Wright was made the grand high tototem of this planet?

Mr. Simmons. No, sir; you have your titles wrong. We had no tototem, and he was just designated at that time as chief of staff to the president or whatever the title the head of the organization would assume.

Mr. Campbell. He was to be the whole thing in the air, or at the head of the planet or dominion?

Mr. Simmons. Well, he was to have been the active executive, under the general direction of the president.

Mr .Campbell. Certainly; he was still subject to some satrap, or the imperial wizard of the invisible empire?

Mr. Simmons. No, sir; you are wrong. We have not gotten up in the air nor under the water yet. That organization was never consummated.

Mr. Campbell. He was selected or was in contemplation for this position?

Mr. Simmons. Well, yes, sir.

Mr. Campbell. That was the dominion that was to be formed?

Mr. Simmons. Yes, sir; that is true in that organization, but that organization was not to be in anywise connected with the Knights of tl e Ku-Klux Klan.

Mr. Campbell. That was not to be a Ku-Klux adjunct?

Mr. Simmons. No, sir.

Mr. CAMPBELL. Nor of the organization——

Mr. SIMMONS (interposing). It was to be encouraged in the patriotic service it was to render to the aerial interests of this country.

Mr. CAMPBELL. Were men required to be members of the Knights of the Ku-Klux Klan in order to become citizens of this planet or of this dominion?

Mr. SIMMONS. No, sir; the only requirement there was to be was that a man must be a flyer or flyer mechanic, or a citizen who was interested in aeronautics. That was the only proposed condition.

Mr. CAMPBELL. At that time Mr. Wright presented petitions from high military officers petitioning for the development of this organization?

Mr. SIMMONS. That is, they were supposed to have been signed.

Mr. CAMPBELL. There was a question raised almost immediately as to the signatures attached to some of those petitions, was there not?

Mr. SIMMONS. Some days afterwards. I do not remember exactly the time, but some days afterwards——

Mr. CAMPBELL (interposing). The petitions were presented to you on the stage in an Atlanta theater, before a large audience.

Mr. SIMMONS. Yes, sir; in a theater at Atlanta. Ga.

Mr. CAMPBELL. In a somewhat dramatic fashion?

Mr. SIMMONS. I am not so much familiar with the histrionics of it. You might classify it as in a dramatic fashion. It was at the annual celebration, and at a certain time, he walked out and produced it.

Mr. CAMPBELL. At the right time, he walked out and produced a handful of petitions.

Mr. SIMMONS. It was at a time. Whether it was at the right time, I can not say, but it was when we got to that part, after the speeches.

Mr. CAMPBELL. It was his cue to come on.

Mr. SIMMONS. I suppose so; yes, sir.

Mr. CAMPBELL. And he presented the imperial wizard of the invisible empire with those petitions?

Mr. SIMMONS. Yes, sir.

Mr. CAMPBELL. Asking the imperial wizard to grant the petitioners that for which they prayed.

Mr. SIMMONS. No, sir; not so much that way. It was a request made to take the lead in organizing this particular institution in the interest of the Air Service of America.

Mr. CAMPBELL. And, thereupon, action was taken upon the petition?

Mr. SIMMONS. I considered the matter, and it was some days after that—I do not remember just how long—I consented, knowing that it would put a great burden on me, but in the interest of this service, I said that I would do my best to help them out.

Mr. CAMPBELL. And you commissioned Mr. Wright to become the head of that organization?

Mr. SIMMONS. There was no commission, because the organization had not been formed. I requested him or designated him to head it.

Mr. CAMPBELL. What designation did you give him? Did he have some rather attractive title?

Mr. SIMMONS. Nothing more than he had on his door the title " Chief of staff to the Knights of the Air."

Mr. CAMPBELL. Chief of staff to the Knights of the Air?

Mr. SIMMONS. Yes, sir; as he represented himself to be an experienced air man, and I wanted men who had knowledge of this thing.

Mr. CAMPBELL. How long had you known him before you wished him this commission and gave him this title?

Mr. SIMMONS. It was some time in the later part of the winter. I do not remember exactly when he first came to Atlanta, but it was possibly in February or possibly early in March. I had received some letters from him before he came down there. He came down there and told me about the air service of this country. He told me about the enormous sums of money that the Government had spent to create an air service, and said that it was going to rack and ruin, and that the flyers were not having opportunities to practice. He said that organizations at many of those places, including Philadelphia and New York, had discussed this matter seriously, and that he had spent some money of his own trying to get Congress to do something.

Mr. CAMPBELL. I am directing your attention to this for the purpose of asking whether or not you made any inquiry as to his standing or credibility before you gave him a position in your organization?

Mr. SIMMONS. He wore the uniform of a major in the Air Service, and I considered that a recommendation when he presented himself to me.

Mr. CAMPBELL. I think you stated or somebody stated that your suspicions were aroused very soon after he presented these petitions as to the authenticity of certain signatures.

Mr. SIMMONS. Some days afterwards.

Mr. CAMPBELL. How many days afterwards.

Mr. SIMMONS. I can not state exactly. I kept no memorandum of that.

Mr. CAMPBELL. That petition was presented on May 6.

Mr. SIMMONS. Yes, sir; the sixth day of May.

Mr. CAMPBELL. You ascertained soon after that that Gen. Pershing denied hrving signed the petition?

Mr. SIMMONS. That information came to me through a report that came to me through a newspaper reporter.

Mr. CAMPBELL. Did you ask for a report, or was this simply a newspaper reporter who came to you and said that he had no authority and that Gen-Pershing was denying the signature?

Mr. SIMMONS. That next morning after I got this information—this reporter came to see me in the latter part of the afternoon——

Mr. CAMPBELL (interposing). The next morning after you had what information?

Mr. SIMMONS. This news report. The next morning I was at the office, and I asked Mr. Clarke to come into my office. I said to him. "Have you seen anything of this report from Gen, Pershing?" He said, "Yes; but only what I saw in the paper." I said, "Where is Maj. Wright?" He said, "Out in town somewhere. I do not know where." I said, "As soon as you see Maj. Wright, you send him to me." Sometime during that day, I do not remember now the time, Maj. Wright came into the office, and was sent into my private office.

Mr. CAMPBELL. That was before he was commissioned as a Knight of the Air?

Mr. SIMMONS. No, sir; that was about the time. The Knights of the Air was something we had in mind, and it had not been organized. I said. "Major, what about Gen. Pershing or this thing in the paper?" He said, Col. Simmons, you need not bother about that. I have taken the matter up with Gen. Pershing, and Gen. Pershing says that he did not deny the signing of the petition, but that he has refused to accept office in the organization," I said, "Major, we do not want to get things twisted up here. Be certain about what you do, and let us do the thing right." He said, "You can count on me to do that."

Mr. CAMPBELL. You let it go at that?

Mr. SIMMONS. For the time being.

Mr. CAMPBELL. And he was given an office in your organization?

Mr. SIMMONS. In the Knights of the Air.

Mr. CAMPBELL. And he was sent out to do missionary work?

Mr. SIMMONS. He was sent out or employed by Mr. Clarke in the propagating work in order to give him something to do, as he seemed to be up against it, until we had time to get the thing incorporated and a constitution and by-laws provided.

Mr. CAMPBELL. The idea was that he was to work among his friends, or among the aviators, and secure them as members of the klan, and in that way add a few additional dollars to the funds?

Mr. SIMMONS. Not necessarily; he was to do other work, too.

Mr. CAMPBELL. What other work was he to do besides propagation work?

Mr. SIMMONS. To get into touch with the different aerial clubs in the country until we got the organization plans all worked out. He was to get to the various clubs intelligence of such an organization so as to get their cooperation in the formation of the Knights of the Air.

Mr. CAMPBELL. But one of the chief purposes in securing his services in the field, or in the propagation work, was to secure additional members for the Knights of the Ku-Klux Klan?

Mr. SIMMONS. Of course, that is a matter to be presumed. If Mr. Clarke, in the propagation department, secured a man or employed a man to work in that department, it would be for that work, of course.

Mr. CAMPBELL. He took Mr. Wright on for that work with your consent?

Mr. SIMMONS. Mr. Clarke announced to me one day that he wanted to give and would give Mr. Wright a position there so that he would have employment and would be making something. Of course, the Knights of the Air had no funds, and he could do this work and make a livelihood while the other organization was being developed. I said, "That is your department, and I have no suggestions to make."

Mr. CAMPBELL. So all of the questions you have submitted here to members of this committee this morning to be propounded to Mr. Wright did not suggest themselves to you while he was getting members for the Knights of the Ku-Klux Klan?

Mr. SIMMONS. No. sir; those suggestions have come in since then. I will frankly make the statement to you, Mr. Chairman, that my suspicion was somewhat aroused as to the authenticity of certain signatures on those petitions, but under the oath of this organization we will not condemn any man on mere suspicion, and we waited to make careful investigations as to Mr. Wright, not taking any action because we were bound to him. He came to us recommended, as he said, as a thirty-second degree Scottish Rite Mason, and a member of other lodges I am a member of, wearing the insignia and uniform of a major, and with those things in mind, while a man's suspicions may be aroused he will take no action until those suspicions have been thoroughly confirmed, and when they had been confirmed, and time and contact with the man confirmed those suspicions, then his services were disconnected.

Mr. CAMPBELL. They were confirmed after you discovered some of his letters in the Hearst papers?

Mr. SIMMONS. No, sir. Oh, no; they were started before the Hearst papers ever started this. I think it was in the month of August, or possibly July; I do not remember.

Mr. CAMPBELL. Was he summarily excommunicated from the Knights of the Ku-Klux Klan?

Mr. SIMMONS. That is my understanding.

Mr. CAMPBELL. Did you issue the order?

Mr. SIMMONS. My understanding was that it was either in July or August—I can not remember now which—Mr. Clarke announced to me, "We will have to get rid of C. Anderson Wright." I said, "What is the matter, Mr. Clarke? What is the trouble?" He said, "Well, Colonel, he won't do and we can not use him." I said, "Well, you are handling that proposition and you look out for that—to safeguard the best interests of our organization."

Mr. CAMPBELL. Now, that was solely with respect to his activities in the propagation work—he could not use him in connection with that work?

Mr. SIMMONS. Yes; his official connection with the klan.

Mr. CAMPBELL. What I am inquiring about now is this: After all these things you raise here in questions that are to be propounded to him he still remained a Knight of the Ku-Klux Klan? You did not ask the local counsel or the local—what is the name?

Mr. SIMMONS. The cyclops.

Mr. CAMPBELL. The cyclops or the terrors—what are they; holy terrors or just terrors?

Mr. SIMMONS. No; they are just plain terrors.

Mr. CAMPBELL. You did not ask that the cyclops and the terrors of the klan to which he belonged locally take up his case and deny him the right of membership?

Mr. SIMMONS. That matter had not been gone into as to what action, if any, had been taken by this local klan. I had not been apprised of that, and the matter came on right here in August; and following the meeting of the supreme executive committee, immediately following that, I went North; and following that I was down sick with the work I had to do and had no opportunity to do that.

Mr. CAMPBELL. Then, summing it all up, while he was useful, sending in the shekels to the klan treasury and to Clarke, he went on in good standing and without question?

Mr. SIMMONS. I think the record will show he sent in very few shekels; very few, sir.

Mr. CAMPBELL. Is that the reason Clarke said he would not do?

Mr. SIMMONS. Well, now, I can not tell you Mr. Clarke's reasons. The only statement to me was, "He won't do." That is my knowledge of it.

Mr. CAMPBELL. If he was not sending any names, of course he was not answering Clarke's purpose.

Mr. SIMMONS. Now, that is a matter Mr. Clarke will have to answer.

Mr. CAMPBELL. Have you since this morning taken into account the responsibilities that rest upon you as the imperial wizard with respect to the finances of the organization?

Mr. SIMMONS. Put your question again, please.

Mr. CAMPBELL. With respect to knowledge of or control over the finances that have been committed to your care as the Imperial wizard?

Mr. SIMMONS. You say you are disposed to go further?

Mr. CAMPBELL. Have you given the matter any consideration?

Mr. SIMMONS. Yes.

Mr. CAMPBELL. Since this morning?

Mr. SIMMONS. I have thought about it the best I could.

Mr. CAMPBELL. Do you know now what has happened to all the funds that came into the imperial treasury amounting, from the time of its organization, to about $250,000, which should have had your scrupulous care and attention?

Mr. SIMMONS. You have reference to funds, sir, before Clarke's contract or afterwards?

Mr. CAMPBELL. I have reference to before and after. Before Clarke's contract you took in, according to the figures that you have submitted here, in round numbers, $151,000, and since then you have taken in $170,000 in round numbers. There is left in your treasury now about $12,000 in cash and you account for assets in the neighborhood of about $20,000 or $25,000. Now, where has the rest of the money gone; who has got it?

Mr. SIMMONS. To my knowledge, sir, all moneys that have been received by this organization have been disbursed in and for the interests of the organization in its development.

Mr. CAMPBELL. Are there receipts and vouchers for those expenditures?

Mr. SIMMONS. To my knowledge there are.

Mr. CAMPBELL. Where are they?

Mr. SIMMONS. They are among the files in the office, with the exception of a period in the history of this organization before the Clarke contract, possibly three years ago. I do not remember now, when a lot of the memorandums and accounts were lost in moving from one office to another late one evening, and I have never been able to recover them, and I have been trying in what time I have had since then to reconstruct from my knowledge just the contents of those records.

Mr. CAMPBELL. You have filed here a very accurate statement—that is, you give it down to cents—of your receipts prior to the contract with Clarke. To be specific, I think——

Mr. SIMMONS (interposing). I have never compiled, to my knowledge, any statement of that. I have been working on it.

Mr. CAMPBELL. You filed one here with the committee—a statement of receipts prior to the contract with Clarke of $151,088.72.

Mr. SIMMONS. You must remember that the record will show that when I filed that exhibit I made the statement I could not vouch for the actual correctness of the figures. I had not had time to go over it and produce the facts.

Mr. CAMPBELL. How did you come to get the 72 cents in if there was some uncertainty as to the amount that had been received?

Mr. SIMMONS. I did not put the 72 cents in.

Mr. CAMPBELL. Who furnished you these figures or who made up this statement?

Mr. SIMMONS. I judge Mr. Furney made that out from the office. I was sick at the time and I asked for a statement.

Mr. CAMPBELL. Mr. Furney is a bookkeeper?

Mr. SIMMONS. Yes; he has been the bookkeeper since Mr. Clarke has had charge of the propagation department.

Mr. CAMPBELL. You filed it here on the assumption it was correct?

Mr. SIMMONS. No, sir. I made the statement that I could not vouch for the accuracy of these financial statements, as I had had no opportunity to check over them.

Mr. CAMPBELL. Do you say now that this is a larger or smaller amount than was received?

Mr. SIMMONS. It is larger amount—much larger.

Mr. CAMPBELL. How do you account for the bookkeeper's returns being larger than the actual receipts?

Mr. SIMMONS. That is a matter that took place before the bookkeeper was connected with the work, and I was sick at the time, and the records that I have were boxed up and have been since we moved the office, and it was based upon, I judge, his best knowledge or his suppositions along that line in order to rush these statements out; but I will say to you, sir, that prior to Clarke's coming into the organization and taking charge, that amount is much in excess of what the order received.

Mr. CAMPBELL. This did not represent $10 a member—this $151,000?

Mr. SIMMONS. No, sir; we did not have that number of members.

Mr. CAMPBELL. You did not have that many members?

Mr. SIMMONS. No, sir; nothing like that. And prior to that time, in the early development of the organization, I would judge that the average initiation fee would be about $6. In many places it was $5 and in a good many places it was $6.50 and the robe had to be furnished, back in the early days.

Mr. CAMPBELL. You have not attempted at any time to hold out to the public that you only had a few members, have you?

Mr. SIMMONS. Oh, no. There has been no occasion for any attempt along that line.

Mr. CAMPBELL. On the contrary, you have held out to the public the idea that you had a very large number of members?

Mr. SIMMONS. Well, no; I have not. I do not think I have.

Mr. CAMPBELL. You stated to this committee, either Thursday or Friday, rather a clever covert threat that if this committee did anythnig to the Knights of the Ku-Klux Klan that hundreds of thousands of klansmen would appear in the next election to strike us hip and thigh.

Mr. SIMMONS. No; you have misread that. Mr. Chairman.

Mr. CAMPBELL. Oh, no.

Mr. SIMMONS. I meant the purpose of it.

Mr. CAMPBELL. What I refer to is the "hundreds of thousands."

Mr. SIMMONS. Well, the hundreds of thousands there—that statement is altogether incorrect. We have not a membership exceeding 100,000.

Mr. CAMPBELL. You have not?

Mr. SIMMONS. No, sir.

Mr. CAMPBELL. Why did you say, then, that you would get after us with hundreds of thousands of ku klux?

Mr. SIMMONS. It was not the intention to say that, and when the typists ran that off hurriedly, that may have been one of those things I struck out.

Mr. POU. I did not understand Col. Simmons as making that statement.

Mr. SIMMONS. And I certainly did not make it in any way as a political threat.

Mr. RODENBERG. I think it was made in reference to the New York World.

Mr. SIMMONS. Yes; it was made in connection with the New York World.

Mr. CAMPBELL. It was in connection with what the New York World had undertaken, and that it might be that the New York World was trying to get the Republican administration into a trap.

Mr. SIMMONS. Yes, sir.

Mr. CAMPBELL. And if they succeeded in doing that, then the hundreds of thousands of Knights of the Ku-Klux Klan would get in their work later on?

Mr. SIMMONS. Yes; but, honestly, Mr. Chairman, if that word "hundreds" appears there——

Mr. CAMPBELL. I was not disturbed by the statement at all.

Mr. SIMMONS. No, sir.

Mr. CAMPBELL. Except to challenge your attention to the "hundreds of thousands of knights" that were involved in the matter.

Mr. SIMMONS. I ask that it be read verbatim. I remember in the writing that word "hundreds" appears, and I struck it out because it was not in conformity with the facts. I am glad you brought this out, so as to correct it.

Mr. CAMPBELL. Did you say it has been stricken out?

Mr. SIMMONS. I said that in one of the writings in the preparation of this manuscript where it appears I struck it out. Now, that correction which I made may have gotten into some of the other manuscripts when it was being run off by the stenographer.

Mr. CAMPBELL. You mean the use of the words "hundreds of thousands?"

Mr. SIMMONS. Yes; the "hundreds of thousands," As far as I am concerned, the New York World may have said we had millions or hundreds of thousands and would do this, that, or the other thing, but there is nothing to that, Mr. Chairman; not a thing, sir.

Mr. POU. Col. Simmons, I will ask you a few questions. First, I believe I will take up the matter of the initiation donation or fee, or whatever it may be called, which at this time, I believe, is $10.

Mr. SIMMONS. Yes, sir.

Mr. Pou. How does that fee compare with the fees of other eleemosynary, charitable organizations in size or amount?

Mr. Simmons. Well, sir, to my knowledge, it is the lowest fee of any standard eleemosynary organization with which I am connected.

Mr. Pou. My recollection is that in my early manhood I was taxed $14 to join a fraternal organization. You have knowledge of the fees of other similar organizations?

Mr. Simmons. Yes, sir.

Mr. Pou. And you say this is the lowest?

Mr. Simmons. The lowest; and even during the war period, when others were raising their fees, we did not raise.

Mr. Pou. Has there ever been, so far as you know, any complaint from the members of the klan with respect to the amount of the fee charged?

Mr. Simmons. No, sir; absolutely none. I have often made the statement, however, to our field men that if any man, after he comes in, is dissatisfied, "pay his money back to him and sever his connection." I have given that instruction repeatedly.

Mr. Pou. It would seem that these criticisms as to the amount of the fee have come almost entirely from gentlemen who are outside of the klan and who do not belong to it.

Mr. Simmons. Yes; who do not belong; and it has never cost them a cent.

Mr. Pou. Now, Colonel, by questions that have been asked here—you have been asked quite a good deal about the money that has been taken in—I imagine you must be a very wealthy man.

Mr. Simmons. Well, I would judge so myself. I would think so.

Mr. Pou. I believe I will ask you the question, as a matter of fact, about what do you consider yourself worth?

Mr. Simmons. You mean financially?

Mr. Pou. Yes.

Mr. Simmons. Well, sir, I have no financial status. I have given my life for the last six years to the development of this organization, the expenses of myself and family to be covered. I held a position which I resigned to take up this work at the instance of its incorporators, to take it up without pay, and they at that time agreed to underwrite me for $200 a month, which never did materialize. When I had spent all the money I had in the bank and called upon them, they flickered or failed; and I have labored, as a matter of patriotic service, in bringing it thus far without any stipulated income, only the expenses to be met, so I could go ahead with the work. I have tried to steer this thing as far from any commercialized impressions as possible. The position that I resigned to devote my life to this work was worth about $10,000 a year to me, and I had paid up my debts and had a little money in the bank. When they asked me to resign all business connections, I did; and since that day I have devoted myself to this work without any stipulated compensation, and what money was to be used was for my expenses and my family and in the furtherance of the institution; and up until the time Mr. Clarke came into the work I had to go out and make that money myself; that is, in the work itself. That is a brief statement of it.

Mr. Pou. Very little of this money has found lodgment to your credit?

Mr. Simmons. No, sir; only as it is to be used—I have had no personal pocketbook for six years. Whatever money I could make on the outside was used in the furtherance of this organization, paying its obligations and its debts.

Mr. Pou. You started out with the purpose of building up this organization practically without help?

Mr. Simmons. Yes, sir.

Mr. Pou. And through the means of your initiative and constructive ability the organization now numbers close to 100,000?

Mr. Simmons. Well, sir, I would say 95,000, or somewhere along there. I can not be altogether accurate in that, but that is approximately it.

Mr. Pou. Is it or not a fact that an impartial audit of the books of the Ku-Klux Klan made by certified public auditors and dating from June 1, 1920, to October 1, 1921, will show the total income of the klan, the total amounts paid out, giving each item, and that all these amounts paid out were in the legal and lawful conduct of the klan, and that it will also show the bank balance and the completed audit will balance?

Mr. Simmons. Yes, sir; it will show that.

Mr. Pou. Is it also a fact that an audit of the books and rough record of the klan for the five years previous to June 1, 1920, will show approximately the total income. of the klan for that period and the amount paid out, and that all such payments and expenses were in the legal and lawful conduct of the klan; also that the total amount of the klan for the 5-year period previous to June 1, 1920, was approximately $15,000, or an average of $7 per member for 2,500 members?

Mr. SIMMONS. Well, a careful audit, to take the time necessary to produce such an audit, will show all that approximately, and I would say that that amount you name there would be somewhere in the latitude of the correct amount of the income through that period. Certainly, it could not have been much above that.

Mr. CAMPBELL. Will you explain the words " in trust," which appear in the receipt issued to a member joining the klan?

Mr. SIMMONS. I have a copy here of the receipt, which I would be glad to turn over to the committee, with a duplicate attached to it. This has been a matter which has been brought up here, and I am glad that you asked that question. I will explain to you that in these receipt books, so called, there is an original and a duplicate. The duplicate stays in the book, so that we can check the man who got this application and received this money. The original, or the white sheet, is given to the applicant when he pays his money, and this states, " Official certificate of donation." I will read this, and then I can get to your point:

" This certifies that ——— has donated the sum of $10 to the propagating fund of the Knights of the Ku-Klux Klan (Inc.), and same is accepted as such and as full sum of ' klectokon,' entitling him to be received, on the acceptance of his petition under the laws, regulations, and requirements of the order, duly naturalized and to have and to hold all the rights, titles, honors, and protection as a citizen of the invisible empire. He enters through the portals of a klan to be instituted at ———, State of ———; date, ———, 19——. Received in trust for the Knights of the Ku-Klux Klan (Inc.) by ———"; that is, whoever received it.

Now, that is done for this reason: If a field man—and I have had experience in the work of other fraternal organizations where I have had to check them up—goes out and takes in money or collects initiation fees and gives no receipt, the man would show up with a claim that he had paid the money, and so on; and this was to show, as evidence, that if that man knocked down any money, he must, when he finishes up and uses all the certificates in one of these books, turn the stubs in, and then we check against those stubs. He received this money—the agent, or the member who takes the application—in trust, and it must be turned in; and if he does not turn it in, then we have it on him as misappropriating or misusing the funds.

(The certificate referred to follows:)

This certifies that ——— has donated the sum of $10 to the propagating fund of the Knights of the Ku-Klux Klan (Inc.), and same is accepted as such and as full sum of " klectokon," entitling him to be received, on the acceptance of his petition under the laws, regulations, and requirements of the order, duly naturalized and to have and to hold all the rights, titles, honors, and protection as a citizen of the invisible empire. He enters through the portal of a klan to be instituted at ———, State of ———; date, ———, 19——.

Received in trust for the Knights of the Ku-Klux Klan (Inc.).

By Kl. ———, K. O. I. E.

[Imperial seal, Knights of the Ku-Klux Klan.]

Official certificate of donation.

Mr. POU. Reference has been made during this hearing to some sort of military organization connected with the klan. I believe at Norfolk, Va. Do you know anything about such military organization; and if so, what comment or explanation do you care to make?

Mr. SIMMONS. I remember a reference, I believe, in one of these letters that brought out the fact regarding a military organization referred to in that letter at Norfolk. You will notice in our constitution and laws where it says that there shall be a military organization, and so on. That military organization to this order is what the patrol is to the Shrine and the Uniform Rank is to the Knights of Pythias, and the Woodmen of the World and other fraternal orders who have a uniform rank or a military feature, and it is simply a uniform rank and is not in any wise to be construed in the sense of what you would call a real military organization. However, what instructions we give in there, in order to make the boys efficient in their drilling, is to be, of course, military instruction so as to train them in matters of drill.

Mr. RODENBERG. Mr. Pou, will you allow me to ask there this question: Does your military organization appear in a different uniform from the klan?

Mr. SIMMONS. The military organization has not been established yet. We have never organized a military organization. We have not had time to get to that.

Mr. POU. Reference has been made from time to time concerning the assistance in the administration of the law, as it was put, by the Ku-Klux Klan. Now, I ask you this question, is it contemplated that the Ku-Klux Klan as an organization shall aid in the administration of the law or is considered simply an individual obligation of the member?

Mr. SIMMONS. Altogether an individual obligation. We teach in the order respect for law and its righteous enforcement, and it is an individual obligation absolutely.

Mr. POU. And there has never been any threat of the head of the klan going to a judge or prosecuting officer and saying, " Here is the klan, we are back of you," or anything of that kind?

Mr. SIMMONS. No, sir.

Mr. POU. And what you are teaching is, in fact, part of the make-up of a good citizen?

Mr. SIMMONS. That is it, sir; absolutely.

Mr. POU. Have you withheld anything connected with this organization, Col. Simmons?

Mr. SIMMONS. No, sir; I do not think of anything touching any information. I have tried to answer every question as fully as I can.

Mr. POU. You have not felt at any time intimidated by the fact that during a part of the time of your examination you were confronted by the head of the Secret Service of the United States on one side and a gentleman detailed from the Attorney General's office on the other?

Mr. SIMMONS. Well, no; I have not felt any intimidation. I certainly have had, it looked like to me, every courtesy extended.

Mr. POU. I believe this is the first time in the history of the Rules Committee that it has had such honor conferred upon it.

Mr. SIMMONS. Those fellows, I understood, were here, and they looked, as I have seen them, pretty nice looking fellows. They do not seem to be so terrible. I am glad to meet them and to know them.

Mr. POU. You saw the Sherlock Holmes of America sitting over there in front of you, Mr. W. J. Burns, I suppose?

Mr. SIMMONS. I was conscious Mr. Burns was present; but it has been a fair deal all the way through.

Mr. POU. I think this is the first time it has been announced publicly that a detail from the Attorney General's office has been sent to listen in on a congressional hearing; it may have been that such a thing has taken place, but I do not recollect it within 21 years' service.

Mr. SIMMONS. This is my first experience in a thing like this, in fact, I have never had a case in court in my life.

Mr. POU. Notwithstanding the fact that you have been confronted with these high dignitaries, you have tried to make a full and complete statement, as far as you could, withholding absolutely nothing?

Mr. SIMMONS. Well, sir, under my physical condition I have done my best to be fair, square, and honorable, and I shall continue, and if there can be, as a result of this, anything brought out that is not right, I again state and reiterate, give me a chance to make it right.

Mr. POU. I believe I have no further questions to ask Col. Simmons.

Mr. SNELL. I have very little I want to ask about. In this paid advertisement, over the colonel's name, in the Chicago Daily Tribune of Tuesday, August 16, under the second heading, it says:

" In order that there may be absolutely no doubt in the public mind as to the real purposes and object and work of this organization, I quote herewith section 3, article 2, of the constitution and laws of the Kn ghts of the Ku-Klux Klan," etc.

The third heading in that paragraph reads in this way:

" Third, to aid and assist in the execution of all constitut'onal laws."

I would like to have the colonel tell us, in a few words, just exactly what that means.

Mr. SIMMONS. Your question has been largely answered, but possibly I could add to it as it was put to me a few moments ago, sir. That has reference to our teachings, the imparting to the citizen of his duties and responsibilities as a good citizen, and that I hold myself individually ready at any time to assist, on the call of my country, my State, and of my community to answer the call for the enforcement of law, if I am called, and seek to protect the peace and security of the community. That has reference to our teachings along the line of good citizenship and the righteous enforcement of law.

Mr. SNELL. It definitely speaks here about the object and work of the organization.

Mr. SIMMONS. Yes, sir. You know, we teach, sir, to our members, as they come in, the high ideals of citizenship, and that is an object of this organization, and as a result this teaching has an application on a citizen's life on the outside.

Mr. SNELL. I think you stated that in nearly all the communities where you have lodges they were composed largely of the most representative citizens that were there.

Mr. SIMMONS. Yes; that is my knowledge.

Mr. SNELL. And that they were working for the uplift of the community. Now, if that is so, why is it that nearly all of the alleged activities take place at night and under cap and gown, so to speak—under a mask?

Mr. SIMMONS. Well, now, sir, I can not explain to you what is in the minds of those parties that are responsible for those allegations. I can not explain that.

Mr. SNELL. What is your publicity department doing to create a different impression in the minds of the people in regard to these activities you are charged with?

Mr. SIMMONS. What is our publicity department doing?

Mr. SNELL. Yes; to overcome that unfair reputation.

Mr. SIMMONS. We are doing everything that is humanly possible. We have first disavowed these things, and if we have membership in those sections we have done our best to get at the truth and facts in an investigation.

Mr. SNELL. After a man has taken your oath, would he ever come and tell on the other members of the klan, as a usual thing?

Mr. SIMMONS. He is required to tell if that member has used his membership in violation of law, and we do not condone, in any sense of the word, any acts of violence in contravention of the law. There may have been individuals who have done it, but I am speaking of the organization now and not acts that nobody can reach.

Mr. SNELL. How many charters have been withdrawn?

Mr. SIMMONS. How is that?

Mr. SNELL. How many charters of lodges have been withdrawn that disobeyed the rules of the organization?

Mr. SIMMONS. To my recollection there have been only two charters that have been revoked—that is, done away with.

Mr. SNELL. Have any individuals been dropped?

Mr. SIMMONS. Oh, yes, sir.

Mr. SNELL. By your order?

Mr. SIMMONS. Oh, yes, sir; for different violations of our laws, and there have been numbers of them dropped for failure to pay their dues and meet their obligations to the organization.

Mr. SNELL. You said a little while ago that if anyone was not satisfied with the order and wanted his donation back, you would issue him an order to pay back his initiation fee.

Mr. SIMMONS. I have given that instruction.

Mr. SNELL. Did Mr. Wright receive his back?

Mr. SIMMONS. I do not know whether—he has never expressed himself to me that he is dissatisfied. The first I heard of it was here, but if Mr. Wright wants his back he can get it, or anybody else. Maybe that will help him out a little.

Mr. SNELL. Colonel, who gave you the exhibits you have filed?

Mr. SIMMONS. Those exhibits were brought to my sick room the day that I left Atlanta, recently.

Mr. SNELL. Were they compiled in your office by your own men?

Mr. SIMMONS. I judge so. They were brought over by the secretary of the organization to my residence.

Mr. SNELL. And still you have no reason to believe they are correct?

Mr. SIMMONS. Well, I say this: I judge they are, in the main, correct, but from what you have read to me there, or the committee, there are certainly some things in there that are in excess. This thing came on hurriedly and we have not had any time, and not being able to be at the office, why, there is some discrepancy.

Mr. SNELL. I understood from the question Mr. Pou asked that the receipts, which you thought were correct. were only $25,000 up to the 1st of June, 1920. Was that the correct amount, or practically correct, Mr. Pou?

Mr. POU. The question I asked was this:

"Is it not also a fact that an audit of the books and rough records of the klan for the five years previous to June 1, 1920, will show approximately the total income of the klan for that period and the amounts paid out, and that all such payments and expenses were in the legal and lawful conduct of the klan? Also that the total income of the klan for the five-year period previous to June 1, 1920. was only approximately $15,000, or an average of $7 per member for 2,500 members?"

Mr. SNELL. I thought it was $25,000 instead of $15,000. Here is a statement that the colonel filed as Exhibit C, which he says was made up by his own secretary, and this appears at the top:

"All records previous to June 15, 1921, are in memorandum form, no books to that time being opened. These records will be properly booked when turned over to accounting department; same are held by Col. W. J. Simmons, and due to ill health and urgent business he has been unable to attend to this duty. The approximate amount involved in the above is: Receipts, $151,088.72; disbursements, $102,502.53; bank balance, $48,585.10."

Now. I can not understand why the colonel should file this statement, made up in his own office, as Exhibit C, if it was ten times out of the way.

Mr. SIMMONS. I will endeavor to assist you to understand me.

Mr. SNELL. That is what I want to get at.

Mr. SIMMONS. Yes, sir. I make the statement, if I understand you in reading that——

Mr. SNELL (interposing). I have read just what you handed in yourself. They were not my words.

Mr. SIMMONS. I can not remember saying that, and I can not remember all of those statements.

Mr. SNELL. Do you want to see it?

Mr. SIMMONS. No; I will take your statement, but the fact of the business is this: The amount of the receipts from the beginning of the organization up to June 1. 1920—what was the amount?

Mr. SNELL. $151,088.72.

Mr. SIMMONS. I know no matter who made up that statement, even if an angel from heaven made it, I know that that amount there is away in excess of what the receipts were.

Mr. SNELL. Your own man would not deliberately make up anything of that kind?

Mr. SIMMONS. No; he would not deliberately have done it. but he possibly had wrong impressions as to the amounts and the number of members.

Mr. SNELL. It is hard for us to reconcile the two statements you make. saying that it was not to exceed $15,000, while your own man—and you file his statement as an exhibit—says $151,000.

Mr. SIMMONS. I realize the predicament the committee is in on that point, but if you will give me time——

Mr. CAMPBELL (interposing). The committee is not in a predicament.

Mr. SIMMONS. Well. the gentleman just said something about the difficulty in reconciling the two statements.

Mr. SNELL. It is hard for us to reconcile the two statements. but I am not in any predicament about it.

Mr. SIMMONS. I think the explanation there is ambiguous. and that that statement. while I have not had an opportunity to study those statements thoroughly. has reference to the work in Clarke's contract.

Mr. SNELL. You had no contract with Clarke up to that time?

Mr. SIMMONS. I can not get all those things in my mind, but I can do this for this committee: If I have an opportunity. I can construct a statement of the receipts and disbursements of this order from the start up to Clarke's contract. I can prepare you a statement, and I will prepare it under oath as to the accuracy. I am willing to do that at any time this committee desires it.

Mr. SNELL. Mr. Williamson in his statement said there was a very good set of books from the 1st of June down to the present time and that they had furnished him every opportunity and accorded him every privilege he asked when he examined them. If I remember correctly, he looked over Clarke's books at that same time and they showed receipts of about $225,000. You said that at the time Clarke took over the contract you had about 5,000 members, as I remember it.

Mr. SIMMONS. Well, it is very indefinite there, but something from 2,500 to 5,000; I can not tell.

Mr. SNELL. And that you now have in the vicinity of 95,000.

Mr. SIMMONS. Somewhere along there.

Mr. SNELL. If you only had 90,000, that would show that Clarke had gotten 85,000 members for you?

Mr. SIMMONS. Well, yes; something like that.

Mr. SNELL. I should suppose, then, that with $8 a member, which you say he received from each one, his books would show receipts and expenditures of $680,000 instead of $225,000.

Mr. SIMMONS. Evidently; but I have not examined his books at all; I do not know.

Mr. SNELL. I have reference to Clarke's books, which were examined by Mr. Williamson, but you do not know anything about them?

Mr. SIMMONS. No; I was sick at the time and was not at the office at all all the time the departments were there and Mr. Williamson was there.

Mr. SNELL. I understand you to say that each man pays a tax of 45 cents per quarter?

Mr. SIMMONS. There is a per capita tax on the local organizations that goes into the general fund of the organization of 45 cents per quarter.

Mr. SNELL. That would be $1.80 a year?

Mr. SIMMONS. Yes, sir; and not $3, as stated here by some.

Mr. SNELL. I do not find any caption in your receipts that shows the amount received under that head.

Mr. SIMMONS. Well, I do not know about that.

Mr. SNELL. That must amount to quite a large sum at the present time, with 80,000 or 90,000 members.

Mr. SIMMONS. If the per capita tax is promptly paid and fully paid, but we have had a great deal of trouble in getting the local organizations—all of them are new—to respond to that. I would rather estimate now, sir, that there is possibly in the neighborhood of $75,000 or $100,000 due this organization by way of unpaid per capita tax.

Mr. SNELL. How much?

Mr. SIMMONS. Possibly from $75,000 to $100,000. I just make that merely as a rough estimate.

Mr. SNELL. I should think, as long as it does not show it has been received, that there must be that amount of money coming in, based on those figures.

Mr. SIMMONS. It may have been included in some other item.

Mr. SNELL. There is not enough money to take care of it, because your total receipts are only $137,228.75.

Mr. SIMMONS. You must remember that many of our local organizations have not had to pay the per capita tax, because they have come in right recently; they have not paid because it is not due.

Mr. SNELL. I understood you to say that the supreme treasurer could draw checks as well as yourself.

Mr. SIMMONS. He can if they are countersigned by myself.

Mr. SNELL. I understood that a lot of th's money that you could not explain may have been paid out by the supreme treasurer, and for that reason you did not understand it, but if you countersign the checks I suppose you would know what the payments were for.

Mr. SIMMONS. Not always what it is paid for, because I will countersign a half dozen checks for certain bills to be paid. I say, "How many checks do you need?" He will say, "a half dozen," and I will countersign them, and then as those bills are paid the imperial treasurer signs his name.

Mr. SNELL. If you countersigned them before he drew them, how do you know he did not draw money from the klan treasury to pay this lawyer in this Texas case?

Mr. SIMMONS. What lawyer in the Texas case?

Mr. SNELL. In the Atlanta case, I mean.

Mr. SIMMONS. At that time the checks were drawn by myself, under the regulations or the resolution of the supreme executive committee.

Mr. SNELL. That could not have taken place under those circumstances?

Mr. SIMMONS. No, sir; I would have signed the checks, then.

Mr. SNELL. How long has he been signing them?

Mr. SIMMONS. Since the last meeting of the executive committee, the 1st of August.

Mr. SNELL. Then most of these other expenses must have been met prior to that time?

Mr. SIMMONS. Yes, sir.

Mr. SNELL. Would you not have been familiar with them?

Mr. SIMMONS. That is true, but I was familiar with them only in a general way, but not as to details, because I have been out and in there.

Mr. RODENBERG. I have just a few questions, Mr. Chairman. Did I understand you to say this morning, Mr. Simmons, that you do not keep a complete record of all the members of the klan at the headquarters in Atlanta?

Mr. SIMMONS. No, sir. We have begun here right recently to compile a record, but we have not been keeping a record of the individual membership.

Mr. RODENBERG. Of course you could not possibly collect your per capita tax unless you knew.

Mr. SIMMONS. Of course the per capita tax is paid in by the secretary of the local organization, as in all other organizations.

Mr. RODENBERG. Do you have a printed roster of your members?

Mr. SIMMONS. No; not to my knowledge, unless it is on one of these addressograph machines, for the use of the officers in mailing out letters.

Mr. RODENBERG. Do your local klans maintain a printed roster?

Mr. SIMMONS. Not to my knowledge, sir.

Mr. RODENBERG. Do you know of any order, other than the Ku-Klux Klan, that does not maintain a printed roster?

Mr. SIMMONS. Put that question again.

Mr. RODENBERG. Do you know of any other organization, other than the Ku-Klux Klan, that does not maintain a printed roster of its membership?

Mr. SIMMONS. Well, to my knowledge; yes, sir.

Mr. RODENBERG. Do you?

Mr. SIMMONS. That is, what you call in printed form?

Mr. RODENBERG. A printed roster, a complete roster of all the members. Do you know of any headquarters, the grand headquarters of any order in this country, that does not have a complete record of its entire membership?

Mr. SIMMONS. No; I am not familiar with the workings of the officers in the headquarters of the various fraternal orders.

Mr. RODENBERG. Is there any injunction issued by you to any of the klans not to keep a printed roster?

Mr. SIMMONS. No, sir; nothing; the matter has never even come up.

Mr. RODENBERG. There is no secrecy maintained about your roster of membership, is there?

Mr. SIMMONS. No, sir; only it is left to the discretion of the local organization.

Mr. RODENBERG. Do you know of any klan that belongs to your organization that has ever given publicity to its membership; the roster of its membership?

Mr. SIMMONS. I do not recall any at this particular time; there may have been, but I do not recall it.

Mr. RODENBERG. It is not a part of your plan to conceal the list of membership from the public, is it?

Mr. SIMMONS. A good many of those things are left with the local organization, what is for the best interests of the local organization's work.

Mr. RODENBERG. You simply maintain a card index system at the headquarters?

Mr. SIMMONS. Yes, sir; usually of the officers, and up to right recently, two or three months ago, when we began to construct a file and get the lists in.

Mr. RODENBERG. Mr. Simmons, you are familiar with the publication known as the Searchlight, are you not?

Mr. SIMMONS. Well, I know of the paper being published.

Mr. RODENBERG. Who publishes that?

Mr. SIMMONS. The Searchlight Publishing Co. is the style of the company and Mr. J. O. Wood is editor, I think, and general manager.

Mr. RODENBERG. Is that publication friendly to you?

Mr. SIMMONS. Well, I can not say that it is friendly; it is an independent paper, and it has published several articles in the interest of the organization, as well as other articles. It is an independent newspaper.

Mr. RODENBERG. Have you ever employed the columns of that paper to give expression to your views on any subject?

Mr. SIMMONS. No; I have not, other than just articles touching upon the principles of the organization that they would ask me about.

Mr. RODENBERG. On July 2 an article appeared in the Searchlight purporting to be an interview with you, and I want to read this to you.

Mr. SIMMONS. All right, sir.

Mr. RODENBERG (reading):

" For the edification of those who do not know, allow me to state that the Knights of the Ku-Klux Klan has not yet started to work, and may not do so for at least one year yet. We do not intend to start any definite activity until we have sufficiently organized to make sure of success.

" To those who love fireworks—rhetorical or otherwise—allow me to suggest that they wait quietly until the Ku-Klux Klan actually starts work. We are keeping records and making plans. The day of our activity has not yet arrived."

Is that an authentic interview?

Mr. SIMMONS. No, sir; that is not my interview, and I will call Mr. Wood down on it, as editor of the paper.

Mr. RODENBERG. That is not an interview of yours, then?

Mr. SIMMONS. No.

Mr. RODENBERG. You deny its authenticity?

Mr. SIMMONS. Yes, sir; I deny its authenticity and that wording.

Mr. RODENBERG. Then I shall not press the question. I was very anxious to know just what you meant by the expression, " fireworks, rhetorical or otherwise."

Mr. SIMMONS. Those who know me, sir, know that is not one of my expressions.

Mr. RODENBERG. I was particularly anxious to know what you had reference to when you said, " We are keeping records and making plans." I wanted to know the character of the plans, and I was about to ask you whether the language employed carried with it an implied threat to those who were criticizing you.

Mr. SIMMONS. No, sir.

Mr. RODENBERG. But you repudiate the interview?

Mr. SIMMONS. Those are not my words.

Mr. RODENBERG. I do not believe I have anything further to ask.

Mr. GARRETT. Mr. Simmons, one thing I do not know that I got clearly in mind was about the use of the fund of $19,000 that was referred to by the chairman, which came out of the amount accumulated by the $2 that went to the organization. I got the impression from the whole hearing here that the $8 which went to Clarke and his organization of propagation was utilized for obtaining members.

Mr. SIMMONS. Yes, sir.

Mr. GARRETT. And that whatever you had spent out of this fund, amounting to some $19,000, was paid for lecturers who instructed those who had become members?

Mr. SIMMONS. Yes, sir.

Mr. GARRETT. Did I get the right impression?

Mr. SIMMONS. Yes; special lecturers sent out for instructing in special ritualistic work and doctrines and teachings; 'n other words, as the word implies, as instructors. That has to do with the training and development of the organization after it has been chartered. When an organization is chartered it is no longer within the realm of the propagation department, and then we send these men out for the purpose of instructing those men and teaching them in ceremonial work and grounding them in the faith and principles of the organization.

Mr. GARRETT. That is all.

Mr. CAMPBELL. I believe that is all, Mr. Simmons.

Mr. SIMMONS. All right. Mr. Chairman, I wish to again thank you all for your courtesy, and I ask that Mr. Wright be put back on the stand at your discretion.

Mr. GARRETT. I move that we have an executive session.

Mr. CAMPBELL. The committee will retire to an adjoining room for a moment.

(The committee retired, and upon resuming its open session the chairman made the following statement:)

Mr. CAMPBELL. The committee is of the unanimous conclusion that no witnesses will be recalled at this time, and that no other witnesses will be called at this time. At a subsequent time, the committee will meet and decide on its further action in the matter. At present the committee is adjourned.

Mr. TAGUE. Mr. Chairman, before the committee adjourns I just want to ask the indulgence of the committee. I am not going to read this letter, but one day last week Mr. Etheridge, I believe he calls himself, appeared before this committee and made a statement in which he brought in the name of Miss Riordan, a school-teacher in Atlanta, Ga. Miss Riordan was not here and has not been here, but she has sent a letter to Representative Ryan, who was detained at his home on account of illness. Mr. Ryan asked me to have this letter inserted in the record of this hearing.

Mr. GARRETT. Mr. Chairman, just a moment: I do not think Mr. Etheridge brought Miss Riordan's name into this matter, but I think that Mr. Thomas, of the New York World, first mentioned Miss Riordan's name.

Mr. TAGUE. I did not hear Mr. Thomas refer to her, but I did hear Mr. Etheridge. At any rate, this lady's name, without her knowledge or consent, has been brought into this hearing. She has had no part in it, and her name has been used, according to her letter, in a false light, and she wishes to appear before this committee in a right light.

Mr. POU. If my friend will pardon me, I suggest this, that he leave this letter with the chairman. The hearings have been formally closed for the time being, and we can decide at a subsequent meeting whether the letter shall be made a part of the record.

Mr. TAGUE. That is satisfactory to me, or, at any rate, it will be satisfactory as long as I give the committee this letter.

Mr. CAMPBELL. The committee will stand adjourned.

(Thereupon, at 4.30 o'clock p. m., the committee adjourned.)